INSIGHT ⊙ GUIDES

AUSTRALIA

www.insightguides.com/Australia

⊙ Walking Eye App

Your Insight Guide now includes a free app and eBook, dedicated to your chosen destination, all included for the same great price as before. They are available to download from the free Walking Eye container app in the App Store and Google Play. Simply download the Walking Eye container app to access the eBook and app dedicated to your purchased book. The app features an up-to-date A to Z of travel tips, information on events, activities and destination highlights, as well as hotel, restaurant and bar listings. See below for more information and how to download.

MULTIPLE DESTINATIONS AVAILABLE

Now that you've bought this book you can download the accompanying destination app and eBook for free. Inside the Walking Eye container app, you'll also find a whole range of other Insight Guides destination apps and eBooks, all available for purchase.

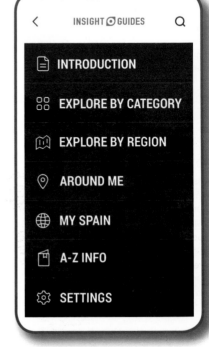

DEDICATED SEARCH OPTIONS

Use the different sections to browse the places of interest by category or region, or simply use the 'Around me' function to find places of interest nearby. You can then save your selected restaurants, bars and activities to your Favourites or share them with friends using email, Twitter and Facebook.

FREQUENTLY UPDATED LISTINGS

Restaurants, bars and hotels change all the time. To ensure you get the most out of your guide, the app features all of our favourites, as well as the latest openings, and is updated regularly. Simply update your app when you receive a notification to access the most current listings available.

Shopping in Oman still revolves around the traditional souks that can be found in every town in the country – most famously at Mutrah in Muscat, Salalah and Nizwa, which serve as showcases of traditional Omani craftsmanship and produce ranging from antique khanjars and Bedu jewellery to halwa, rose-water and frankincense. Muscat also boasts a number of modern malls, although these are rare elsewhere in the country.

TRAVEL TIPS & DESTINATION OVERVIEWS

The app also includes a complete A to Z of handy travel tips on everything from visa regulations to local etiquette. Plus, you'll find destination overviews on shopping, sport, the arts, local events, health, activities and more.

HOW TO DOWNLOAD THE WALKING EYE

Available on purchase of this guide only.
1. Visit our website: www.insightguides.com/walkingeye
2. Download the Walking Eye container app to your smartphone (this will give you access to both the destination app and the eBook)
3. Select the scanning module in the Walking Eye container app
4. Scan the QR code on this page – you will be asked to enter a verification word from the book as proof of purchase
5. Download your free destination app* and eBook for travel information on the go

* Other destination apps and eBooks are available for purchase separately or are free with the purchase of the Insight Guide book

Contents

THE BEST OF AUSTRALIA: TOP ATTRACTIONS

Discover Australia's unique attractions – exciting adventure activities, absorbing museums, vast empty landscapes, and indigenous culture... here, at a glance, are our top recommendations.

△ **Sydney Harbour.** The Opera House is deservedly on everyone's list as a must-see attraction in Australia – it's on the Unesco World Heritage list, after all – and when you combine it with the iron bulk of Sydney Harbour Bridge, you have one of the great vistas of the world. See page 107.

▽ **Canberra's Museums and Galleries.** Gathered around Lake Burley Griffin is what collectively amounts to the most impressive collection of educational and cultural showpieces in Australia. See page 149.

▽ **The Great Barrier Reef.** More than 2,000km (1,240 miles) of mostly pristine coral gardens and rich aquatic life, the Reef rewards divers, snorkellers or those who simply gaze through glass-bottomed boats. See page 236.

△ **Uluru.** Rising out of the parched red centre of the country, Uluru (Ayers Rock) is the dramatic touchstone of this ancient continent. It's a sacred site to its Aboriginal custodians, and worth travelling thousands of kilometres to see. See page 264.

◁ **Melbourne's Music Scene.** A host of brilliant venues large and small helps to make this the finest music city in Australia. See page 164.

△ **Australia's Wineries.** In a nation rich in high-class, picturesque wineries, the Barossa, Clare and Coonawarra regions stand out as some of the finest. See page 78.

▽ **Kakadu National Park.** Of the numerous National Parks, this one is unmissable with its mixture of indigenous flora and fauna along with ancient Aboriginal culture. See page 258.

△ **Port Arthur.** Tasmania's grim penal settlement provides something of a crash course in Australia's colonial history. The setting, ironically, is stunning. See page 299.

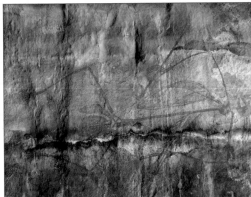

△ **Wildflowers in Western Australia.** Springtime, beginning in September, is when the countryside around Perth and southern Western Australia is awash with technicolour blooms. See page 290.

▷ **Boxing Day at the MCG.** Up to 100,000 spectators and fans turn out to this world-famous Melbourne stadium for the beginning of a five-day test match, an epic even in the cricket world. Even if you don't follow the sport, go to the stadium for the party atmosphere. See page 163.

THE BEST OF AUSTRALIA: EDITOR'S CHOICE

Perfect Australian beaches, illuminating galleries and fascinating historical towns; here are the best things to do on your visit Down Under.

Fraser Island.

BEST ISLANDS

Fraser Island, Qld. There are endless beaches on this giant sand bar. See page 224.

Kangaroo Island, SA. Seals, penguins, echidnas, kangaroos, emus and koalas all live here. See page 203.

Lord Howe Island, NSW. This heavily forested isle has numerous walking trails, as well as diving and snorkelling facilities. See page 132.

Magnetic Island, Qld. Just over the water from Townsville but a world away. See page 222.

Maria Island, Tas. Maria Island is vehicle-free, so pack walking boots or hire a mountain bike at the ferry point. See page 300.

Tiwi Islands, NT. Accessible only by boat or plane through organised tours, the islands are rich in Aboriginal culture. See page 263.

Diving off the islands of Queensland.

BEST BEACHES

Bells Beach, Vic. This beach is famed world-wide for its spring surf contest. See page 171.

Cable Beach, WA. A ride on a camel train along the beach at sunset is a great experience for kids. See page 287.

Maslin Beach, SA. The backdrop of sandstone cliffs makes this family-oriented beach one of the most beautiful in the state. See page 195.

Noosa, Qld. As well as being an excellent surfing beach, Noosa benefits from a national park on one side and a shopping strip on the other. See page 219.

Shark Bay, WA. A World Heritage Site, Shark Bay has marine wildlife galore. Hand feed dolphins at the bay's Monkey Mia. See page 283.

Noosa Beach, Queensland.

Whitsunday Island, Great Barrier Reef. As far as beaches go, Whitehaven is pretty unbeatable, and it's open for camping, too. See page 239.

Wineglass Bay, Freycinet NP, Tas. This is a breathtaking sweep of white sands and azure sea. The best views are from Wineglass Bay lookout. See page 300.

BEST GALLERIES

Tiled artwork decorates Melbourne.

Aboriginal rock art galleries at Kakadu, NT. The rock art galleries, particularly at Nourlangie and Ubirr rocks, display some of the earliest paintings by man. See page 258.
National Gallery of Australia, Canberra. Repository of many of the finest artworks in the country. See page 151.
National Gallery of Victoria, Melbourne. The gallery has been split over two sites; one houses national and one houses international works. See page 164.
South Australian Museum, Adelaide. Extensive Aboriginal and Pacific exhibits and a broad survey of regional natural history. See page 192.

BEST MARKETS

Central Market, Adelaide. A covered area packed with more than 200 shops, the main attraction is the wealth of local produce that SA is famed for. See page 193.
Queen Victoria Market, Melbourne. A buzzing place where locals after fresh produce or deli specialities mix with tourists seeking souvenir clocks in the shape of Australia. See page 165.
Bondi Markets, Sydney. The Bondi Markets have helped establish more than a few of the most successful Sydney fashion designers. See page 116.
Fish Market, Sydney. The ultimate seafood experience, Sydney's Fish Market has fish auctions, market stalls, restaurants and even a cookery school. See page 113.

Adelaide's famous covered market.

Sovereign Hill is an open air museum in Golden Point, a suburb of Ballarat, Victoria.

BEST COLONIAL TOWNS

Ballarat, Vic. An old gold-mining town. The Eureka Centre re-creates the day in 1854 when gold was discovered. See page 175.
Broome, WA. The timber dwellings of Chinatown serve as a reminder of Broome's pearling days. See page 286.
Hahndorf, SA. Pretty German town established in 1839 in the Adelaide Hills. See page 195.

Richmond, Tas. One of the very best preserved Georgian towns in all of Australia. See page 299.
The Rocks, Sydney. Site of the first European settlement, today The Rocks is virtually an open-air museum. See page 108.
Charters Towers, Qld. Attractive former gold-mining town with splendid colonial buildings. See page 221.

Campbell's Cover in The Rocks, Sydney.

Tamarama Beach, New South Wales.

Federation Square, Melbourne.

Murchison Gorge, Kalbarri
National Park.

Kangaroos on Esperance Beach.

DOWN UNDER

You can call it the world's largest island, or
the Earth's oldest continent. Either way,
Australia is a place like no other.

An Australian kookaburra.

.H. Lawrence once said "Australia is like an open door with the blue beyond. You just walk out of the world and into Australia." Australians like to think of their country as God's own – or Godzone in the vernacular. Since the turn of the millennium this philosophy has taken on a new resonance as a whole series of travails (of almost biblical proportions) has assailed the country. There has always been fire, but in February 2009 it took on a tragic dimension when bushfires destroyed a great part of the state of Victoria and took scores of lives. The heatwave at the start of 2013 cause more fires across Victoria and New South Wales, and forced the Australian Bureau of Meteorology to add another colour band to its temperature chart – for temperatures over 50 degrees Celsius (122 degrees Fahrenheit). There have always been floods, but they attained a new scale when the fatal inundation in January 2011 affected 75 percent of Queensland. Even plagues of locusts have been sweeping the land. This might cause some to question the purpose of living at the far ends of the Earth, but for most Australians it provokes only a pause for thought to cherish their unique challenges.

Weano Gorge in the Karijini National Park, Western Australia.

This country of extremes is used to doing things the hard way. People have been inhabiting this daunting continent for around 50,000 years, and they know that for every down, there's an upside to living in one of the most remarkable places on Earth. Try waking up to the bush dawn, as the kookaburras begin their maniacal laughs and the golden light pierces the gumtrees. That is one of the great outdoor experiences in Oz. In Sydney, a dawn stroll along the harbour as the first ferries roll past the Opera House will convince you that this may well be the most gorgeous city on Earth. The very differences that permeate Australia's land, culture and history have also given it a sin-gular strength and durability. When the British colonists and convicts first arrived in the 1780s, they attempted to re-create the places and cultures of their homeland, but the strangeness of the landscape, including the heat, rain (or endless droughts), expansive landscape and the otherness of it all meant that they could only ever be partially successful.

Today, Australians tend to be thankful for their distance from Europe and the United States, and embrace their (relative) proximity to Asia. The quirks of their homeland – the egg-laying mammals, the ghostly trees, the savage deserts, the spiders, even the menagerie of deadly snakes – have become a source of endless fascination.

The Twelve Apostles as seen from the Great Ocean Road.

AN ANCIENT LANDSCAPE

Australia has been a continent for around 50 million years. But the history of the land can be traced back much further, to a time when the world was young.

Hawks Head Lookout, Kalbarri National Park.

Australia's topography, so forbidding to the first European settlers in the late 18th century and so compelling to more recent arrivals, takes us back to the earliest history of our planet. Certain rocks have been dated back 3,500 million years, while large chunks of the landscape suggest continental movements dating back more than 1,000 million years.

Whereas much of Europe and the Americas have the landscapes of youth – snow-covered peaks, rushing waterfalls, geysers, active volcanoes, giant gorges and mountain lakes – Australia's blunted, stunted, arid lands speak of an age that must be treated with respect. It is a land in which even the animals and plants, developed in isolation, are strikingly different.

Forces of nature

The last great geological shifts in Australia took place some 230 million years ago, before the Permian period. It was then that the forces of nature convulsed the Earth's crust and created alpine ranges whose peaks extended above the snow line. Since then, modest convulsions on the eastern and western fringes have created low ranges (now known as tablelands), and volcanoes have occasionally erupted – but, generally speaking, Australia was already a sleeping giant when the rest of the world's landforms came into being. Barring unforeseen geological circumstances, it will also be the first continent to achieve equilibrium, a flattening of the land to the point where rivers cease to run, there is no further erosion, and landscape becomes moonscape.

Australia began to take shape 50 million years ago when it broke away from the great continent known as Gondwanaland. This landmass at one time incorporated Africa, South America and India. Australia broke free and drifted north at first, reshaping itself into a continent. The centre was rising from a shallow sea to unite what had been a series of islands. One of these islands, the Great Western Plateau, had been the only constant during much of this change, sometimes partly submerged but always the stable heart of the continent. Today that plateau spreads over almost half the continent, a dry and dramatic expanse of pristine beauty. It spreads from the west coast to beyond the West Australian border, taking in the Kimberley and Hamersley ranges, the Great Sandy Desert, Gibson Desert and the Great Victoria Desert, and, although its topography has changed greatly, it houses the artefacts of ancient times.

A rock found near Marble Bar in the far northwest yielded the remains of organisms which lived 3,500 million years ago – the oldest form of life yet discovered. A dinosaur footprint is frozen in rock near Broome, and in the Kimberley, once a coral reef in a shallow sea, landlocked ocean fish have adapted to fresh water.

While much of the west is brown and featureless, every now and then something crops up to whet the appetite, perhaps because it is such a contrast with the surroundings. People will drive great distances to have a look at geological oddities. In the case of Wave Rock, 350km (220 miles) to the west of Perth, it's the edge of a granite outcrop, about 15 metres (50ft) high, that is curling over along a length a little over 100 metres (330ft), looking as if a giant wave had petrified mid-action. This distinctive shape derives from a process that commenced about 60 million years ago from a softening of some sections of the granite and subsequent water erosion, which eventually led to Wave Rock emerging from the ground.

Similarly, the magnificent Bungle Bungles on the southern edge of the Kimberley at the top of Western Australia are probably the most dramatic result of erosion in the country. This is a sandstone range that stretches 450km (280 miles) and occupies 640 sq km (247 sq miles) in the Purnululu National Park. The peculiar dome shapes of the peaks are dramatic enough, and when combined with the striping effect caused by alternating layers of orange and grey rock (according to the ferrous content), you have a heart-stopping site, unlike any other in the world. It was recognised as a World Heritage Site by Unesco in 1987.

Being so far from the main population centres, relatively few visitors or, indeed, Australians, ever get to see Bungle Bungles. Tourists are much more likely to find themselves at the country's more famous World Heritage-listed rock: Uluru. This, too, is sandstone, but just one monolithic form, the tip of a rocky equivalent of an iceberg, where the majority is hidden below the surface. The strength of Uluru lies in its homogeneity and in the absence of the flaws that have allowed the forces of erosion to eat away at the rocks that would once have surrounded it. The fact that

it is surrounded by many kilometres of flat desert heightens the contrast.

The Lowlands

The central eastern lowlands, stretching south from the Gulf of Carpentaria and bounded by the Great Dividing Range to the east, form a sedimentary basin that has often been encroached upon by the sea. Although this is a catchment area of 1.5 million sq km (600,000 sq miles) for rivers running inland off the eastern range, much of the water is lost through evaporation or into the vast chain of salt lakes

Wild flowers in the Hamersley Gorge, Pilbara.

FLORA AND FAUNA

Australia's vegetation is dominated by the eucalyptus, the humble gumtree, which can be found in more than 500 different forms. It's hard to escape the smell, feel and sight of this tree, which is most often stunted, knotted and offers little shade. Australian marsupials have developed in isolation in extraordinary ways, and into 120 different species – from the red kangaroo and the gliders that fly between trees, to tiny desert mice. The platypus and echidna are the world's only egg-laying mammals; the Queensland lungfish can breathe both above and under water. Australia has clear links to a time when the world was young.

and clay pans. The largest of the salt lakes, Lake Eyre, is also the lowest part of the continent at 15 metres (50ft) below sea level. For much of the time it is a lake in name only. However, with above-average rainfall in recent years, numerous tour operators have set up special sightseeing trips to see the lake with water and the concomitant surge in birdlife.

Much of the lowlands are so exceptionally harsh and inhospitable that it is difficult to imagine that beneath the surface lies the Great Artesian Basin, from which bores are tapped to provide water for livestock. The most ancient

where the rain falls and where the air stays relatively cool. Once you're across the range, everything dries out and becomes desert.

Mount Kosciuszko, at 2,230 metres (7,315ft), is the highest point in the Great Dividing Range, but equally majestic are the rainforests of the north and the moors of Tasmania.

The Glass House Mountains in southern Queensland were formed by volcanoes about 20 million years ago; they are formed from plugs of hardened magma piped up the centre of peaks that have subsequently eroded away. The granite belt bridging the Queens-

Mungalli Falls, near the town of Atherton in Queensland.

part of the basin area is the Flinders Ranges of South Australia, in which there are rocks and remains dating back 1,000 million years.

The Highlands

Because of its immense age, Australia can no longer boast a true alpine range. The Great Dividing Range that runs parallel with the east coast for more than 2,000km (1,250 miles) is as diverse as any found on Earth, tropical at one end and subalpine at the other. It is a series of "fold mountains", where tectonic plates have collided and buckled.

The Great Dividing Range dictates the climate of eastern Australia. The narrow strip between the range and the Pacific Ocean is

land–New South Wales border and the Warrumbungle Mountains was born in similar circumstances.

Australia's last active volcano died only 6,000 years ago – just a few ticks on the geological clock. In Tasmania the effects of volcanic activity and two ice ages have created a distinctive wilderness. This can be seen in the Nut at Stanley, another of the nation's many geological oddities. This 150-metre (490ft) -high plug of volcanic rock was formed in similar fashion to the Glass House Mountains.

For a variation on the theme, make a trip out to the Undara Lava Tubes in outback Queensland, 130km (70 miles) west of the Atherton Tablelands. In this case it is the absence of volcanic rock that is significant. When the long-extinct Undara volcano erupted around 190,000 years ago, streams of lava spread across the countryside and, as the surface of the rock cooled, the lava inside flowed on, leaving hollow tubes behind, up to 20 metres (65ft) in diameter. These were soon absorbed into the landscape and remained undiscovered until some of the tubes collapsed.

The Coast

The coastline of Australia is as spectacular and as varied as the centre. It ranges from the

Repeated El Niño events since 2000 caused mayhem, bringing increased rainfall over northern Australia and extended drought elsewhere. The latter has caused major anguish to river systems and has accentuated the danger of bushfires in those parts of the country already susceptible to them. There's little doubt that the devastating fires that hit Victoria in February 2009 were exacerbated by years of dry conditions.

Elsewhere, water is the problem. Tropical cyclones have regularly wrought havoc on the north and east coasts, most notably Cyclone

The dramatic Tasmanian coast.

limestone cliffs at the edge of the Nullarbor Plain to the jagged rock formations of Tasmania and western Victoria, from the mangrove swamps of the north to the spectacular beauty of the Great Barrier Reef – a lagoon which runs almost 2,000km (1,250 miles) down the Queensland coast and contains more than 2,000 coral reefs.

At risk

Australia manages to avoid the major fault lines that cause such trouble for its earthquake-plagued neighbours. It's pretty short of active volcanoes, too. Although there are plenty of other natural hazards to deal with, most are climate-related.

Tracy, which ripped into Darwin on Christmas Eve 1974; and Cyclone Yasi, which just missed Cairns in 2011, but still brought lots of rain and winds. There have been several storms in tropical Queensland, including Cyclone Larry, which hit the Innisfail and surroundings in 2006.

Further south, when droughts do break, they tend to do so with a vengeance. Rainfall at the end of 2010 and beginning of 2011 caused floods in southern Queensland that affected an area greater than France and Germany combined. Nothing happens by halves in Australia. Luckily, the Australian spirit is indomitable, and the local people work hard to recover quickly from events like these.

DECISIVE DATES

c.50,000 BC
The first Australians arrive, overland from New Guinea.

8000 BC
Returning boomerangs are used for hunting.

9th century
Seafarers from China possibly reach Australia's north coast.

1290s
Marco Polo's journal refers to a land south of Java, rich in gold and shells.

1606
Dutchman Willem Janszoon lands on the western side of Cape York Peninsula – the first verifiable European landing.

1642
Abel Tasman names the west coast of Tasmania Van Diemen's Land.

1688
English buccaneer William Dampier lands on the northwest coast.

1770
Captain Cook lands at Botany Bay, then sails northward, charting 4,000km (2,500 miles) of coast.

1773
The first picture of a kangaroo is seen in Britain.

1788
First Fleet arrives in Sydney Cove with a cargo of convicts.

1790
Second Fleet arrives.

An Australian propaganda poster from World War I.

1793
First free immigrants arrive.

1801–3
Matthew Flinders proves Australia is a single island by circumnavigation.

1813
Australia's own currency is established. The first crossing is made of the Blue Mountains.

1817
The name Australia is adopted (instead of New Holland).

1829
First settlers land at Fremantle, and found Perth two days later. Western Australia becomes a colony.

1830
All Aborigines in Tasmania are rounded up and herded into reserves.

1831
Publication of *Quintus Servinton*, the first Australian novel, by

Henry Savery, a former convict.

1838
The Myall Creek Massacre: 28 Aborigines are butchered by white farmers.

1851
Gold discovered, first in NSW and then Victoria.

1854
Battle at the Eureka Stockade between state troopers and miners protesting against licence fees.

1855
Van Diemen's Land becomes Tasmania.

1859
European rabbits are introduced near Geelong; by 1868 they have eaten most of western Victoria's vegetation.

1860
First south–north crossing (Melbourne to Gulf of Carpentaria), by the Burke and Wills Expedition.

1861
The first Melbourne Cup horse race is watched by 4,000 people.

1868
The transportation of British convicts ends.

1880
Bushranger Ned Kelly is captured and hanged.

1883
Silver is discovered at Broken Hill, NSW.

1891
Delegates from the six colonies meet in Sydney to draft a constitution.

1893
Gold rush in Kalgoorlie, Western Australia.

1896
Athlete Edwin Flack represents Australia at the first modern Olympic Games.

1901
The six colonies join together to become a federation, the Commonwealth of Australia.

1914–18
330,000 Australians serve in World War I; 60,000 are killed, 165,000 wounded.

1915
Australian troops take a major part in the Gallipoli siege; more than 8,000 are killed.

1928
Royal Flying Doctor Service is founded in Queensland.

1932
Sydney Harbour Bridge opens.

1942
15,000 Australians are captured when Singapore falls to Japan. Japanese bomb Darwin.

1950
Immigration peaks at 150,000 new arrivals.

1954
Elizabeth II is the first reigning monarch to visit Australia.

1959
Danish architect Jørn Utzon wins the competition to design Sydney Opera House.

1967
Aborigines are finally granted Australian citizenship and the right to vote.

1973
Sydney Opera House is completed. Australian Patrick White wins Nobel Prize for Literature.

1974
The town of Darwin is flattened by Cyclone Tracy.

1985
Uluru, Kata Tjuta and the surrounding desert (now a National Park) are returned to Aboriginal control.

1986
The Australian film *Crocodile Dundee*, starring Paul Hogan, grosses $116 million in the United States.

1995
Australians protest strongly over French nuclear testing in the South Pacific.

1999
Australians vote against becoming a republic.

2000
Sydney hosts the Summer Olympic Games.

2002
A bombing in Bali by Islamist extremists kills 88 Australians.

2006
Melbourne hosts the Commonwealth Games.

2008
Prime Minister Kevin Rudd apologises to the Stolen Generations (Aboriginal children forcibly taken from their families to be raised by whites).

2009
Bushfires in Victoria claim 173 lives.

2010
Julia Gillard is the first woman to be elected Prime Minister.

2011
Queensland is devastated by floods over 1 million sq km (386,000 sq miles).

2012
Australia wins a seat on the United Nations Security Council.

2013
Heatwave causes more devastating bushfires across Victoria and New South Wales. Sydney has its hottest day on record – 45.8°C (114°F).

2014
Lindt café siege in Sydney claims three lives.

2015
Malcolm Turnbull becomes 29th Prime Minister.

Sydney Opera House under construction, 1966.

Australian aboriginal, from
Ebenezer Sibly's 'Universal System
of Natural History'.

J. Ihle Delt.

J. Chapman Sculpt.

An exact Portrait of
A Savage of Botany Bay.

DREAMTIME AND DISCOVERY

Living in harmony with the land, Australia's Aborigines developed a culture rich and complex in its customs, religions and lifestyles, which was abruptly interrupted by the arrival of the British in 1788.

Long before the ancient civilisations in the Middle East, Europe and the Americas flourished, and more than 50,000 years before European, Asian or Middle Eastern navigators recorded visits to the shores of "the Great South Land", Australian Aborigines occupied this continent – its arid deserts and tropical rainforests, and especially its major river systems and coastal plains and mountains. Estimates by anthropologists put the population of Aborigines, prior to 1770, at more than 300,000.

The ancient traditions of these people are based on a close spiritual bond with every living thing and with the land as represented in rocks, rivers and other geographical features.

The dawn of creation

Dreamtime is the basis of all traditional Aboriginal thought and practice, informing their cultural, historical and ancestral heritage. Dreamtime was the dawn of all creation, when the land, the rivers, the rain, the wind and all living things were generated. The individual exists within an eternal Dreaming, only attaining physical embodiment through a mother and briefly existing on Earth before returning to the Dreamtime continuum. The place of birth is key in relating an individual to a specific region or clan.

Tribal elders are responsible for maintaining the clan's group identity through its totemistic belief system. Each clan forms special bonds with a totem, usually an animal or a plant that acts as a protector and a symbol of group identity. Through special ceremonies and other social and religious practices, the elders transmit their knowledge to younger generations.

A cave painting of a turtle on Ubirr Rock at Kakadu in the Northern Territory.

EARLY EXPLORERS

The Greeks, the Hindus and Marco Polo had all speculated upon the location and nature of the "Great South Land". The Arabs, Chinese and the Malays had probably come and gone, as had the Portuguese. The Dutch came, looked and left, disappointed at not finding "uncommonly large profit". At the end of the 17th century, the English explorer and privateer William Dampier was appalled by the bleak landscape of the northwestern coast, inhabited by "the miserablest people on earth". The fertile east coast was missed by just a few kilometres by both the French explorer Louis Antoine de Bougainville and the Spaniard Luis Vaez de Torres.

Aborigines have always celebrated the adventures of their Dreamtime spirit heroes through paintings, songs and sacred dances. Rock paintings are of special significance, bearing the strongest psychological and ritual values. As Aboriginal language was not written, these paintings, along with the oration of legends by tribal leaders, were the main media for passing Dreamtime stories from one generation to the next.

The Aboriginal ceremony of celebrating with song and dance is called *corroboree*. For centuries the male dancers have been experts at mimicking the movements of animals; with these skills they reconstructed legends, heroic deeds or famous hunts. Bodies were elaborately painted, and songs were chanted to the accompaniment of music sticks and boomerangs clapped together.

Basic dance themes deal with hunting and food gathering, or sex and fertility; sometimes they take a humorous vein, but more often they deal seriously with the business of life. Some tribes use a long, hollow piece of wood which, when blown, emits a droning sound. This is the didgeridoo, whose sound is said to resemble the calling of the spirits.

An engraving depicting a night-time Aboriginal corroboree.

CAPTAIN JAMES COOK

James Cook was stern and hot-tempered; physically, he was tall, dark and handsome. He was also, in the parlance of his time, a "tarpaulin", an officer who had prospered without the boost of an aristocratic birth.

Born in 1728, the son of a Yorkshire farm labourer, at age 18 he was apprenticed into the North Sea colliers. Enlisting in the Royal Navy in 1755, he distinguished himself as a navigator and a master, particularly on the St Lawrence River in Quebec, Canada, during the Seven Years' War with France.

A courageous and proud man, Cook was driven more by a sense of duty and personal excellence than by greed or God. All supplies of fresh food which his crew obtained he "caused to be equally divided among the whole company generally by weight, so the meanest person in the Ship had an equal share with myself [Cook] or anyone on board." As for the soul-snatching men of the cloth, he would never permit a parson to sail on any of his ships. Reflecting during his homeward journey upon the state of the Australian Aborigine, he took a remarkably enlightened view, writing the classic description of the noble savage: "In reality they are far more happier than we European; being wholly unacquainted with not only the superfluous but the necessary Conveniences so much sought after in Europe… the Earth and sea of their own accord furnishes them with all things necessary for life."

Aborigines believe that a person's spirit does not die with their last breath, and that ceremonies are essential to ensure that the spirit leaves the body and becomes re-embodied elsewhere – in a rock, a tree, an animal, or perhaps another human form. This explains why such significance has been attached to the retrieval of cadavers or body parts from museums around the world, returning them to the country of their birth and performing the ceremonies to finally bring the spirit to peace.

Each person is the centre of an intricate web of relationships which give order to the entire world. In the late 18th century, this delicate relationship with the land was thrown out of kilter with the arrival of the Europeans. Aboriginal culture had prepared the people for many things they might expect to face in life – except the coming of the white man.

The impact of Captain Cook

When James Cook, a 41-year-old Royal Navy lieutenant, dropped anchor in 1770 in an east-coast bay that so teemed with exotic new life forms he decided to call it Botany Bay, he verified by flag and map an idea that Europe had long suspected.

Cook had been sent by the Admiralty to Tahiti, at the request of the Royal Society, to observe a transit of the planet Venus. Among the company of 94 on his second-hand coal ship *Endeavour* were Daniel Carl Solander and Joseph Banks, two great botanists of the age.

After leaving Tahiti, Cook sailed southwest to New Zealand and spent six months charting both islands. He was then free to return to England by either the Cape or the Horn. Instead, he and his officers decided upon a route that would lead towards the unknown, the fabled South Land.

On 28 April 1770, *Endeavour* anchored in Botany Bay for one week. No naturalists before or since Solander and Banks have ever collected in such a short time so many new specimens of plant, bird and animal life. Meanwhile, the sailors ate their fill of seafoods, causing Cook at first to name the place Stingray Harbour Bay. He later changed it to Botany Bay because of Solander and Banks' discoveries.

A claim for the king

Sailing north, Cook sighted and named (but did not enter) Port Jackson, Sydney's great harbour-to-be. On 22 August, at Possession Island off the tip of Cape York, he hoisted the British colours and claimed the whole of the eastern side of the continent under "the name of New South Wales" for George III.

Upon reaching London in 1771, Cook reported to the Admiralty that he had found the east coast of New Holland, but not the Great South Land – if indeed such a place existed. During his voyage of 1772 to 1775, he destroyed the historical myth of the Great South Land by using the westerlies to circumnavigate the Antarctic. In 1779, he died at the hands of Polynesians in the Hawaiian islands.

Captain James Cook.

THE NEW SETTLERS

The transportation of convicts was phased out between 1840 and 1868. By 1860, the continent had been divided into five separate colonies, with each exhibiting (at times) more loyalty to Mother London than to any neighbouring siblings. A major force within the colonies was the "squatocracy", the rich officers, emancipated convicts and free settlers who had followed the explorers into the fertile hinterlands. They had simply laid claim to or squatted upon enormous tracts of land, often 8,000 hectares (20,000 acres) or more. Like the merino sheep they introduced to their stations, the squatters both lived off and were the fat of the land.

The First Fleet

In May 1787, 11 small ships of the First Fleet under Captain (later Governor) Arthur Phillip sailed from Portsmouth. Eight months later, the 1,000 passengers and prisoners arrived at Botany Bay. Three-quarters of them were convicts, since Britain had been forced to find a new dumping ground for rebels, poachers, prostitutes and murderers after it lost the New World colonies in the American War of Independence. The auguries for Australia's future were not those of the Promised Land.

A quick survey showed two things: Cook's

A painting of ships of the First Fleet in Sydney Cove.

A TOUGH BEGINNING

Officers, marines, transportees, sheep, goats and cattle were disgorged in 1788 into a cove that is now overlooked by the Sydney Opera House. The surgeon-general to the fleet rhapsodised that Port Jackson was "the finest and most extensive harbour in the Universe." It is said that even the convicts raised a cheer of joy. It is also noted that two Aborigines shouted "Warra! Warra!" (Go away!); no one heeded. Thus the colony stumbled to life. It was a rough beginning. The English authorities did not provision the expedition well; many of the tools were next to useless, and their crops failed to thrive in the unusually sandy soil.

description of the place was far too generous; and two ships of the Comte de la Pérouse were also there, possibly shopping for a new continent on behalf of France's Louis XVI. Phillip hurriedly sailed 20km (12 miles) up the coast to Port Jackson and raised the flag for George III on 26 January 1788.

After 30 months of isolation, locked in by the natural prison of the alien bush and suffering from a lack of decent supplies, the settlement was down to half rations. When a ship finally appeared, to their despair, it was carrying not supplies but 222 elderly and ill female convicts. Fortunately, the supply ships of the Second Fleet were close behind.

The birth of Sydney

The tents at Sydney Cove were eventually replaced by brick and timber huts. Phillip tried to lay out a town along orderly lines, but conformity was not in the nature of its inhabitants. Short cuts soon became streets and, despite later attempts at order, the convenient jigsaw that resulted can still be observed today as the ground plan of Sydney's high-rise pile-up.

Sydney Town expanded west towards the fertile farming lands of Parramatta, but was still hemmed in by the impenetrable escarpment of the Blue Mountains. Explorers fanned out by land and sea to open new pastures and farms, and to establish even more isolated and savage prisons, such as Norfolk Island. This small piece of land in the Pacific originally figured in British strategy as a potential source for flax, needed to create sails. Unfortunately, the island became known as a hellhole of corporal punishment.

Conditions weren't that much better in Sydney. In 1804, prisoners at Castle Hill Reserve rose against the government. Some 200 convicts set out to capture Parramatta, then tried to seize the ships in Sydney Harbour. Troops swiftly quelled the rebellion at what became known as the Battle of Vinegar Hill. Nine of the ringleaders were hanged and another nine received between 200 and 500 lashes from the whip.

New South Wales was still costing London dearly (£1 million in the first 12 years), but it was turning a profit for its local landowners and the officers of the NSW Corps, otherwise known as "the Rum Corps". The Corps resisted the extortionate demands of trading-vessel masters, and developed its own monopolies. The colony had become such a vat of drunkenness, and the demand for Bengal rum (which the Corps controlled) was so great that rum almost became the currency of the colony.

Captain Bligh fails again

Governor William Bligh (of *Bounty* fame) was despatched to clean up the Rum Corps' act, and to encourage free settlers to come to Sydney. However, the Corps, at the bidding of farmer and officer John Macarthur, pulled the second of the famous mutinies in Bligh's career, and in 1808 deposed him.

New South Wales and its penal settlements

from the inhuman conditions was to commit murder in the hope of being hanged.

Transportation to Australia's penal settlements ceased by 1868. By then, 160,000 convicts had arrived; only 25,000 were women, a distortion which left its stamp on the harsh, frontier society for decades. These pioneers made few concessions to each other and none to the original inhabitants of the land.

No Man's Land

When the First Fleet arrived, no war was declared against the indigenous people. The

A painting of the view of Parramatta, showing the barracks and Sydney Cove.

at Moreton Bay (now Brisbane), Norfolk Island and Van Diemen's Land (Tasmania) entered the 19th century with a reputation as "hell on Earth" – a reputation that the British hoped would serve as a deterrent to crime.

Forgers, unionists, and petty thieves caught stealing bits of muslin or loaves of bread were thrown together in Australia, when death at the end of a noose would often have been more merciful. In attempting to escape, some inadvertently became the interior's first explorers. They fled into the bush; some believed that China lay beyond the Blue Mountains or that a colony of free men dwelt inland. On Norfolk Island, the only guaranteed method of escape

HUNTERS AND GATHERERS

Aborigines lived in clans of 10 to 50 or more people. To survive the harsh Australian landscape, men hunted and women were fishers and gatherers. A good hunter knew intimately the habits of the creatures he stalked, was an expert tracker and understood the seasons and the winds. Each tribe recognised the local landmarks and their links with the rich mythology of Dreamtime. Various geological aspects were sacred sites with their own personality and significance. The Aborigine considered himself, nature and the land inseparably bound and interdependent. In this state of unity, he (and she) achieved a balance with the environment.

British government simply declared the land *terra nullius* – literally, land belonging to nobody – based on the notion that the territory lacked human habitation and could therefore be obtained for free. The first settlers to arrive on Australia's remote shores could not understand the Aboriginal people's nomadic lifestyle or their profound connection to their tribal lands. It seemed that they came and went without reason across the sparse landscape.

European settlers occupied the land; Aboriginal resistance was met with savage reprisals.

The list of convicts on the ship Merchantman from Portland to Western Australia, June 1864.

Those living in the vicinity of Port Jackson were the first to lose their lands, and, as settlement expanded, so began the cycle of attack and reprisal. Previously unknown European diseases brought death and misery to the Aboriginal people, while survivors were reduced to living in abject squalor around the periphery of the settlements. An ugly war of attrition prevailed, and massacres were exacted upon people who often had taken no part in any transgressions.

As the spread of settlement advanced, Aboriginal people ejected from their tribal lands were forced into territory belonging to their neighbours – adding internal conflict to an already difficult predicament. Either way, spears stood no chance against bullets.

Domestic exploration

A continent of 7.7 million sq km (3 million sq miles), much of it searing desert or dense scrub, could not be explored easily. Before the crossing of the Blue Mountains in 1813, most significant exploration took place by sea. Two British sailors, Bass and Flinders, guessed correctly at the separation of Tasmania from the mainland. The French ships of Baudin in 1802, and later of Dumont d'Urville in 1826, scared the colonial authorities into establishing settlements in Tasmania and Western Australia respectively. Once the Great Dividing Range was penetrated in 1813, the drive for new lands, minerals and the glory of being "first there" – wherever "there" happened to be – lured men and women on.

Early explorers believed that the westward-flowing rivers of the NSW interior led towards a vast inland sea. In 1830 Charles

LUDWIG LEICHHARDT

Many early explorers blended courage and folly, but few as spectacularly as Ludwig Leichhardt. In 1844, Leichhardt, a 31-year-old Prussian draft dodger, launched an ambitious northwesterly expedition, despite the fact that he could neither shoot nor see very well; he also had a poor sense of direction. His expedition ran into innumerable difficulties, with provisions lost, and three men speared (one fatally) by natives. Fourteen months after their departure, and long after being given up for dead, Leichhardt and his party staggered into their destination, Port Essington (Darwin). These "men from the grave" were fêted as national heroes; the Prussian government even pardoned Leichhardt for his military desertion.

In April 1848, Leichhardt set out again, this time aiming to trek from Roma in southern Queensland to the Indian Ocean. His party of seven men and 77 beasts was never seen again. The search continued for years, spurred on by finds of skeletons, relics and pack horses. Stories of a wild white man living among Queensland Aborigines in the 1860s suggested that one member, Adolf Classen, might have survived for some time. In all, nine major searches were conducted for survivors or evidence of Leichhardt's party. The desert has never relinquished the tale of their fate; however, the city of Sydney has named one of its suburbs after him.

Sturt and his party set out on the Murrumbidgee River, following its current into the Lachlan and Murray rivers, finally reaching Lake Alexandrina near the South Australia coast. After travelling more than 1,000km (600 miles), they were within sight of the sea, but were unable to reach it. Instead, they had to row back against the current toward their starting point. Their 47 days' rowing, on meagre rations and against flood tides, left Sturt temporarily blind, but is one of the most heroic journeys in Australian exploration.

By 1836, the vast river systems were charted. Tasmania had been explored, and the genocide of its natives had begun. A decade later, most of New South Wales, half of Queensland, and the southern and northern coasts had been thoroughly explored.

However, as late as the 1870s and 1880s, explorers were still having first-contact encounters, often with surprising results. In 1869, South Australia's surveyor-general, G.W. Goyder, surveying the land that was eventually to become Darwin, was invited to a corroboree by the local Larrakia people, who performed word-perfect renditions of 'John Brown's Body', 'The Glory, Hallelujah' and 'The Old Virginia Shore'.

They had learned the words not from "whitefellas" but from the Woolna people who, in turn, had memorised the tunes spying on surveyors working near the Adelaide River.

Heroes and villains

The 19th century is rich in tales of intrepid adventurers. Some of them were driven by the urge to explore unknown territory, but most were motivated by dreams of finding riches. One such tale of misadventures is now deeply ingrained in Australian folklore.

In August 1860, Robert O'Hara Burke and W.J. Wills left Melbourne with a well-equipped team and a camel train (imported from Afghanistan). Their intention was to be the first party to cross the continent from coast to coast.

Burke was brash, inexperienced, supremely confident. Too impatient to wait for the supply camels to keep up, he took Wills and other team members, Grey and King, with him; from Innamincka on Cooper's Creek, he forged ahead in 60°C (140°F) heat. They reached the Gulf of Carpentaria in February 1861 and immediately began retracing their footsteps. Grey died along the way. The three emaciated

survivors finally reached their earlier camp at Innamincka where they had left another companion, William Brahe. But Brahe, who had waited four months for them, had departed only seven hours earlier. After rejecting the assistance of local Aborigines, Burke and Wills died in the Stony Desert. Only King, cared for by Aborigines, survived to tell the story. The Dig Tree is so called because when Brahe's party left camp, they left instructions carved into a tree that provisions were buried nearby. The tree still attracts tourists to this remote pocket of southwest Queensland.

A depiction of farm life.

LACHLAN MACQUARIE

The initial brutality shown to convicts was tempered by the reforms of Governor Lachlan Macquarie (1810–21), by the influence of some emancipists (freed convicts), and by a growing prosperity through trade. Macquarie, a paternalistic autocrat, stifled the Rum Corps' monopoly on the import of spirit, established the colony's own currency (1813) and first bank (1817), and encouraged the first crossing of the Blue Mountains (1813). His programme of public works and town planning (265 projects in 11 years) owes much to Francis Greenway, an emancipist transported to Sydney for forgery, who became the colony's leading architect.

FROM GOLD RUSH TO WORLD WAR

After gold was discovered in the 1850s, a sudden influx of immigrants set out to make their fortune. A similar boom of outlaws set out to relieve them of it. Then, in 1901, the six quarrelling colonies became a nation.

In 1851 Edward Hargraves, an Australian forty-niner (a fortune seeker of the 1849 California gold rush) returned home. He was certain, given the geological similarities he had observed between California and Australia, that gold must exist in New South Wales. Unbeknown to him, gold had been found 10 years earlier by a Rev. W.B. Clarke, but news of the discovery was suppressed. Upon seeing the gold, the Governor, Sir George Gipps, had said: "Put it away, Mr Clarke, or we shall all have our throats cut!"

The announcement on 15 May 1851 of "Gold Discovered!" near Bathurst, 170km (106 miles) west of Sydney, sent shock waves through the Australian colonies. The rush of prospectors to Bathurst was so great that the population of Victoria immediately nosedived. Melbourne employers offered a £200 reward for the discovery of gold near *their* city.

By July the prize had been claimed, and before the end of the year incredibly rich fields were in production in Victoria at Ballarat, Bendigo and Castlemaine. For the businessmen of Melbourne, the finds were a mixed blessing. While the prices of flour, blankets, bread, shovels and mining gear doubled and tripled, there was often no one to sell them. Melbourne and Geelong were almost emptied of able-bodied men.

The Roaring Days

The scene in the goldfields was one of frantic activity, where teams of four or six men worked a claim, digging, shovelling, washing and cradling from dawn to dusk. When the miners hit town, they careened around the streets on horseback or in cabs. At one Melbourne theatre, reported an eyewitness, the actors "were obliged to appear before the footlights to bear a pelting shower of nuggets – a substitute for bouquets

Painting depicting gold panning in Australia.

– many over half an ounce, and several of which fell short of the mark into the orchestra."

Gold rushes flared like bushfire around the continent during the next two decades, and then sporadically for the rest of the century. The last great find was the Kalgoorlie-Coolgardie field in Western Australia in 1892–93.

It was not only the shop assistants of Sydney and the sailors of Port Phillip who caught gold fever. In 1852 alone, 95,000 hopefuls from around the world flooded into New South Wales and Victoria.

The Eureka Stockade

At Ballarat, near Melbourne, the early gold diggers smarted under the imposition, whether they struck gold or not, of a £1-a-month licence fee. Raids by thuggish police who enforced the licence fee *and* collected half the fine from defaulters added to their rancour.

In October 1854 a miner was kicked to death by a local publican, who (despite strong evidence against him) was cleared of the crime. Mass meetings attended by up to 5,000 miners railed against these injustices. The men demanded the granting of universal franchise and the abolition of licence fees. They formed the Ballarat Reform League and on 29 November made a bonfire of their mining licences.

The lieutenant-governor of Victoria, Sir Charles Hotham, sent in the "traps" (policemen) and troopers. Five hundred diggers built a stockade and swore to "fight to defend our rights and liberties". In the early hours of 3 December 1854, a force of 300 infantry, cavalry men and mounted police savagely attacked the sleeping stockade, whose defenders had dwindled to 150. Within 15 minutes it was all over. Six soldiers and 24 miners were dead.

Eventually an amnesty was proclaimed for the rebels, and the licence fee was abolished. While the incident is replete with tragedy and

The site of the 'Eureka Stockade'.

BUSHRANGERS AND REBELS

The gold rush created a new boom in bushranging, or highway robbery. Many an "old lag" (ex-convict), as well as poor settlers, saw that gold need not necessarily be dug from the ground. The proceeds from holding up a stagecoach or gold wagon could be good, and the work was a lot cleaner than digging. One Victorian gang in 1853 relieved the gold escort of 70,000g (more than 2,400oz) of gold and £700 in cash; three gang members were sent to the gallows.

In the 1860s the most famous of the "Wild Colonial Boys" were the bushrangers Ben Hall, Frank Gardiner and John Gilbert. Well-armed and superbly mounted – often on stolen racehorses – they pulled off audacious raids. In

November 1864, Hall's gang of three, working the Sydney–Melbourne road, rounded up 60 travellers at once. Then came the prize for which they were waiting – the armed mail coach. While one bushranger covered the 60 captives, Hall and Gilbert shot the police guard and robbed the coach. Several of the captives came out of the bush, not to aid the police, but to watch the shoot-out.

From their first appearance, bushrangers were often sheltered by the rural poor, many of whom were descendants of political transportees. Their strong republican sentiments led them to regard some of the outlaws as rebels against the same enemy – the British, Protestant landlords and civil authorities.

some farce, the Eureka Stockade and its flag continue to evoke the ideals of revolt against colonialism and bourgeois authority. As Mark Twain commented, Eureka was "the finest thing in Australian history... another instance of a victory won by a lost battle."

The Federation is born

In September 1900, Queen Victoria regally proclaimed that, on 1 January 1901, not only a new century but also a new nation would be born.

A federal government for the six Australian

Strong box used by gold commissioners for storage and carriage of gold in the 19th century.

colonies was generally welcomed. Under the new Constitution the Queen remained head of state, retaining power over all foreign affairs. British parliamentary legislation could overrule any laws passed by the Commonwealth, and legal appeals ultimately were settled in London. Few Australians objected to this arrangement, for each of the six colonies felt more at ease in its dealings with the motherland than with the other colonies.

For her part, Britain did not let the new nation escape the interests of imperialism. She expected, and got, continuing support in her military involvements, and ample returns on her substantial investments in Australia.

The quest for a capital

The new nation needed a capital. Sydney and Melbourne each wished it to be in its own state, and neither of the long-standing rivals would permit it in the other's. After considerable backbiting, a separate Australian Capital Territory was established at a point between the two cities, 320km (200 miles) from Sydney on the beautiful Monaro Tablelands. Some suggested naming the capital Shakespeare – hardly an appropriate choice, considering the anti-intellectual cultural cringers who formed a vocal part of the Australian population. In 1913 the Aboriginal word "Canberra", meaning "meeting place", was chosen instead.

The Great War

When Britain declared war on Germany on 4 August 1914, Australia, as a member of the British Empire, was automatically at war, too. The response by both Labor and Liberal parties was immediate. By the end of October the First Australian Infantry Force of 20,000 volunteers had been despatched to Europe via Egypt. Many were to die at Gallipoli.

The Australian "Diggers" (soldiers) were deployed in France, on the Western Front, from April 1916. In the grisly attacks, through mustard gas and frozen winters, their losses were appalling – 23,000 dead in nine weeks in the First Battle of the Somme, 38,000 at Ypres, 10,000 at Bullecourt. The new nation was being cut down. Indeed, so was some of the old nation; more than 420 Aboriginal soldiers served in the war, largely from Tasmania's Bass Strait islands.

Many Australians were now questioning the sense of supporting Britain in what they saw as a "sordid trade war". But a deciding factor was the presence at Australia's helm of a feisty and dogged little man who was loved and loathed with equal passion: William Morris ("Billy") Hughes, or "the Little Digger".

In 1916 Hughes pledged a supply of 16,500 Australian troops a month. Such a number could be raised only through conscription – previously, recruitment was voluntary. The proposal was defeated narrowly in a referendum, and Hughes was expelled from his own Labor Party. He set about forming a national coalition government and held a second referendum in December 1917. He was defeated but bounced back, winning a seat at the Versailles Peace Conference.

Of the 330,000 Australian troops who fought in the war, 226,000 (68.5 percent) were casualties, a greater percentage by far than suffered by any other Allied nation.

The Great Depression

Between 1929 and 1933 every government in Australia, both state and federal, was thrown out of office by an electorate deciding to "give the other mob a go – they couldn't be worse." But unfortunately they could do no better, for the Great Depression had arrived. Thirty percent of the country's breadwinners were on "Susso" (sustenance benefits). Wearing World War I surplus greatcoats, hundreds were tramping the Outback roads as "swagmen" looking for rural work.

Australia's economy was based heavily upon the export of wheat and wool, and upon continued borrowings from Britain. When world prices for primary products slumped by 50 percent, and when Britain withdrew £30 million from the Australian economy, the result was traumatic, especially for the poor.

Sir Otto Niemeyer of the Bank of England was despatched to scold Australians for living at an unsustainably high standard, to advise wage cuts and retrenchments, and to make sure that

Ned Kelly surrounded by police.

THE KELLY GANG

Ned Kelly was born in 1854 and grew up among impoverished Irish farmers near Benalla, northern Victoria. He first ran foul of the law in 1877, when he shot a constable in the wrist. Teaming up with his brother Dan and two friends, Joe Byrne and Steve Hart, he fled to the bush and turned outlaw. The following year, in a shoot-out at Stringybark Creek, Ned killed three of a party of four police who were hunting him. From then on, the Kellys became part of Australian folklore. Ned saw himself as a Robin Hood, a defender of the free against the oppressive British overlords. Instead of robbing coaches, his gang bailed-up whole towns, cutting the telegraph and robbing the bank before escaping.

The gang hid out in the Wombat Ranges, but in June 1880, on hearing that a train-load of police was on the way to arrest them, they captured the town of Glenrowan, Victoria, and held the townsfolk prisoner in the hotel. A furious shoot-out erupted between the Kellys and the cops. Wounded, Ned donned his suit of home-made armour and attempted to escape. Instead, he stumbled into the police who at first thought they were seeing a ghostly apparition. Ned was shot down but not killed. The police torched the hotel and the other three members of the Kelly Gang died within rather than surrender. Four months later in Melbourne, Kelly was sentenced to death. He was hanged on 11 November 1880.

the interest was still paid on the loans.

World War II

When Britain again went to war against Germany in September 1939, Australia once more automatically entered the conflict. A Second Australian Infantry Force was raised and despatched to the Middle East.

In 1939 Australia's prime minister, the leader of the United Australia Party, was Robert Gordon Menzies, a clever, witty barrister and a deeply conservative Anglophile. He had earned the nickname "Pig-Iron Bob" by selling pig iron to the re-arming Japanese, of whom Australia had become increasingly nervous.

While Australian air, land and sea forces fought in Britain, the Mediterranean, North Africa, Greece and the Middle East, Japan began to move south, first into French Indochina. Australian forces were sent to Malaya, the Dutch East Indies, Darwin and Rabaul (New Guinea) to try to stem the tide of the Japanese invasion forces.

In Canberra, Pig-Iron Bob was reviled for his Chamberlain-like pre-war appeasement of the Axis powers. By October 1941 a Labor Government under John Curtin was in power.

Australian and New Zealand troops on the way to Gallipoli in 1915.

THE CHINESE INFLUX

The vast majority of gold-diggers were British, but the Chinese were also numerous. In the five years from 1854, more than 40,000 flocked to the Victorian fields. The Chinese lived in their own communities, were diligent labourers, and produced only one Chinese bushranger, San Poo.

By 1887, Asian immigration was stifled. Australia inaugurated "the White Australia Policy" with federation and nationhood in 1901. The Immigration Act allowed an impossibly tough dictation test in any European language to be given to all non-European arrivals. It was not until 1966 that there was any genuine reversal of this race-based exclusion.

A nation comes of age

The Japanese attack on the United States at Pearl Harbor confirmed Australia's great fear: to be isolated in an Asia at war. When Singapore fell on 15 February 1942, 15,000 of the 130,000 captured troops were Australian. The country was faced with the fact that a distant and beleaguered Britain could be of no real assistance against an imminent Japanese invasion.

Japanese planes bombed Darwin on 19 February and Broome on 3 March. Arms and food caches were established in the northern regions of the continent. Australia faced the very real threat of invasion by Japanese troops.

The Australian war cabinet outraged Prime Minister Winston Churchill by diverting the

7th Australian Division from the defence of British Burma to the New Guinea and Pacific theatres. If it is true, as is commonly said, that the Australian nation was born at Gallipoli, it is no less true that with the fall of Singapore Australia finally came of age.

The end of the war

The tide began to turn against Japan in May 1942, when a combined fleet of American and Australian forces checked the Japanese at the Battle of the Coral Sea. The US victory at Midway in June assured Allied control of the Pacific, but on New Guinea, Japanese foot soldiers were closing in on Australia's main base at Port Moresby. After months of guerrilla combat and hand-to-hand jungle fighting, the Australian troops finally pushed them back.

Of the 1 million Australian servicemen and women who enlisted, almost 10,000 died in Europe and more than 17,000 in the Pacific. Of those taken prisoner by the Japanese, 8,000 did not survive the Japanese camps. An Aboriginal complement of more than 3,000 bravely served in the forces, despite official discouragement early in the war.

A wrecked Japanese plane after the Battle of the Coral Sea, 1942.

THE DEATH TOLL OF GALLIPOLI

While Australia's troops trained in Egypt, Winston Churchill (then First Lord of the Admiralty in London) conceived a plan to relieve Turkish pressure on Russia's troops by forcing an entrance to the Black Sea. He wanted to capture the Dardanelles, and ordered the waiting Australian, New Zealand, French, British, Indian and Gurkha divisions to attack from the sea. The Turks, warned of British intentions, entrenched themselves in fortified positions along the ridges of the Gallipoli Peninsula. Their commanders (Mustafa Kemal and the German Liman von Sanders) were able to direct their fire upon the exposed beaches below without exposing their own troops to much risk.

From 25 April 1915, when they landed, until 20 December, when they withdrew, the Allied forces were pinned down to the near-vertical cliffs and narrow coves. There was both horrendous carnage and epic heroism. During the eight months of fighting at Gallipoli, 78,000 were wounded and 33,500 killed on the side of Britain and its allies. Of the dead, 8,587 were ANZACs (belonging to the Australian and New Zealand Army Corps). Almost as many French died at Gallipoli, and twice as many Britons, Indians and Nepalis fell. On the other side, 250,000 Turks died in battle. Nevertheless, out of this baptism by mud, shrapnel and gallantry arose Australia's first coherent sense of nationhood and identity.

Sculpture at the National Gallery of Victoria.

THE MODERN ERA

Over the past 60 years, Australia has witnessed a trebling of the population, industrial booms and economic slumps, rigid conservatism and progressive liberalism.

Australian history since World War II has been an up-and-down saga – a rise to undreamed-of affluence in the 1950s and 60s when the wool prices boomed, followed by unexpected cracks in the great suburban dream. Today the image of the country as a conservative, Anglo-Saxon society somehow finding itself lost in Asia has been completely recast. But the road towards a cosmopolitan, liberal, middle-class Australia has been tortuous. For a small country – population-wise – of which it was said "nothing ever happens", there has been a succession of booms, recessions, political crises, wars, culture shocks and social changes.

The 1940s were the most difficult years in Australia's history, the long war against Japan emphasising the country's vulnerability. The war also shook up Australian society internally; many women served in the armed forces, or worked in factories or office jobs that had previously been reserved for men, and were reluctant to go back to the old inequality between the sexes.

Radical post-war changes

In 1946, Australians voted an activist Labor government, led by Ben Chifley, into power with plans for an expanded social welfare programme. In quick succession, Chifley set up a government-owned airline, took initiatives in housing and education (the Australian National University was opened in Canberra), and ordered massive work projects such as the Snowy Mountains Scheme, which provided hydroelectric power for southeast Australia.

The most radical and revitalising change, however, occurred in immigration. The spectre

Migrants sail into Sydney Harbour in 1949.

GOVERNMENT AND POLITICS

Australians are triple-governed – by local councils, and at the state and federal levels. According to polls, most people feel that politics is the least trustworthy of professions. Many people believe that a nation of nearly 24 million people can't produce enough talent to run three levels of government. Judging by the acres of newsprint and airspace devoted to the topic, the nation is obsessed with politics, though no more than a few thousand people are members of political parties. Everyone votes because they have to: federal law made it compulsory in 1924; unless you have a good excuse, you will receive a small fine for not voting.

of a Japanese invasion in World War II convinced Australians that the country's population must increase. Labor's immigration minister, Arthur Calwell, embarked upon one of the most spectacular migration programmes of the 20th century. Half of the assisted migrants were to be British, but the other half could come from anywhere – as long as they were white. More than 2 million migrants arrived between 1945 and 1965, helping Australia's population to leap from 7 to 11 million.

The nation still clung to its White Australia policy, and Calwell himself was a racist. (He

Queen Elizabeth II and Australian Prime Minister Robert Gordon Menzies arrive at a state banquet in Canberra during the Queen's tour of Australia in 1954.

made the infamous wisecrack, when asked whether he would permit Asian immigration, "Two Wongs don't make a white.") The policy was modified slowly in later years until it was formally abolished in 1973. So rapid has been the overturning of these anachronistic attitudes that at the present time one-third of all immigrants are Asian.

The "boring" 1950s

Still, mainstream Australian culture changed slowly. In the 1950s, Australia remained a rigid society, one which had grown up in comparative isolation and was complacent

and illiberal. It was still dominated by men, despite the post-war challenge from women: male rituals like sport, drinking and brawling predominated; homosexuals were persecuted as "poofters" and anyone with a beard or long hair was dubbed a "weirdo". Male values such as "mateship" were extolled, while "the missus" was expected to stay at home and look after the kids. It seemed, visually and ethically, a very working-class society, a land of boots and felt hats, of men in dank pubs calling each other "mate" or "sport".

The churches, especially the Roman Catholic Church, dominated morals; divorce was legal, but it was condemned and hard to obtain. Abortion remained illegal, the province of backstreet doctors. The nation was burdened with a suffocating puritanism which Australians labelled "wowserism". Censorship was strict: James Joyce's *Ulysses* and D.H. Lawrence's *Lady Chatterley's Lover* were banned, and had to be smuggled into the country. The language was stamped with prejudices, many directed at migrants and refugees ("reffos").

Politically, the decade is referred to as the "Boring Fifties". A revived conservative party – known as the Liberal Party (although it was formally and ideologically unrelated to its British namesake and often far from liberal in its literal sense) – was led by the rabid Anglophile Robert Menzies. He proclaimed himself "British to his boot-straps" and was able to tap into the growing Cold War hysteria, attacking the Labor Party for being riddled with Communists.

When rising unemployment threatened to turn the Liberals out of office, Menzies decided to plump for safe, middle-of-the-road policies that would disturb neither extreme of the electorate. The Labor Party split in 1955 on ideological lines and effectively kept itself out of power for another 17 years.

"Development" became the national slogan; there were posters everywhere stressing peace, prosperity and progress, and even the arrival of rock'n'roll from the United States didn't seem to disturb the social equanimity. There were a few rebel groups, such as the bodgies (male) and widgies (female), who did such radical things as ride motorcycles and listen to Elvis, but it was hardly more than a milk-bar menace. Another nonconformist group was the Sydney "Push", a group of freethinkers and libertarians who gathered at pubs and coffee shops and scorned the suburban coma ward that surrounded them. They wrote poetry and bawdy songs and, though mainly a male group, produced two remarkable women – Germaine Greer, author of *The Female Eunuch*, and the late Lillian Roxon, author of the first *Rock Encyclopedia*.

The affluent 1960s

Meanwhile, Australia had begun turning itself from a nation of primary industry (sheep, wheat and cattle) to one of manufacturing. Between 1940 and 1960 the number of factories doubled; fridges, washing machines, vacuum cleaners and cars became available to the great mass of the population for the first time.

By the mid-1960s, Australians were enjoying (after the Americans) the highest standard of living in the world. They were also living in the most urbanised nation on Earth, with three-quarters of the population in cities – more than half of that on the eastern seaboard.

Barry Humphries as Dame Edna Everage, 1976.

THE FLIGHT OF THE FREE SPIRITS

Every year from the late 1950s onward, thousands of young Australians left on their equivalent of the Grand Tour of London and other cities in Europe, seeking excitement and the sort of mind-broadening experience which was unavailable at home.

They could hardly be blamed. The newsreels of the time, seen now, are embarrassingly nationalistic, racist and sexist. The pubs closed at 6pm sharp each weekday, producing the infamous "six o'clock swill", when men crammed into bars and guzzled as much as they could between the end of work and closing time (women wouldn't have been allowed in even if they'd wanted to). Off-course betting was illegal, so SP (starting price) bookmakers flourished alongside sly-grog joints, where liquor could be bought after hours. There is another side to the story, too. During the prosperous 1950s Australia enjoyed the most even income distribution of any Western industrialised nation.

Well into the 1960s, the district of Earls Court in London became an Aussie ghetto; unique talents like Barry Humphries, Clive James and Robert Hughes all fled Australia. The nation's best artists and writers – Patrick White, Germaine Greer and Sidney Nolan among them – turned themselves into expatriates.

Links with the Old Country were weakened when Britain joined the European Economic Community; trade with the US and Japan grew to fill the gap. The 1951 ANZUS security treaty brought Australia and New Zealand securely within the USA's sphere.

In the meantime, the shape of Australian society was being entirely changed. In the early 1960s the number of white-collar workers exceeded, for the first time, the number of blue-collar workers, and then streaked far ahead. This booming group typically lived in comfortable suburban homes, owned cars

Gough Whitlam, Australian politician, campaigning in 1972.

and TVs, had bank accounts, and voted Liberal (Australian for "Conservative"). Australia, regarded for so long as a working man's paradise, had transformed itself (almost unnoticed) into one of the most middle-class nations in the world.

But, amid the prosperity, many were dejected over the fate of Australia and the consequences of its new-found wealth. Donald Horne wrote a book called, with heavy irony, *The Lucky Country* – a land that had squandered its opportunities and abandoned its best egalitarian traditions to wallow in complacency. The Australian social ideal of communality was changing and with it, apparently, the Australian character.

Cracks began to appear in the bland facade of Australian contentment. In 1962 Australia became involved in the Vietnam War; in the next 10 years she sent 49,000 conscripts, chosen by lottery, off to the jungles of Southeast Asia – where 499 were killed and 2,069 wounded. As in the United States, the antiwar movement breathed life into all forms of liberalisation, pushing Australia into an era of crisis and questioning.

Political change in the 1970s

When the Labor Party, led by Gough Whitlam, finally won office in 1972 under the slogan "It's Time", it seemed to many that a clean break with the past had occurred and a promising new, progressive era was about to begin.

Labor moved quickly to abolish military conscription, to end Australia's involvement in Vietnam, to recognise China and to begin

THE SPIRIT OF THE 1960S

Student power, the women's movement, black power and sexual liberation groups began challenging the conservative consensus. The rigid censorship of books and films was slowly dismantled, allowing Australians the opportunity to pore over previously forbidden classics of literature such as *Lolita* and *Portnoy's Complaint*. Aborigines had been allowed to vote in federal elections in 1967, but a "freedom bus" drove through Queensland and New South Wales in protest against the deep-rooted, systematic discrimination against black people. At the same time, it was found that 10 percent of Australians were living in chronic poverty; they included Aborigines, single parents, and the sick, disabled and jobless.

At the same time, migrants began transforming the staid British social customs of their host country. At an obvious level there was the introduction of delicatessens, continental European food, open-air cafés, new varieties of music and a hectic sort of cosmopolitanism hardly imaginable before World War II. More profoundly, the migrants also opened Australians up to new ideas and new ways of looking at the world that have gradually altered the national character. Spurred on by the new spirit, a revived Labor Party argued for new policies on a grand scale, and was led by its most inspiring politician for years, the towering, bushy-browed, charismatic Gough Whitlam.

the long process of reconstructing the social welfare system. Everything appeared to happen at once, with plans under way for a universal health-care system, increased support for the arts (resulting in a spate of Australian films), and the formal end of White Australia.

But Whitlam didn't reckon on the economic and social impacts of big government spending. He managed to win another election in 1974 but was confronted with a sudden and unexpected world recession provoked by an oil price hike. Australians suddenly faced growing inflation and unemployment,

election, consolidated his power and swore he would take politics off the front page.

Stability under Labor – the 1980s and 90s

In 1983 a new Labor era began when Australians voted in a government led by Bob Hawke, an ex-union leader, ex-Rhodes scholar and ex-world champion beer drinker (2.5 pints in 11 seconds). Hawke later wrote that this feat did most for his political career in a country "with a strong beer culture". The Labor Party became more right-wing, economically liberal and in

Germaine Greer at a women's liberation march in Sydney's Hyde Park, 1972.

and the government was beset by a series of damaging scandals.

Labor was hobbled in its programme by a conservative majority vote in the Senate. In 1975 the Liberal-National Country Party opposition, led by Malcolm Fraser, used this power to deny the government its money supply. Whitlam refused to resign, and the nation was thrust into a grave political and constitutional crisis. This was resolved in a controversial manner: the governor-general, Sir John Kerr, as the Queen's representative in Australia, dismissed Whitlam and called another election. It was an act that many considered illegal – in spirit, if not in the letter of the Constitution. Fraser won the subsequent

closer touch with the increasingly powerful white-collar unions and business.

For the next 13 years, Labor ruled with little challenge (with Paul Keating taking over the prime ministership in 1991). Consensus became the catchword, with the government brokering historic accords between business and unions, promising unprecedented industrial peace, and finally introducing a national health-care system for all, Medicare.

This new-look Labor government had to deal with an ever-sliding Australian economy, starting off with a series of devaluations of the Aussie dollar (the "Pacific peso", as it wryly became known). Under Keating, Labor presided over a push towards free-market policies, yet was able to maintain some degree of social justice by keeping Australia's welfare system intact.

Diplomatically and economically, Australia linked itself much more closely to Asia, while on the home front Asian immigration was stepped up, shifting the emphasis away from European immigration. Women were admitted to more positions of power, and Aboriginal land rights (control over their native homelands) was put on the national agenda. The celebration of the Bicentennial of British settlement in 1988 was a landmark of Australian self-confidence, but also a cause for some

in 1996 voted in a Liberal-National coalition government, led by the determinedly conservative John Howard. In economic matters, Howard advocated a freer market and smaller government. Conservatism also held out in the 1999 referendum, in which Australia voted against becoming a republic and (by the narrowest of majorities) opted to keep the Queen as head of state.

The new millennium

Australia's economic outlook has improved steadily with the globalisation initiatives of

Sydney Harbour Bridge decorated with the Olympic rings, 2000.

national soul-searching. In 1992, a High Court ruling, known as the Mabo case, finally abolished the historical fiction of *terra nullius* – the colonial doctrine that said Australia was uninhabited when the British colonists and convicts first arrived – and opened the way to Aboriginal land claims.

The 1980s and 1990s saw a flowering of the Australian arts, with local film-makers and writers increasingly taking on an international profile. Australians also began talking seriously about becoming a republic at last – an initiative driven by the news that Sydney would host the Olympic Games in 2000.

Despite the steady achievements of these years, Australian voters wearied of Labor and

successive recent governments, a booming resources industry and the often controversial privatisation of the transport, energy and communications monoliths. In recent years the Australian dollar regained considerable ground against the US greenback, reaching parity in 2010. The country celebrated its new-found confidence in the euphoria of Sydney's staging of the 2000 Olympics. Dubbed the "best Games ever" by the IOC president, the Games were an unequivocal success, both as a mark of Australia's sporting prowess and as the ultimate high-profile evidence of Australia as an attractive travel destination.

There were clouds on the horizon, however. Howard championed a foreign policy more closely aligned with that of the United Kingdom and the United States. He then committed troops to the war in Iraq despite widespread public disquiet. A perceived connection of this presence to a spate of terrorist attacks across the Western world was reinforced by the 2002 Bali bombings, in which 202 people died, including 88 young Australians.

John Howard went on to become Australia's second longest-serving prime minister after Robert Menzies. A buoyant economy and a disorganised Labor party helped keep

crisis, and while prudent financial management was to be expected, the aversion to reform was not. As the 2010 election loomed, the party's power brokers did the numbers and ousted Rudd as leader in favour of Julia Gillard. In a knife-edge result, and only with the help of a handful of independents, Julia Gillard became Australia's first female prime minister in September 2010 – nicely coinciding with the tenure of Australia's first female Governor General, Quentin Bryce. Despite Australia's ongoing economic strength, Gillard's minority government has struggled to

Australian Prime Minister Michael Turnball.

him in office; however, an increasing disillusionment among the electorate, exacerbated by the government's treatment of refugees and its refusal to sign the Kyoto Agreement on climate change despite overwhelming evidence of global warming, finally saw Howard and his Liberal-National coalition ousted in 2007. Howard suffered the ultimate ignominy of losing his own seat after 11 years as prime minister.

The Labor Party, led by centre-left Kevin Rudd, took power, surfing a wave of expectation of change. In retrospect, these expectations may have been too high. Rudd was helming one of the few countries to escape largely undamaged in the global financial

maintain support. However, she can be proud of a number of successes, including Australia's appointment to the UN Security Council in 2012.

In 2013, the Liberal/National Coalition, led by Tony Abbott of the Liberal Party, won the federal election. In 2015, after a leadership spill, Malcolm Turnbull became Prime Minister and was hoped to lead the Coalition to victory at the next election. In the first quarter of 2016, the Australian dollar remained at a six-year low due to falling oil prices and the strengthening of the US dollar, among other factors. While unsettling for Australians, the country's appeal as a destination for foreign visitors remains strong.

Centre Place, Melbourne.

Lifeguards on the Sunshine Coast, Queensland.

THE URBAN AUSSIE

Most of the population live in cities and suburbs, and most of them on the coast. But that doesn't stop Australians dreaming of the wide-open Outback.

According to myth, the "true Aussie" is a sun-bronzed stockman or jillaroo, riding the Outback range with a trusty sheepdog – which is like imagining all Americans to be tobacco-chewing cowboys, and Frenchmen going about in berets and striped shirts. Truth be told, Australia is the most urbanised country on Earth, with 80 percent of the population living in cities (66 percent in the state capitals). The Great Australian Dream, still enjoyed by a huge portion of the population, was to live on your own plot of land, with a brick house with a red-tile roof, and host a barbie in the backyard. The dream was founded on the belief that home ownership leads to a better life and is an expression of success and security. However, today's rising property prices are dashing this dream for many. Not willing to let dreams pass them by, many an Australian is happy to simply adapt and be content with an inner-city apartment and to travel the world instead.

Family enjoying a barbie in their backyard.

Clinging to the coast

Most Australians now work in office jobs, and wouldn't recognise a trough of sheep dip if they fell in it. And although many still see the Outback as somehow embodying the most distinctive part of the country, relatively few have visited it, let alone considered living there. Even Patrick White, who set famous novels such as *Voss* in the furthest red-sand-and-spinifex deserts, never actually saw them (he got his images from his friend Sidney Nolan's paintings). White settled in Sydney's eastern suburbs, thousands of kilometres from the Red Centre.

The fact is that Australians have clung to the coast rather naturally, shrugging off the priggish, cramped and tight-lipped spirit of the first British settlers and openly embracing the more

RISING TENSIONS

Events like the Bali bombings of 2002 and the wars in Iraq and Afghanistan have caused racial and religious tensions to shift. Where previously Aboriginal groups were the scapegoats for the ills of urban Australia, now the sizeable Muslim communities are being targeted as troublemakers, despite living peacefully in Australian cities for decades. Racially motivated beach riots erupted in the Sydney suburb of Cronulla in 2005, and in 2009 Indian students protested against racist attacks. For a place that professes an idyllic paradise of sun and opportunity for all, it is a worrying development.

sensual and hedonistic spirit of their Mediterranean environment. At least in the 21st century, the coast – and specifically the beach – has a far more powerful claim on Australian souls than the Outback. "How shall I put this delicately?" asks Sydney writer Robert Drewe. "Most Australians of the past three generations have had their first sexual experience on the coast. So is it surprising that for the rest of their lives the sexual and littoral experiences are entwined in their memories; that most Australians thereafter see the beach in a pleasurable light?" It is to the sea that Australians return at each cru-

Sydney's Gay and Lesbian Mardi Gras.

cial stage of their lives: as young kids, on honeymoon, as parents. It is to the sea that they were taken as children, and to the sea that they return in old age, to the endless retirement villages of the Queensland shores.

How could it really be otherwise, in a country with such a climate and geography? It would take a serious effort of will not to lap up the perfect skies, the sea breeze, the glorious mounds of prawns and oysters, the bodies laid out on the sands and saturated in SPF 30+. Under the Antipodean sun, more austere national traits succumb to the easy-going, tolerant, obsessively casual Australian manner. It's no surprise to see a first-generation immigrant from Glasgow turn into a surfie overnight,

or the daughters of black-shrouded Muslim women lolling bikini-clad in the outdoor beer garden of a pub.

Leisure has become crucial to the Australian way of life – while working from 9 to 5 provides the means, it is at the weekends when Aussies truly come into their own, and few other places give people such opportunities to use their leisure well. Nature is close in Australia as nowhere else: in Sydney, with its 70 metropolitan beaches; in Melbourne, with one-third of its area devoted to parkland; or in Darwin, where 4-metre (13ft) crocodiles are regularly fished from the harbour. Some visitors still arrive expecting kangaroos to hop across the tarmac. This may not be so, but even in the red-brick back blocks of suburbia a national park might begin at the end of the road, and residents may keep an eye out for funnel-web spiders, possums in the roof and snakes in the garden.

Despite the occasional natural menaces, relaxation is part of the territory in Australia. It takes something truly grim to rouse most people to anger – and there's always a swim, or a beer, or a crisp Chardonnay to calm them down. From railway workers to restaurant waiters, the most common response to questions these days is a breezy "No worries", "Too easy" or "Not a problem" – the latest incarnations of the 1950s slogan "She'll be right, mate". Politics is a matter to shake your head at ("The bastards are all the same" is the common refrain at election time). Economics, however, has become a matter of fascination, and taxi drivers and supermarket clerks can talk with authority on economic rationalism and exchange rates.

THE RISE OF GAY CULTURE

Visitors hoping to find the "last refuge of unselfconscious masculinity" – as Ocker Aussies term it – may be disappointed. In recent times, gay culture has exploded in the country – especially in Sydney, which now has a higher concentration of gay residents than San Francisco.

At the first Gay Mardi Gras parade in 1978, police blockades were set up and 53 marchers were taken into custody. Today, the annual parade is the highest-attended event in the country, luring 300,000 to watch floats of fabulously attired folk having fun.

From convicts to democrats

Every country is shaped by its past, and few have had a stranger start than Australia's, as the dumping ground for Britain's petty criminals. As Robert Hughes remarked in *The Fatal Shore*, it's one of the great ironies of history that a land founded by felons should evolve into one of the world's most law-abiding societies. Few cities of equal size around the world are as safe, tidy and downright civil as Australia's.

Social commentators have tried to draw conclusions from the country's awkward origins: that the convict legacy instilled a disdain for settlers after the 1850s, or the wave of immigrants from the rest of the world a century later. Although the convict stain was once a matter of horror – an ignoble memory that any respectable society would excise, particularly from school books – the opposite is true in Australia today. Anyone who can dig up a convict ancestor now wears the fact as a badge of honour. In Sydney's Hyde Park Barracks Museum, schoolchildren eagerly type their names into a computer bank to see if they too bear the felon's mark.

Sydneysiders, of course, are more likely to come up trumps in this game of ancestral

Shoppers at Rundle Mall, Adelaide.

authority, leading to its powerful union movement, or that it led to a blunt conformism, accepting serious curtailments of civil liberties for most of the 20th century. Hughes comes up with the formula "skeptical conformists": Australians like to think of themselves as rowdy rebels, talking big at the pub or behind authority's back, but obey with little question when it comes to the crunch. Other (more jaded) social commentators might say that Australia's beginnings as a penal colony have made it a corrupt place from day one.

As diverting as such theories are, the truth is that few modern Australians can really trace their lineages to convict times; most are the descendants of free English, Scottish and Irish rivalry, since theirs was the original convict settlement. Melbourne, being established by free settlers, has always seen itself as having a more respectable and cosmopolitan flavour.

There lies another of the great Australian stories: the antagonism between the two major redoubts of the urban Aussie: Sydney and Melbourne. Both have their distinctive character, both have world-leading attractions, and both are worth a lingering visit.

Colonial machismo

The traditional image of Australians as sturdy bush workers may have little to do with modern life, but it has been a robust stereotype. It's the local version of the great frontier myth that crops up in the United States, parts of South America and South Africa. By the 1890s, writers, poets and painters were suggesting that a distinctive national spirit had been forged in the great empty wilderness, and that this "New Man" was typified by a Kiplingesque mishmash of colonial values: naturally democratic, excelling at sports, blunt in his language, sardonic, self-reliant, independent, and not over-educated or burdened by musty traditions. Above all, an Aussie trusted his mates, who were bound to one another by an almost mystical bond. This image transmuted over the years from the miners of the gold rushes to the Outback drover and the ANZAC Diggers of Gallipoli.

The one obvious drawback of this stereotype was that it did not include women. The contribution of women on the frontier, in the arts, or in the factories during wars, tended to be brushed aside, so that by the 1950s Australia had earned a reputation as one of the most sexist societies in the developed world. The worst manifestation of the crass male spirit was known as the "Ocker Aussie" – the beer-swilling, pot-bellied, narrow-minded, gay-bashing, provincial redneck, who watched footie at the pub while the sheila stayed at home minding the kids. Barry Humphries satirised the type with Bazza MacKenzie, the simple-minded tourist who was always ready for a schooner and a chunder. Paul Hogan, as Crocodile Dundee, refined and introduced the persona to the world.

Like the long-ingrained racism, sexism abated with the general loosening-up of society in the 1970s. Aussie women have always been strong characters – perhaps even more blunt, independent and self-reliant than the men so loudly proclaimed themselves to be, out of sheer necessity – so in recent years they have easily taken the lead in many fields. Still, as in other Western nations, women remain sadly under-represented in politics and top management positions.

Australian dreams

Perhaps the myth dearest to the Australian heart is that theirs is the most naturally democratic of societies – the frontier past, and distance from the Old World, have naturally levelled Aussies to equals.

Certainly the outward signs are there: waiters may still call you "mate"; taxi drivers can still get cranky if you sit in the back seat instead of up

front (as a social equal would); and public officials, even prime ministers, are often known by their first names. The other side of the egalitarian coin is known as the "tall-poppy syndrome": a national resentment of high achievers and an inescapable urge to bring them down.

But is Australia a classless society? Patently not. There may be none of the rigid divisions of the British or the gross inequalities of the American system, but there are serious divisions of wealth and opportunity – and many believe that the gaps are increasing. According to pessimists, the great settler's dream of Australia

Street dancing in Perth.

as the "millennial Eden" is being eroded. In a haphazard way, Australians have committed themselves to avoiding the errors of Europe and the US, and guaranteeing an unusual measure of social justice. But Australians are becoming increasingly materialistic, and less generous in their vision of society as a place where the weaker are protected. Australia's great narrative historian, Manning Clark, had a bleak vision of his compatriots before he died in the 1990s: "Mammon had infected the ancient continent of Australia," he intoned, in the manner of an Old Testament prophet. "The dreams of humanity had ended in an age of ruins."

Just don't try telling that to any Aussies on a sunny day. They'll already be at the beach.

Surfing off the Queensland coast.

LIFE IN THE BUSH

**The old stereotypes of rural Australia are disappearing
quickly, but there's still a distinct attitude of mind
among those who live "out there".**

Ten-year droughts, dramatic floods, bush-fires whistling through the scrub – the same natural processes that allowed the Aborigines to eke out an existence from the land have made life unpredictable for most farmers. Yet despite constant threats of bankruptcy, few give up. They stick to the land, aided by their own brand of black humour and the solace of Saturday night at the pub.

Rural Australia – sometimes referred to as West of the Divide, The Bush, Back o'Bourke, Beyond the Black Stump or The Mulga – is, in some respects, an Antipodean myth. Most Australians rise each morning to spend another day at the factory or office, a far cry from the days when men tramped "the Wallaby Track" (the old sheep station shearing circuit), with belongings in a "swag" on the shoulder and a faithful blue-heeler cattle dog padding alongside.

Mustering cattle on Delta Downs, north Queensland.

Changing attitudes

The image of a roving jackaroo is a romantic one, and it wouldn't be out of place in the work of one of the country's literary folk heroes, Andrew Barton "Banjo" Paterson. His poem, *The Man From Snowy River*, is a tale of derring-do in the Victorian high country that still resonates with Australians and visitors today.

The other great turn-of-the-20th-century bush writer, author and poet Henry Lawson, had a more ambivalent and, arguably, grounded view of the bush. After a wretched childhood on the western New South Wales goldfields, Lawson kept returning to the bush to reinforce his dislike of it. He hated the unrelenting grey-green of the eucalyptus, the monotony and hopelessness (his word) of the countryside. Lawson railed against the heat on the track

to Hungerford, the "bloody flies", the thieving publicans, the greedy bosses, the arrogant squatters and the brutal police. He did, however, love the "bush battlers", the staunch early unionists and the great Outback tradition of mateship – male-bonding in the wild. These tough men often reciprocated his admiration, and many felt that Lawson, through his writing, was speaking for them.

Perhaps because of the residual influence of Lawson's writings, many visitors and even some urban Australians seem to believe that the Outback and its 170,000 farmers and graziers are stuck in an 1890s time warp. In fact, Aussie farmers are highly mechanised agribusiness people, mustering cattle by helicopter and trail bike, flying their own planes, and adept at using the internet to run their businesses. It's true, however, that workers on the stations put in long hours day in, day out, and often live in difficult conditions.

Another blind spot commonly found concerns the colour of cowboys. The best stockmen have always been black, although until the 1960s they were often paid half of what white workers received. As jackaroos, boundary riders, shearers and trackers, Aborigines have contributed skill and labour to Australia's rural prosperity, particularly in the Northern Territory

a good deal of truth in them. And there's a helpfulness in the bush that is not always immediately apparent to the visitor, thanks to a little bush mischief on the side. Any enquiry for directions, for instance, can be met with a slow "buggered-if-I-know" reply, followed almost immediately with an entertaining series of precise directions. Australians would never deliberately misdirect visitors, for, in the Outback, misdirection may result in death, by either starvation or thirst.

Visitors from overseas wanting to "go bush" will find many specialised tourism operators

Jackeroos still manage the herds with the help of a horse and hound.

Driving in the Outback is best accomplished with a 4-wheel-drive vehicle.

and Western Australia. Furthermore, with the granting of land rights, Aborigines have taken over some of the cattle stations and found a degree of independence.

Despite all the changes of the past 100 years, it is still another world outside the Australian cities. But you don't need to trek all the way to the Outback to find a country mentality; it can be found in any small rural town where the architecture is at least semi-colonial and which services a broad rural area.

Bush mischief

Many of the old clichés about laconic, resourceful, friendly country people still have

catering for just that urge. Everything's available, from luxury air, bus and rail tours to motorised four-wheel-drive backpacker parties.

The Outback has resorts ranging from remote fishing camps to the accommodation conglomerates at Uluru (Ayers Rock) offering everything from camp sites to five-star luxury.

For extra authenticity it's worth seeking out one of the stations that accepts guests and gives them a flavour of what it's like to muster cattle or round up sheep in the sometimes inhospitable land of the Outback. The official tourism site for Queensland, for example, offers a range of options (www.myqldholiday.com.au).

Celebrating Australia Day.

A MULTICULTURAL SOCIETY

In the past 50 years the population has doubled and diversified. Immigrants have not always found it easy, but today's rich ethnic mix is seen as one of Australia's assets.

When a survey in 1939 showed that the Australian population was comprised of 98 percent Anglo-Celtic stock, local newspapers proudly proclaimed that Australia was the most British country on Earth. In this monochromatic society, the only unusual accents were those of the new chums from corners of Ireland or the Scottish highlands. On the dinner table, foods were rarely more exotic than Yorkshire pudding, and Christmas was a time for huge Dickensian meals of roast beef or pork, no matter how brutally hot and tropical the weather.

All that changed after 1945, when Australia embarked on one of the most ambitious and successful immigration programmes of the modern era. The migrants were drawn first from the Mediterranean and Baltic countries of Europe; since the 1970s immigrants have come from around the world. Since the programme began after World War II, more than 6 million settlers from almost 200 countries have chosen to make Australia their home.

A group of young Muslim women wear hijabs made from the national flag on Harmony Day.

Immense diversity

Almost one-quarter of the population was born overseas; 15 percent speak a language other than English at home. In recent years, more than 40 percent of settler arrivals have come from Asia, with the British and Irish down to 14 percent. The humanitarian programme is gradually adding even more diversity to the population. In the 1990s, most of these arrivals came from the Balkans; lately African arrivals have topped the list.

Just as the United States and Argentina were transformed by immigration in the 1890s, so the post-war influx has radically changed the structure and habits of Australian society. Take a seat on the Manly ferry or a Melbourne tram and you're as likely to be sitting next to the daughter of a builder from Athens as you are to a journalist from Naples or a car salesman from Thailand. There is a wonderful sense of cultural diversity to be had across Australia. Multiculturalism was first the guiding principle of Australia's immigration policy, but has become a cornerstone of Australian society in general. Aussies prize tolerance and respect for all cultures and races.

Although a multicultural society is a *fait accompli*, balancing the demands of such a heterogeneous population can be a delicate task. There have been missteps along the way, but since so many people have chosen Australia as their homeland, there is a strong motivation to work together and find solutions to ethnic or racial problems. Ethnic traditions and loyalties are respected and encouraged, but the first loyalty must be to the Australian legal and parliamentary system; multiple languages are promoted, but English is the official tongue of the country; coercive cultural practices, such as arranged marriages, are illegal.

The closing door

Even as late as the 1970s, Australia welcomed almost anyone who applied as an immigrant. These days, more emphasis is laid on skills:

such categories as age, employability, English-language skill and so on, although concessions are sometimes made for immigrants willing to move to less popular states or far-distant country regions. Employability usually gets the highest weighting because of the greater contribution skilled migrants make to the economy.

The New Australians

When Australia became a nation in 1901, racial purity was top of the agenda; the notorious White Australia policy, instituted by the Immigration Restriction Bill, was one of the first

Dancers at an Indian wedding in Sydney.

of the 190,000 target set for 2014–15, 128,550 places were reserved for skilled migrants, with 60,885 places in the family category and 565 for special eligibility migrants. .As a result of taking an additional 12,000 people from Syria and Iraq, Australia's humanitarian intake in 2015–16 (over 25,000) is the largest since World War II.

If the statistics are cold, the issue isn't. Immigration is still a major point of debate within Australian society; scarcely a week goes by without a politician, academic, or public personality adding to the discussion.

The immigration process can be laborious. Applicants are tested for their suitability to settle successfully, assimilate into the community and find work. Points are allocated for

measures to be passed by the new parliament. It would govern migration for decades, and was not formally overturned until 1973.

Thus the first wave of non-British immigrants, brought over in the 1950s and 1960s, was drawn from Europe – mostly from Greece and Italy. Some 275,000 of these "New Australians" arrived in those years – although now, of course, they are Old Australians. Some 5 percent of the population is now of Italian descent, while Melbourne is often touted as the second-largest Greek city in the world.

The polyglot nation

Even during the 19th century, there had been some exceptions to Australia's monoculture. A large Chinese population came to Australia during the gold rushes of the 1850s (and survived the bitter resentment of Anglo miners, which occasionally erupted into violent attacks).

Several wine-growing valleys of South Australia, settled by Silesians in the 1840s, are still Teutonic in ethos. Remote Broome at the top of Western Australia was once full of Japanese pearlers. But these areas remained exceptions to the rule until the boom in different cultures that Australia received in the 1970s, once it truly opened its doors to the rest of the world, particularly to Asia. By the 1990s, one-third of

offenders in this category is British tourists overstaying their visas.

If media coverage is any indication, asylum-seekers – mainly Kurds from Iraq, Afghanis, Syrians, Iranians or Sri Lankan Tamils – arriving by boat from the Indonesian archipelago are a major concern. The Howard government's Pacific Solution, whereby asylum-seekers are processed offshore, is still contentious and skirts the edge of the country's obligations under international law. Labor has essentially followed the same policy since 2007, as have the following Liberal governments.

Greek parade for Australia Day.

all immigration was from Asian countries, and the proportion has increased steadily. The new arrivals do not always find it easy to adapt, but their cultural influence is increasingly obvious in all regions of the country.

Other ways of settling

For those for whom all legal avenues have failed, or who are too desperate to go through the lengthy process, there is illegal immigration – often by arriving as a tourist and then overstaying the visa. It is estimated that there are about 60,000 like this, many of whom remain undetected for years. When apprehended, they face the choice of rapid departure or mandatory deportation. The single biggest group of

As a result of these waves of immigration, over 2 million Australians speak a language other than English when they are at home. An ethnic radio and television broadcasting network – Special Broadcasting Service (SBS) – began in the 1980s to transmit in many languages (with television programmes subtitled in English), and SBS Television's evening news has the most wide-ranging foreign coverage of all the stations in Australia.

Overall, the Australian experience of immigration has been one of the most successful in history: the massive influx has been absorbed into society with remarkably little friction. Indeed, many optimists see this diversity as the key to the country's vitality.

A rock painting in Kakadu National Park.

ABORIGINES TODAY

Captain Arthur Phillip reported that the first words the Australian Aborigines said to his men in 1788 were "Warra! Warra!" (Go away!). Given the subsequent cultural attrition, their first reaction was remarkably prescient.

Interest in the Aborigines is often piqued by modern Aboriginal art. The symbolism found within these paintings has helped generate interest in learning about a culture that is vastly different from any other.

In much of Aboriginal art, it all comes back to the land. For Aboriginal groups, land rights have always been a top priority. The land is a crucial part of their being and their culture, and the responsibility for protecting significant sites is central to their spiritual life. Yet the Aborigines have been forced from their traditional homes, and have seen sacred sites mined, built on, flooded or destroyed.

There have been a few attempts at partial restitution. The Northern Territory Land Rights Act (passed in 1975) allowed Aborigines to make claims to swathes of the Outback on the basis of traditional ownership. The act also gave them significant control over mining and other activities. Royalties from mining activities were distributed to various Aboriginal groups, and land rights acts have been passed in various states in an attempt to right the wrongs of history.

Creating Aboriginal crafts.

Growing resentment

There is a perception that Aboriginal dissent did not surface until the 1960s and 1970s, but in fact an Aboriginal rights association existed in Sydney as early as 1924. The Melbourne-based Australian Aborigines Advancement League petitioned King George V for special indigenous electorates in 1932. If colonial Australians believed (as many did) that Aboriginal people owed them a debt of gratitude for having brought civilisation to *terra nullius*, they were disabused by the Aboriginal Progressive Association manifesto of 1938. Issued on the 150th anniversary of the landing of the First Fleet in Botany

HOW ABORIGINES LOSE OUT

Aboriginal Australians are the country's most disadvantaged group. Statistics tell the sad story: the average life expectancy for Aborigines is 10 years shorter than that for other Australians; they have three times the infant mortality rate and a far higher incidence of both communicable diseases, such as hepatitis B, and lifestyle diseases such as heart failure; an unemployment rate six times the national average; half the average income level; and a large proportion living in substandard housing or temporary shelters. Aborigines are also 16 times more likely to be imprisoned than other Australians.

Bay, this document declared 26 January a day of mourning. "You took our land away from us by force," the manifesto said. "You have almost exterminated our people, but there are enough of us remaining to expose the humbug of your claim as white Australians to be a civilised, progressive, kindly and humane nation. By your cruelty and callousness towards the Aborigines you stand condemned in the eyes of the civilised world."

Political awareness grew steadily from the 1930s, culminating in the Freedom Rides of the mid-1960s, when activists rode in buses through Outback Queensland and New South Wales

self-determination. This allowed Indigenous Australians to make decisions affecting their future, retain their cultural identity and values, and achieve greater economic and social equality.

The Department of Aboriginal Affairs was established in 1972, followed by the Aboriginal Development Commission (ADC) in 1980. The underlying concept was to bring economic independence to indigenous people by fostering business enterprises, but it didn't happen overnight. In 1988, while the rest of Australia celebrated 200 years of settlement at the Bicentennial, Aboriginal activists staged peaceful pro-

Aboriginal boy.

bringing their message to remote communities. Demonstrations resulted in violent clashes with police, pushing the Aboriginal plight on to the front pages and into middle-class homes.

Various lobby groups began to champion Aboriginal political rights. The first positive step came in 1949, when the Chifley government passed an act confirming that those who could vote in their states could vote for the Commonwealth. Aboriginal people in all states (except Queensland and Western Australia) had been entitled to vote in state elections since the 1850s; they didn't vote because no one told them they could.

By the early 1970s, this new-found political consciousness forced the government, led by Gough Whitlam, to develop a new policy of

test marches. White Australians were forced to admit that, for the Aborigines, the colonial invasion had been an unmitigated disaster.

Rights and wrongs

The public agenda changed in 1992, when the High Court of Australia overturned the legal fiction of *terra nullius*. The judges agreed that native title had always existed for land that had been continuously occupied by Aborigines; in 1993 the government set up a Native Title Tribunal to regulate claims. However, because 19th-century missionaries moved Aboriginal peoples around, often splitting up clans by force, few Aboriginal groups could prove continuous occupation of their lands.

Aboriginal industry has been promoted by politicians, community activists and Aboriginal leaders. Most promising has been the creation of successful Aboriginal businesses, from shopping centres and cattle stations to craft shops.

The problems facing the Aborigines who live in remote communities – illiteracy, unemployment, low wages, ill health, alcohol and drugs – resist simple solutions. A strong interventionist policy of cracking down on alcohol and delinquency in the Northern Territory, which was introduced by the Howard government, has not improved this complex situation..

Sport has seen several outstanding performers, including Evonne Goolagong-Cawley, who became a Wimbledon tennis champion, and athlete Cathy Freeman, who won a gold medal in the 2000 Olympics.

Music has always been central to Aboriginal culture and there has been a steady flow of acts who have crossed over into the commercial mainstream, from Jimmy Little in the 1960s to Yothu Yindi in the 1980s, on through Kev Carmody, Tiddas, Archie Roach and, the newest breakout phenomenon, Geoffrey Gurrumul Yunupingu.

Geoffrey Gurrumul Yunupingu entertains the crowd.

Perhaps the biggest step towards some type of reconciliation occurred on 13 February 2008, when, amidst a national outpouring of emotion, Prime Minister Kevin Rudd issued a formal apology to the Stolen Generations in a speech broadcast live around the nation.

Success stories

Many Aborigines have successfully entered Australian society on their own terms. Neville Bonner became a senator of the Commonwealth Parliament and pastor Sir Doug Nichols was appointed Governor of South Australia. Oodgeroo Noonuccal (formerly Kath Walker) was a prominent artist and author, while writers such as Herb Wharton and Evelyn Crawford are immensely popular.

THE STOLEN GENERATION

Between 1910 and 1970, police and welfare officers forcibly removed up to 100,000 children from their parents. The idea was to assimilate mixed-blood Aboriginal children into European society. They were fostered into white homes and forbidden to speak their own languages. Most were given physically demanding or menial jobs, many suffered abuse, and nearly all experienced psychological damage. The stories of these sad children, known as the Stolen Generations, were brought to public awareness by a 1997 government report, 'Bringing Them Home'. Prime Minister Kevin Rudd formally apologised to the Stolen Generations in 2008.

ABORIGINAL ART

From Dreamtime to polymer paints, the artworks being created by modern Aborigines carry the symbolism of thousands of years of myth and tradition.

It's contemporary yet traditional. It's today but it's timeless. Attaching a single label to modern Aboriginal art can be as difficult as establishing the meanings behind the symbols. But it does provide us with a unique cultural vision of Australia. The explosion in Indigenous Australian art began in the early 1970s as a spark in Northern Territory, first in various groups in Arnhem Land and in the desert community of Papunya, west of Alice Springs. In Arnhem Land, missionaries encouraged tribal people to paint their designs, derived from traditional rock art and body decoration, on bark panels stripped from trees. Meanwhile in central Australia, teacher Geoffrey Bardon introduced polymer paints, producing an entirely new genre of art: the strongly symbolic dot style was born. Today the National Gallery in Canberra, all the state galleries, and many private galleries in all the major cities feature desert and Top End art.

Other Aboriginal communities have also earned distinguished reputations for their artisans: Tiwi islanders for their carving and distinctive painting; representations of WA's Kimberley region, as characterised by artists Rover Thomas and Paddy Carlton; and the blazing acrylics from Eubana Nampitjin of Balgo Hills. Works by the late Emily Kngwarreye put the central Australian community of Utopia on the map; her niece Kathleen Petyarre continues that tradition with her intricately detailed paintings, prints and batiks, which can be viewed at numerous galleries throughout Australia.

The Aboriginal Memorial, created by artists from Ramingini in the Northern Territory, is constructed of 200 hollow log bo coffins and can be seen in the National Gallery of Australia.

A Tiwi Island man creates a bold artwork. With its strong patterns and use of colour, Tiwi art is recognised as being ver attractive and highly collectable.

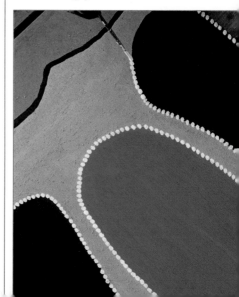

An Aboriginal bark painting of a funeral ceremony with kangaroos on Croker Island, painted by Melangi de Milingibi. The image is used on Australian banknotes.

Inside Art Mob, an Aboriginal art gallery and shop in Hobart, Tasmania.

BUYING THE ART

In an industry with a turnover in the millions of dollars, the Aboriginal art market is rife with opportunists trying to rip off the buyers and/or the artists. As a buyer, you can take a few simple steps to avoid the common pitfalls. Prime amongst them is establishing the authenticity of the work. Ideally, buy direct from the artist or their community, an Aboriginal art and craft centre or a reputable dealer – look for membership of the Indigenous Art Trade Association or the Australian Commercial Galleries Association – and always ask for a certificate of authenticity and/or photographic provenance of the work. That way you can establish the title, the artist's name, community and language, the date of the work and the story behind it. After that, consider (with reference to the quality and price of other works by the artist) whether you are getting value for money. In recent years there have been several instances of exploitation of artists by unscrupulous traders, so enquire whether the dealer subscribes to an industry ethical code, such as the Australian Indigenous Art Code of Conduct.

Modern Aboriginal art is often created to evoke the culture of the Dreaming, without any strong connection to a particular Dreaming story or song.

Detail of Aboriginal bowl bearing an intricate pattern, burnt into wood.

A potter at work in Nguiu, Bathurst Island, Northern Territory.

An Opera Australia production of 'Salome' at the Sydney Opera House.

THE ARTS

In music, drama, literature, film and the visual arts, Australia has absorbed influences from around the world and now has its own distinctive voice.

There's good reason to believe that a fair number of visitors enjoy the opera or an orchestral concert whilst in Australia. This isn't to argue that Opera Australia is the best company in the world or that the Sydney Symphony has that something extra to get musical celibates across the line. Or perhaps it is, at least in the latter case, because what both these companies have is the Sydney Opera House as a home base. It's a Unesco World Heritage Site and dominates the harbour. It's the place all first-time visitors want to see, many going on the guided tour. The logical next step is to see a performance.

So what will you see? With both companies it will be work fit to grace any stage. In 2014, an American, David Robertson, became a chief conductor of the Sydney Symphony Orchestra (SSO). That same year he conducted the controversial but highly acclaimed MET premiere of John Adams' Death of Klinghoffer. In 2015, his projects with SSO included a Schumann's symphony cycle and Beethoven's Missa Solemnis among others.

The award-winning author Peter Carey.

Opera Australia splits its time between Sydney and Melbourne and tours with the odd production further afield. It stages everything from high-profile and popular shows, such as Britten's *Midsummer Night's Dream* directed by Baz Luhrmann, through to chamber productions of challenging new Australian work. In 2016, Opera Australia celebrates 60 years. Queensland, Adelaide, West Australia and Victoria all have their own opera companies, while every state has its own orchestra.

Classical music is, of course, very much part of the Western tradition – indeed, many of the pieces performed today predate the European discovery of Australia. When those first settlers arrived, almost all their cultural pleasures were transplanted from the mother country, much like their language, skills and crops. Indigenous Aboriginal culture, which dates back at least 50,000 years, was largely ignored.

The first stirrings of a specifically Australian cultural identity came in the 1890s and coincided with an upsurge in Australian nationalism. This was reflected initially in literature. It was the period when *The Bulletin* magazine's school of poets and short-story writers was founded, spearheaded by balladeers such as "Banjo" Paterson, who wrote *The Man From Snowy River* and *Waltzing Matilda*, and Henry Lawson, Australia's revered short-story writer. Their work celebrates the bush, mateship,

Aussie nationalism and the triumph of the underdog, usually at the expense of the ruling Anglophile "bunyip aristocracy". Joseph Furphy wrote his novel *Such Is Life* at this time, capturing the world of rural dwellers in a style not dissimilar to Mark Twain's. Marcus Clarke's *For the Term of his Natural Life* was more of a potboiler, but did provide a gripping portrait of convict life in 1830s Van Diemen's Land (Tasmania).

Literature

Steele Rudd began his *On Our Selection* series in 1899, about life on poverty-stricken bush properties and featuring the characters Dad and Dave, who lived on for years in the wider world of radio and cinema. A little after Rudd, C.J. Dennis started celebrating city larrikins in his poems about Ginger Mick and The Sentimental Bloke (1915).

This creative leap was the start of a distinctive Australian literature, which continued strongly in the 20th century through the novels of Henry Handel Richardson, Miles Franklin, Christina Stead, Ruth Park and the towering, Nobel-prize-winning Patrick White. Today's high fliers include Peter

'Neighbours' character Harrold Bishop, played by Ian Smith

THE SOAPS

Very little locally produced television finds its way beyond the shores of Australia, with the major exception of soap operas, which have consistently found an audience in the UK. *Home and Away* has been limping out of Sydney since 1987, but the one show from which so many impressionable viewers have drawn their image of suburban Australia is *Neighbours*. Such is the level of its following that an entire industry has evolved to serve the legions of fans who visit Melbourne. Various organised tours run to "Ramsay Street", and there's even a weekly Neighbours-themed pub quiz in a St Kilda hotel.

Carey, Kate Grenville, Tim Winton and David Malouf. Australians are some of the most voracious book buyers in the world, and they flock to the many literary festivals in Australia.

Theatre

In theatre, Louis Esson began writing plays in a self-consciously Australian idiom in the 1890s, but it took a long time before any groundswell of home-grown drama could be detected. Ray Lawlor's *Summer of the Seventeenth Doll* (1955) was the first portrayal of clearly Australian characters to break out internationally and is still revived periodically. The 1970s saw an exponential expansion of Australian theatre as a wave of politically active writers filled the fringe theatres in the main cities. These writers inexorably moved into, and became, the mainstream. David Williamson is the best known of these and is still writing today. Of the next generation, Louis Nowra, Hannie Rayson and Joanna Murray Smith are consistently producing interesting work.

All the big cities have theatre companies, usually with a state-funded flagship accompanied by a range of smaller fringe enterprises. The Sydney Theatre Company is currently run by playwright Andrew Upton (married to actress

Bell stood down after 25 years as the company artistic director.

Dance

Dance was one of the first disciplines in which colonial Australian culture began to reconnect with the country's indigenous population. Composer John Antill wrote *Corroboree*, a ballet suite, in 1946; it was performed as such in 1950, touring the country over the next decade. It combined Aboriginal and Western forms to great acclaim. Today the Bangarra Dance Company does the same thing; the company

Actors from Belgium's Theatre Royal de la Monnaie perform 'Babel' as part of the annual Sydney Festival.

Cate Blanchett) and offers a strong programme occasionally bolstered by some of Blanchett's Hollywood friends tempted by a spell on the boards in the Harbour City.

The large commercial theatres tend to be clogged up with clone musicals from Broadway or London's West End, with the odd homegrown production, such as *Priscilla Queen of the Desert*, going the other way.

The great anomaly of the Australian stage is the Bell Shakespeare Company. In 1990 John Bell effectively revived the role of the actor/manager, which had died out as a concept everywhere else, by setting up a company to tour Shakespeare around the country. It's still going and producing three shows a year. In 2015,

is directed and run by Aboriginal people. The company tours extensively in Australia and overseas, as does the Melbourne-based Australian Ballet, which presents both classical and contemporary repertoire. Cutting-edge smaller companies include Chunky Move, which leads the way in harnessing modern technology to complement its performers.

Painting

A recognisable school of landscape painting in Australia emerged in the late 19th century, personified by Sir Arthur Streeton, Tom Roberts and the Heidelberg School (named after the Melbourne suburb, not the German town), which pioneered Australian impressionism. Today there is an art trail in the vicinity and, nearby, the Heide Museum of Modern Art. This property was, for a spell, the haunt of Albert Tucker, Joy Hester and probably Australia's best-known painter, Sidney Nolan. Nolan was one of a group of figurative painters working after World War II, identified as part of the Australian School. His series of paintings on Ned Kelly, the outlaw bushranger, became national icons.

In the early 1970s Sydney became the centre for an abstract expressionist movement that drew upon earlier painters such as Ian Fairweather and Godfrey Miller. Local artists were soon experimenting with hard edge, colour field and lyrical expressionist modes. A new breed of younger painters looked up to Brett Whiteley as the poster boy for artists living the rock'n'roll lifestyle.

In Melbourne, painter and printmaker Fred Williams established himself as the most important landscape artist of the post-war years with his haunting, semi-abstract depictions of the Outback.

Perhaps the best-known contemporary Australian artist is Tracey Moffatt, born in

Mandawuy Yunupingu of Aboriginal band Yothu Yindi.

ANTIPODEAN RHYTHMS

Australia has become as well known for its rock bands as its films; the pub music scene, especially in Melbourne and Sydney, is extraordinarily healthy. Performers such as Nick Cave, Wolfmother and the Temper Trap started off on the pub circuit and now enjoy international success. Others that made it big overseas include the Seekers, the Bee Gees, AC/DC, Midnight Oil, INXS and Men at Work. The Aboriginal band Yothu Yindi, with didgeridoos and tribal dancers, is unmistakably Northern Territory. One of Australia's best-known exports (in Europe, at least) is Kylie Minogue, a former teenage soap star and now pop icon. At home the dance scene is pumping, and acts such as Pendulum have taken off overseas.

There are two particular musical fields in which Australians have twisted the popular American styles into something distinctly antipodean. Bush ballads may have died out, but American country and western music took off in the rural areas of Australia in the 1940s and 50s. Local singers adopted names like Tex Morton and Slim Dusty and began writing songs about outlaws, pubs, and the country myths of girlfriends past. Slim Dusty's *The Pub with No Beer* was a huge hit. More recently, Keith Urban has become a global star, while Kasey Chambers is the biggest name locally. Meanwhile, a hip-hop scene is blossoming, with Adelaide's Hilltop Hoods and Sydney's Bliss 'n' Eso leading the charge.

Brisbane in 1960. Her painterly films and photographic works have won international critical acclaim and been widely exhibited. She is symptomatic of a whole wave of artists working across various media who set out to challenge not just with the message, but also with the medium.

Brisbane's impressive new Gallery of Modern Art leads the way in this field, but Sydney's Museum of Contemporary Art and Melbourne's Australian Centre for Contemporary Art have consistently supported adventurous work. The multi-million-dollar Museum of

range from period pieces (Gillian Armstrong's 1979 version of the Miles Franklin classic, *My Brilliant Career*) to George Miller's 1996 talking pig, *Babe*; to Baz Luhrmann's dazzling dance comedy *Strictly Ballroom* (1992), and David Michôd's crime thriller *Animal Kingdom* (2010). The latest blockbuster, Miller's *Mad Max Fury Road*, scooped up six Oscars at the 2016 Academy Awards.

Australian actors Nicole Kidman, Cate Blanchett, Toni Collette, Geoffrey Rush, Eric Bana, Guy Pearce and Hugh Jackman have all become big names in Hollywood.

A still from 'Rabbit-Proof Fence'.

Old and New Art, just north of Hobart, opened with a bang at the beginning of 2011.

Film

Soldiers of the Cross (1899) is said to be the world's first feature film and, like the more famous *The Story of the Kelly Gang* (1906), was made in Australia. It took several more decades, however, for local cinema to find its voice; it wasn't until the 1970s that films emerged onto the world stage with the likes of *Mad Max* and *Picnic at Hanging Rock*. Progress was swift thereafter, and, with a burst of dramatic talent and new government incentives, the film industry became Australia's biggest cultural export. The most celebrated films to come from Australia

Some actors and directors prefer to create work that reflects the realities of modern Australia. Since 2000, for instance, a spate of indigenous-themed films has been released, including *Rabbit-Proof Fence* (Philip Noyce's 2002 look at the Stolen Generation of Aboriginal Australians) and *The Tracker*, whose director, Rolf de Heer, won international praise for *Ten Canoes*, the first Australian film to feature an entirely indigenous cast and to be spoken entirely in indigenous languages. *Samson and Delilah* (2008) portrayed the desperation of Aboriginal youth in central Australia; the film won the Caméra d'Or (Gold Camera Award) for best first feature film at the 2009 Cannes Film Festival.

MODERN AUSTRALIAN CUISINE

It took a long time to happen, but food in Australia is now distinguished for its quality, imagination and a truly multinational diversity.

Not so long ago, the term "Australian cuisine" conjured grisly images of meat pies, Vegemite sandwiches and sausage rolls. Not anymore; Australia is now a trendy paradise for foodies. Few places in the world have restaurants with such variety, quality and sheer inventiveness. From formal dining rooms to tiny beach-side cafés, menus explore the merging of Australia's bounty of native ingredients with international culinary traditions. Even the most basic corner diners, which once served up hamburgers and chips, now dish up focaccia with fresh King Island cheeses and exotic fruits.

In fact, Australia's culinary establishment may be the most adventurous in the world. Nearly every city has seen a swarm of "Mod Oz" restaurants with inventive chefs at the helm and an audience of willing epicures. This renaissance is due to two factors: the wealth of superlative Australian produce – including native foods – and the plethora of international cuisines brought to Australia by its immigrants. The mix of traditional flavours from around the world has inspired a flurry of innovation.

The Australian palate, like the nation, is relatively young, and the current sophistication follows a bleak culinary history. The early settlers struggled to maintain their stolid British or Irish diets, subsisting on salted meats – either roasted, stewed or baked into pies. Various early recipes indicate that native animals were eaten but, apart from kangaroo (whose tails make a fine soup), were rarely appreciated. The unfamiliar harshness of the Australian bush bred tough bellies used to tinned beef and damper (the most basic bread of flour, water and a pinch of salt).

Oysters for sale at Sydney Fish Market.

During the gold rush days of the 1850s, Chinese immigrants recognised the potential for cultivation and grew a great variety of herbs and vegetables. On some occasions, their industry saved white mining camps from starvation. Even the tiniest country town still has its Chinese restaurant, which for decades saved the citizens from complete culinary deprivation.

Even in the 1960s, the only things approaching an Australian cuisine were a couple of sweet confections – pavlova, a meringue pie shell filled with fruit and cream, and lamingtons, sponge cubes covered with chocolate and coconut. Of course, there was always Vegemite – the black, salty yeast spread that most Aussies were weaned on, though abhorred by most others. Thanks to the climate, the "barbie" (barbecue) did become an Australian institution, but British roast dinners were turned out every Sunday; and on Christmas Day, in steaming hot summers, the hot roast turkey graced every table.

Culinary immigration

The massive migration from Mediterranean countries after World War II made the first real dent on Australia's palate. Italians in particular helped revolutionise cooking,

in the Pacific Rim are found in rural villages almost as often as in major cities. Diners enjoy pristine teppanyaki Japanese dining rooms, and take-away lakhsa stalls. Singapore-style food courts have sprung up everywhere; even local supermarkets now stock Thai and Indian ingredients. Lemongrass, chilli, coriander and cardamom give new depth and flavour to many essentially European dishes.

Not that Australia has tossed off its British culinary heritage altogether. Your fish'n'chips might still come in folded newspaper, but inside is fresh-grilled barramundi instead of

An upmarket restaurant in Melbourne.

introducing wary Aussies to the wonders of pasta, garlic and olive oil. Today, each capital city has its share of Italian restaurants serving authentic, well-priced food: in Melbourne, Lygon Street is the heart of Little Italy; in Sydney, it's Norton Street in the Leichhardt neighbourhood.

This was only the beginning. The extension of immigration in the 1970s added myriad new cuisines. The great melting pot – or perhaps more appropriately, salad bowl – of Australian society meant that restaurants were suddenly opened by Lebanese, Turkish, Balkan, Hungarian and Spanish chefs. But the biggest impact by far has been made by the Asians. Restaurants featuring the cuisine of every country

deep-fried cod. And although pies'n'peas are now thankfully low on the food chain, you can still get the Australian version at the occasional retro-chic diner.

Going local in the kitchen

The foundation of Australian cuisine is the quality and variety of its ingredients. Without them, all of the exotic spices and exciting recipes in the world would still result in dismal dining. Locally sourced produce, meats and fish are highly sought after. Aussies were slow to recognise the wealth of seafood in their waters, but now a range of fresh fish is on every menu. Small farms devote themselves to gourmet beef and poultry, while the quality of everyday vegetables rivals that grown on organic farms in Europe or the United States. Far from pining for imports of French cheese, Greek olives or Italian wine, Australians produce their own, which are often rated superior to the imports.

Australia can be divided into regions that are known for particular produce: King Island cream, Sydney rock oysters, Bowen mangoes, Coffin Bay scallops, Tasmanian salmon, Illabo milk-fed lamb. Each state has its acknowledged specialities. Tropical Queensland produces a wealth of exotic fruits, like Bowen

and cultivated native foods. Finally, Western Australia has received rave reviews for its superb new wines from the southwest and for goat cheeses.

Towards a flavourful future

Established chefs who pioneered the Australian culinary adventure are being joined by a new generation of emerging talent eager to further explore gustatory possibilities. At top restaurants such as Sydney's Quay, customers make reservations months in advance. But kitchens throughout Australia are being taken over by

Fruit vendor at Yungabarra markets.

mangoes and papaya, succulent reef fish, mudcrabs and Moreton Bay Bugs (shellfish, not insects). From The Northern Territory come the white-fleshed barramundi and Mangrove Jack, while in Darwin, sample buffalo burgers and crocodile steaks. New South Wales has Hunter Valley wines, Balmain Bugs and perfect Sydney rock oysters. Victoria produces some of the tenderest meats, such as Gippsland beef and Meredith lamb, Mallee squab and corn-fed chicken. Tasmania is one of the least-polluted corners of the globe, and has gained national attention for its salmon, trout, cheeses, oysters and raspberries. South Australia is home to the Barossa Valley wine industry, Coffin Bay scallops, olive oils, tuna

chefs in their 20s who are rated as highly as those far senior in both age and experience.

There is much flavour and excitement to be found in unpretentious neighbourhood restaurants, as well. Pub grub is as often spring rolls with satay dipping sauce or bruschetta with tomatoes, feta and basil as it is a meat pie or hamburger. Australians have a passion for pizza and will top a thin crust with everything from emu to pineapples to tandoori chicken. Local restaurants offer Moroccan-spiced chicken breast, chicken parmigiana, and lamb shank with red cabbage on the same menu. The wine and beer list at even the most humble restaurant will be more than adequate. Non-licensed establishments usually welcome BYO customers.

Bush Tucker Meets the Locavore Movement

As Australia's culinary consciousness matured, it looked inward to the foods native to its shores.

The phrase "Bush Tucker" has become the buzz word for truly Australian ingredients, referring to edible flora and fauna found in the great storehouse of the Outback. Possum, quandong fruit, eels, bush tomatoes, emu and even witchetty grubs were common items on the Aborigine menu. The natives thrived on these foods for 50,000 years, but the arriving Europeans dismissed them as uncivilised.

When the restaurant scene exploded in Australia in the 1990s, many restaurants began to incorporate native elements into their elegant recipes. Chefs happily experimented with riberries, bunya nuts, wild rosellas and Kakadu plums. High-end restaurants featured main courses which used ingredients from the Outback in ways the Aborigines never imagined (and not just because they did not own Cuisinarts).

Much of that frenetic energy has simmered down. Modern Australian cuisine ("Mod Oz") has been tempered to mean appreciating and incorporating indigenous ingredients without ignoring the conventional pantry. There is still an obvious delight in using the more unusual ingredients in ways to satisfy the curious gourmand. Every major city has at least one restaurant with distinctive Bush Tucker courses. Along with standard offerings like lamb short loin with spinach soufflé, fine-dining menus will feature roasted emu wrapped in prosciutto and seared kangaroo rump with seasonal vegetables. Sweet potato mash is served alongside salads of warrigal and samphire greens. Wattle seed, pepper leaf and lemon myrtle join thyme and oregano as seasonings. Meanwhile, pubs serve deep-fried crocodile bites and pizza with kangaroo topping along with the expected meat pies or fish and chips.

The change in the concept of Bush Tucker reflects an evolution in the Australian attitude towards food. Culinary writers and food industry analysts see an increasing interest in nutrition and in ways of using local ingredients and simple preparation techniques in cooking both at home and in restaurants. Those incorporate Australian

ingredients, but that now often means foods from other cultures and traditions which have taken root in Oz.

The emphasis now is as much on how and where foods are grown as on what they are. "Grow and Buy Australian" is the new movement. Chefs and home cooks seek out locally sourced ingredients grown by sustainable methods. Consumers want to know that their produce was grown without pesticides and that their beef was grass-fed, their chickens free-range and their fish wild-caught. Farmers' markets are springing up like mushrooms after a heavy rain in city centres as

Kangaroo steaks.

well as country towns. Increasingly, consumers want to meet the person who planted the lettuce, made the cheese or picked the fruit. Websites supply consumers with links to Australian raised, grown or produced food and drink that aren't available in local shops.

Chefs are responding to diners' interests for healthier menu items. "Hyper-local" is the new restaurant buzz-phrase for a chef who maintains his or her own garden for produce and herbs. Others have arrangements with farmers for regular purchases of fresh produce, cheeses and meats. For restaurants, with their notoriously slim profit margin, buying locally is usually more economical. For their customers, it means fresher, healthier food.

AUSTRALIAN WINES

The Australian wine scene might be a late bloomer, but it has quickly earned the respect of the wine world's cognoscenti for the consistent quality delivered by the major labels and the mature treatment of varietals by the smaller producers.

When Australian wines first appeared on the international scene, they were considered a novelty. But now, each of the six states and both territories boast vineyards and wineries. The great differences in climates and soils, often even within a few kilometres, create conditions for a range of wines as vast as the continent.

Although more than 140 varieties of grapes are cultivated Down Under, Europeans found no native grapes. Cuttings of plants from the Cape of Good Hope arrived with the First Fleet in 1788. By the 1850s, grapes were being grown in most Australian states. When the phylloxera epidemic (which decimated Europe's vineyards in the 1870s) spread to Australia, strict regulations and quarantine limited the damage. As a result, vines that were planted in Australia before the epidemic are some of the oldest in the world. That said, most of the nearly 2,500 wineries in Australia are less than 30 years old.

The most popular red grapes are Shiraz, Cabernet Sauvignon and Merlot, while Chardonnay, Semillon and Riesling are the most popular whites. Once a mainstay of the industry, fortified wines – largely Muscats – still have a small but loyal following. "Stickies" is the name for golden sweet dessert wines made from grapes deliberately affected by Noble Rot, which concentrates their flavours and sweetness.

Australia is the sixth-largest producer of wine in the world and the fourth-largest exporter, selling to more than 100 countries and contributing about A$5.5 billion to the nation's economy. The largest export market by volume is the UK, which imports more than 250 million litres (66 million gallons) of Australian wine annually. While the value of wine export to the US fell by 8 percent in 2014, the US and

Early morning sun on the vines, Barossa Valley.

Canada are still the most lucrative markets for Australian wine. Coming up fast is China; an expanding economy has turned China into the fastest-growing wine market in the world and the fourth-largest export market for Australia.

Economic and climatic challenges

The Australian wine industry faces challenges from an oversupply of wine and grapes, the global economic downturn and a strong Australian dollar. There's also another obstacle not so easily dealt with: global warming. The continent is already at the edge of the sustainable grape-growing environment and most of Australia's 62 wine-growing regions are highly susceptible to climate change.

Australians thrive on challenges and, with the fate of one of their favourite luxuries and one of their most important exports at stake, this is one they take on with exceptional energy and enthusiasm. Wineries like Henschke in the Barossa and d'Arenberg in McClaren Vale, Tyrrell's in the Hunter Valley north of Sydney and Sandalford in West Australia draw on up to six generations of experience.

One advantage for Australian wine makers is the lack of the regulations that define so much of European wine-making. This leaves them free to innovate with flexible wine-making

With elevations of 2,200 metres (7,000ft), it's the highest land in Australia. As conditions throughout the rest of the grape-growing world deteriorate, the microclimate in the Snowys should develop as one of the best for grape cultivation. Growers think this will give them up to a century of compensation for predicted climate change.

Flying vintners

Since the harvest in Australia is six months earlier than in the northern hemisphere, wine makers and grape growers can visit other wine

Wine barrels.

practices. Growers lead the way in "canopy management", artificially controlling the heat and humidity of vineyards. Organic and sustainable viticulture and planting drought-resistant varieties are popular.

Mother Nature may be playing a role in climatic adaptation. Cleggert Wines in Langhorne Creek in South Australia has cultivated Australia's first indigenous grapes. Malian and Shalistan are both the result of natural genetic variations of Cabernet Sauvignon grapes, which were noticed and propagated by the wine maker. Whether this was a genetic accident or an evolutionary response to conditions is a matter of debate.

Growers are buying property in the Snowy Mountains in southern New South Wales.

regions internationally when those areas are busy with production. The passing on of proven techniques elsewhere to Australia's "flying wine makers" is evened out by the introduction of Australian ideas and innovations, particularly in France, Spain and Italy.

The 2015 harvest was 1.67 million tonnes with some modest and patchy strengthening in average winegrape prices and exports.. That still leaves an enormous inventory of existing vintages. Most of that consists of wines for which Australia is well known, particularly Shiraz, Cabernet and Chardonnay. However, those are wines which are produced equally well in many other places and create a marketing challenge for the Australian wine makers.

Expanding the market

To avoid becoming stereotyped as producers of a limited range of wines, Australians are exploring the potential of other grapes. They are planting European varieties like Barbera and Chenin Blanc, and some exotic varieties only a true oenophile would recognise, like Saperavi from Southern Russia and Spain's Doradillo, both of which are being cultivated in Victoria.

In the Granite Belt in Southeast Queensland, wine makers use the "Strange Bird Wine Trail" to market unfamiliar European varietals. The

Shiraz. This area was not affected by the phylloxera epidemic, and as a result, it has some of the oldest vines in the world. It's fitting then that the National Wine Centre of Australia is in Adelaide. The multimedia exhibits, demonstration vineyard and tasting room present an overview of the wine-making process and the delectable results. Nine distinct regions are within 90 minutes' drive of the Centre. Barossa Valley, Adelaide Hills and McLaren Vale are the best known, but Langhorne Creek is considered a hidden gem. It is home to about 20 wineries, including Bleasdale, where the Potts

Wither Hills winery in Blenheim provides wine tasting experiences.

map points out wineries which bottle alternative varietal wines like Tempranillo, Malbec and Silvaner, which are rarely found on bottleshop shelves. While the immediate goal is to develop a domestic market for these wines, the long-range plan is to create wines fine enough to challenge their historic producers.

The grand tour

Wine tourism is a major industry, with each wine region uncorking new initiatives to attract visitors. Wine-lovers will have far more tasting rooms (also called cellar doors) to visit than the time or fortitude to do them justice.

South Australia produces more than half of the nation's wine, and focuses on Cabernet and

family has been making wine since 1860, and Zontes Footsteps, where enthusiastic newcomers produced their first vintage in 2003.

Victoria boasts five diverse wine regions within an hour of Melbourne. Most of the wineries offer amenities beyond their liquid attractions. Cafés, spas, fine dining, luxury accommodation, even art galleries are part of the experience. The Yarra Valley has the oldest vineyards and there is a definite Mediterranean influence which reflects the approach by Italian wine makers who arrived in the 1860s. Meanwhile, the Geelong region along the Great Ocean Road in the southwest corner of Victoria takes advantage of climate and soil similar to Bordeaux and Burgundy.

New South Wales has the broadest range of climates in Australia, from the Alpine conditions of the Snowy Mountains to the coastal breezes of Shoalhaven Coast and the cool conditions of the Southern Highlands. With over 130 wineries, Hunter Valley, a two-hour drive north of Sydney, is the most established region, with a reputation for exquisite Semillon and Shiraz and acclaimed Chardonnay and Verdelho. Tourists can visit the Visitors' Information Centre in Pokolbin for maps, information and a chance to sample a few wines. It's also possible to sample many of

Shiraz grapes from the Barossa Valley.

the region's wines at the many tasting centres in and around Pokolbin. The Small Winemakers Centre, Boutique Wine Centre, Hermitage Road Cellars and the Hunter Valley Winegrowers are cellar doors showcasing smaller wineries which emphasise their individual approach to their art. South of Sydney, the Shoalhaven Coast is home to Coolangatta Estate, which was started in 1822. Nearby Kladis Estate is a relative newcomer, just 25 years old. Australian wine guru James Halliday ranks both as 5-star wineries.

The Australian Capital Region, while technically and politically independent, is physically within New South Wales. Clonakilla Estate at Murrumbateman routinely produces the finest Shiraz-Viognier red blend (like Côte de Rotie) made in Australia.

For many years wine aficionados ignored Queensland's wines. The region produced well-respected wines until the 1930s when the domestic market turned to the southern states. Not until Ballandean Estate near Stanthorpe in the Granite Belt started producing wine commercially in 1970 did attention once again shift northward. Queensland wines are considered lighter, crisper and fruitier than varietals from other states. The most established region is the Granite Belt. Three hours west of Brisbane and the Gold Coast, it is 1,000 metres (3,000ft) above sea level and is the only area in Queensland with four distinct seasons. The crescent of higher ground from the Sunshine Coast Hinterlands to Brisbane's Scenic Rim and the Gold Coast Hinterland is home to several dozen new, small wineries. For a completely different experience, wineries near Cairns make wines from tropical fruits like mango, passionfruit and bush lime.

The southwest corner of Western Australia is home to more than 170 wineries in nine distinct regions. It is known for its Cabernet Sauvignon but it also has a reputation for Sauvignon Blanc and Zinfandel. With vines planted as early as 1829, viticulture in the Swan District, which stretches from the east side of Perth northward, predates both Victoria and South Australia. The headliner region is Margaret River. Surrounded on three sides by the Indian and Great Southern Oceans, it has a distinctly Mediterranean climate and powerful Cabernet and Merlot. It also has the most well-developed and comprehensive tourism industry.

The island of Tasmania has a cool climate which lends itself to producing excellent sparkling wines. The sometimes fickle Pinot Noir enjoys the maritime influence and thrives here. Most of the 60 or so wineries are very small operations run by passionate vintners. The Jansz Vineyard, with its connection to the French Champagne house Roederer, is credited with bringing attention to Tasmania's sparkling potential. Wineries are clustered around Hobart on the Tasman Sea on the eastern side of the island and Launceston and the Tamar River to the west. On the east coast, Frogmore Creek is noted for its sustainable, organic viticulture techniques, while its wines have won awards for their compatibility with Asian cuisine.

WHERE SPORT IS SUPREME

If you want to join the locals for a pint and a chat, you'll need to know how the local team is getting on.

Arguably, sport was the language in which Australians first shouted: "Hey world, here we are!" Wherever people gather – in pubs, clubs, the workplace or around the barbecue – sport tends to be the major topic of conversation. They bet on it and brag about it, they eulogise or verbally flay its performers, analyse its conduct and speculate about its future. One thing they never do is tire of it.

The golden 1950s

The sports fixation reached its apogee in the 1950s, a period when Australia dominated in world swimming and tennis, and arrived as a force to reckon with in track and field, cycling, boxing, sculling and golf. The climax came in 1956: Australia dusted the United States 5–0 in the Davis Cup tennis final, while at the Melbourne Olympic Games, Aussie athletes won 35 medals – 13 gold, eight silver and 14 bronze – an astonishing number for the small population.

Australia has always punched above its weight at the Olympics, and continues to produce track and field stars. For many proud Aussies it all culminated in Cathy Freeman's gold-medal-winning run in the 400 metres at the Sydney Olympics in 2000.

The cricket mania

It's only in summer, when cricket grabs the public's imagination, that Australians are more or less united in their sporting focus. Spectator interest settles squarely on the national team in its Test Match encounters with the West Indies, India, Pakistan, New Zealand, South Africa and, most crucially, England.

A Test Match takes up to five days to complete; even then it frequently finishes in a draw. Yet the game is followed with religious zeal. Radios blare

Aaron Finch bats at the Manuka Oval, Canberra.

out the ball-by-ball commentary at the beach; pub discussions focus on the diving catch in the slips; and cricket is on TV, day in, day out. In the more than 100 years since Australia played its first Test series against England, nobody has been better at the game than a slightly built fellow by the name of Donald Bradman. "The Don" was to cricket what Pelé was to football or Babe Ruth was to baseball.

A Test series is played over three to five matches, with the battlegrounds moving between Sydney, Melbourne, Adelaide, Brisbane and Perth. Ground capacities range from 30,000 to 100,000; lovers of the game say there are few greater sporting moments than to experience the opening over of an England v Australia Test before a capacity crowd. The Australian team was the top-ranking team for most of the 1990s and 2000s but has recently slipped in the rankings. Probably nothing hurt quite so much as the thrashing the England team handed out when they toured Australia in 2010.

If a five-day Test sounds too much to take in, consider watching a "limited-over" or one-day game. As the name implies, these are quick affairs that come and go in a heated rush and often wring participants and spectators dry with tension and drama. A standard one-day game gives each side 50 overs to bat and 50 to bowl,

League (AFL) game; thousands more follow on TV. September's AFL grand final is one of the great sporting experiences.

Rugby League

In Sydney and points north, footie of a different kind is the winter preoccupation. Rugby League started as a professional alternative to Rugby Union. It's played in a half-dozen provinces of a half-dozen countries, and to that degree qualifies as an international sport. League attendances are nothing like as large as those of the AFL, but the Sydney clubs – such as

The Queensland Maroons take on the New South Wales Blues in Brisbane.

while the much newer T20 format gives each side 20 overs and usually lasts about 3 hours.

Aussie Rules footie

On the surface it seems incongruous that a country so fond of cricket, with all its esoteric customs and traditions, could have given birth to a game as apparently anarchic as Australian Rules football. The sport may be virtually unknown beyond Australia's shores, but in the southern states it's a passion, particularly in Melbourne: the city may have only 4 million inhabitants, yet Aussie Rules ranks among the most popular football leagues in the world. It is estimated that each winter weekend in Melbourne, one person in 16 attends an Australian Football

St George, the Western Suburbs, Manly and Parramatta – keep their players fabulously well paid through the revenue from their slot machines and licensed clubs. In Brisbane and Sydney, the game found its roots in the working-class inner suburbs and, despite media overkill, hasn't significantly broadened its social base.

Rugby League is a physical rather than cerebral game. You don't have to play this game to feel how much it hurts. The game's appeal rests in its strong gladiatorial image and macho confrontations as pairs of teams slam into one another – although fans believe that a dazzling backline movement resulting in a try (touchdown) is one of the real joys in sporting life.

Two or three times a year in the State of Origin

series, the New South Wales and Queensland teams engage in a brutal battle. The Aussie national side, known as the Kangaroos, regularly hops through tours of France and Great Britain unbeaten.

> *The uncompromising style of defence in rugby prompted one American football coach to observe: "Our guys could never stand up to that sort of constant punishment."*

Rugby Union

According to its devotees, Rugby Union is "the game they play in heaven" – which is remarkable considering its relative popularity in New South Wales and Queensland, where angels are in short supply. If you enjoy rugby, watch the Wallabies (the national side) in action, especially if there's a spare ticket for a Bledisloe Cup match, which sees the Wallabies face up to the mighty All Blacks from New Zealand.

game first kicked off more than a century ago among British migrants, then more or less stagnated until post-World War II, with the arrival of migrants from Southern Europe. Now most clubs in the National Soccer competition – the A League – are dominated by players from the

Christopher Ikonomidis celebrates with fans after Australia wins the 2018 World Cup qualifying match at Allianz Stadium, Sydney.

At club level, Rugby Union projects a social spirit often lacking in the professional codes. The game has a "silvertail" (upper-crust) image based partly on its strength in the universities and private schools. The "flying Ella brothers" of the 1970s were a contradiction to the class rule, three gifted Aboriginal athletes from Sydney's inner southern suburbs who all wound up wearing the gold shirts of the Australian team.

Soccer

The history of soccer in Australia bears little comparison to other forms of football. The

Italian, Greek, Croatian, Slavic, Maltese, Dutch and Macedonian communities. The national team, the Socceroos, continue to edge their way up the international ladder, and their success in the 2006 World Cup – the first World Cup they qualified for since 1978 – helped revive the sport's popularity at home. They have enjoyed mixed success since then, however.

Great individualists

The 1950s and 60s brought forth a rash of tennis talents, including Rod Laver, John Newcombe, Evonne Goolagong-Cawley and Pat Cash. Recent hopes, including Adelaide's Lleyton Hewitt, have not managed to reach the same heights consistently.

Australian golfers have generally kept their end up, and Greg Norman, "the Great White Shark", was a phenomenon. Today Jason Day is the pick of the bunch.

But it has been those sports which pit the individual against the elements which have brought out the best in Australians. It's not surprising that swimming has been a top sport: kids are tossed into the pool almost as soon as they can walk. In the 1950s, Dawn Fraser became Australia's darling as much for her cheeky anti-establishment attitude as her victories. In the 1970s, Shane Gould followed in her wake, with a slew

one of the world's greatest-ever surfers. Names like Nat Young and Tom Carroll have permanent niches in a national surfing hall of fame.

Australian motor racing has produced Formula 1 world champions in Jack Brabham (three-times winner) and Alan Jones. Yet the real local heroes of the track are the V8 touring car drivers. The class attracts heavy sponsorship for its championship series, the highlight of which is the Bathurst 1000 held in October, an endurance event that attracts an international field of drivers. The Formula 1 Grand Prix is held on Melbourne's Albert Park circuit in early March.

Jockey Michelle Payne on Prince of Penzance.

of Olympic medals.

Australia's most recent swimming superstar is Ian Thorpe, who won three gold and two silver medals in the 2000 Olympics, and in 2003 became the first swimmer ever to win three consecutive world titles in one event, the 400 metres freestyle. At the 2004 Olympics, "the Thorpedo" added four medals to his Olympic tally: two gold, one silver and one bronze. By contrast, the swim team performed poorly at the 2012 London Olympics, with a total of only 10 medals (including one gold) derided as the worst result in more than 30 years.

Aussies have ruled the waves almost since surfing's inception as a competitive sport, with Mark Richards' four world titles marking him as

A nation of punters

It is often said that Aussies would gamble on just about anything, but there's only one race that captures everyone's imagination and puts millions of dollars through the bookmakers and the agencies of the Totalizator Agency Board (TAB). At 3.30pm Melbourne time on the first Tuesday in November, the whole of Australia stops for the Melbourne Cup. The 3,200-metre (2-mile) event has become an international thoroughbred classic since it was first held at Melbourne's Flemington course in 1861. It's a public holiday in Victoria, and even the process of government is suspended so that the nation's decision-makers can watch the race. In 2015, Michelle Payne became the first woman to win the race.

SURF CULTURE

Introduced to Australia in 1912 by Duke Kahanamoku of Honolulu, surfing has become a way of life for many of Australia's coastal dwellers.

On a good day at Noosa Heads, Manly or countless other Australian beaches, thousands of surfers of all ages and on all kinds of equipment clog the line-ups. Surfing today is as mainstream as tennis, golf, cricket or football, and kids on the coast grow up riding every kind of surf craft imaginable. If you come across a Saturday-morning "nippers" (junior surf life-saving session), with kids who look as if they're barely out of nappies charging in and out of the waves, you would swear they're breeding a new, genetically modified amphibious race here.

The old surf clubs with their prime beach-front positions are still the social hubs of the Australian coast, where you can enjoy a cheap meal or cold beer, or succumb to the dreaded "pokies" (fruit machines), all with unmatched ocean views. The old, framed black-and-white photos of past surf champions peer down, echoing earlier, simpler times. The worldwide boom of the surf industry means that professional surfers have the opportunity to set themselves up financially for life. Young surfers barely out of their teens drive luxury 4WD vehicles and buy mansions.

For a real surf experience, take a lesson, sit under a pandanus tree with a pie and a chocolate milk, go for another surf, then retreat to the surf club for a steak and a beer. Just see if you don't feel strangely good about the world again. Then go to bed, wake up and do it all over again.

Contemplating the waves on Main Beach, along the Gold Coast in Queensland.

King's Beach, at Caloundra, is the perfect place to learn to su the waves are typically small and the locals are friendly. Take your board up near the headland on the northern edge.

The northern end of Bondi Beach has been rated a gentle 4 (with 10 as the most hazardous); the southern side is rated as a 7 due to a rather strong and consistent rip current.

A BRIEF HISTORY OF SURFING

Australian surfing as we know it began at Sydney's Freshwater Beach, when visiting Hawaiian champion Duke Kahanamoku put on his historic display in 1914. However, there is some evidence of a surf culture among Indigenous Australians. The foundation meeting of the Greenmount Surf Club in 1908 paid tribute to a local Aboriginal man, named Churaki, for the many daring rescues he carried out in the surf prior to the club's formation.

Surf life-saving clubs were formed in the early 1900s to protect public safety, and quickly grew as social hubs for the emerging beach culture. Surfboards were built for ocean rescues and manned by teams of earnest paddlers, but proved poorly designed for rough ocean conditions.

Surf clubs remained unchallenged as the pinnacle of beach culture until the 1950s, when a group of Americans visited Australia to coincide with the 1956 Melbourne Olympics. Their surf-riding displays on revolutionary, short, light Malibu boards reverberated around the country. Freshly inspired surfers rejected the conservatism of the surf clubs for the freewheeling lifestyle of the wave-chasing surfie.

In the late 1960s and early 1970s, surfing's image reached an all-time low, associated as it was with laziness, drug use and antisocial behaviour. Beneath the hippy trappings, however, surfer rivalry was pushing the sport to greater heights. In the late 1970s, Australia's success in the first ever international competitions made the dream of pro-surfing a distinct possibility. Today, lucrative careers with million-dollar salaries and worldwide superstardom beckon the most successful surfers.

Olympic swimming champion and pioneer surfer Duke Kahanamoku (1890–1968), a Hawaiian hero, poses for a photograph in 1935.

he mission of Surf Life Saving Australia (SLSA) is to provide safe beach environment throughout Australia. They patrol ̃aches and educate the public about safety.

The SLSA has over 150,000 members, of whom more than 40,000 actively patrol 400 Australian beaches. That makes it one of the largest volunteer organisations in the country.

A koala relaxes at Lone Pine Sanctuary in Brisbane.

ONE-OF-A-KIND WILDLIFE

Australia has been a separate island long enough for
evolution to take a unique path. The result is a range of
plants and animals that are found nowhere else on Earth.

Research findings are thin as to just how many people around the world actually believe that kangaroos are a regular sight on the city streets of Australia. It has become one of those stereotypical notions or urban legends, alongside the idea that most Aussie men are like Crocodile Dundee. Both ideas are popular, and both are almost entirely false. And yet, if you just wander down past the National War Memorial in Canberra, the nation's capital, at dusk, there's a very good chance that you'll find a mob of kangaroos grazing on the lawn.

In smaller towns and settlements, many of which appear to have only a toehold on the harsh antipodean landscape, the bush is often just over the back fence. The proximity of the wild means there's a fair likelihood of encountering a smattering of mammals, birds or reptiles that will surprise and delight a visitor from overseas. Even in the big cities, bereft of kangaroos as they may be, there will be possums to intrigue the tourist and frustrate the locals, whose fruit they eat and whose eaves they burrow into.

Visitors can feed and pet the kangaroos at Lone Pine Sanctuary.

Of the unique animals Down Under, possums, at least, have their counterparts in the Americas (the Virginia opossum); but the Australian kangaroo stands alone. There is nothing like it anywhere else in the world, and there's a reason for that. The sheer age of the Australian landmass and its isolation from other continents allowed its animals and plants to adapt to their unique environment and evolve independently of the rest of the world, unchallenged until the arrival of the European colonists and the onset of the technological age.

Eccentric mammals

For the perfect example of a uniquely evolved animal, take the Australian mammal. Warm-blooded and furred, mammals almost all give birth to live young and suckle them. There are three groups: placentals, marsupials and monotremes.

Elsewhere on Earth the placental group proliferates. However, very few examples of this group can be found among the native Australian fauna. The native dog, the dingo, is one, but was only introduced into Australia by Aboriginal immigrants within the past 20,000 years.

In Australia, marsupials are by far the most prominent group. Marsupials give birth to partially formed embryos which remain secure in a pouch until they are strong enough to survive independently. Most marsupials are herbivorous, but there are some that include insects, small reptiles or smaller mammals in their diets. The larger members of the carnivorous group include the Tasmanian devil and the Tasmanian tiger (thylacine). The latter, however, is now extinct (except in the minds of a a handful of die-hard environmentalists who believe that a few lone individuals survive in the Tasmanian wilderness).

It is the herbivores that abound in the land Down Under, including the shy koala, which is not even remotely related to the bear family; many varieties of possum, including the ringtail and the sugar glider; the wombat; and the macropods, or hopping marsupials, such as the kangaroo, wallaby and potoroo. Sadly for visitors just

A Boyd forest dragon perches on a tree near Kuranda.

SAVING AUSTRALIA

Similar to movements in other parts of the world, a coordinated conservation movement emerged in Australia in the late 1970s, around the time of the nationwide campaign to protect Tasmania's Franklin River from being dammed.

The eco-movement gathered impetus during the 1980s, and is now well known. Environmental activists have managed to ensure many wild places are now safe for future generations to enjoy. Notable victories include the protection of such landmark destinations as Fraser Island, Kakadu, the Daintree Rainforest, Tasmania's Southwest National Park and the Great Barrier Reef.

passing through, these species tend to be most active at dawn and dusk. Unfortunately, the typical Australian visitor is most likely to encounter these crepuscular creatures on the road, as a fleeting glimpse in the headlights of a vehicle.

The koala's habit of sleeping openly in the forks of gum (eucalyptus) trees made it an easy target for colonial hunters seeking koala fur. So great was the slaughter that urgent steps were taken to save the koala in the 1920s. This laid-back marsupial is now a completely protected animal. The wombat is related to the koala, but instead of making its home up a tree and dining on gum leaves, it uses its powerful digging paws to make burrows under stumps, logs or in creek banks. It lives on roots, leaves and bark.

Monotremes are a unique and extraordinary group of animals. Rather than giving birth to live young, they lay eggs. However, they then suckle their young and display many other mammalian traits. The amphibious duck-billed platypus is a monotreme, as is the echidna (also known as the spiny anteater). These two species are the only examples of living monotremes, although the fossil record suggests that monotremes were once widespread.

Snakes and lizards

Reptiles figure prominently in Aboriginal legend, particularly the venomous snakes such as the taipan, tiger snake, death adder and brown snake. Non-venomous species are also plentiful, as are lizards, which range from the tiniest of skinks to goannas more than 2 metres (6ft) long. Among the more exotic is the frill-necked lizard, which erects a frock of skin around its neck when confronted with danger. Don't confuse the frill-necked lizard with the bearded dragon, which has a mane of prickly spines. The blue-tongued lizard hunts snails and insects, often in city gardens. The eponymous blue tongue is often displayed as a bluff against danger.

Australia also has more than its share of frogs and toads, the most famous of which is the cane toad. Although it's not even a native, the cane toad has brought a whole lot of trouble.

Sea life

Queensland's Great Barrier Reef is a wonderland blessed with numerous fish, shell and polyp species peculiar to Australian waters. But you don't have to go snorkelling in the Reef to sample the coastal wildlife; a scramble over any coastal rock platform will reveal shellfish, starfish, anemones, crabs and even the occasional octopus. Raising your eyes to the open sea may reward you with sightings of dolphins and whales. The latter follow migratory paths along the west, south and east coasts according to season. Sharks and lethal box jellyfish are the ones to avoid.

Bird life

Australia's early explorers were as intrigued by the birdlife they saw in the skies as they were by the kangaroos and koalas found on the ground. Flocks of raucous parrots and cockatoos can be found plundering the fruit trees. They include brilliantly plumed rosellas and lorikeets. The eccentric bowerbird builds a structure or bower to win the attention of a female. He adorns his court with brightly coloured trinkets (preferably blue) such as stones, glass or objects collected from gardens and houses.

Eagles, hawks, crows and cuckoos of native origin all thrive, while the variety of habitats allows for many species of waterfowl. Some were hunted by the early settlers, and development has consumed many coastal habitats. Luckily, protective measures have saved many species from extinction.

Nature reserves

If you don't have time to spend weeks in the bush spotting creatures in their natural environment, a suitable compromise is a visit to any of the larger nature reserves that exist on the fringes of the cities. Otherwise you can go to any of the city zoos, such as Sydney's Taronga Park or the Melbourne Zoo, or their rural offshoots

– Western Plains Zoo in Dubbo or Healesville Sanctuary – and see most forms of local wildlife.

Plant life

From Queensland's steamy jungles to the delicate blossoms of New South Wales, there is no end to the variety of plant life. Like many animals, Australian flora has been affected by the introduction of foreign trees, grasses, shrubs and other plants. Some of these have flourished unchecked, completely altering the ecological balance. In the cities, the replanting of native trees has encouraged bird and insect life to return to these areas.

Scuba diving in Cairns.

TREES OF LIFE

From a stroll through the leafy outer suburbs of Sydney to a bushwalk in the jarrah forests of Western Australia, you can easily expose your senses to the great Aussie bush. Just the range of eucalypts is immense, from a low, stunted, scrub-like bush to the towering species of the highland woodlands. The mountain ash eucalyptus, found in the forests of Victoria and Tasmania, is the tallest flowering plant on Earth, growing to 70–90 metres (230–300ft) or more. Ghost gums appear silvery-white under the light of the moon, while rock-hard ironbarks are capable of blunting the toughest timber saws. Australia draws its national colours from the gold and green of the hardy acacia, or wattle – it is usually

one of the first species to rejuvenate after bushfires.

Most Australian trees have very hard timber, which made clearing the land an extremely arduous task for the early settlers. In Tasmania, the Huon pine was found to be one of the best building timbers ever, and was especially prized by boat-builders. Western Australia's jarrah and the tough karri are also superb construction timbers. The jarrah forests are currently under threat from mining and foresters, and scientists are exploring ways to combat a disease called "dieback" that has affected the forests. A concerted effort to replant some of the tree life laid waste in the name of agricultural development is currently in process.

DANGEROUS WILLDIFE

Australia has many creatures that are hazardous to humans, but it's a two-way street. Humankind has been responsible for wiping out countless species, and we're only now realising the destruction we've caused.

The second most famous interlopers onto the Australian mainland (after the First Fleet) were the cane toads. These giants were introduced in Queensland in 1935 to eradicate beetles that were attacking the key sugar-cane crop. The toads were unsuccessful in their official goal, and unfortunately they also wreaked havoc on local insect species. Even worse, the cane toad is toxic to anything that tries to eat it, giving it a privileged location on the food chain.

The cane toad is now spreading relentlessly across the country. Its story highlights the dangers of introduced species. Rabbits, foxes and cats have caused untold damage over the last 200 years, as have starlings and mynah birds. One stowaway starfish is estimated to have spawned 100 million descendants in Victoria's Port Phillip Bay.

The problem is that most introduced species thrive in an environment where they lack natural predators but enjoy a ready supply of food. Foxes and feral cats prey on small native mammals, rabbit s destroy crops, wild pigs destroy vegetation around watercourses, and starlings, introduced to control caterpillars that were eating fruit crops in the Melbourne hinterland in 1857, began to feast on the fruit themselves.

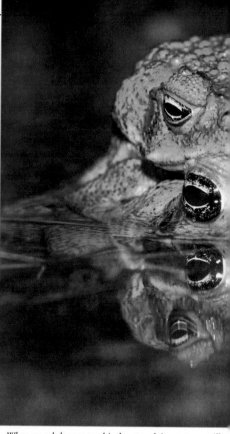

When an adult cane toad is threatened, it secretes a milky-white fluid known as bufotoxin from glands behind the ey This toxin is a Class 1 drug under Australian law; there ha been human deaths due to the consumption or licking of cane toads.

The starling is a threat to the native flora and fauna of Austral. WA has gone to great lengths to limit the bird's territory.

Although cute, rabbits are an invasive species and a serious threat to crops.

...the past 100 years, bites from Sydney funnel-web spiders ...ve caused 13 deaths, and seven of those were children. ...kily, since an anti-venom was developed in 1981, there ...ve been no casualties. If you are bitten by any large, black ...der while in Australia, seek medical attention immediately.

93

A saltwater crocodile.

AUSTRALIA'S NATURAL-BORN KILLERS

Australia is a land where lethal killers abound…or crawl or slither or float or dive. Scorpions hide beneath rocks across the continent, great white sharks devour the occasional abalone diver off South Australia, saltwater crocodiles stalk fishermen (as do box jellyfish) in the Northern Territory, the venomous blue-ringed octopus waits on the reefs, and the funnel-web spider lurks in the gardens of suburban Sydney.

And as if that weren't enough, Australia possesses more species of venomous snakes than any other country on Earth. It is home to 40 snake species, and 12 of them, like the stunning copperhead, can inflict a fatal wound. The inland taipan, or fierce snake, takes the prize as the world's deadliest snake: it is 50 times more venomous than the cobra. This rich reptilian diversity is not limited to the mainland: 32 known species of venomous sea snakes reside offshore.

However, dangerous liaisons between humans and these creatures are rare, with most sightings of killer animals confined to city zoos. In the wild, most animals prefer escape to confrontation with potentially lethal human beings.

An inland taipan (Oxyuranus microlepidotus), the most venomous snake in the world, is almost never photographed due to its extremely shy nature.

The Big Red sand dune on the edge of the Simpson Desert.

A glorious jacaranda tree, a common sight along the Central Coast in spring.

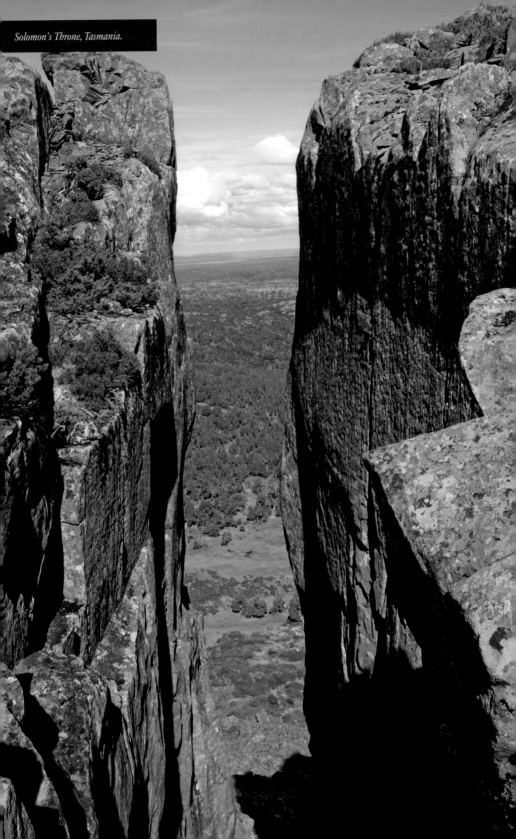
Solomon's Throne, Tasmania.

INTRODUCTION

A detailed guide to the entire country, with main
sites cross-referenced by number to the maps.

The vast Australian landscape.

Australia has some fantastic cities: Sydney, with its glorious harbour and the twin icons of the Opera House and the Harbour Bridge; Melbourne, famed for its laneways, cosmopolitan café culture and plethora of sporting arenas; Brisbane, characterised by its subtropical colonial architecture; Canberra, full of museums and galleries; Adelaide, and its great churches and parks; Perth, with its river and atmospheric old port; Hobart, and its colonial heart and mountain backdrop; Darwin, known for its frontier town flavour.

Every country has cities, but no other country has a vast Outback with Uluru at its parched red centre. Nowhere else has the Great Barrier Reef, the Kimberley in northern Western Australia, the pristine wilderness of Tasmania, or the alpine splendour of the Great Dividing Range.

So make the most of the cities and enjoy the coast. The popular image of Aussies as surf-loving beach dwellers is not without a grounding in truth. There are, after all, thousands of kilometres of unspoilt beaches. But the rewards for those who dig a little deeper are many. Australia's Aboriginal population thrived for 50,000 years without the need for cities, and they spread across this entire continent, leaving tantalising fragments of rock art as their only record. You shouldn't limit your Australian experience to the well-trodden path.

Great Barrier Reef.

So visit Sydney, but go to the Blue Mountains as well, or get right out to the isolated old mining town of Broken Hill. Visit Melbourne, but don't forget to go up into the high country and drive along the Great Ocean Road. See Brisbane and then consider stopping at the Reef, the islands and Daintree's tropical rainforest. From Canberra, head up to the Snowy Mountains. After Adelaide, visit Barossa wine country or the underground desert dwellings of Coober Pedy. Perth has the Kimberley to the north and the ancient forests and wineries of Margaret River to the south. Hobart gives access to the wonders of Freycinet National Park or Cradle Mountain, and the remarkable Port Arthur Penal Settlement. Darwin is the jumping-off point for Kakadu, with its rich Aboriginal culture, tropical wetlands and saltwater crocodiles.

And always, so far from all of these, but essential for anyone really wanting to taste the difference of this ancient land, is Uluru, the rock at the heart of the real Australia.

Australia

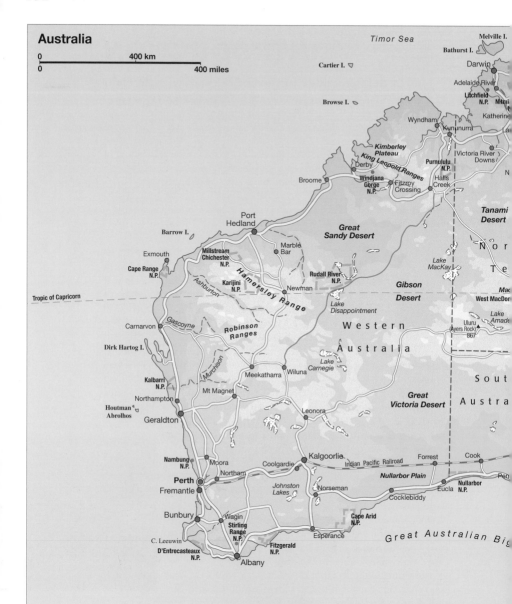

0   400 km

0   400 miles

Timor Sea

Melville I.

Bathurst I.

Cartier I. ▽

Darwin

Adelaide River

Litchfield
N.P.   Nitmi

Browse I. ◊

Katherine

La

Wyndham

Kununurra

*Kimberley
Plateau*

Victoria River
Downs

N

King Leopold Ranges

Derby

Purnululu
N.P.

Broome

Windjana
Gorge
N.P.

Fitzroy
Crossing

Halls
Creek

Port
Hedland

Marble
Bar

*Great
Sandy Desert*

*Tanami
Desert*

Barrow I.

Lake
MacKay

N o r

T e

Exmouth

Millstream
Chichester
N.P.

Rudall River
N.P.

*Gibson
Desert*

Mac

West MacDo

Cape Range
N.P.

Karijini
N.P.

Newman

Ashburton

Hamersley Range

Lake
Disappointment

Uluru
(Ayers Rock)
867

Lake
Amade

Tropic of Capricorn

Carnarvon

Gascoyne

*Robinson
Ranges*

W e s t e r n

A u s t r a l i a

S o u t

Dirk Hartog I.

Murchison

Meekatharra

Wiluna

Lake
Carnegie

Kalbarri
N.P.

Mt Magnet

*Great
Victoria Desert*

A u s t r a

Northampton

Leonora

Houtman
Abrolhos

Geraldton

Nambung
N.P.

Moora

Coolgardie

Kalgoorlie

Indian Pacific Railroad

Forrest

Cook

Northam

Nullarbor Plain

Pen

Perth

Fremantle

Johnston
Lakes

Norseman

Eucla

Nullarbor
N.P.

Bunbury

Wagin

Cocklebiddy

Stirling
Range
N.P.

Cape Arid
N.P.

C. Leeuwin

D'Entrecasteaux
N.P.

Fitzgerald
N.P.

Esperance

Great Australian Big

Albany

I N D I A N   O C E A N

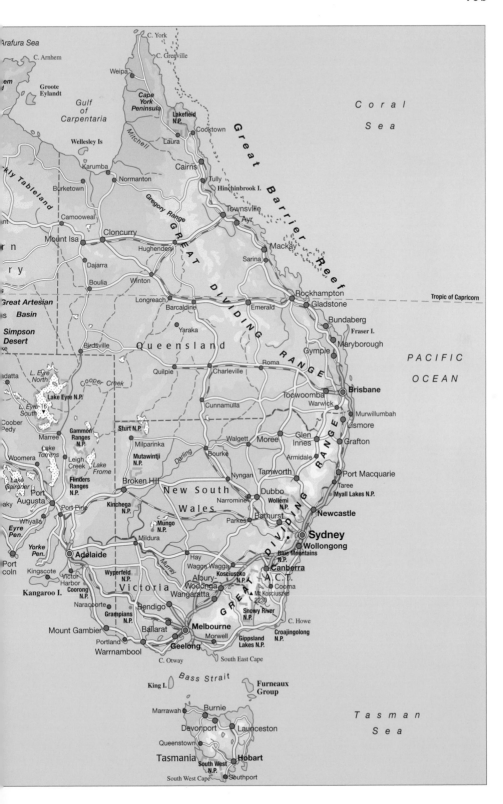

The Opera House.

SYDNEY

The glittering harbour with its coat-hanger bridge, the pearly sails of the Opera House, the bronzed life-savers at Bondi Beach... most of the symbols that define Australia are located in Sydney.

Sydney is where Australian indulgence finds its most spectacular backdrop, a city where leisure has been elevated to an art form. Yet Australia's largest metropolis, with four-and-a-half million people, can still baffle expectations. The natural beauty of the harbour and beaches often stands in stark relief to the man-made landscape: the narrow, traffic-clogged streets, the lacklustre architecture of its inner city, the endless orange-roofed expanse of its suburbia. However, if this is your first stop in Australia and the flight path of your aircraft takes you in a loop west of the city, with the Opera House and the Harbour Bridge cast in miniature against the harbour, chances are you'll be smitten.

Sydney's origins

To its critics – who mostly live in its traditional rival, Melbourne – Sydney is all glitz, obsessed with superficial show and appearance above substance. But none of this seems to matter to most Sydneysiders, and even less to visitors. The city continually lures many of the wealthiest, smartest and most artistically talented from the rest of Australia, and increasingly, the world, while real-estate values go through the roof. Everybody wants to live in "the capital of the Pacific Rim".

Yet few of the world's great cities have had such an unpromising start.

On 26 January 1788, a fleet of 11 ships under the command of Captain Arthur Phillip landed a seasick gaggle of male convicts while the local Aborigines threw stones in a vain attempt to drive them away. The officers pitched their tents east of the freshwater Tank Stream at Sydney Cove, with the prisoners and their guards to the west (creating a social division that lasts to this day, with the wealthier suburbs of the east versus the have-nots of the west). Two weeks later, the women convicts disembarked, with a few children in

Main Attractions
Harbour Bridge
Opera House
Botanic Gardens
Sydney Tower
Bondi Market
Blue Mountains

North Sydney Olympic Pool.

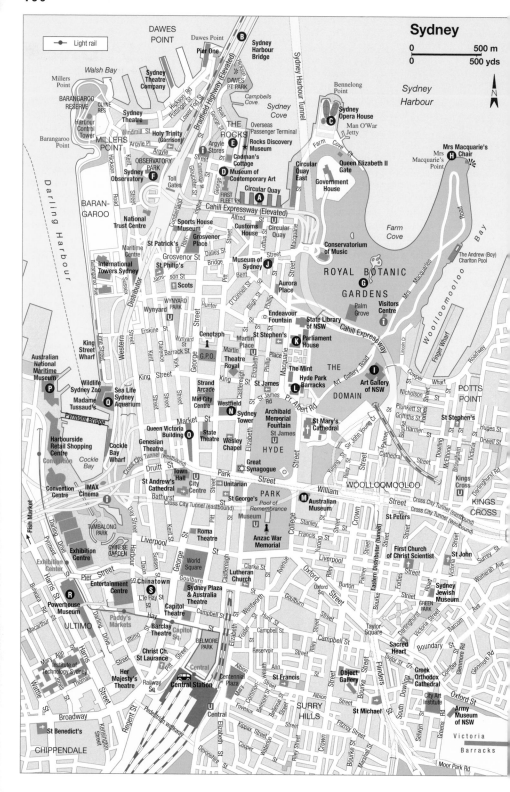

Sydney

Light rail

0   500 m
0   500 yds

tow (some of whom had been born during the 11-month voyage).

Today the site of these early landings is one of the most visited spots in Sydney: **Circular Quay** Ⓐ. This is the gateway to **Sydney Harbour** and the place where everyone should begin a visit. Ferries, Jetcats, water taxis and tour boats of every stripe plough in and out of its docks, taking passengers up and down the grand waterway of Port Jackson, described by Phillip as "the finest harbour in the world, where a thousand ship of the line may ride with the most perfect security." To get a feel for Sydney, hop on a ferry, take a seat outside and don't get off at all; all ferries eventually return home to the quay. There's a great view of Sydney's two familiar icons.

The Harbour Bridge

First to be constructed was the **Harbour Bridge** Ⓑ. The widest single-span bridge in the world, it was erected during the depths of the 1930s Depression as a symbol of hope in the future. It became dubbed the Coat Hanger, the Toast Rack and the Iron Lung (the latter for the number of people given work on its construction, which kept Sydney breathing). These days, despite dire predictions that rust is rotting it away from the inside, the bridge is still the major link between Sydney's northern and southern suburbs (there's also an underground tunnel).

The southeastern pylon on the Harbour Bridge is home to the **Pylon Lookout** museum (tel: 02-9240 1100; www.pylonlookout.com.au; daily 10am–5pm), which leads up to a viewing platform with superb views of the harbour and city. Small-group guided climbs to the bridge's summit, each lasting 3.5 hours, can be booked through BridgeClimb (tel: 02-8274 7777; www.bridgeclimb.com; daily). Unless you're seriously scared of heights, spend the cash and do the climb. You'll forget all about the deeply unattractive jumpsuits that are compulsory for safety once you see the priceless view from the top.

The Opera House

The second symbol began construction in 1959, and today is probably the most photographed site in Sydney. The **Opera House** Ⓒ (tel: 02-9250 7777; www.sydneyoperahouse.com; guided one-hour tours daily between 9am–5pm; a two-hour backstage tour including breakfast is limited to 12 visitors, daily at 7am) is without a doubt one of the world's most spectacular buildings (or, as art critic Robert Hughes would have it, "the biggest environmental site-specific sculpture south of the Equator"). It was designed by Jørn Utzon, a Dane, after an international competition – although nobody at the time quite knew how it would be built. It was the first large-scale project to make extensive use of computer technology, but, even so, the construction was fraught with difficulties. Costs escalated. Utzon became caught up in the petty-minded moneygrubbing of Australian politics, and resigned in disgust in 1966. A state lottery raised the necessary cash, and by the time the completed building was opened by the Queen in 1973, it cost A$102 million – 15 times its initial

TIP

Take a ferry from Circular Quay to Cockatoo Island. It's a 20-minute journey out towards Parramatta and the reward is a jumble of 19th-century prison buildings – part of the Unesco World Heritage-listed Australian Convict Sites – and the remnants of a massive 20th-century shipyard. Bring a picnic with you and wander at leisure.

View of Sydney Harbour.

Bunting flutters on the old warehouses at The Rocks to celebrate Australia Day on 26th January.

budget. But few have ever complained about the price since. The Opera House became an immediate icon for Australia's new-found cultural independence.

Also overlooking the harbour, the Gothic Revival style is exemplified by **Government House** (tel: 02-9228 4111; www.sydneylivingmuseums.com.au; guided tour only, every half-hour; generally Fri–Sun 10.30am–3pm, check website; free), the state governor's residence which is also open to the public. The ground-floor state rooms have some beautiful 19th- and 20th-century furniture and decoration.

Apart from the docking ferries, Circular Quay is a lively scene, packed with buskers, pedlars and office workers relaxing on their lunch breaks during the day, and busy with after-work drinkers and dining tourists at night. Just around the waterline lies the **Museum of Contemporary Art** **D** (MCA; tel: 02-9245 2400; www.mca.com.au; daily 10am–5pm, Thu till 9pm; free), its squat form enlivened by a new extension. The ground-floor restaurant and the café and sculpture terrace on the fourth floor offer spectacular harbour views.

Weekend market, The Rocks.

Those interested in Australian art might enjoy Daniel Boyd's work featuring reinterpretations of Aboriginal and Australian-European history or that of Rosalie Gascoigne who uses mostly found materials.. But even if the contemporary art scene isn't your thing, the museum won't disappoint: there's always a mix of fresh styles and interesting new exhibitions.

The Rocks

Behind the MCA sits Sydney's most historic district, known as **The Rocks** **E** after the sandstone bluffs from which the first convicts cut golden bricks for public buildings (take a look up the **Argyle Cut**, slicing straight through the cliffs – the pick marks are still easily identifiable). Almost immediately the area became the colony's main port, and warehouses grew up along the waterfront, backed by merchants' shops, offices, hotels, banks, bars and brothels that went along with the seafaring trade of the 19th century. Respectability always eluded The Rocks, and by the 1960s the area had long outlived its original mercantile function.

Today The Rocks is virtually an open-air museum, where you can absorb Australia's early history with a leisurely stroll – although the entire area is now unashamedly devoted to tourism. Avoid the markets on a Saturday unless you want to be stuck there for hours dodging the crowds. If you really want to visit, make it an evening excursion – you'll be spoilt for choice in overpriced but top-notch restaurants.

Sydney's oldest buildings

Next to the MCA is the tiny stone **Cadman's Cottage** (daily 9am–5pm; free), built in 1816 and believed to be Sydney's oldest building, now housing a museum. Only a small number of buildings remain from the first half of the 19th century. Many more date from the Victorian era, when cargoes of wool, wheat and gold provided a rich source of income that allowed architectural flourishes of the period to blossom. The contrast between these ornate buildings and the simple, embellished stonework of the Georgian era is striking.

The Argyle Cut passes the **Argyle Centre** (a convict-era storehouse that is now a boutique shopping centre) and the **Garrison Church**, and eventually leads up a steep path to **Observatory Hill**. Although a fort was built on the hilltop in 1803 for officers in case of a convict uprising, the oldest building still standing is the Signal Station, which was erected in 1848. In 1855 the hill became the site for the **Sydney Observatory** **F** (tel: 02-9271 0222; www.sydney observatory.com.au; daily 10am–5pm, night sessions also available, bookings essential; free), which began as a time-keeping device. Since 1982 the Observatory has been a museum of astronomy, with an imaginative **3-D Space Theatre** (daily, check times).

Today Observatory Hill is a lovely picnic spot with fine harbour views, making it a favourite viewing point for tourists and locals to watch the fireworks on New Year's Eve. Further towards Millers Point lies a network of narrow streets that have traditionally been home to wharf workers. The **Hero of Waterloo** (Lower Fort Street) and **Fortune of War** (George Street) compete for the honour of being Sydney's oldest pub, with the **Palisade** (Bettington Street) one of the most atmospheric.

The Botanic Gardens

Following the waterline in the opposite direction from the quay leads you past the Opera House to the **Royal Botanic Gardens** **G** (tel: 02-9231 8111; www. rbgsyd.nsw.gov.au; daily sunrise–sunset; free) – a vast, voluptuous collection of antipodean flora, including some truly majestic Moreton Bay figs. Hidden amongst the sculpted lakes and exotic fronds is an excellent café-restaurant. If you decide to picnic on the lawns, be warned – the strutting, long-beaked ibis are notorious lunch burglars.

From **Mrs Macquarie's Point** **H** one gazes out at the tiny island of Fort Denison. This is also the site of the summer Open Air Cinema (one month every year; tel: 1300-366 649; www.stgeorgeopenair.com.au), where you can sip champagne and watch a recent film from a screen that seems

Ken Done (pronounced as in bone) is a popular local artist and designer who has a gallery in The Rocks exhibiting his paintings. A shop sells clothes, ceramics and other items featuring his work.

View of Sydney Harbour and the Bridge taken from Observatory Hill.

Harbour-hopping

Sydney's green-and-yellow harbour ferries are perhaps one of the city's most pleasant forms of public transport.

A surprising amount of the city can be seen by hopping from wharf to wharf. A five-minute ride directly opposite Circular Quay (the main ferry terminal) leads to the North Shore suburb of **Kirribilli**, where the prime minister and governor-general have official residences (and both are known to pop in to the legendary Kirribilli fish-and-chip shop for a meal beneath the bridge pylons).

On the other side of the bridge, **McMahons Point** is believed to have the best view in Sydney; running up to North Sydney, **Blues Point Road** has a string of much-favoured cafés. Only a bit longer is the ride to **Cremorne Point**, a dramatic promontory with a harbourside walk to Mosman (considered to be one of the best hikes in Sydney), where a ferry can be caught back to the quay.

Also accessible by ferry is **Taronga Park Zoo** (tel: 02-9969 2777; www.taronga.org.au; daily

A harbour ferry approaches Circular Quay.

9.30am–4.30pm). Surrounded by virgin bush, this must be one of the most beautiful zoo sites on Earth, with another heart-stopping panorama of the city (taronga is an Aboriginal word for "view across the water"). The collection of more than 5,000 animals includes all the local critters (this is your best chance to see a platypus, and many a snake that you would rather not encounter in the wild). In summer, classical, jazz and swing concerts are held in the zoo's gardens.

Around half of Sydney's beaches are within the harbour (some have shark nets set up). One of the best is **Balmoral**, which also has the famous Bathers' Pavilion restaurant on its shores. **Nielsen Park** at Vaucluse is a favoured picnic spot, while **Lady Jane** allows nude bathing. **Camp Cove**, on the southern side near the harbour entrance, permits topless bathing and is popular with families.

The most famous ferry ride of all is to **Manly**; it crosses through the open sea between the Heads, and on a rough day waves can dwarf the boats. The name was given by Captain Phillip in 1788 when he was struck by the "manly" bearing of the Aborigines he met there. In the 1930s, the isthmus became Australia's favourite holiday resort "seven miles from Sydney and a thousand miles from care." The family atmosphere has lingered. There is an 11km (8-mile) harbourside walk to the Spit from here (catch a bus back). On West Esplanade are **Manly Art Gallery and Museum** (tel: 02-9976 1419; www.manly.nsw.gov.au; Tue–Sun 10am–5pm; free), with a good selection of Australian paintings, and **Oceanworld** (tel: 02-8251 7878; www.manlysealifesanctuary.com.au; daily 10am–5.30pm) where visitors can watch sharks and stingrays being fed.

From Circular Quay a high-speed catamaran, the RiverCat, speeds down the river to **Parramatta** ("where the eels lie down" in the original tongue) – technically a city in its own right, although Sydneysiders persist in calling it a suburb. Parramatta still has several colonial buildings scattered around, including Old Government House (tel: 02-9635 8149; www.oldgovernmenthouse.com.au; Tue–Sun 10am–4pm); an Explorer bus meets the RiverCat at the docks and transports passengers to the attractions.

Acting as a tourist attraction and famous Sydney icon, the harbour ferries transport more than 38,000 Sydneysiders into the city every day for work and they provide the quickest route to some seriously popular suburbs.

to rise out of the harbour. You'd be hard-pressed to find a more beautiful backdrop to a cinema, but get in quick because tickets sell out fast.

Paths continue through the gardens to the **Art Gallery of New South Wales ❶** (tel: 1800-679 278; www.artgallery.nsw.gov.au; Thu–Tue 10am–5pm, Wed 10am–9pm; general admission free). This imposing edifice is crowned with the celestial names of Leonardo da Vinci, Michelangelo, Botticelli and the like, although not one of these artists is represented in the collection. What the gallery does contain is the country's finest grouping of Australian art, and the garden setting makes it perfect for an afternoon of browsing.

Sydney's **Central Business District** – the CBD, as many refer to it – is an oddly anonymous hodgepodge of glass skyscrapers and architectural styles from the past two centuries, all squeezed onto a street plan drawn up in Georgian times. It is best seen by strolling up Young Street from the quay, past the 1846 classical revival **Customs House** (tel: 02-9242 8551; www.sydneycustomshouse.com.au; Mon–Fri 8am–midnight, Sat 10am–midnight, Sun 11am–5pm; free) – now a cultural forum with an on-site lending library, a city model of Sydney and a rooftop restaurant – evoking Sydney's early days as a great imperial port.

Museum of Sydney and Macquarie Street

You then pass the **Museum of Sydney ❶** (tel: 02-9251 5988; www.sydneylivingmuseums.com.au; daily 10am–5pm), which has entertaining sight-and-sound exhibits from the city's earliest days to today. Built on the site of the original Government House, remnants of the foundations (unearthed by accident in 1983) can now be seen inside the museum.

Cut over to Macquarie Street for a view of official Sydney: in quick succession come the **State Library** (tel: 02-9273 1414; www.sl.nsw.gov.au; Mon–Thu 9am–8pm, Fri 9am–5pm;

Sat 10am–5pm; free), which contains some of the most important archives of Australiana; **Parliament House ❶** (tel: 02-9230 2111; www.parliament.nsw.gov.au; Mon–Fri 9am–5pm; free) – the seat of the New South Wales state government; **Sydney Mint;** and **Hyde Park Barracks ❶**.

The barracks now houses one of Sydney's most popular museums (tel: 02-8239 2311; www.sydneylivingmuseums.com.au; daily 10am–5pm). Designed in 1817 by convict architect Francis Greenway and completed in 1819, the building was first used to house hundreds of prisoners. Exhibits relating to the convict system include a re-creation of the prisoners' cramped canvas-hammock sleeping quarters.

At the end of Macquarie Street lies **Hyde Park**, with the powerful Art Deco **Anzac War Memorial**. To the east of the park on College Street stands the **Australian Museum ❶** (tel: 02-9320 6000; australianmuseum.net.au; daily 9.30am–5pm), the oldest (1827) and one of the largest in the country. It is the foremost showcase of Australian natural history, and also

TIP

Almost every December the Domain – the stretch of open parkland just south of the Botanic Gardens – hums with the only major music festival devoted solely to antipodean acts: Homebake. All the greats of the Australian and New Zealand music scene have headlined. There is also a cinema pavilion and comedy stage.

The clock tower of the Sydney Central Railway.

An installation at the Museum of Sydney symbolises links between Aboriginal and European cultures.

Sharks circle above at the Darling Harbour Aquarium.

includes an extensive Aboriginal section. Only a fraction of its collections is ever displayed, but the museum mounts ever-changing exhibitions designed to captivate visitors (and children in particular).

Sydney Tower

Cut back across Hyde Park towards Pitt and George streets, the two main arteries of the CBD, and where you'll find some very respectable shopping. The controversial needle of **Sydney Tower** (www.sydneytowereye.com.au; daily 9am–10.30pm) is regarded as a phallic eyesore by many, but it has great views from the summit, and your ticket includes a "4D" film about Sydney. The Skywalk, where you walk on the tower's exterior, is a must for thrill-seekers.

Covering an entire city block is the **Queen Victoria Building** (tel: 02-9265 6800; www.qvb.com.au; Mon–Wed, Fri–Sat 9am–6pm; Thu 9am–9pm; Sun 11am–5pm; free). Built during the 1890s Depression as Sydney's main market, the arcade was lovingly restored in the 1980s. The stained-glass windows, Byzantine

arches and plaster ornamentation have made the QVB, according to Pierre Cardin, "the most beautiful shopping centre in the world". For comparison, cross George Street and drop into the Strand Arcade (tel: 02-9265 6800; www.strandarcade.com.au; Mon–Wed, Fri 9am–5.30pm, Thu 9am–9pm; Sat 9am–4pm; Sun 11am–4pm), a smaller but, arguably, just as exquisite Victorian arcade.

Darling Harbour

The controversial monorail that once ran to **Darling Harbour** is no longer in operation, so you'll have to make the 10-minute walk on foot. In the 1800s, this was the back door to Sydney, where most trading ships docked. It is now a touristy collection of shops, restaurants and family attractions. It's still the largest of the city's modern developments, although the neighbouring Barangaroo site will dwarf it once it's completed sometime around 2020. The **Maritime Museum** (daily 9.30am–5pm, Jan until 6pm; tel: 02-9298 3777; www.anmm.gov.au; permanent collections free) and the **Chinese**

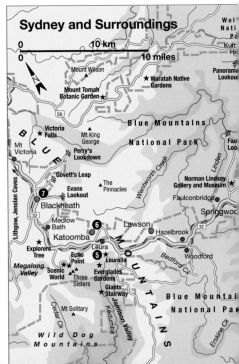

Garden were joined in 2012 by **Madame Tussaud's** (tel: 02-9333 9240; www.madametussauds.com/sydney; daily 9am–8pm), where Kylie Minogue, Nicole Kidman, Wolverine and others are on display. Another new arrival is the Darling Quarter Theatre (www.monkeybaa.com.au), focusing on introducing young people to the arts.

One of the most popular harbourside attractions is Wild Life Sydney Zoo (tel: 1800-206-158; www.wildlifesydney.com.au; daily 9.30am–6pm), where you can see animals such as koalas and kangaroos, venomous spiders and snakes in their natural habitat. The tropical rainforest enclosure, where you can walk amid thousands of brightly coloured butterflies, is a highlight.

Right next door is the **Sea Life Sydney Aquarium** (tel: 02-8251 7800; www.sydneyaquarium.com.au; daily 9am–8pm). Emerging fresh from a $10 million renovation, with 14 new themed zones in 2012, this is the best place to see Australia's extraordinary aquatic life without getting wet – or eaten. As well as crocodiles and tanks full of multi-coloured tropical fish, the Aquarium

has transparent tunnels that take you underwater for a spectacular, fish-eye journey through various habitats teeming with sea creatures – the Great Barrier Reef, a seal sanctuary and the Open Oceanarium – where sharks, sea turtles and stingrays glide alongside.

For years, Sydney's casino, not far from the Maritime Museum in Pyrmont, was regarded by many Sydneysiders as an embarrassment. Since a redevelopment and rebranding unveiled in 2011, **The Star** (tel: 02-9777 9000; www.star.com.au; 24 hours), as it is now known, has been embraced by locals, not least for its clutch of fine restaurants, which include an outpost of über-hip New York restaurant chain, Momofuku.

Transfer to the Light Rail at the casino and get off two stops later at the **Fish Market** in Pyrmont (tel: 02-9004 1100; www.sydneyfishmarket.com.au). The ultimate seafood experience, Sydney's vast Fish Market mixes fish auctions, market stalls, restaurants and a seafood cooking school. Behind-the-scenes tours run on Mondays, Wednesdays, Thursdays and Fridays

Sydney Tower is often referred to by locals as Centrepoint Tower.

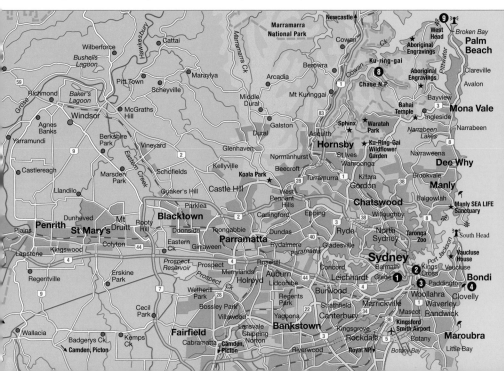

TIP

The Sydney Visitors'
Centre at Darling
Harbour (tel: 1800-067
676) is located behind
the IMAX Theatre, under
the expressway. It is
open 9.30am–5.30pm
for general advice, free
leaflets, maps and
brochures and
information about tickets
for a variety of city
attractions. It also sells a
range of Australian-
made souvenirs.

From here you can take the Light Rail back to Paddy's Markets, which leads to the **Powerhouse Museum** (tel: 02-9217 0111; www.maas.museum. com; daily 10am–5pm), a huge space devoted to science and technology, with lots of interactive displays. From there, it is a short stroll back into Sydney's **Chinatown** Ⓢ, with its wall-to-wall Asian food.

Away from the centre

In many ways, it is the assortment of inner-city suburbs (as they are oddly called) that shows Sydney at its most genuine. In the late 19th century, row after row of terraced houses were thrown up as cheap accommodation for workers – usually with small gardens, tight porches and elaborate iron-lace decorations. In the early 20th century several families at a time would squeeze into these places, but as soon as they could, most moved out to the more spacious outer suburbs in search of the Aussie dream. But from the 1970s gentrification began apace.

In the inner west lies **Glebe** ❶, whose main thoroughfare, Glebe Point Road, is lined with boutiques and cafés – many catering to students from the nearby **University of Sydney**, a leafy haven built in a self-conscious Oxbridge style. Harbourside **Balmain** was once the raunchiest of working-class suburbs, with industrial dockworks and 41 pubs, one for every 366 residents. There are now some 20 pubs, and the leafy ambience is decidedly more up-market. It can be reached by regular ferry from Circular Quay, and is an ideal spot for a Sunday stroll (the 19th-century waterfront residences are particularly impressive – they featured in Peter Carey's novel *Oscar and Lucinda*).

Kings Cross

The inner east is more of a mixed bag. In Victorian times, **Kings Cross** ❷ was an elegant, tree-lined suburb; in the 1920s and 1930s "The Cross" was Sydney's bohemian mecca, but the Vietnam War and the drug boom turned it into the city's sleazy red-light strip, albeit now on the decline. The recent addition of a horde of backpackers' hostels has hardly lifted the atmosphere.

Despite the grotty backdrop, The Cross also houses some of the city's most popular nightspots and best restaurants, not to mention a smattering of exclusive members-only (unless you're a gorgeous blonde, model or musician) bars. Don't be too wary of the area. It is worth exploring, and a bit of common sense will keep you safe. The southern side of Darlinghurst Road is much more appealing than the main drag, and the side streets and neighbouring suburbs of **Potts Point** and **Elizabeth Bay** are filled with grand old mansions and pretty, well-maintained homes. **Victoria Street** houses more great eateries, fashionable bars and chic fashion stops.

Oxford Street is one of Sydney's most iconic thoroughfares, although the Darlinghurst end in particular has seen better times.

Traditionally this is the heart of gay Sydney, particularly where Oxford Street meets Taylor Square. Gay-friendly

The less salubrious side of Kings Cross.

Kings Cross has been home to many people
WEALTHY, RESPECTABLE, IMPOVERISHED, BOHEMIAN AN JUST PLAIN CRIMINAL.
Residents know well the nuances of its streets.

clubs, bars and shops snuggle happily together here, and every February the area hosts the **Sydney Gay and Lesbian Mardi Gras** parade. Thousands of Sydneysiders line the street, peek over balconies and try and nab a spot on a roof terrace while the flamboyant floats, processions, dancers and acts sashay past. A million more watch the event on TV from the comfort of their living rooms. This is all the more remarkable, given that homosexuality was illegal in NSW until 1982. Prejudices seem to have been swept aside and locals of all backgrounds come out to applaud the efforts of the carefully constructed party.

Paddington

As Oxford Street enters **Paddington** ❸, the change in atmosphere is quite palpable. For many years now "Paddo" has been a popular address for young Sydneysiders. The colonial-style housing is chic (although not cheap!) and the boutiques, bars and restaurants that line Oxford are a weekend opportunity for the well-heeled and even better-dressed to show off their trendy tastes. It is not unusual to see the Paddo elite rummaging around the **Paddington Bazaar**, Sydney's oldest market, held in the grounds of the Uniting Church on a Saturday (10am–4pm), dressed in head-to-toe labels, straight from the covers of Vogue. However, the addition of Bondi Junction's huge shopping mall in 2004 hit Paddo hard. The Sydney faves of Sass & Bide and Scanlon & Theodore survive, but more and more owners of small businesses are paying their last month's rent and closing up shop as they struggle to compete with the convenience of Bondi Junction or meet the ludicrously high rent rates. But if you love to people-watch almost as much as you love shopping for shoes, you will appreciate the community feel of Oxford Street – and it beats being stuck in an air-conditioned mall when there is sunny Sydney weather to soak up.

As you reach the summit of Oxford, before it heads along the dual carriageway to Bondi, you hit **Centennial Park**. A favourite spot all year round for those wanting some greenery, whether you want to run, rollerblade, picnic, cycle, horse ride or just relax in a café with a coffee in the company of some very yummy eastern suburbs mummies, you can do it here. Great all year round, in midsummer the Centennial is also home to the Moonlight Cinema (www.moonlight.com.au), a delightful opportunity to watch new blockbusters and old classics while lounging on a comfy beanbag in the park. Take a picnic (there are some great delis on Oxford) and a bottle of wine and relax in the great outdoors. It's an unmissable treat for a Sydney summer night.

Bondi Beach

From Paddington, it's a short bus or taxi ride to any of the eastern beaches – of which the most famous is certainly **Bondi** ❹ (pronounced Bond-eye). It was from this great arc of sand in the late 1880s that the first Sydney "cranks" braved the ocean – breaking

TIP

There are a lot of galleries in Paddington's backstreets where you can browse through the works of local artists, sculptors and photographers. Some of the smallest streets, such as Stafford Lane and Union, Broughton and Duxford streets, are very attractive, lined with pastel-coloured Victorian terraces with ornate wrought-iron balconies.

Colonial shop fronts and houses in Paddington.

Australia has more than 11,000 beaches; if you look hard enough, you'll find one all to yourself.

Children learn to surf and swim from a very young age.

an old law that forbade swimming during daylight hours as indecent. The breakthrough came in 1902, when Manly newspaper proprietor William Gocher defied the ban and invited arrest. A similar challenge to the ban came the following year from a Waverley clergyman and a respectable bank clerk, and crowds of Sydneysiders soon followed suit. In 1906, the world's first life-saving club was set up, and 20 years later, crowds of up to 100,000 people were reported at Bondi on summer days. With its wide golden sands, ragged sandstone headlands and reliably fine rollers, Bondi had become another potent Sydney icon. Its status was further enhanced during the 2000 Olympics when Bondi played host to the beach volleyball competition.

The beach is at its best, not surprisingly, in summer. Activity kicks off at dawn, with the joggers on the promenade, bodybuilders by the shore and surfies catching a few waves before work. Sun-worshippers arrive early, closely followed by busloads of tourists. The Bondi Pavilion opens up, selling ice creams and souvenirs; picnickers

arrive with their fish and chips; and the activity continues until well after dark, when lovers take over the sands.

Bondi is also a suburb. **Campbell Parade**, the main beachfront thoroughfare, is a motley string of 1930s-era storefronts that seems to resist all improvement ("one of the great disappointments of Sydney," according to the writer Jan Morris). In the mid-1990s, talk of a Bondi Renaissance began as the suburb leapt to new heights of fashionability, and strings of New Australian restaurants opened on the North Bondi end. But still, the parade hangs on to its raffish, sand-gritted personality – and most Sydneysiders really would have it no other way.

The **Sunday Bondi Markets**, held each week 10am–4pm in the grounds of the Bondi Beach Public School, have helped establish many successful Sydney designers, and young hopefuls set up stalls each week in hope of being discovered. As if to emphasise the link, the streets behind the busy tourist trap of the parade are now lined with the fashionistas' boutiques, and are a great place to bag an expensive one-off.

Beaches of the Eastern suburbs

Despite its historic and iconic status, however, the face of Bondi is changing. Slightly further away from the city than is comfortable – especially in summer when the 40-minute bus ride can take twice that time thanks to the throngs of tourists – Bondi is being eclipsed by some of the other eastern suburbs beaches, which are just as beautiful (although all much smaller than Bondi), but don't attract the crowds. The easiest way to see them all in a day is to walk the coastal path. **Coogee** is your best option to start from in summer because it is quicker to get to from the city on a bus.

After a face-lift, Coogee (once known as a poor cousin to trendy Bondi) is coming into its own with great restaurants and bars popping up

all the time. The beach itself is flanked by the historic Wylie's Baths, and although the waves are not for surfers, there's many a boogie boarder to be found at the weekend.

Following the coast along, you'll see the small beach of **Gordon's Bay**, after which you will hit **Clovelly**. Including a saltwater swimming pool and one of the best kiosks on the strip (try their milkshakes), Clovelly is popular with families because it is sheltered from the big waves and is also great for snorkelling. The Clovelly Hotel pub is also well known for its fantastic lunch and dinner menu – best served on one of their two decks – and if there is a big sports game on, it will play on one of their massive screens.

Continue on through the stunning Waverly Cemetery until you come to **Bronte**. As well as being home to Aussie director Baz Luhrmann (and the late Heath Ledger), Bronte attracts parties of people throughout summer thanks to a crowd of free gas barbecues and some killer surf.

Next up is **Tamarama** beach, before you turn the corner to find yourself at Bondi. The walk is best in summer when there is little wind and before the sun hits its peak but, just in case, there are plenty of cafés and kiosks along the way to sustain you. If you are here in November, do not miss Sculpture by the Sea, a free exhibition of contemporary sculpture, which starts at Bondi and runs all the way to Bronte.

Watsons Bay

North of Bondi, New South Head Road runs to **Watsons Bay**, whose pub has the finest outdoor beer garden in Sydney, with views across the bobbing yachts to the city skyline. Next door is Doyle's, Sydney's oldest and best-known fish restaurant. It is a bit of a hike up to **South Head** at the mouth of Port Jackson, but well worth it.

The route back to the city goes through one of the most exclusive suburbs, **Vaucluse**. At its centre is a

magnificent mansion, **Vaucluse House** (www.sydneylivingmuseums.com.au; Fri–Sun 10am–4pm), built in 1827 for the statesman, poet and explorer William Charles Wentworth. The tearooms are charming, as are the garden picnic grounds. Swanky **Double Bay** is synonymous with Old Money, although there is also a large Central European contingent that has made the grade.

The Blue Mountains

Just 65km (40 miles) west of Sydney lie the **Blue Mountains**, the range that divides the populous, beach-fringed coastal plain from Australia's notoriously flat, harsh interior. It was an effective barrier to the colony's first explorers, whose efforts to conquer this section of the Great Dividing Range were thwarted by the rugged sandstone cliffs. The footsteps of the trio who (in 1813) successfully found the narrow passes are now followed westwards by the main route out of Sydney, the **Great Western Highway**. Today those three pioneers – Blaxland, Wentworth and Lawson – are remembered in the names of towns along the highway

Many beach hotels offer swimming pools right next to the ocean, just in case you prefer your water without salt and waves.

Shops on Campbell Parade.

FACT

The original owner of Vaucluse House, William Charles Wentworth, was born in 1790. The son of a convict, he took part in the first successful inland exploration across the Blue Mountains – the town of Wentworth Falls is named after him – became a radical politician and co-founded the colony's first independent newspaper, The Australian, in 1824.

The three sisters rock formation in the Blue Mountains National Park.

as it winds up into the mountains. It was not until the 1920s that this "rude peculiar country" took off as a holiday destination for fashionable Sydneysiders. Small European-style guesthouses sprang up, catering to honeymooners and families escaping the summer heat. In 1932, a group of bushwalkers came across a farmer about to cut down a gorgeous blue gum forest in the Grose Valley. They begged him to stop, and in the end offered to buy the land. It was the beginning of a movement that has since protected almost 1 million hectares (2.5 million acres) of Australia's most magnificent wilderness.

Despite the almost impenetrable barrier the Blue Mountains presented to early travellers, they are a sandstone plateau reaching a height of only 1,100 metres (3,600ft). Erosion has caused the stone to fall away to form sheer cliff faces punctuated by picturesque waterfalls. The **Blue Mountains National Park** (tel: 02-4782 3653; vehicle charges apply), totalling 247,000 hectares (610,400 acres), is well served by bushwalking tracks and picnic and camping spots. Small towns are riddled with fine

restaurants, old-style cafés and antiques stores catering to weekenders.

Leura

As you drive up from Sydney, first stop should be **Leura** ❺, a classic Blue Mountains hamlet; it's a tidy, picturesque railway town that makes an ideal lunch break. The region's main town, **Katoomba** ❻, is perched on the edge of the Jamison Valley, and shows off its natural wonders to the best advantage at **Echo Point**, which overlooks one of the state's most photogenic rock formations, the **Three Sisters**. Always busy with tourists, Echo Point has a well-equipped tourist information centre. A great place to take a breather before or after a hike, it might also be wise to take a picnic.

High on the list of breathtaking experiences is the **Scenic Railway** that winds down into a tree-clad gorge and is claimed to be the world's steepest railway. There are many footpaths for one-day walks in the area – an excellent choice is hiking down the Golden Stairs to the rock formations known as the **Ruined Castle**.

Katoomba has a giant cinema with a screen as tall as a six-storey building; its feature on the Blue Mountains, The Edge, is quite stunning.

Some 10 minutes' drive further west along the highway looms the **Hydro Majestic Hotel**, an Art Deco-style former casino that catered to high society in the 1920s and was recently restored. **Blackheath ❼** has some of the best guesthouses and restaurants, along with rewarding walks and the unmissable **Govett's Leap**, a spectacular lookout over the Grose Valley.

The village of **Mount Victoria** is the highest in the Blue Mountains. As in so many of the surrounding settlements, the preservation of historic buildings, especially along Station Street, makes this spot a pleasure to wander through, or bed down for the night in one of the beautiful cottages – priceless views guaranteed.

Jenolan Caves

As the road drops from the mountains down the steep Victoria Pass, it narrows to cross a convict-built bridge that was part of the first road through to the rich wool, wheat, cattle and sheep country to the west. A little way on, and 46km (29 miles) south of the highway, the magnificent **Jenolan Caves** (tel: 1300-763 311; www.jenolancaves.org.au; daily, times vary) is a mighty series of underground limestone halls encrusted with stalactites and stalagmites. In the 1920s this was the premier honeymoon spot for young Australians, who regarded the arduous journey and difficult conditions as a badge of honour.

On the highway, 12km (7.5 miles) past the Jenolan Caves turn-off, signposts point to a monument to the ingenuity used in solving one of the 19th century's greatest engineering problems at **Lithgow**. It is the railway line that originally conquered the steep descent out of the Blue Mountains, known as the **Zig-Zag Railway** – so named for its unique method of overcoming the almost sheer

mountain side. The zig-zag line was finished in 1869, but was abandoned in 1910 for a more modern descent. Dedicated train buffs restored the line to give day excursions travelling back into railway history; trains have been temporarily suspended, but check the website for updates (tel: 02-6355 2955; www.zigzagrailway.com.au).

Colonial towns around Sydney

Picturesque colonial towns also cluster on the eastern edge of the Blue Mountains. Peppered with historic buildings, the atmosphere of these hidden settlements is truly unique. Acting like a kind of time capsule of Australian colonial history, the **Hawkesbury** area was established in 1794 when settlers arrived to farm their 12 hectares (30 acres). Many of the descendants from these pioneers still work and live in the district, giving it a truly rustic Aussie atmosphere.

There are countless bushwalking and camping opportunities in the town of **Windsor**, as well as the new Hawkesbury Regional Gallery (The Deerubbin

Leura's Everglades gardens integrate local and European trees and plants.

The picturesque town of Leura.

TIP

Leura's National Trust-owned Everglades gardens (37 Everglades Avenue; tel: 02-4784 1938; www.everglades.org.au; daily 10am–5pm), designed in the 1930s by Danish landscaper Paul Sorenson, integrates local and European trees and plants and offers stunning views over the Jamison Valley. Bring a picnic or indulge yourself in the popular tea room.

Centre; tel: 02-4560 4441; www.hawkesbury.nsw.gov.au; Mon, Wed–Fri 10am–4pm, Sat–Sun 10am–3pm; free), but its main appeal is the atmospheric colonial architecture, the venerable Macquarie Arms Hotel and a lively Sunday street market. **Richmond** has a handful of fine Georgian streetscapes and offers camping, canoeing and swimming.

Closer to Sydney, on the southwestern edge of the conurbation, lie several more historic towns. In 1805 John Macarthur was granted nearly 2,000 hectares (5,000 acres) to raise sheep in **Camden**, the beginning of the nation's wool industry. The Camden-Campbelltown-Picton region is still known as Macarthur Country, and **Camden Park House** (1835) is owned by descendants of John Macarthur; it is open to groups by appointment (tel: 02-4655 8466; www.camdenparkhouse.com.au) – with an open day in the third week of September. Camden (pop. 8,000) is the centre of a dairy region focused on the Nepean River Valley.

Lying 16km (10 miles) southwest of Camden, tiny **Picton** also has numerous remnants of 19th-century settlement. Upper Menangle Street is listed by the National Trust as "representing a typical country town street" of 100 years ago. It is a fine base from which to explore the scenic surrounding region.

North of Sydney

An hour's drive north of Sydney lies one of New South Wales' most beautiful national parklands, **Ku-ring-gai Chase National Park** ❽ (tel: 02-9472 8949; vehicle charge payable). Hundreds of Aboriginal carvings dot the cliffs here, which often give sweeping views of the countryside and Cowan Creek: the easiest to reach are on the **Basin Trail** off West Head Road. At the mouth of the Hawkesbury River is **Broken Bay** ❾, a favourite recreational area, where boaters and picnickers flock at weekends.

Palm Beach, home of the Aussie TV soap *Home and Away*, is one of Greater Sydney's smarter neighbourhoods, and its beach is rated highly by surfers. If you're short of time, you can visit this area by seaplane; these leave from Rose Bay in the city, landing in Pittwater.

An old farmstead in the Hawkesbury area.

ROYAL NATIONAL PARK

Only 32km (20 miles) from Sydney, the **Royal National Park** (tel: 02-9542 0648; daily sunrise–8.30pm) was established in 1879 and is the world's second-oldest national park – after Yellowstone in the United States.

The Royal packs incredible natural diversity into a relatively small area, offering riverside picnic spots, great surf beaches, clifftop heathland walks, rainforest cycle tracks and much more. The park also has more than 60 camping sites.

A daily entrance fee is charged, so an annual pass may prove more economical if you're planning to spend a lot of time visiting the national parks. There is a strict code of care when it comes to conserving the natural beauty of the parks, so read up on the rules and live by them while you're there.

NEW SOUTH WALES

New South Wales's greatest asset is its diversity. From Sydney you can head north for tropical banana plantations, south for snowcapped mountains or west for the expanses of the Outback.

The Hunter Valley at dawn.

There's a lot more to Australia's most populous state than its capital city. While Sydneysiders may have the harbour as their playground, elsewhere in the state you can unwind by hiking in the rainforest, diving at a coral reef, or just counting the cattle as they come in for the muster. Similarly, while Sydney may be enjoying a balmy day, there may be snow on the southern Alps and dust storms sweeping across the sunbaked towns in the western Outback, while monsoons flood the lush farming country of the northeast.

The Pacific Highway

For generations, the Pacific Highway has been Sydney's escape route to the sun. Generations of Sydneysiders have made the regular pilgrimage up the coast, fleeing the winter chill, the big-city hustle, or just the tedium of the everyday. Not so long ago, the road passed through country that was still largely undeveloped: after the outskirts of Sydney thinned out into nothingness, you were in a place where the bush and the breezes did most of the talking.

These days, the Pacific Highway has been transformed into a traffic-laden artery that cuts through expanding coastal towns and seafront subdivisions. However, motorists may still enjoy a flickering parade of gum-trees in the late afternoon light, along with occasional glimpses of the Pacific Ocean's white-lace hems (despite its name, the Pacific Highway is generally several kilometres from the coast). The highway is currently being upgraded, due to be completed in 2020 (for details see www.rms.nsw.gov.au/projects).

At a pinch, you can make the drive to Queensland in 12 hours, but it's much better to take some time to explore the unpredictable patchwork of boutique wineries and old-fashioned milk bars, country pubs and fish'n'chips shops, fabled surf spots and vast tropical plantations. Three days is the bare minimum needed to sample at least some of the coast, but if you want to do some serious exploring, five days is recommended.

The trip north starts at Sydney Harbour Bridge. Northbound traffic soon throttles down into the four lanes of the Pacific Highway; at peak hours, this artery is clotted every few minutes at stop lights and suburban intersections, although at other times it flows freely. After negotiating past the cars of the well-heeled upper North Shore, you finally hit the beginning of the Newcastle Freeway at **Wahroonga**.

Where the highway crosses the **Hawkesbury River** at **Brooklyn**, a vista of ridges, valleys and arms of open water spreads east and west. This is a popular weekend playground for many Sydneysiders, who rent cabin cruisers and drift among the bays and inlets. Many companies offer cruises; a highlight is the Hawkesbury Cruises, the local service departing from Brooklyn (www.hawkesburycruises..com.au).

Upstream lies **Wiseman's Ferry**, where former convict Solomon Wiseman opened the first ferry across the river in 1827. A free car ferry takes you to the rugged bush-clad sandstone cliffs of **Dharug National Park** (tel: 02-4320 4200). Walkers, cyclists and horse riders can travel a stretch of the Great North Road, literally carved out of the rock by convicts in the 1830s.

The commercial hub of this central coast region (a mixed bag of retirees, new industries and Sydney commuters) is a detour away at the not-terribly-alluring **Gosford**. But beyond the urban sprawl are the orchards and forests of the **Mangrove Mountain** area, plus a string of beautiful beaches to escape to. Nearby is the **Australian Reptile Park** (tel: 02-4340 1022; www.reptilepark.com.au; daily 9am–5pm).

At **Doyalson**, the Pacific Highway heads along a ridge between the ocean and **Lake Macquarie**. Frequently overlooked by tourists, the lake (particularly its western shore) is a fascinating relic of a past age, when working folk could afford water frontages. The mining village of **Wangi Wangi**, for many

years the retreat of the artist Sir William Dobell, is a classic example of lake-shore charm.

The Hunter Valley

The second-largest city in New South Wales, **Newcastle**, was long burdened with a reputation as an unsophisticated industrial hub. But when steel production stopped in 2000, the town worked hard to reinvent itself as a cultural centre. Helped by a lively waterfront development, beautifully preserved heritage buildings and a large student population to liven things up, it is developing as a destination in its own right. Newcastle also makes a great base to explore the region, with easy access to the boating and bushlands of Lake Macquarie to the south and expansive, wild Myall Lakes to the north, not to mention its own impressive surf beaches. As a bonus, there are the prosperous wineries of the lower **Hunter Valley ❶**, one of Australia's premier wine-growing districts.

Many of the area's hillsides were originally settled in the pursuit of coal. Coal mining is still a thriving

The Redback spider is the most venomous in all of Australia. Luckily the antivenom is commercially available.

The coastal road.

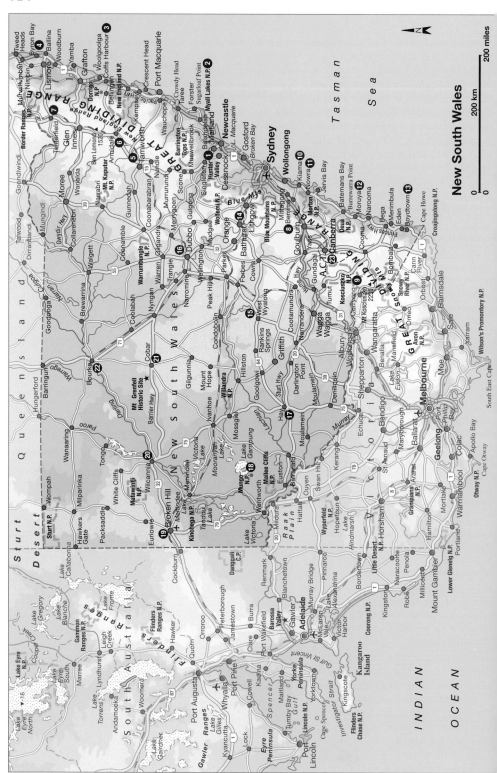

New South Wales

local industry, along with aluminium smelters, giant open-cut mines and power stations, providing a surprising flipside to the area's famed wine industry. Turning off from Newcastle, you reach **Maitland**, a city rich in historic buildings. From there, the road leads through one winery after another, with most of them gathered around **Pokolbin**.

As the highway heads deeper into the valley, the pace of life slows down. **Singleton** is an appealing mixture of modern and old civic buildings and private homes.

The town of **Scone** (rhymes with *own*) is pretty but unremarkable save for its horsiness. This is the home of thoroughbred stud farms, horse shows and the sport of polo. Much of New England is squatter territory, where the sons and daughters of the landed gentry (or those aspiring to it) continue the traditions of Mother England: good riding skills, political conservatism and bad dress sense. Scone hosts several major polo tournaments, of course.

While the Hunter Valley is very pleasant to visit, its scenery is not that spectacular; in high summer, its low hills can become unbearably hot. Many wine buffs now prefer to head an hour's drive further east to visit the lesser-known vineyards around **Mudgee**. The picturesque village of **Gulgong** makes an ideal base; it was the childhood home of the poet Henry Lawson, and has a centre devoted to him, as well as a pioneer museum.

Port Stephens

Back on the Pacific Highway, north of Newcastle the road crosses the Hunter River at Hexham and skirts the western shore of **Port Stephens**. Two-and-a-half times the size of Sydney Harbour and blessed with both calm swimming coves and ocean beaches perfect for surfing, Port Stephens is home to a number of popular resorts such as the sophisticated **Nelson Bay**, and quieter settlements such as **Tea Gardens** and **Hawks Nest**. The bay's most famous attraction is its large population of bottlenose dolphins. Between May and November it also offers whale-watching opportunities. The aquatic reserves at **Fly Point** and

Milking a tiger snake.

Segenhoe Stud Farm, Scone.

Whales and Dolphins

Watching a pod of dolphins splashing just beyond the breakers turns a day at the beach into something very special.

The coast of New South Wales is one of the best places to see whales and dolphins in the wild. While dolphins frolic near the beach, the whales' winter migration takes them along the length of the state's coastline. Over the past few years, stray whales have spent several days in Sydney Harbour, to the delight of ferry passengers.

Humpbacks travel north along the coast from about May, heading into the warm waters off the Queensland coast and returning south between September and November. Other species that are sighted less frequently include southern right whales, false killer whales, orcas, minke and, very occasionally, blue whales, the biggest creatures on the planet.

All the major holiday towns along the coast offer whale- and dolphin-watch cruises. Whale tours at Eden, deep on the state's south coast,

A pod of dolphins off the New South Wales coast.

have a fascinating edge to them, a little like visiting the scene of a crime with the criminal who did the deed. Until the 1930s, the town of Eden was a whaling station, and the various species of whales were all hunted in a gruesome alliance between killer whales and whaling boats. Paradoxically, Eden was one of the first towns in the state to develop a whale-watching industry, and its whaling history, the depth of knowledge that these operators bring to their task and their obvious affection for "their" whales make this more than just a wildlife tour.

A two-hour drive south of Sydney, Jervis Bay has a pod of resident dolphins, and the relatively placid waters of the bay make this a prime viewing spot. To the north of Sydney, Port Stephens, Coffs Harbour and Byron Bay all offer their own whale- and dolphin-watching cruises.

Whale-watching tips

Unlike the fast, acrobatic dolphins that never seem to idle for long, whales move slowly. On a whale-watch trip, the vessel will probably venture out into the open sea, where it will spend a good deal of time stopped and pitching in the waves while watching the whales. For anyone who suffers from motion sickness, this is not an ideal situation. If you are subject to seasickness, take medication well before you set foot on the boat.

An excursion is typically full of competitive anticipation, as children and adults alike vie to be the first to catch a glimpse of the quarry. However, once a whale is sighted, vessels are not allowed to approach closer than 100 metres (330ft). Whales are curious creatures and they will often swim closer to a stationary vessel, but you can't count on a close-up look. Larger vessels with an upper deck will usually give you a better vantage point; the best place to stand is usually forward of the bridge.

Unfortunately, much of the action with whales and dolphins takes place below the water, and out of sight if you're standing on the deck of a boat. But if the vessel is properly equipped with the right equipment, you can tune in and listen to what's happening below. Whales and dolphins communicate via high-pitched squeaks and whistles. Whales, in particular, are known for their beautiful songs, and the humpback is one of the most vocal of all the whales. If your vessel has a hydrophone, an underwater microphone, you can listen to them talking over the public-address system.

Halifax Point are popular with divers, and the surrounding bush offers ample walking trails.

Myall Lakes to Macksville

About 40km (25 miles) north of Port Stephens you reach Bulahdelah, the gateway to the beautiful **Myall Lakes ❷**. Preserving these aquatic pearls as a National Park was an early victory for conservationists. Paperbarks, palms and other wetland vegetation crowd the shores, while the waterways are filled with bird life. Surrounding the chain of lakes is national parkland where nature-lovers may camp in the wild. The beaches at the tiny community of **Seal Rocks** are some of the most scenically exquisite along the whole NSW coast and benefit from different outlooks, so there's always one to suit the prevailing winds.

Seal Rocks has the first of a string of beaches at the northern end of the lakes leading to the holiday resort of **Forster**, the southernmost of the North Coast beach towns. Travelling north also entails crossing river after river, for the NSW coast is crenellated with the mouths of waterways which carry runoff from the Great Dividing Range. The further north you go, the more romantic the rivers become, their shores wilder, their bars and tides more spectacular.

Taree, about a two-hour drive from Newcastle, is a thriving market town in the dairy-rich **Manning Valley**. The beautiful Manning River runs through the middle of town and, if you follow it west to **Elands**, after an hour's drive you find yourself at **Ellenborough Falls**, one of the highest single-drop waterfalls in Australia.

The Manning and other valleys of the mid-North Coast are timber centres providing native woods and pine from vast forests which stretch westwards onto the New England Plateau. Here the highway winds through many kilometres of forest, and for a change of scene it is worth a detour along the well-made coast road from

Kew to **Port Macquarie**. These are some of the prettiest beaches in the state, with rocky outcrops and golden sands. On the western side of the road there is yet another chain of ocean lakes, ideal for fishing and boating.

However, tourism has taken its toll on the landscape at Port Macquarie (a former penal settlement, founded in 1821, and still full of historic sandstone buildings). Garish motels, retirement villages and timeshare resorts dot the headlands, and red-brick suburbia has taken over the flatlands to the west. But for all its superannuated qualities, there is still much to like about Port – good restaurants, top-quality accommodation and easy access to uncrowded beaches. **Wauchope**, a few kilometres up the Hastings River, is worth a visit for **Timbertown,** an award-winning replica of an old sawmilling village.

The highway again snakes inland and through the forests. It is worth making the 24km (15-mile) detour to take in the resort of **Crescent Head** – a pretty, peaceful town with fine surf and good golf. For a real escape, head south from Crescent on the old dirt coast road for

TIP

The views from the lookout tower at Cape Hawke in Booti Booti National Park (20km/12 miles south of Forster; www.environment.nsw.gov.au/nationalparks) are spectacular. You can see south to the foot of Barrington Tops. The park has walking trails, a picnic area and camping facilities, but only Elizabeth Beach is patrolled by volunteer life-savers during the swimming season.

To lessen the impact of walkers, national parks in New South Wales provide boardwalks over fragile terrain.

10km (6 miles) to a grassy headland and beach known as **Racecourse**. There's no sign, but a ranger will appear from nowhere after a day or two to collect a modest camping fee. Given the joys of an empty beach, uncrowded waves and occasional dolphin sightings, the minimal fee is a gift.

Nearby is the town of **South West Rocks**, perched on a picturesque headland, and the famous **Trial Bay Gaol**, which held convicts and, later, German war internees.

Continuing northwards, a distinctly tropical feel begins to permeate the air and, from **Macksville** on, banana plantations are a common sight and a good proportion of houses are built on stilts, Queensland-style, in order to catch the cooling breeze and keep things dry. Everywhere the dominant colour is a lush green, and the roadside signs tell you this is paradise. It isn't, but it's a step in the right direction. While you're filling the tank in Macksville, pop around to The Star pub, which sits right on the banks of the Nambucca River, as pretty and profane an ale house as you'll find anywhere.

Just south of Macksville, the small town of **Scotts Head** presents a long, clean beach and a caravan park.

Coffs Harbour and Bellingen

The timber port of **Coffs Harbour** ❸ is reputed to have Australia's best climate, and has developed into a major centre of North Coast tourism. Unfortunately, most motorists know Coffs only as the city of the Big Banana, another manifestation of Australia's bizarre tourist gigantism. Those with a taste for adventure can join whitewater professionals for a day of rafting action on the nearby **Nymboida River**.

Coffs is more or less the midway point between Sydney and Brisbane – around seven and six hours' driving distance, respectively. Travellers often plan to stay here overnight only, but end up staying a week. The town is alive with restaurants and pubs, particularly in the strip from the jetty to Park Beach. Parasailing, four-wheel-drive tours, the beach, golf and galleries fill the days.

The beach at South West Rocks.

Inland, the Bellingen Valley offers scenic pleasures quite different from the coast. Some parts of this valley, particularly the pebbled river banks, look more like parts of temperate Europe than east-coast Australia.

The beautiful village of **Bellingen** (which features dramatically in the climax of Peter Carey's novel *Oscar and Lucinda*) is, along with Nimbin to the north, the heart of alternative culture in NSW, although concessions have been made to capitalism since the real-estate boom hit and idyllic communal farms became worth millions. Bellingen retains a relaxed atmosphere and a strong alternative bent. Browse the local arts and crafts at the Old Butter Factory or the beautifully restored Hammond and Wheatley Emporium department store. If you're in the area in August or October you can take in the local jazz or global music festivals.

Bellingen to Ballina

From Bellingen, take the Dorrigo Road to the small town of **Dorrigo**, a great base for exploring the **Dorrigo National Park** (tel: 02-6657 2309). The park is a fragment of the massive rainforest that covered the area until the 1920s, when loggers clear-felled in their search for Australian cedar, a timber so valuable it was known as red gold. From the Dorrigo Rainforest Centre (tel: 02-6657 2309; daily 9am–4.30pm), you can take a number of walks, including the Skywalk, a wooden walkway stretched high over the forest canopy that is also open for nocturnal excursions.

The Pacific Highway swings inland yet again through the forests, this time emerging at **Grafton**, a lovely old town shaded with jacaranda trees (a wonderful sight in late October and early November) and situated on a bend of the Clarence River, 65km (40 miles) from its mouth. Grafton has some delightful 19th century architecture enhanced by its wide, tree-lined streets. This is flood country, and the houses close to the river are tropical bungalows on stilts. Like several towns away from

the coast, Grafton has been bypassed in the tourist boom, and prices for food and lodging are still reasonable.

North of Grafton, the highway follows the line of the Clarence River across flatlands to the coast, with rambling old houses peering out from behind fields of sugar cane. The village of **Maclean**, built on several hills a few kilometres upriver from Yamba, is quaint, quiet, and a great spot from which to view the workings of the Clarence with its fishermen and cane haulers. Fifteen minutes down a straight bitumen road is the resort of **Yamba**, once a sleepy hollow and now filled with shoddily built weekenders and more garish motels. But the pub on the headland and the beaches spread below are first-rate. Down the coast a few kilometres from Yamba, the village and famous surf point of **Angourie** is renowned for its rocky coastline and Blue Pools.

After a stretch of alternating river and cane scenery, the Pacific Highway clips the coast again at **Ballina**, the southernmost beach town in a string reaching to the Queensland border,

A rainforest waterfall in Dorrigo.

FACT

The strife of Byron: Coastal erosion has long been a problem in Byron Bay and continues to threaten beach-front properties in Byron Bay and pit homeowners against the local council, who favour a policy of a "planned retreat" from those structures that tumble into the water rather than maintaining protective sea walls.

Surf school will teach you all the moves.

collectively known as the Summerland Coast. Ballina, the scene of a minor gold rush in the 19th century, has now found more consistent treasure as a bustling tourist centre and fishing port.

The Highway now heads due north through magnificent rolling hills, but the alternative coastal route takes in some equally breathtaking coastal scenery, including the village of **Lennox Head**, ranked as one of the top 10 surfing spots in the world (the big waves come from May to July).

Byron Bay

The area's big tourist magnet is **Byron Bay ❹**, the easternmost town in Australia and a popular tourist destination.

In the 1960s, Byron was still a quiet rural community with an alternative bent. Today, its magnificent setting, with almost 30km (19 miles) of sandy beaches fringed by a fertile hinterland, has made it a mecca for the rich and the famous. Some, like global music star Jack Johnson, own property here; others ensconce themselves in the area's impressive array of luxury retreats.

The town is just as popular with the less well-off, who spend their time bodysurfing or relaxing in the sun, a laid-back lifestyle that has made the town a magnet for unemployed youth. In a classic case of biting the hand that feeds it, the local council has been battling to limit the number of visitors, but thus far without success.

Come to town on a crowded festival weekend and you may even sympathise with the council. Byron has a packed roster of festivals, devoted variously to blues, writers, films, jazz, and many more besides, during which times the town can get uncomfortably full.

However, the town's growth has not marred its natural beauty. While the beaches are a major attraction, the hinterland features a number of national parks and nature reserves, including **Tyagarah** and **Broken Head** nature reserves, **Arakwal National Park** (tel: 02-6620 9300) and **Cape Byron Headland**. Then of course there's the underwater world. Byron's most famous dive spot, the **Julian Rocks Aquatic Reserve**, is considered second only to the Great Barrier Reef on the east coast. This is where temperate

PARK LIFE

With more than 600 national parks or nature reserves in the state under the aegis of the NSW National Parks and Wildlife Service, you won't find it difficult to find a patch of accessible nature. At 44 of them you will have to pay a daily entry fee for your vehicle. Everywhere else you're free to come and go as you please. Where there is a fee, it's sometimes a matter of purchasing a "pay and display" ticket, so make sure you have plenty of coins on you. It is worthwhile calling the park office (telephone numbers provided in the text) ahead of your visit to check whether there are current fire restrictions that could mean all or part of the park is shut. For full information on any or all of the parks, visit www.nationalparks.nsw.gov.au.

and tropical waters meet, giving divers the opportunity to view an astonishing array of marine wildlife. A few gruesome incidents where divers have been taken by sharks has done little to lessen its popularity.

The best-known attraction in Byron's hinterland is **Nimbin**, Australia's original alternative community, the town where the 1973 Aquarius Festival launched Australia's hippy culture. While much of the town is still caught in a 1970s time warp, with luridly painted houses and shops and the scent of patchouli in the air, its drug community has moved on from marijuana to hard-core heroin. The overt drug peddling makes many visitors uncomfortable, and they tend not to linger.

A better option is to spend some time exploring the local area. The winding roads between Nimbin and Lismore, through undulating landscape covered in lush rainforest, offer some of the most scenic drives in the state. These pockets of rainforest, left untouched by the early settlers, were the focus of Australia's first anti-logging protest in the late 1970s.

Mount Warning

The rich soil in the area is a legacy of the giant, shield-shaped volcano that once covered the entire area. The remnant of its central vent is a 1,157-metre (3,780ft) peak called **Mount Warning** in English, **Wollumbin** (Cloud Catcher) in the local Bandjalung language. Its peak is the first spot in Australia to catch the rays of the rising sun, and offers dazzling views over the district. Also worth exploring are the **Border Ranges National Park** (tel: 02-6632 0000; vehicle entry fee) and the **Nightcap National Park** (tel: 02-6627 0200), including the 100-metre (328ft) -high Minyon Falls.

The border town of **Tweed Heads** has only recently emerged from the shadow of its flashier sister across the Queensland border, Coolangatta, but the tourist boom now proceeds apace. The end of one journey is the beginning of the next. As you cross the Tweed River, the North Coast of NSW falls behind, and what opens ahead is a very different beast: the Gold Coast of Queensland.

The lighthouse at Cape Byron, the easternmost point of Australia.

Two Pacific Gems

Norfolk Island and Lord Howe Island are lush green specks on the vastness of the Pacific Ocean.

Two of Australia's tiniest tourist areas are also among the most attractive. Although Norfolk and Lord Howe are South Pacific islands, these are not atolls of palm trees and corals.

The sea life around the islands is quite phenomenal. In the surrounding waters, warm and cool currents collide, spawning a wealth of marine creatures including giant clams, sea turtles, clownfish, lionfish, tuna, butterfly fish and a wrasse known as the doubleheader, a species that is unique to the islands' waters. It's not surprising that diving is a major draw to the islands.

A rich and fascinating cultural heritage, relaxed lifestyle and rolling green pastures characterise **Norfolk Island**, 1,700km (1,050 miles) northeast of Sydney and covering about 35 sq km (13.5 sq miles). No one lived here until a British penal settlement was established in 1788. The prison island became known for its harsh and cruel conditions.

Lord Howe Island.

The most bizarre event in Norfolk's history occurred after the British Government decided, in 1852, that the settlement was too expensive to maintain and evacuated all the inhabitants. At about the same time, on remote Pitcairn Island the descendants of the *Bounty* mutineers and the Polynesian women they took with them from Tahiti in 1789 (after dumping Captain William Bligh) were finding it difficult to grow enough food for their increasing population. So they were relocated to Norfolk Island in 1856, although a few later returned to Pitcairn.

Today there are about 2,000 people on the 3,500-hectare (8,750-acre) island, but many of them share the same set of Bounty surnames. Indeed, so many Christians, Quintals, Youngs, McCoys, Adamses, Buffetts, Nobbses and Evanses crowd the telephone book that it's the only one in the world to publish subscribers' nicknames.

Norfolk is a self-governing territory within Australia. The tourist clutter of **Kingston** is the island's only town. Tax-free shopping here is very cheap, especially for fashionable wool and cashmere sweaters.

Down by the waterfront, the buildings of the early settlements are still in good condition – some are still used as government offices. The evening sound-and-light show along these buildings, which are remnants from a savage time, is well worth your while.

Norfolk Island doesn't promise a wild time. However, you feel close to history here, and there is enough to do to warrant several days' stay. Diving is a popular activity, and Fletcher Christian's descendant Karlene Christian, at the Bounty Dive Shop, offers daily diving groups.

Lord Howe Island

About 900km (560 miles) to the west, crescent-shaped **Lord Howe Island** is only 11km (7 miles) long and 2km (1.25 miles) wide, with a population of about 300. Visitors usually travel on bicycles.

This heavily forested and partially mountainous isle often has a cap of cloud on Mount Gower (875 metres/2,870ft), at the southern end. There are numerous walking trails, many birds and some unique vegetation. It is advisable to take a tour with a local guide, since it takes a resident expert to decipher the island's rich botany and bird life.

New England

At **Murrurundi** the New England Highway climbs up, leaving the Hunter Valley to enter the Great Dividing Range, the vast upheaval which separates the coastal plains from the tablelands along the entire length of New South Wales. The town itself is set in a valley of the Liverpool Ranges, and seems constantly shrouded in mist.

The road winds into the ranges and onto the New England Plateau, eventually reaching the city of **Tamworth ❺**. This pretty town is the largest in the northwest, with a thriving economy based on sheep and cattle. Tamworth's role as a commercial centre for outlying farms and ranches prompted a local radio announcer to establish a promotion on the cowboy theme. In the early 1970s he organised a country music festival and started calling Tamworth "the country music capital of Australia". At first, residents were wary of being stereotyped, but the annual festival is now the town's major draw, attracting thousands of fans every January. If you're in the area, it is worth a detour to Tamworth just to dine at Monty's (Armidale Road; tel: 02-6766 7000), one of Australia's best regional restaurants.

Not far from Tamworth, along a road that follows the bends of the Peel River, is the old gold-mining town of **Nundle**. Abandoned diggings and the ghostly town make it worth a detour. North of Tamworth, the New England Highway passes through spectacular country with rugged peaks and long plains dotted with quaint old mining towns. In **Uralla** you'll find the grave of the legendary bushranger Captain Thunderbolt, shot during a battle with police at nearby Kentucky Creek in 1870.

As its name suggests, the **New England Tableland** bears striking similarities, in both topography and climate, to the old country: England. Its altitude gives it frosty mornings nine months of the year, occasional snow and a year-round freshness.

Nowhere is this more evident than in the city of **Armidale ❻**, a scholarly town greened by parks and gardens, with two cathedrals and tree-lined streets. As well as the University of New England, Armidale has one other college and three boarding schools,

TIP

Follow Scenic Drive 19 for about 11km (7 miles) east out of Uralla, until you reach the privately owned village of Gostwyck, known for its merino wool. Beautiful little Gostwyck Chapel, set on the banks of a willow-edged stream, is covered with trailing vines that blaze red around April.

A perfect picnic spot.

FACT

The Anaiwian Aboriginal people have called Armidale home for 10,000 years, with other tribes also using the area as a meeting place. The Aboriginal Cultural Centre and Keeping Place (128 Kentucky Street) has a good collection of artefacts, an art gallery and workshops.

A stained-glass window in Penrose Park.

establishing it as the major NSW seat of learning outside Sydney. The student population has given Armidale an air of youthfulness in contrast to its stately Victorian architecture.

The highway out of Armidale leads along a ridge to the watershed of the Great Dividing Range, 1,320 metres (4,330ft) above sea level, at **Guyra**, then on to the junction with the Gwydir Highway at **Glen Innes**, famous for its fine gemstones. Almost a third of the world's sapphires are mined in this area and, although most of the good spots are on commercial lease, you can search for sapphires, garnets, jasper, agate and numerous other stones at many places. The town itself has magnificent ornate buildings and is fringed by five lovely parks. The mist-shrouded **New England National Park** (tel: 02-6657 2309), east of Armidale, is beautiful.

Tenterfield ❼ is the next major town along the route, once chiefly famous as "the birthplace of Federation" (because Sir Henry Parkes first called for the Australian colonies to unite in a speech made in the School of Arts here in 1889), but now more

famous as the birthplace of Peter Allen's grandfather. The late, expatriate Aussie singer topped the charts in the early 1980s with a soppy eulogy to his grandfather called *Tenterfield Saddler*. For all that, it is a rather ordinary country town in which there is not a great deal except memories.

The Southern Highlands

The Hume Highway is the main road from Sydney to Melbourne, along the inland route. **Mount Gibraltar**, a denuded volcanic plug known locally as the Gib, rises above Mittagong and the surrounding terrain, marking the gateway to the Southern Highlands. Few people take the time to stop in Mittagong; they're heading either for the limestone Wombeyan Caves nearby, or the collection of picturesque country towns that have made the Southern Highlands a favourite weekend getaway for Sydneysiders.

The first town you'll come to is **Bowral**, 5km (3 miles) from **Mittagong**, which combines wide small-town streets with elegant big-city-style boutiques. A fashionable resort for well-to-do Sydneysiders in the 1880s, it is still favoured by a similar crowd today, which explains why the town has one of the most sophisticated dining scenes outside Sydney. Other attractions include the **Tulip Festival** in September–October and the International Cricket Hall of Fame (tel: 02-4862 1247; www.bradman.org.au; daily 10am–5pm) on St Jude Street, which includes a permanent exhibition dedicated to Australia's most revered sportsman, cricketer Don Bradman, who died in 2001. The nearby **Mount Gibraltar Reserve** offers the chance to spot wombat and brush-tailed possum

The gem of the Southern Highlands is **Berrima ❽**, a small village preserved just as it was in the first half of the 19th century. It is off the Hume Highway, about 8km (5 miles) west of Bowral and most of it is protected by historic trusts. The township was established in 1831, and today many of its impressive old sandstone buildings have been converted to antique and craft galleries; most of those with historical artefacts are open from 10am to 5pm daily. These include the Surveyor General Inn (1834), said to be the oldest continuously licensed pub in Australia; the Court House (1839), now the information centre and museum (tel: 02-4877 1505; www.berrimacourthouse. org.au; daily 10am–4pm; free); the Gaol (1839), now a prison rehabilitation training centre; the Church of Holy Trinity (1849); and St Francis Xavier's Roman Catholic Church (1851).

Goulburn

The big country town of **Goulburn** is located 200km (120 miles) southwest of Sydney, about midway between the Southern Highlands and the national capital of Canberra. For most of its life Goulburn has been a staging post for travellers along the Hume Highway. In 1992 a bypass ended all that, and Goulburn today is a much more relaxed place without the trucks rumbling through. Its Georgian homes and two classical cathedrals belie its history as a centre of police action against the bushrangers who plagued the surrounding roads in the 19th century. **Towrang Stockade**, 10km (6 miles) to the north, is sparse ruins today; outlaws like Ben Hall and Frank Gardiner gave this once-formidable penal settlement a wide berth.

Iron hitching posts still stand outside some of the graceful commercial buildings on the main street of **Yass**. Hamilton Hume, the explorer after whom the Hume Highway is named, spent the last 40 years of his life here; his **Cooma Cottage** can be inspected (tel: 0414-774 686; www.coomacottage.com.au; Thu–Sun 10am–4pm) and his tombstone can be visited in the local cemetery.

Gundagai, where the Hume crosses the Murrumbidgee River, has one of those quintessentially Australian names that songwriters find irresistible – it features in a number of tunes, from the classic *Road to Gundagai* to *When a Boy*

from Alabama meets a Girl from Gundagai. The town has a colourful history – it was moved from its original site after one of Australia's worst flood disasters in 1852, when 89 people died – and was the favoured hunting ground for the bushranger Captain Moonlight, who was tried at the courthouse in 1879. The town's most famous attraction is the statue of the dog on the tuckerbox, a statue that has retained Aussie icon status long after the poem that inspired it has been forgotten.

The Snowy Mountains

Some might argue that the Snowy Mountains don't really live up to their name. They're not particularly snowy, at least by international standards – the ski resorts at **Perisher Blue**, **Thredbo** and **Charlotte Pass** often rely on snow-making machines for backup during the short ski season. Nor are the peaks particularly impressive. Although it dominates the skyline, Australia's highest mountain, **Mount Kosciuszko** (pronounced *koz-ee-oss-ko*) is a not-quite-soaring 2,230 metres (7,315ft) high and can

Donald Bradman's statue at the eponymous museum.

SIR DONALD BRADMAN

Australia's finest cricketer and batsman, Donald George Bradman, affectionately known as "the Don", was born in Bowral in the Southern Highlands in 1908.

Bradman attracted attention at an early age, batting golf balls against a local water tank with only a thin strip of wood. He made his Test cricket debut in 1928, at the relatively young age of 20. Two years later, he scored a record 334 not out in a Test against England and, in a match against Queensland, the highest first-class innings ever achieved (452 not out) – a record he would continue to hold until 1959.

Bradman's international career spanned 20 years, during which he played in 52 Tests and captained the Australian team for more than a decade. His unequalled reputation stems from his unique batting average of 99.94 runs per innings – he made more than 35,000 runs throughout his career. Sadly, in his final Test, he famously needed only a further four runs to reach an average of 100, but was dismissed for a duck (zero runs) on the second ball.

Bradman retired from the game in 1948 and continued to work as a stockbroker as well as serving as a selector for the Australian cricket team. He died in 2001 in Adelaide at the age of 92; eight years later he was inducted into the ICC Hall of Fame.

TIP

On an average day, you'll have to wait your turn for a photo opportunity by the cairn that marks the busy summit of Mount Kosciuszko. But there's a grassy knoll a little further down where you can sit on the granite rocks and enjoy the view.

be conquered on a gentle hike. However, **Kosciuszko National Park**  (tel: 02-6450 5600; vehicle entry), the largest protected area in the state, is well worth a visit, with a number of beautiful walks, some of which can be accessed by the Thredbo ski lifts.

Whether you're coming down the Monaro Highway from Canberra or along the Snowy Mountains Highway from the coast, the town of **Cooma**, at the intersection of the two highways, makes a good base and has a number of nice heritage buildings.

Some prefer to base themselves at **Jindabyne**, 60km (37 miles) west of Cooma on the shores of the lake of the same name. The original town of Jindabyne is buried under the lake – a picturesque history that made it the perfect setting for Ray Lawrence's acclaimed film, *Jindabyne* (2006). Intrepid divers explore lake-bed remnants, including abandoned trucks and the few homesteads that weren't relocated before flooding.

The creation of Lake Jindabyne was part of the Snow River Hydroelectric Project, a 25-year, A$820-million scheme to provide energy for Sydney, Melbourne and the rest of southeastern Australia while diverting water to irrigate vast stretches of the Riverina district west of the mountains. Regarded as one of the great achievements of civil engineering, 100,000 people worked on the scheme, mainly immigrants from 30 different countries.

The timber town of **Tumut** on the Snowy Mountains Highway is known for its autumn colours and it's May Festival of the Falling Leaves.

South of Tumut, the highway enters the Kosciuszko National Park and skirts the eastern shore of **Blowering Reservoir**, venue of numerous water-ski and speed-boat records, including the fastest (510kph/317mph) and longest (1,673km/1,040 miles) runs.

Further on, the **Yarrangobilly Caves** (tel: 02-6454 9597) have become one of the Snowy Mountains' leading attractions. About 260 caves have been discovered in a 2.5km by 12km (1.5 by 7.5-mile) limestone belt around the 300-metre (1,000ft) -deep Yarrangobilly River valley. Few caverns anywhere can rival the variety and beauty of

Thredbo, Snowy Mountains.

their calcite formations. Six caves are open to the public for inspection, five of them by guided tour only.

The road climbs rapidly into **Kiandra**, 90km (56 miles) from Tumut. Now a desolate road junction, it has two 19th-century claims to fame: it was the site of Australia's highest goldfield (1,414 metres/4,639ft), and the location of its first ski club. In fact, the 15,000 miners who lived in tents and shanties on these slopes around 1860 were holding competitive ski races before anyone in Europe. They strapped fence palings – "butter pads" – to their boots, to move around the surrounding countryside in the winter months.

Travellers proceeding towards Melbourne should turn west at the Kiandra junction. The road climbs to **Cabramurra**, the highest town (about 1,500 metres/4,900ft) in Australia. From this point, it's downhill 63km (39 miles) to the park's western gateway of **Khancoban**. From January to April, this road is a delightful trail through fields of wild flowers, forest stands of mountain ash and snow gum, a number of lovely blue lakes, and frequent herds of kangaroos.

The South Coast

NSW's South Coast remains less developed than its northern counterpart. The occasional boutique winery and eco-resort are more subtle, but amid its authentic mix of fishing ports and vacation towns, steel mills and cheese factories, primal forest and coal works, there's plenty to justify the journey. Those travelling **Highway 1** (the Princes Highway) are at times only a short detour away from a windswept peninsular national park or an island whose best-known denizens are little penguins. Furthermore, because the highway south stays close to the coast, it is more scenic than the better-known Pacific Highway north from Sydney.

Departing the metropolis, the Princes Highway spectacularly skirts the rim of the **Illawarra Plateau** until descending suddenly to **Wollongong**,

a major industrial city in an impressive natural setting. Some may argue that the smokestacks of the nation's largest steel works provide an unsightly backdrop to the otherwise pristine scene of surf and sandstone cliffs, but the heavy industry is the bread and butter for around 10 percent of Wollongong district's population of over 290,000.

That population is spread along 48km (30 miles) of coastline from Stanwell Park in the north to Shellharbour in the south, but is mostly concentrated in the southern Wollongong and **Port Kembla** townships, which have a steel works, a copper smelter and an artificial harbour.

Back in 1797 explorer George Bass anchored in tiny **Kiama Bay** and remarked on a "tremendous noise" emanating from a rocky headland. Today, the **Blowhole** is the most popular attraction of the fishing and market town of **Kiama** ❿. When seas are sufficiently high to force water geyser-like through a rock fissure, the spout can reach an amazing 60 metres (200ft) in height. Beware – visitors have been swept to their death off these rocks.

A monument in Jindabyne to Sir Paul Edmund Strzelecki (1797–1873), the Polish explorer.

Thredbo village before the snow arrives.

The bridge leading to Kangaroo Valley.

Many people enjoy the water by boat.

Kangaroo Valley

Southwards, a short distance of 20km (12 miles) west of **Berry** (the Town of Trees), is **Kangaroo Valley**, a lovely historic township set in an isolated vale among heavily forested slopes. Established in 1829, today it is a favourite haunt of picnickers, bushwalkers and spring wildflower lovers. The **Pioneer Museum Park** (tel: 0421-930 214; www. kangaroovalleymuseum.com) at Hampden Bridge contains a reconstructed 1880s dairy farm, a settler's hut and pioneering farm equipment. Kangaroo Valley is also the gateway to the magnificent **Morton National Park** (tel: 02-4887 7270; vehicle entry), which encompasses a large part of the Shoalhaven escarpment.

Nowra ⓫ is the hub of the Shoalhaven district, 162km (101 miles) south of Sydney. A regional farming centre and an increasingly popular focus of tourism, this river-bank city is 13km (8 miles) from the mouth of the Shoalhaven River. Regional attractions include HMAS *Albatross*, Australia's last naval air training station and host to the Fleet Air Arm Museum, which,

as well as housing a fine collection of military treasures, offers views across the working base from its verandah (tel: 02-4424 1920; www.navy.gov.au; daily 10am–4pm); **Greenwell Point**, where fresh oysters can be purchased from local growers at the cooperative; and the **Nowra Raceways**, three separate modern tracks for horse racing, trotting and greyhounds. The horse-racing track is known as Archer Raceway after the home-bred winner of the first two Melbourne Cups (1861 and 1862). Archer's stall is maintained as a veritable shrine at Terrara House, now operating as a functions venue east of the town.

Jervis Bay

Surrounded on all sides except the southeast by 50km (30 miles) of headland and beaches, **Jervis Bay** (pronounced *Jar-vis*) is one of the South Coast's idyllic holiday spots. Once a port that rivalled Sydney Harbour (Port Jackson) as the colony's most important harbour, these days it's home to the Royal Australian Naval College, HMAS *Creswell*. Technically,

this is part of Australian Capital Territory – co-opted under an act that stipulated the capital must have access to the sea – but that matters not a jot to tourists who are drawn here by the bay's blindingly white, tranquil beaches, the rugged cliff-side landscapes, and the heaths, wetlands and forests that fringe the bay. Picnic in the **Booderee Botanic Gardens** (tel: 02-4443 0977; daily Oct–Apr 9am–5pm, May–Sept 9am–4pm, Dec and Jan holidays 8am–6pm), Green Patch or Illuka beaches, or sign up for a bush-tucker tour with the Wreck Bay Aboriginal Community. The clear waters and varied marine life, including soft corals, sponge gardens and giant cuttlefish, also make it a popular destination for scuba divers.

Ulladulla is a rapidly growing beach resort and fishing port which supplies much of Sydney's fresh fish daily, but hurry on through to allow time to visit Murramarang National Park and Pebbly Beach. At dawn and dusk you are almost certain to be joined by a mob of kangaroos bouncing around on the foreshore,

charming food out of visitors and posing for photos.

Batemans Bay is a popular tourist, crayfishing and oystering centre at the mouth of the Clyde River. The wildlife refuge on the Tollgate Islands, just offshore, is frequented by penguins. At **Old Mogo Town**, east of the Princes Highway near Mogo, 12km (7.5 miles) south of Batemans Bay, an old mine, a steam engine and a century-old stamper battery (ore crusher) attract modern-day fortune-seekers to this compact gold-rush theme park. Kids will love **Mogo Zoo** (tel: 02-4474 4930; www.mogozoo.com.au; daily 9am–5pm), a privately owned zoo specialising in endangered animals, including snow leopards, jaguars, Bengal and Sumatran tigers, and a pride of white lions.

Moruya ⑫, like Nowra to the north, is established several kilometres inland on the tidal waters of a river mouth. Its first home, Francis Flanagan's Shannon View (1828), is still occupied, and the Uniting Church (or Wesleyan, as it was known in the past) was built in 1864 of local granite.

TIP

One of the finest vistas in Australia is to be had from Cambewarra Lookout (650 metres/ 2,120ft up) in Morton National Park, just past the village of Kangaroo Valley, where a sweeping landscape of escarpment rainforest interspersed with tracts of dairy farmland greet the eye. There is also a tea room here for refreshment while you gaze.

One of the beaches at Narooma.

The 130-year-old granite quarry on the north side of the Moruya River once supported a town of its own. Among its notable clients has been Sydney Harbour Bridge.

As the Princes Highway winds through the hills into **Bodalla**, 38km (23 miles) south of Moruya, it's hard to miss the little town's **Big Cheese**. Some 4.5 metres (15ft) high and equally wide, it was sculpted from metal in early 1984 to bolster the community's image as a cheese-making centre. The region's two largest cheese manufacturers produce almost 10,000 tonnes of fancy and cheddar cheese annually.

The waters off the Eurobodalla area, around the small coastal resort towns of **Narooma** and **Bermagui** – especially those around **Montague Island**, 8km (5 miles) off Narooma – yield record tuna, shark and kingfish catches. **Central Tilba**, 29km (18 miles) southwest of Narooma, is a beautifully preserved hamlet. Each of the village's two dozen wooden buildings, classified and protected by the National Trust, is as it was in the late 19th century. The ABC Cheese Factory is open (tel: 02-4473 7387; daily 9am–5pm; free) for cheese tasting, and ancient equipment is on display. Central Tilba was established in the 1870s when gold was discovered on Mount Dromedary. There are fine coastal views from the 825-metre (2,700ft) mountain top, reached by a walking track.

Bega

The lush dairy country continues around **Bega**, the far South Coast's biggest town, and famous for its eponymous cheese. There's probably a bylaw that forbids visitors to leave without sampling the local product: play it safe and take in a factory tour and cheese tasting at the Bega Cheese Heritage Centre (tel: 02-6491 7777; www.begacheese.com.au; daily 9am–5pm; free).

Merimbula and its sister town of **Pambula**, on the so-called Sapphire Coast, offer fine surfing, boating, fishing and oystering. Crucially, there is also a choice of unspoilt safe beaches, which makes this a prime summer

Northeys Store at Hill End, built in 1873, is still an active retail outlet.

HYAMS BEACH

The best-known of all the Jervis Bay beaches is Hyams, on the southern shores of the bay, which has the whitest sand in the world (according to the *Guinness Book of Records)*. The bay's sparkling waters, its underwater topography of arches, caves and rock stacks, and a marine population that includes groupers, wrasses, sharks, cuttlefish and sea dragons, also make this one of the state's finest dive sites.

Most of the dive sites are located on the seaward faces of the northern and southern headlands that guard the approaches to the bay. Shore diving is possible from Hyams Beach and Green Patch, but the best sites require a boat.

Dive operators in Huskisson can usually supply all the gear, as well as providing regular boat trips.

destination for families, many of them from across the border in Victoria. **Eden**, the last sizeable town before you cross the Victoria state border, is located on **Twofold Bay**, once a thriving whaling port and now host to whale-watching tours. The **Eden Killer Whale Museum** (tel: 02-6496 2094; www.killerwhale museum.com.au; Mon–Sat 9.15am–3.45pm, Sun 11.15am–3.45pm) on Imlay Street recalls those 19th-century days.

During its whaling era, Eden had stiff competition as a port from **Boydtown** ⑬, established in 1842 by the banker-adventurer Ben Boyd on the south side of Twofold Bay. Boyd dreamed aloud that his settlement would one day become the capital of Australia. He established a steamship service to Sydney and erected many buildings, but in 1850 his empire collapsed. Boyd went bankrupt, fled Australia to the Solomon Islands, and was never heard from again.

All that remains of the grand scheme today are the **Seahorse Inn** – a magnificent building with stone walls a metre (3ft) thick, Gothic arches and hand-carved doors and windows – and **Boyd's Tower**, a 31-metre (102ft) sandstone lighthouse built in 1846 but never lit. The 8,950-hectare (22,110-acre) **Ben Boyd National Park** (tel: 02-6495 5000; vehicle entry charge) encompasses the coastal headlands north and south of Twofold Bay. Its highlights include stunning red sandstone cliffs, rich animal and bird life, and lovely wild flowers.

Western slopes and plains

The route due west from Sydney, along the Great Western Highway, passes through the Blue Mountains and enters the vast grazing land beyond. **Bathurst** ⑭, Australia's oldest inland city, was a major pastoral centre even before the heady gold rush of the 1850s, although its elegant 19th-century buildings and its lively student population, courtesy of the local campus of Charles Sturt University (split between Bathurst and Wagga Wagga), give it a more sophisticated ambience than one might expect.

Bathurst Courthouse is home to the Bathurst Historical Museum.

TIP

Spring blossoms transform Cowra's Japanese Garden in early October, when it becomes the focus of *Sakura Matsuri*, the town's annual cherry blossom festival. The festival also features traditional Japanese foods, arts and crafts, kite flying, tea ceremonies, martial arts and *shakuhachi* flute recitals.

There's a packaged gold-rush experience at **Bathurst Goldfields** on the city's scenic **Mount Panorama**, where old-time diggings have been set up, and gold-panning demonstrations are given. A bit more authentic is do-it-yourself panning at **Hill End** or **Sofala**, ghost towns north of Bathurst. Take a drive around the town and inner suburbs to see the civic buildings and grand mansions built from the profits of Australia's first gold rush.

In Bathurst, the scenic drive around Mount Panorama becomes a world-class motor-racing circuit for the 1,000km (600-mile) touring car and V8 race in October. Just over 50km (30 miles) west of Bathurst is the intensively photographed village of **Carcoar**, where more than 20 restored colonial buildings nestle in a picturesque little valley.

The highway runs through mainly sheep and wheat country to **Cowra**, a prosperous agricultural centre on the Lachlan River, which has a remarkable link with Japan. During World War II, Japanese prisoners of war interned in a camp there attempted a mass break-out during which nearly 231 of them were killed. The care local people gave to the graves of the prisoners so impressed the Japanese that they repaid them with the gift of a classical garden. The **Cowra Japanese Garden** (tel: 02-6341 2233; www.cowragarden.com.au; daily 8.30am–5pm) is a colourful oriental showpiece in the gold-brown central west of New South Wales.

Wagga Wagga

South of Cowra lies **Wagga Wagga**, shortened to Wagga (rhyming with *logger*) by just about everyone. Although it may seem like a sleepy country town, Australia's most populous inland city has several attractions, including the impressive Botanic Gardens, which have a walk-through aviary with over 300 bird species; the **Wagga Wagga Art Gallery** (tel: 02-6926 9660; www.waggawaggaaustralia.com.au; Tue–Sat 10am–4pm, Sun 10am–2pm; free), which houses the National Art Glass Collection; Charles Sturt University, which runs a prestigious wine course

The Wagga Wagga railway station.

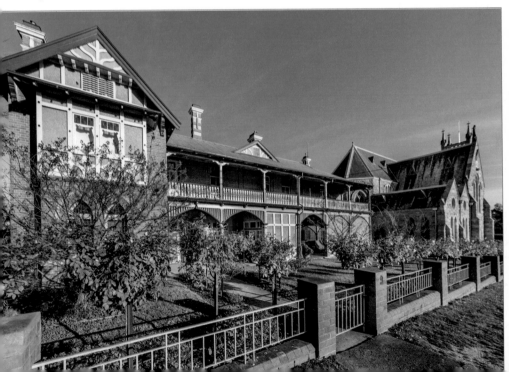

from its on-campus winery; and even a sandy river beach, on the banks of the Murrumbidgee close to the town's main street.

From either Cowra or Wagga the highway westwards becomes a basic two-lane blacktop, running fairly straight for 1,000km (600 miles) or so, until the approaches to Adelaide. Here you enter the true "sunburnt country", the "land of sweeping plains" of Dorothea Mackellar's famous poem. If you've yet to see any kangaroos, you'll probably spot them here – although they're likely to be caught in the glare of your headlights. Those cute warning signs have a serious purpose: 'roos are a dangerous hazard on these roads, particularly at night.

The harshness of the elements is burnt into the wild-west appearance of **West Wyalong** ⓑ, 161km (100 miles) west of Cowra. Motorists should spurn the bypass and drive down the main street of the former gold-mining town. The quaint town of **Orange** is, predictably, a fruit-growing centre – but, not so predictably, the crops are apples, cherries and grapes that are made into quality wines (the town was named after the Duke of Orange). The extinct volcano **Mount Canobolas**, 14km (9 miles) southwest of Orange, has become a 1,500-hectare (600-acre) flora and fauna reserve with walking trails, picnic areas, waterfalls and a 360-degree view of the countryside from the summit.

Classic 2000 film comedy *The Dish* put **Parkes** on the map, or at least reminded us of a key episode in its history. The town, 93km (58 miles) west of Orange, is famous for its Observatory, housing a 64-metre (210ft) radio telescope which played a crucial cameo role in the 1969 moon landing. The Visitor Centre explains all (tel: 02-6862 6000; daily 8.30am-4.15pm; free).

The **Ophir Goldfields**, 27km (17 miles) northeast of Orange, were where Australia's first payable gold was discovered in 1851 and are now an official fossicking area. Banjo Paterson's birthplace is marked by a memorial 3km (2 miles) off the highway on the Ophir Road.

Dubbo

The Mitchell Highway runs through undulating terrain around **Wellington**. The **Wellington Caves**, 8km (5 miles) southwest of the town, have huge stalagmite formations in their limestone caverns. The last truly productive agricultural area is around the thriving city of **Dubbo** ⓰, in the middle of the wheat belt, with large sheep and cattle properties and irrigated farms.

Dubbo's main attraction for tourists is the **Western Plains Zoo** (tel: 02-6881 1400; www.taronga.org.au; daily 9am–4pm), which is an excellent wildlife park partnered with Sydney's Taronga Park Zoo. Animals are placed in settings as near as possible to their native conditions, and penned by moats rather than cages or fences. Australia has an inordinate number of jails as tourist attractions,

Taronga Park Zoo was officially opened in 1916.

The Japanese Garden at Cowra.

TIP

Serious birdwatchers can expect to find close to a hundred species at Willandra Creek, which flows along the edge of flat and arid Willandra National Park. You may also see grey and red kangaroos here, the largest of Australia's marsupials.

and Dubbo is no exception: the **Old Dubbo Gaol** (tel: 02-6801 4460; www.olddubbogaol.com.au; daily 9am–4pm), which was closed in 1966 after almost 80 years, has been restored (complete with gallows) and is open for guided tours.

Narromine, 39km (24 miles) on from Dubbo and on the edge of the western plains, is a major citrus-growing area, and the local Citrus Packers Co-operative will let visitors have a look around. The terrain here provides thermal air lifts, making the area ideal for gliding. In the **Macquarie Valley Irrigation Area**, the town of **Trangie** is the centre of a large cotton-growing industry, and visits can be arranged to the nearby Auscott Cotton Farm. Harvesting and ginning take place from late April to June, the best time to visit.

The scenery starts to turn dry at **Nyngan** on the Bogan River, where the Barrier Highway begins. Here motorists should start keeping an eagle eye on the fuel gauge. There's only one fuel supply (at Hermidale) over the 128km (80 miles) to Cobar;

only one stop (at Topar) between Wilcannia and Broken Hill; and few service stations from there to Yunta in South Australia.

Hay and Willandra

It's a desolate drive on to **Hay** ⑰. Banjo Paterson's bitter poem *Hay, Hell and Booligal* was inspired by the almost treeless horizons and the sun-parched tedium, broken only by the sight of an occasional emu, goanna or flock of budgerigars. The town, about halfway from Sydney to Adelaide, is a well-watered oasis on the banks of the Murrumbidgee River. For many years it was an important river crossing on the stock route to Victoria; it also served as a major link in the legendary Cobb and Co. passenger coach network and is now the centre of an extensive horticultural and wool-producing area. An old Cobb and Co. coach, used until 1901, is on display at the coach-house, corner of Lachlan and Moppett streets, and Hay's Gaol Museum has a great array of pioneering memorabilia.

Balranald is another spot of green on the Murrumbidgee. Head north to visit the **Willandra Lakes World Heritage Site**, a 370,000-hectare (950,000-acre) system of Pleistocene lakes that contains evidence of Aboriginal habitation in Australia, stretching back 50,000 years. The dry lakes contain ancient hearths and middens, and the world's oldest cremation remains – a first sign of civilisation. The most accessible part of Willandra is **Mungo National Park** ⑱ (tel: 03-5021 8900; vehicle entry fee), about 150km (93 miles) north of Balranald. Its star attraction is the **Walls of China**, a geological phenomenon of 30-metre (100ft) -high walls of variegated sand running for 30km (19 miles).

A good base for visiting the park is the sleepy town of **Wentworth**, once one of the interior's most important towns. Its position at the confluence of the Murray and Darling rivers

Broken Hill's redundant Junction Mine.

meant it controlled the river trade between NSW, Victoria and South Australia until it was superseded by the coming of the railways. It is a pleasant enough base, although most of the so-called attractions, such as Old Wentworth Gaol and Pioneer World, can easily be skipped.

Broken Hill

Head north from Wentworth for 265km (165 miles) and you'll reach New South Wales' most remote outpost: **Broken Hill** ⑲. In this far corner, locals set their watches to South Australian time, half an hour behind. Although it belongs to NSW geographically and administratively, most of Broken Hill's trade and communication is conducted through Adelaide, which lies much nearer than faraway Sydney.

The city looms large in Australia's industrial history, with legendary unions eventually dominating the city by means of the Barrier Industrial Council. Its mineral wealth played the largest part in changing the nation from a strictly pastoral

outpost to a more industrial base. With most of the streets named after minerals, it's impossible to escape the town's mining past You can even see reproductions of mine workings at **White's Mining Museum** (tel: 08-8087 2878; daily 9am–5pm), off the Silverton Road.

But not everything in Broken Hill is related to the great black hill. This Outback town has become an unlikely font of the arts, renowned for several locally famous painters including the late Pro Hart, Jack Absalom and Hugh Schulz. Among the 27 galleries in the city, **Pro Hart's** (tel: 08-8087 2441; www.prohart.com.au; Mon–Sat 9am–5pm, Sun 1.30pm–5pm; free) is the most quixotic. Besides a wide range of paintings by Hart himself, it also houses much of his private collection, which includes works by Monet, Rembrandt, Dalí, Picasso, Dobell, Drysdale and Tom Roberts.

An extraordinary art experience is located 45 minutes' drive from town at the Living Desert Reserve. A collection of sandstone sculptures is arrayed

Cooling-off time in Bell's Milk Bar, Broken Hill.

The Walls of China in Mungo National Park.

HOW THE HILL BEGAN

It all began in 1883 when boundary rider and amateur geologist Charles Rasp stumbled across a lump of silver ore on a rocky outcrop he described as a "broken hill". From the claim that he and his syndicate pegged grew the nation's largest company, the Broken Hill Proprietary Co. Ltd (now multinational giant BHP Billiton).

Although it diversified widely and had completely moved out of Broken Hill by 1939, BHP is still spoken of with distaste in the city for its abrasive attitude to the workforce – the stuff of legend. "The Hill" turned out to be the world's largest silver, lead and zinc lode, and, while other mining towns have tended to peter out over the years, is still going strong. It has yielded more than 147 million tonnes of ore from its 8km (5-mile) -long lode.

FACT

Visitors to Mutawintji who know what they're looking for can still find Aboriginal "barbecues" – small mounds where they would cook their meat and where the accumulation of hot animal fats bonded the soil into an erosion-resistant clump.

in the evocative landscape, with a trail winding between them. The reserve closes at sunset.

Broken Hill has also become a centre for one of Australia's unique institutions – the **Flying Doctor Service**, which transports medical care across the vast distances of the Outback by aircraft.

At night, head for the licensed social clubs to play the pokies (poker machines). The city's social life revolves around the Musicians, Sturt, Legion and Social Democratic clubs, which welcome visitors and have good facilities.

In red, rocky country it may be, but Broken Hill still has its beach resort at **Menindee Lake**, 110km (68 miles) away. This is the city's part-natural and part-artificial water-supply system, or at least it is when long-term drought hasn't dried it up. The lake and a system of other lakes and channels cater for boating and swimming; it combines with the adjacent **Kinchega National Park** (tel: 08-8080 3200; vehicle entry fee), home to many water birds.

Sunset over a lake in Kinchega National Park.

The restored ghost town of **Silverton**, a mining centre 23km (14 miles) from Broken Hill, is not just an attraction for tourists; it's becoming a regular star in Outback film epics. With repainted shop and hotel signs, it has appeared in *A Town Like Alice*, *Mad Max 2* and *Razorback*. Also in the Silverton area is the 100-year-old **Daydream Mine** (tel: 08-8088 5682; www.daydreammine.com.au; tours daily 10am, 11.30am), where visitors can walk down into the old workings.

For the brave traveller with a bit more time, it's possible to drive right off the beaten track from Wilcannia to Broken Hill, with a detour through the opal fields. It's a rewarding diversion, but not one to be taken lightly because of its lack of sealed roads and limited fuel and water.

Mutawintji National Park

From Broken Hill, it's about 265km (165 miles) northeast to **Mutawintji National Park** (tel: 08-8080 3200), a surprising patch of greenness in the barren Bynguano Ranges. Strange and colourful rock formations surround ancient Aboriginal campsites, tools, engravings and paintings, which are explained in films shown at the visitor centre. Visitors must check in with the resident ranger on arrival. There are camping facilities, but no power. Ranger-guided tours are available during the cooler months.

White Cliffs, 297km (185 miles) from Broken Hill, is a lunar landscape of craters created by opal diggings, and where fossickers with permits can scrounge. Many residents live underground to escape the winds and extreme temperatures; some of them don't mind showing off the interiors of their white-walled subterranean settlements, which can be surprisingly luxurious. The best accommodation at White Cliffs is an underground motel or subterranean bed-and-breakfast.

The historic buildings and wharf remnants at **Wilcannia** ⓴, 98km

(61 miles) south of White Cliffs, are reminders of the days when its position on the Darling River made it a major inland port and earned it the title of Queen City of the West.

Take the highway from Wilcannia to Cobar, and about 40km (25 miles) before town, you'll find the turn-off to the **Mount Grenfell Aboriginal cave paintings** (tel: 02-6836 2692). Drive 30km (19 miles) along a good dirt road to the cave, a shallow overhanging rock shelter, for rare examples of the techniques of pigments applied by finger, in human, bird and animal outlines, and hand stencils.

Cobar

Cobar ㉑ typifies the resilience of the area's people as well as its hardy flora and fauna. From being a riproaring town of 10,000 people and 14 hotels not long after copper mining began there in the 1870s, its fortunes have fluctuated: 100 years later its population was less than 4,000 and only one mine was operating; today the figures are 7,000 people and four mines. The Eleura

lead, zinc and silver mine (which was opened in 1983) boosted the town's population and economy. The **Great Cobar Heritage Centre** (tel: 02-6836 2448; Mon–Fri 8.30am– 5pm, Sat–Sun 9am–5pm), in an old two-storey mining company office, gives a fascinating insight into the area and its people.

Cobar's Great Western Hotel is the epitome of country hotels, with its massive first-floor verandah. Classification by the National Trust means that the exterior retains its original timberwork and iron lace but, on the inside, accommodation has been transformed into modern, motel-style units.

North of Cobar, the Mitchell Highway meets the Darling River at the small and pleasant township of **Bourke** ㉒. Once an important port, Bourke has become immortalised in the colloquial expression, "out the back o'Bourke", signifying a place so remote that it is exceeded only by going "beyond the black stump". Take in the emptiness that surrounds Bourke, and you'll get a sense of what the Outback really means.

Camels can cope well in the Outback's harsh conditions.

The Mad Max 2 Museum, Silverton.

Aerial view of Parliament House.

CANBERRA

The capital of Australia is a place conceived by accident, built by bureaucrats and located on a compromise. Considering all that, it's a remarkably pleasant place to visit.

During one of his visits to Australia's national capital, the Duke of Edinburgh declared that Canberra ㉓ (pop. about 380,000) was "a city without a soul" – a royal snub the citizens of Canberra have never forgotten. In January 2003, raging bush fires spread into the city, destroying 530 homes and 30 farms, and killing four residents. The community spirit in the aftermath demonstrated that even if Canberra lacked soul, its residents still had hearts. But it is not a dearth of soul that troubles Canberra – the city is missing a sense of purpose. Like many administrative capitals, it is an artificial city, constructed not around any existing settlement, but simply out of thin Monaro air.

Purpose-built city

The reason Canberra was built at all can be traced to colonial jealousy: in 1901, at the time of the federation of the six Australian colonies, there was intense rivalry (which still exists) between Sydney and Melbourne over which was the chief city of Australia. The founding fathers solved the problem by the deciding to build a new capital. The search for a site lasted from 1902 to 1908, and is known as The Battle of the Sites. Ultimately a small and hitherto undistinguished valley in the southern tablelands of New South Wales was selected as the site.

Visitors often complain that they can never find the centre – even when they are actually standing in it. Canberra, the political, diplomatic and administrative capital of the Commonwealth, is simply not built as a commercial city, and so far it has stubbornly refused to look or act like one. In fact, what it looks most like, apart from a spread of pleasantly wooded suburbs, is a kind of semi-dignified Disneyland, complete with a **Captain Cook Memorial Water Jet** Ⓐ which flings water 140 metres (460ft) into the air. Visitors are either impressed

Main Attractions

Parliament House
Old Parliament House
Questacon
National Gallery
National Museum of Australia
Australian War Memorial Museum

The façade of Parliament House.

Free guided tours of Parliament House take about 45 minutes and include both Houses, the Great Hall and the roof.

or bemused by the city's uncluttered, circular road system that tends to lead the unwary around in circles. Of equal wonder is the absence of external TV antennae and the lack of front fences – both decreed aesthetically incompatible with Canberra's image.

Similarly, new homes are supplied with young native trees in order to promote the city's reputation as a leafy suburbia. In contrast to the absence of urban planning in other Australian cities, Canberra's character does impress. As a result, the capital is a city of showcase architecture. The main attractions are clustered in close proximity to **Lake Burley Griffin**, and a walk around the lake will provide great views of the city and parliaments.

Although the city is Australia's capital, it can seem surprisingly casual, with low-key security. The best times to visit are spring, when it's green and covered with blossom and wattle, and autumn, when the weather is balmy and the yellowing leaves of the deciduous trees are strikingly beautiful.

Parliament House Ⓑ (daily 9am–5pm), which cost more than A$1 billion and is adorned with many art and craft works. It will be celebrating its 30th anniversary in 2018. It was completed in 1988, just in time for the bicentennial celebrations. It is built into the side of Capital Hill on the lakeside, its roof grassed in order to blend in, and to allow Australians to walk over their representatives. Free public tours are offered at 10am, 1pm and 3pm. You can also view the transcript of the National Apology speech delivered in 2008 by then Prime Minister Kevin Rudd to the Aboriginal Stolen Generations.

When parliament is sitting, anyone can watch the action from the Public Galleries. The livelier of the two chambers is the House of Representatives, and the best time to be there is Question Time. This is generally held at 2pm, for which you'll need to book by calling the Sergeant-at-Arms' office on 02-6277 4889 by 12.30pm on the day required.

Museum of Australian Democracy

Its predecessor, **Old Parliament House** Ⓒ on King George Terrace, now houses the **Museum of Australian**

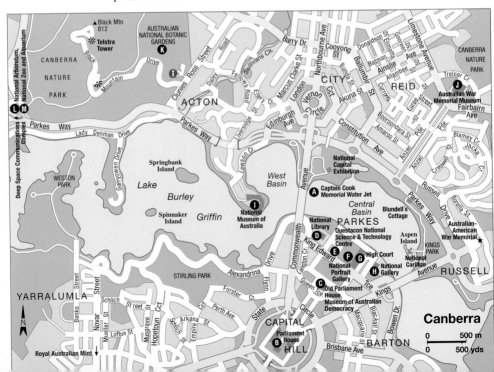

Canberra

0   500 m
0   500 yds

Democracy (tel: 02-6270 8222; www.moadoph.gov.au; daily 9am–5pm) where a guided tour of the old chambers is combined with an insight into salient moments of political history.

When visitors step outside, they are confronted by contemporary politics. At the side of the glass-like pond at the front of the building sits the **Aboriginal Tent Embassy**, first set up here in the 1970s to focus attention on the Aboriginal land-rights campaign. It has been a permanent fixture since 1992. Depending on your point of view, it's either an icon or an eyesore; but it does serve to remind visitors of how many Aboriginal people feel that they do not share equally in the fruits of modern Australia.

National institutions

Also on the lake front, from west to east, are the **National Library ⓓ** (tel: 02-6262 1111; www.nla.gov.au; daily; hours vary, so check website; free), which has 10 million items and whose displays include a model of Captain Cook's *Endeavour* (visit the everchanging display in the Treasures Gallery); **Questacon – The National**

Science and Technology Centre ⓔ (tel: 02-6270 2800; www.questacon.edu.au; daily 9am–5pm), which has many enjoyable hands-on displays; the **National Portrait Gallery ⓕ** (tel: 02-6102 7000; www.portrait.gov.au; daily 10am–5pm; free), which presents permanent and temporary exhibitions; the **High Court ⓖ**, grandiose enough to echo a Moghul palace; and the **National Gallery ⓗ** (tel: 02-6240 6411; www.nga.gov.au; daily 10am–5pm; free), which has the world's largest collection of Aboriginal art, a Sculpture Garden and renowned American artist James Turrell's Within without Skyspace, best viewed at dawn or dusk.

On the Acton Peninsula is one of Canberra's more dramatic structures. The **National Museum of Australia ⓘ** (tel: 1800-026 132; www.nma.gov.au; daily 9am–5pm; generally free but charges apply to some temporary exhibitions) houses an eclectic collection of artefacts. Highlights include the world's largest collection of Aboriginal bark paintings, convict clothing and leg irons. Perhaps the oddest exhibit is the oversized heart of the racehorse Phar Lap, whose record-breaking achievements captured

The National Gallery's Sculpture Garden is freely accessible from the path around Lake Burley Griffin.

The National Museum of Australia.

CAPITAL INSIGHTS

On the opposite shore from the National Library at Regatta Point, just by the bridge, is the **National Capital Exhibition** (tel: 02-6272 2902; www.nationalcapital.gov.au; Mon–Fri 9am–5pm, Sat–Sun 10am–4pm; free) – essential if you want to make sense of the layout of Canberra. The exhibition offers some curious sidelights to the shaping of the capital. According to the original plan, the surrounding hills were to be planted with flowering shrubs in different colours: Mount Ainslie in yellow, with plantings of wattle and broom, Black Mountain in pink and white with flowering fruit trees, and Red Hill – in red, of course. The plan was never implemented with any enthusiasm, although Red Hill does live up to its name, with its springtime flush of scarlet bottle-brush and *Callistemon lanceolatus*.

TIP

Every year during January and February, the National Botanic Gardens host a summer concert series on weekend evenings. The diverse programme includes everything from jazz to hip-hop. Call the Gardens' visitor centre, tel: 02-6250 9540, or visit www.anbg.gov.au for more information.

the country's imagination during the Great Depression until his premature death, apparently due to arsenic poisoning. Children have their own gallery, **KSpace FutureWorld**, at the National Museum. Here they can use touchscreen computers to design cities and vehicles, then watch their designs come to life on a 3D screen.

On Aspen Island, the **Carillon** tower, a 53-bell gift from Britain, plays musical selections to the residents at weekends.

North of the lake, the **Australian War Memorial Museum** ❶ (tel: 02-6243 4211; www.awm.gov.au; daily 10am–5pm; free) has a collection of relics, weapons, documents and photographs.

The city has acquired an impressive range of restaurants and several international-class hotels (such as the fabulous Art Deco Hyatt). Nightlife is improving, too: there are 300 cafés, restaurants and bars, a variety of cinemas and theatres, a casino, and some good music, ranging from classical to rock.

National Botanic Gardens

The **Australian National Botanic Gardens** ❸ (tel: 02-6250 9540; www.

anbg.gov.au; daily 8.30am–5pm; free) at Black Mountain Reserve, contain a huge range of Australian plants over 40 hectares (100 acres), the best of its kind in the country. The surrounding bush is one of the city's great attractions.

The **National Arboretum Canberra** ❶ (Tuggeranong Parkway; www.national arboretumcanberra.com.au) features 100 forests and 100 gardens of threatened and iconic trees from around Australia and the world. There is an impressive nature-themed playground for families and an outdoor amphitheatre.

West of the lake, the **National Zoo and Aquarium** ❹ on Lady Denman Drive (tel: 02-6287 8400; www.national zoo.com.au; daily 10am–5pm) includes a wildlife sanctuary.

In the midst of all the high-minded architectural efforts, Canberra retains considerable charm. It remains one of the few full-size cities in Australia where it's still possible to see kangaroos in the streets. For those who miss out on this spectacle, the nearby **Tidbinbilla Nature Reserve** offers a range of Australian flora and fauna.

Around Canberra

Canberra is a good jumping-off place for outdoor entertainment. There are easy day trips to old mining and farming towns such as **Captains Flat** and **Bungendore**.

A few hours' drive to the south is the **Snowy Mountains ski area**, which offers spectacular bushwalking in summer. About the same distance east is the south coast of New South Wales, with some of the prettiest beaches.

The **Deep Space Communications Complex** at **Tidbinbilla** (www.cdscc. nasa.gov; daily 9am–5pm; free) is active in the command, tracking and recording of a number of NASA space exploration projects, and is open to visitors.

Foodies will want to explore the **Poachers Way** (www.thepoachersway. com.au), a food and wine trail that takes in the region's best restaurants, provedores, artists and wineries – Clonakilla winery is the pick of the bunch).

The Australian War Memorial Museum.

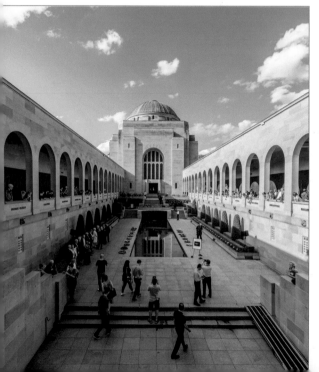

Deep Space Communications Complex at Tidbinbilla.

A statue in Queen Victoria Gardens, Melbourne.

Melbourne at night.

MELBOURNE

The capital of Victoria is Australia's most "European" city, a 21st-century metropolis with an abundance of 19th-century charm and a passion for culture and sport.

That Melbourne continues to feature at or near the top of *The Economist*'s "most liveable city" table never surprises its residents, even if denizens of the harbour city across the border affect disbelief. Melbourne doesn't compete on brash big-ticket items like a beautiful harbour or amazing opera house, but simply and quietly gets on with being the sporting, cultural and dining capital of Australia. It's also a shopping magnet for many Australians, lured by boutiques known for their one-off designs. For visitors, that combination justifies an extended stay.

Newcomers will not find the most picturesque city. The Yarra River isn't the sparkling focal point that rivers are in some cities. Novelist Anthony Trollope considered the Yarra (or Yarra Yarra as it was) during a visit in 1871: "It seems to have but little to do with the city. But it is popular with rowers, and it waters the Botanical Gardens".

River development

Attitudes toward the Yarra River are changing, though slowly. There has been extensive work over the past few years, with the Southgate development, Federation Square and a massive rehabilitation programme at Docklands.

Trollope also complained that "there are no hills to produce scenery, or scenic effect. Though you go up and down

the streets, the country around is flat – and for the most part uninteresting. I know no great town in the neighbourhood of which there is less to see in the way of landscape beauty." Well, say locals, if he'd looked up, he'd have seen the Dandenong Mountains. But Melbourne is more about hidden charms. It has copious parks and gardens to linger in, and leafy suburbs proliferate.

Indeed, suburbs are intrinsic to an understanding of the city. One of Melbourne's most famous exports, Dame Edna Everage, may skewer them

Main Attractions

Federation Square
Block Arcade
Old Melbourne Gaol
Melbourne Museum
Royal Botanic Gardens
National Gallery of Victoria
St Kilda

Flinders Street Station.

Rowers on the Yarra River. Melbourne has a strong sporting history and hosted the 1956 Olympics and the Commonwealth Games in 2006.

mercilessly but this city is the sum of its neighbourhoods. And when Edna was born out of Barry Humphries' appalled fascination with the mono-cultural suburbia he grew up in with its "politics of niceness", nobody could have anticipated that by 2006 the city he scorned would have so thoroughly embraced his creation as to approve the naming of a city laneway Dame Edna Place.

Melbourne versus Sydney

Melbourne now is not the city it was in the 1950s. At that time the majority of Australia's biggest companies were based in the Victorian capital and most overseas enterprises followed suit. Here was the seat of the Establishment where background and connections determined your entry to the corridors of power. There is still some residue of those times; stockbrokers, lawyers, bankers and company directors are more often than not the product of the city's elite grammar schools and colleges. Pitch up at the wrong barbecue and you'll still find men bragging about their private school and casually dropping the names of their more successful classmates.

But the balance of power between the rivals has shifted. Sydney now has the majority of major company headquarters and, with the exception of the mining companies and banks, the trend is in that direction. So Melbourne has had to reinvent itself.

Much of the impetus for this adjustment has come from changes in the population. Migration has always influenced the growth of the city, and the Anglo-Celtic dominance that lasted up to World War II has diminished with consecutive waves of migrants from Italy, Greece, the Balkans, Lebanon, Turkey, China, Vietnam and Eastern Europe. The genteel, refined European tastes of the past are still there, but they have been spiced by a more vibrant and outgoing approach to life.

The Melbourne that Ava Gardner described in the 1960s, while shooting an adaptation of Nevil Shute's *On The Beach*, as the perfect place to make a film about the end of the world, is now a city of cool bars, radical architecture and sophisticated inhabitants.

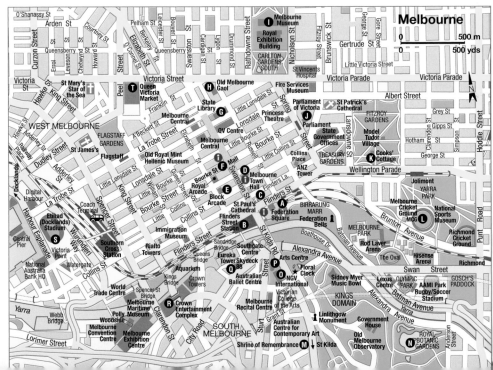

Melbourne's early history

Unlike Sydney, Melbourne was not founded as a penal colony. Instead, early settlers were free men intent on building a new and prosperous life for themselves. In June 1835, John Batman, a land speculator from Tasmania, sailed his schooner into Port Phillip Bay, rowed up a broad river and declared: "This will be the place for a village." With a payment of goods including blankets, mirrors and axes, he persuaded the local Aborigines to "sell" him 600,000 acres (240,000 hectares) of prime land and drew up a document to legalise the purchase. This was later dismissed by the British Government, which accused Batman of trespassing on Crown Land.

A year later, the settlement beside the Yarra was named in honour of Lord Melbourne, Britain's prime minister. The first land sales took place soon after, and small properties at the centre of the settlement sold for £150. Two years later, the same properties were changing hands for £10,000.

It was the discovery of gold at nearby Ballarat in 1851 that propelled the sudden growth in population and prosperity which determined Melbourne's true character. This was also when its role as Australia's financial centre was established. The finds drew thousands of fortune-seekers from Europe, the USA and China; gold fever swept the country. But in time the alluvial gold ran out, and thousands of diggers left the goldfields to make Melbourne their home. The population more than quadrupled in 10 years, and the gold revenue financed new development in a rapidly expanding city determined to grow grand in style.

When Mark Twain visited on a lecture tour in 1895, he was entranced by what he saw: "It is a stately city architecturally as well as in magnitude. It has an elaborate system of cable-car service; it has museums, and colleges, and schools, and public gardens, and electricity, and gas, and libraries, and theatres, and mining centres and wool centres, and centres of the arts and sciences, and boards of trade, and ships, and railroads, and a harbor, and social clubs, and journalistic clubs and racing clubs, and a squatter club sumptuously housed and appointed, and as many churches and banks as can make a living. In a word, it is equipped with everything that goes to make the modern great city."

Ironically, by this time depression was setting in. Federation in 1901 saw the city take on the mantle of political capital until the move to Canberra in 1927. The Depression of the 1930s was followed by a spell of industrial growth and development, given extra impetus by post-war migration. When it hosted the 1956 Olympics, Melbourne was more than ready to take its place on the world stage. Substantial investment in the local equivalent of François Mitterrand's *grands projets* – particularly under Liberal Premier Jeff Kennett in the 1990s – transformed the city and shifted its geographical axis.

TIP

For marvellous city views and a peaceful drink in stylish surroundings right in the heart of the city, try Transit Lounge, the rooftop cocktail bar above the Transport Hotel in Federation Square. There's cool live music most weekends.

Melbourne's skyline.

Federation Square

The completion of **Federation Square**  (tel: 03-9655 1900; www.fed square.com) in 2004 gave Melbourne its first popularly embraced public space. The ornately Victorian **Flinders Street Station** ⓑ had been the city's signature building for years, and "under the clocks" was the traditional rendezvous point for a night out, a practice immortalised in a song of that name by seminal local band Weddings Parties Anything. But station steps are not necessarily the best place to loiter. Federation Square, on the other hand, has plenty of space, places to sit, cafés and bars, and is right opposite the station.

The design of Federation Square has its detractors, some of them vehement, but no one can deny its impact on the city. Built above unsightly railway yards, it serves to unite the Central Business District (CBD) with the Yarra. At its heart is a gently scalloped piazza paved with variegated sandstone, which inclines towards a small stage and a giant video screen. Concerts and public events attract large crowds and there always seems to be something going on.

The buildings behind, designed as "shards" sticking out of the ground, look as if they have been crazy-paved in a combination of glass, stone and zinc. The riches within include a branch of the National Gallery of Victoria – **The Ian Potter Centre** (tel: 03-8620 2222; www.ngv.vic.gov.au; daily 10am–5pm; free), which is one of those buildings that, inside, has an air of unpredictability. Walls are coming at you from all angles and there's no clue as to what may be around the next corner. Somehow it all works; the daylight comes in where it should and the art – all Australian – is displayed sympathetically. The **Australian Centre for the Moving Image** has screenings, exhibitions, even video games; the programming is sometimes populist and always eclectic (tel: 03-8663 2200; www.acmi.net.au; Mon–Fri 10am–6pm, Sat–Sun 9.30am–6pm; cinema times as advertised; free except for some exhibitions and cinema). There is also the **Edge** performance space and a variety of bars, cafés and restaurants.

The Windsor Hotel on Spring Street is a Victorian Heritage Hotel and dates from 1883.

Federation Square.

Behind Fed Square (as it quickly became known) is **Birrarung Marr**, an area of parkland on the river bank designed to acknowledge the original Aboriginal occupants of the land. Rock carvings and sculptural representations of shields and spears reflect the various tribes. Further on, the striking **Federation Bells** installation is worth seeing and hearing, and the passage of a bridge through to the Melbourne Cricket Ground ensures that plenty of people get to enjoy them.

Taking the tram

Melbourne's CBD is on an easily navigable grid and very walkable. Acting as backup is the **Circle Tram**, a free service that operates in a loop round the edge of the CBD. The tram system is one of Melbourne's great resources and, if you pick your route judiciously, a great way to discover the city.

St Paul's Cathedral ⓒ (tel: 03-9653 4333; www.stpaulscathedral.org.au), opposite Federation Square, was built between 1880 and 1891 to a design by William Butterfield, who never bothered to travel from England to see it. The stained glass and tiled floors are among the highlights.

On the other corner of Flinders and Swanston streets, **Young and Jackson's** pub (tel: 03-9650 3884; www.youngandjacksons.com.au) is a Melbourne institution, renowned for the 19th-century nude portrait *Chloe* on the first floor, which was considered rather racy in its day.

Continue down Swanston Street to **Melbourne Town Hall ⓓ**. Typical of the grand public buildings of the gold boom, it comes into its own during the International Comedy Festival every April, when various performance spaces are carved out of its halls and meeting rooms and it takes on a real club atmosphere.

Collins Street crosses Swanston Street at this point and, were you to go uphill past the magnificent **Regent Theatre** – pop into the foyer if it's open – you would come to what's

known as the "Paris end", where a bunch of exclusive boutiques and designer stores tempts the wealthy tourists. To avoid that, go in the opposite direction.

Shopping arcades

Were you to continue walking a couple of blocks, you would be rewarded with the remarkable Gothic Revival facade of the **ANZ Bank Building** at the junction with Queen Street. But before that comes the **Block Arcade** ⓔ (tel: 03-9654 5244; www.theblockarcade.com.au) between Elizabeth and Swanston streets. In this Victorian marvel, thrill to the mosaic floors, etched glass roof, and the original shop fittings. The **Hopetoun Tearooms** (tel: 03-9650 2777; www.hopetountearooms.com.au) has been purveying refreshment to refined shoppers for generations. Wind through to Little Collins Street and cross the road to **Royal Arcade** (tel: 0425-738 042; www.royalarcade.com.au). You'll run the gamut of the slightly cartoonish statues of Gog and Magog, just behind you as you enter.

TIP

Melbourne's city-centre laneways are fundamental to the city's character and appeal. The one-off designer shops, cosy cafés and funky bars are all joined by a vibrant wash of graffiti, including several pieces by Banksy… if you can find them. The City of Melbourne publishes a useful leaflet guide to the laneways to get you started.

Cast-iron details on Powlett Street.

SHOP

Melbourne is peppered
with interesting little
shops and boutiques. To
get a real feel for the city
you might consider
taking a shopping tour
around the less obvious
streets and areas.
Hidden Secrets Tours
operates a number of
"fashion walks" (tel:
03-9663 3358;
www.hiddensecretstours.
com), as well as other
themed tours.

The far end opens into **Bourke Street Mall** , the epicentre of old-style city shopping with the flagship department stores of the Myer and David Jones chains. At the Elizabeth Street end, the old GPO building has been successfully converted into a high-end shopping complex. The Myer store runs back across two blocks and has a bridge over to the bustling **Melbourne Central** retail hub which completely encloses the 1890 Shot Tower.

The Swanston Street entrance to Melbourne Central faces the imposing **State Library of Victoria** (tel: 03-8664 7000; www.slv.vic.gov.au; Mon–Thu 10am–9pm, Fri–Sun 10am–6pm; free), which has had a rather large fortune spent on it in renovations. The **Reading Room** copies the famous one in London's British Museum.

The **QV Centre**, next to the library, is another shopping development, which attempts to emulate the feel of Melbourne's laneways in a more modern structure.

Following Latrobe Street beside the library and turning left on Russell Street, you'll find **Old Melbourne Gaol** (tel: 03-8663 7228; www.old melbournegaol.com.au; daily 9.30am–5pm). This is where Ned Kelly met his end. His death mask is on display along with some of his armour. The building is grimly atmospheric as it is, but extreme thrill-seekers can join a monthly overnight ghost hunt.

Return along Russell Street until you reach Little Bourke Street, Melbourne's **Chinatown**, a buzzing and colourful lane with several good eateries. Turn left on Spring Street and continue to the end, where the **Carlton Gardens** across the road lead up to Australia's first World Heritage-listed structure, the **Royal Exhibition Building**. Access is normally only available for special events, but if you get a chance, nip in and have a look. It's a lovely spot.

Melbourne Museum

On the far side, that striking modern pavilion is the **Melbourne Museum** (tel: 131102 (Victoria only), 1300-130152; www.museumvictoria.com.au; daily 10am–5pm). The largest museum

Bourke Street.

in the country, there is masses to see and it's all presented so alluringly that you can spend hours here without realising it.

The children's section is pitched just right, and other areas appeal to all ages, especially the Melbourne Story Gallery and the Bunjilaka Aboriginal Centre. There's an IMAX cinema too.

Spring Street

Return to Spring Street and the state's seat of government at **Parliament of Victoria House** ⑦ (tel: 03-9651 8911; www.parliament.vic.gov.au; tours Mon–Fri 9.30am, 10.30am, 11.30am, 1.30pm, 2.30pm, 3.45pm; free), another grandiose Victorian pile, which still awaits the dome originally designed for it. Tours are available unless the houses are in session, in which case try for the public gallery.

The **Princess Theatre** opposite Parliament House is typical of its era, even down to the ghost story; ask for details at the box office. Continue along Spring Street to another monolithic public building. This is the **Old Treasury** (tel: 03-9651 2233; www.old treasurybuilding.org.au; Sun–Fri 10am–4pm; free). The permanent exhibits are linked to the history of the building and its role as Victoria's repository of gold. **Treasury Garden**, alongside, simply crawls with possums after dark.

Fitzroy Gardens and the MCG

Walk through to **Fitzroy Gardens**, where, under towering old trees, you will find **Cooks' Cottage** ⑧ (tel: 03-9658 9658; www.thatsmelbourne.com. au; daily 9am–5pm). It's not hard to discover Australia if you were brought up there, you might think. But no, the whole thing was disassembled in Yorkshire, shipped round the world and rebuilt in Melbourne, making it the only 18th-century building in town. Elsewhere, look out for the model **Tudor Village**, sent as a gift from the people of Lambeth in London, grateful for Australian food

parcels during World War II; and the **Fairies Tree**, a tree trunk carved with cute little figures.

Across Wellington Parade, the Melbourne Cricket Ground, better known as the **MCG** ⑨, beckons to sports fans. Try to get in to see some kind of sporting action, but if not, there are tours (Gate 3; tel: 03-9657 8888; www.mcg.org. au; daily 10am–3pm if no event) of the 100,000-seat stadium. The **National Sports Museum** (tel: 03-9657 8879; www.nsm.org.au; daily 10am–5pm) is housed here and has interesting exhibits on cricket, racing, Aussie Rules and the Melbourne Olympics, all enhanced by the latest technology.

South of the Yarra

Return to Federation Square, turn left over the river, and go down St Kilda Road. Directly ahead of you is the grey stone **Shrine of Remembrance** ⑩ (tel: 03-9661 8100; www.shrine.org. au; daily 10am–5pm; free). Built to commemorate the dead of World War I, it is aligned so that once a year at 11am on the 11 November – Remembrance Day – a beam of light shines

The Old Melbourne Gaol also runs night tours four nights a week.

SPORTS SOCIETY

If Australians are sports mad, then Melbourne must be the asylum. It's not just the obsession with the sports themselves, but the determination to make every contest an event.

The first Tuesday of November is a public holiday, because that's when the Melbourne Cup horse race is run. Each year the crowds at Flemington Racecourse seem bigger than the year before. In 2006, the record-breaking 129,000 crowd was not at Cup Day at all, but at the previous Saturday's Derby Day.

Boxing Day cricket invariably sells out at the MCG, but in 2010, for an exciting Ashes series where Australia was pitched against England, the first four days of the test match sold out in advance; that's 400,000 people if everyone turned up.

The Australian Rules football Grand Final at the MCG in September is probably the biggest event of them all. When local teams Collingwood and St Kilda drew in the 2010 final, the match had to be replayed, prolonging cup fever by another week; Collingwood eventually won by 56 points. Aussie Rules dominates Melbourne for seven months of every year. Everyone has to "barrack" for a team, irrespective of age, gender or interest. In this very Victorian sport (10 of the 18 teams are from the state), it came as a shock to learn the majority of the winners between 2000 and 2015 were from other states around Australia.

TIP

A card showing membership of any National Trust organisation from around the world will secure free admission to Old Melbourne Gaol, managed by National Trust Victoria. For those without a card, buying one in Victoria is a cost-effective way of securing reciprocal benefits elsewhere.

on to the Stone of Remembrance and illuminates the word "love". A visitor centre nestles in the shadow of the main building.

Just across the way from the shrine is the Observatory Gate, one of the entry points to the **Royal Botanic Gardens** (tel: 03-9252 2300; www. rbg.vic.gov.au; daily 7.30am–sunset; free). Enthusiasts will enjoy the specialist areas, like the cactus garden or the cycad collection, but many simply wander through the beautifully tended grounds and drink in the tranquillity of the lakeside. There is also an excellent children's garden.

Arts precinct

Return to St Kilda Road and cross over to the bluestone bulk of the **National Gallery of Victoria** (tel: 03-8620 2222; www.ngv.vic.gov.au; Wed–Mon 10am–5pm; free). This is, in fact, **NGV International**, which houses the NGV's collection of work from overseas, as opposed to the Ian Potter Centre at Federation Square which specialises in Australian works. Stick your fingers in the water wall at the

entrance, as generations have before you, and take your pick of the permanent exhibits or the visiting shows (for which a charge is usually levied). Leonard Hall's stained-glass ceiling of the **Great Hall** accounts for all the people lying on their backs within, and beyond is the doorway to the **Sculpture Garden**.

Next door, distinguished by the huge mesh spire above it, is the **Arts Centre** (tel: 03-9281 8000; www. artscentremelbourne.com.au). This cultural powerhouse has three theatres presenting **Melbourne Theatre Company** productions and visiting opera, dance and drama companies. In 2012 work finished on the renovation of **Hamer Hall**, the city's formal concert venue. If you carry on past the NGV and turn right, the striking building with the white geometric shapes all over it is the new MTC Theatre, and just beyond it, the equally new Melbourne Recital Centre.

At the river turn left along the South Bank where the promenade provides good views over the city, but not as good as those from the top of

A country locale for a weekend stroll.

MUSIC CITY

As well as having a throbbing local scene, Melbourne is a must-visit destination for international performers of all genres. It's partly down to the local audiences, who love their music, know what they like, and are also pretty relaxed about trying something new. And it's a lot to do with the venues.

Every inner-city suburb seems to have two or three pubs or clubs where something will be happening most nights of the week. Old favourite the Esplanade Hotel – or "Espy" – in St Kilda will book hundreds of acts a year across its various bars. The Corner in Richmond, the Prince of Wales in St Kilda, the HiFi Bar in the city, and the Northcote Social Club in High Street, Northcote, present big-name overseas acts in intimate settings.

the **Eureka Tower** ⦿ and its Eureka Skydeck 88 (tel: 03-9693 8888; www. eurekaskydeck.com.au; daily 10am–10pm) which, all too predictably, is on the 88th floor.

You may want to cross over the river to visit the absorbing **Immigration Museum** (tel: 131102 (Victoria only), 03-9927 2700; www.immigration. museum.vic.gov.au; daily 10am–5pm), or **Melbourne Aquarium** (tel: 1800-026 576; www.melbourneaquarium.com.au; daily 9.30am–6pm, Jan 9.30am–8pm).

Crown Casino ⦿ (tel: 03-9292 8888; www.crowncasino.com.au; daily, 24 hours; free) on your left seems to go on forever; given the turnover on the tables and through the one-arm bandits, or "pokies" as they're known, the management probably hopes it will. Shops, restaurants, show venues and a cinema can be found inside.

Docklands

The architecturally stimulating **Melbourne Exhibition Centre**, or "Jeff's Shed" as the locals call it, since it was one of Premier Jeff Kennett's projects, comes next. On the river bank beyond is the distinctive outline of historic ship, the *Polly Woodside*, docked in front of the new Convention Centre.

Stay on the path by the water round to **Docklands**, the latest area of Melbourne to be given an overhaul. You cross the river on the serpentine **Webb Bridge** and then follow the path through a sculpture garden that eventually leads to **Victoria Harbour**, with the **Etihad Stadium** ⦿ on your right and glistening new developments of offices, apartments and restaurants on your left. The area is slowly finding its feet but it's worth wandering down for a look if only because it's unlike anything else in Melbourne.

It's time to hop on the Circle Tram clockwise to the junction of Latrobe and Queen streets. Walk north up Queen Street until reaching the extensive sheds of **Queen Victoria Market** ⦿ (tel: 03-9320 5822; www.qvm.com. au; Tue, Thu 6am–2pm, Fri 6am–5pm, Sat 6am–3pm, Sun 9am–4pm). It's a buzzing place where locals after fresh produce or deli specialities mix with tourists seeking souvenir clocks in the shape of Australia.

Melbourne Aquarium.

The famous grounds of the MCG.

Little Italy

A short distance to the north, **Lygon Street** in Carlton, just 10 minutes by tram from the city centre, is sometimes known as **Little Italy**. It was this area that the waves of post-war Italian migrants adopted as their own, and at certain times of the year, such as when the Ferrari team is in town for the Grand Prix, streets are closed and the partying doesn't let up. Today Lygon Street is touristy, but a lively community of professional people and academics from adjacent Melbourne University keeps the place grounded. Coffee bars, bistros, trattorias, noisy pubs and pool rooms, as well as edgy fashion boutiques, contribute to a vibrant atmosphere.

Brunswick Street, a few blocks to the east, is hipper. In the evenings Melburnians drift here from around the city with bottles of wine tucked under their arms, looking for the latest BYO restaurant. They find cuisines from around the world, as well as Modern Australian. Wine bars, pubs with local bands and comedy nights, designer clothes stores, tiny retro fashion shops, gay and lesbian bookshops, artists'

cafés of the type popular in the 1950s and 60s, full of earnest characters confused by daylight, all happily co-exist.

Melbourne Zoo in Parkville, west of Lygon Street, has been a favourite since it opened in 1862 (Elliott Avenue; tel: 1300-966 784; www.zoo.org.au; daily 9am–5pm). It has a comprehensive collection of indigenous animals, displayed in sympathetic surroundings, as well as species from further afield. Its elephant enclosure manages to re-create an Asian setting, and the food court is themed to match.

St Kilda

St Kilda has always meant fun. Often sleazy, frequently illicit, but fun nonetheless. This bayside suburb is Melbourne's urban beach. There's no surf and few would brave a dip in the water, but the sand is clean and the beach-front on weekends is rather like Los Angeles' Venice Beach: rollerbladers and cyclists speed past, models preen themselves in the sun, and body-builders work out on the grass. Fight for an outside table at a beach-front restaurant, or walk along the jetty for a

There are lots of live music venues in Melbourne.

The St Kilda Markets in front of the Palais Theatre.

distant view of the city skyline (there's a café at the end).

Acland Street is famous for its cafés and cake shops. It displays the palate-delighting influences of Mittel Europe, reflecting a strong Jewish presence, but other nationalities are crowding in. At the end of the street, **Luna Park**'s gap-toothed grin invites you to try the clattering roller coaster (tel: 03-9525 5033; www.lunapark.com. au; Sept–Apr Fri 7–11pm, Sat 11am–11pm, Sun 11am–6pm, Jan–Feb Thu 7–11pm, May–Sept Sat–Sun 11am–6pm; charge for rides).

The **Upper Esplanade** hosts a Sunday arts and crafts market, while in **Fitzroy Street** the restaurants take over the footpaths, Mediterranean-style, with their tables and umbrellas.

Williamstown

On the other side of the bay, over the Westgate Bridge (or take a ferry from Southgate), is **Williamstown**, a bayside village with plenty of cafés, restaurants and great views back to the city. On its outskirts lies one of Melbourne's best museums: **Scienceworks** (2 Booker Street, Spotswood; tel: 131 102; www. scienceworks.museum.vic.gov.au; daily 10am–4.30pm), set in the grounds of an old pumping station. Its hands-on displays include House Secrets, which reveals what's really going on under the surface of a domestic environment.

Prahran and South Yarra

North of St Kilda, **Prahran** has one of Melbourne's best markets (163 Commercial Road; tel: 03-8290 8220; www. prahranmarket.com.au; Tue, Thu, Sat 7am–5pm, Fri 7am–6pm, Sun 10am–3pm) and, in **Chapel Street**, a shopping strip that runs from op-shop (charity shop) to designer chic, with prices rising as you move north into South Yarra and affluent Toorak.

Como House (corner Williams Road and Lechlade Avenue, South Yarra; tel: 0407-873 967; www.como house.com.au) is a graceful colonial mansion built in 1847, set in grounds that demand that you go equipped with a picnic. Gardens can be visited Mon–Sat 9am–5pm, Sun 10am–5pm; house tours Sat–Sun in summer at 10.30am, 12pm, 2pm, 3pm and 3.30pm.

FACT

Melbourne was the centre of a brewing revolution over 100 years ago. In the 19th century most Australian beer had been made like British ales, until lighter Continental-style lagers were brewed here by German immigrants. Today lots of "boutique beers" are available, including Three Ravens, Mountain Goat, Bright Brewery, James Squire and Holgate.

Dining in an Italian restaurant on Lygon Street.

Twelve Apostles lookout, off the Great Ocean Road.

VICTORIA

All the destinations in Victoria are within a day's drive of Melbourne – alpine mountains, desert plains, pristine beaches, historic wineries, gold-mining villages and quaint spa towns.

A round 6 million people live in Victoria, the smallest of the mainland states, which makes it heavily populated by Australian standards. Over four million are in Melbourne though, so parts of Victoria can still feel pretty empty. Squashed down in the bottom right corner of the country, its northern border defined over hundreds of kilometres by the Murray River, Victoria is at its emptiest in the northwest, where the Mallee, a semi-arid land of open plains, is given over to sheep, grain and national parks; and in the east, where the end of the Great Dividing Range curls round to peter out a few kilometres short of Melbourne. This high country of timber and cattle farming gets busier in winter as snow opens up the ski fields.

Victoria stuttered into life with the first permanent European settlement at Portland in 1834. Two years later pastoralists started crossing the Murray from the east and, with Melbourne growing, population increase was rapid. Aboriginal numbers, though, fell rapidly as introduced diseases and firearms took their toll.

In 1851 Victoria seceded from New South Wales. Within weeks gold was discovered and the new state's population and prosperity boomed. Indeed, the countryside is still littered with colonial mansions, and the towns with stately public buildings and hotels.

For being such a small state, Victoria manages to pack in a lot of attractions. The Great Ocean Road, the Goldfields and **Wilson's Promontory** are amongst the best known, but there are also coastal resorts, wineries, the inland ports of the Murray and some wonderful mountain scenery to explore. With good roads and comfortable distances to cover, Victoria is an easy state in which to lose yourself.

Main Attractions
Geelong
Queenscliff
The Great Ocean Road
Port Fairy
The Grampians
The Murray River
The Dandenongs
Beechworth
The Mornington Peninsula

Playing in the waves at Torquay.

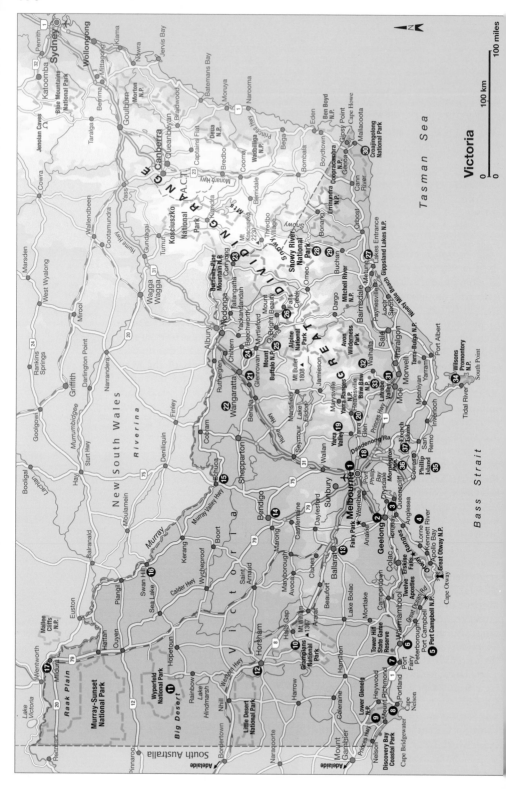

Victoria

West of Melbourne

From Melbourne the Princes Freeway speeds through the plains along the western shore of **Port Phillip Bay**. For a glimpse of opulence, take the exit to **Werribee Park** (www.werribeepark.com.au; Oct–March daily 10am–5pm, Apr–Sept Mon–Fri 10am–4pm, Sat–Sun 10am–5pm; free). In a 60-room Italianate mansion built in 1877 by the pastoralist Chirnside family, visitors can sample a vivid display of flamboyant wealth. The extensive grounds are set off by a sculpture walk mostly made up of past winners of the Helen Lampriere Sculpture Prize. There are more fragrant pleasures to be found in the adjoining **Victoria State Rose Garden**.

Nearby, the **Werribee Open Range Zoo** (tel: 1300-966 784; www.zoo.org.au; daily 9am–5pm) re-creates African savannah, with safari buses carrying you amongst the animals.

Geelong and the coast

As you drive on, the volcanic **You Yangs** dominate the skyline. Get closer to them by detouring to **Anakie**, home of **Fairy Park** (tel: 03-5284 1262; www.fairypark.com; daily 10am–5pm), "Australia's first and oldest theme park", where dioramas from fairy tales unfold by the winding path to the top of a granite crag. It's very low-tech by today's standards, but kids love it and there's an excellent playground, including the irresistible "do not touch this button".

Return to the highway and Victoria's second city. In its early days **Geelong ②** rivalled Melbourne as an outlet for Western District wool and later became an important manufacturing centre. After years of somnolence the city has shaken itself up – particularly by the waterfront, where quirky sculptures and a renovated pier are the focus.

A drive along the waterfront shows Geelong past and present – the old mansions, wool stores and piers, and the new industries, wharves and container terminal. Along the Barwon River are fine homes such as **Barwon Grange** (Fernleigh Street; tel: 03-5221

3906; www.nattrust.com.au; Sept–April 1st, 2nd and 3rd Sun of each month 1–4pm, May–Aug 3rd Sun of the month 1–4pm), refurnished in the style of 1855, when it was built by a merchant shipowner.

For a whiff of nostalgia, take the Bellarine Highway out of Geelong and travel to **Queenscliff ③**. This was "Queen of the Watering Places" in the 1880s when paddle steamers brought the fashionable to the handsome turreted hotels. There is still a haughty grandeur to the place. The Queenscliff fort (King Street; tel: 03-5258 1488; www.fortqueenscliff.com.au; tours Sat–Sun and school holidays, 1pm and 3pm), with red-brick walls and cannon, was built in the 19th century to defend Melbourne against a Russian invasion.

The road on to **Anglesea** meanders through seaside settlements, sleepy in winter and pulsing with life in summer. **Torquay** is the surf centre of Victoria, and **Bells Beach** is famed worldwide for its Easter surf contest. Beyond Anglesea, whose main claim to fame is the mob of kangaroos that live on the golf course, is the start of the **Great**

The winding Great Ocean Road.

Bushwalking in Great Otway National Park.

Beach bollards decorate the sands at Geelong near the town of Port Phillip Bay.

The Great Ocean Road leads past Apollo Bay.

Ocean Road, 200km (125 miles) of the state's most spectacular coastal scenery.

A favourite weekend spot from Melbourne is **Lorne ❹**, set on a picturesque bay with a bush backdrop and several restaurants and shops. The annual Pier-to-Pub Swim in January attracts entrants from across the nation.

In the **Great Otway National Park**, tracks wind through eucalyptus forest and fern gullies to waterfalls and lookouts. Walks vary from a gentle stroll along the St George's River to rock-hopping along to the Cora Lyn Cascades. A three-hour hike up to the **Erskine Falls** can be strenuous, while the less energetic can drive to a lookout.

Along the coast at **Kennett River**, a 6km (3.5-mile) drive leads to the **Grey River Scenic Reserve**. It's a short walk (1.5km/1-mile round trip), one of the best in Victoria, up a fern gully amid towering blue gums.

For a panoramic view of the **Otway Ranges**, turn inland at **Skenes Creek** and drive up into the hills. After 15km (9 miles), turn left into the fern and mountain-ash forest along Turton's Track. When the country opens out again you are on a ridge. On the left, wooded spurs reach down to the sea; on the right are the volcanic lakes and plains of the Western District.

From **Apollo Bay**, with its mixed artsy and fishing vibe, the Great Ocean Road leaves the coast to wind through the forest behind Cape Otway. Find the **Otway Fly** (tel: 03-5235 9200; www.otwayfly.com; daily 9am–5pm), and enjoy a walk through the forest canopy on 600 metres/yds of steel walkway, 25 metres (82ft) above the ground. At **Cape Otway** a tour of the **Lighthouse** (tel: 03-5237 9240; www.lightstation.com; daily 9am–5pm), which has watched over the hazardous entrance to the Bass Strait since 1848, is worthwhile. The setting is sublime.

The Twelve(ish) Apostles

Beyond Princetown lies the spectacular coastline of **Port Campbell National Park ❺**, where breakers have battered the soft limestone cliffs, creating grottoes and gorges, arches and sea sculptures rising from the surf. The road gives only occasional glimpses of the drama below, which includes the stark

rock stacks of **The Twelve Apostles** and the spray billowing through the fallen arch of **London Bridge**. It is an evolving landscape; as over time some of the stumps have collapsed into the sea due to erosion, leaving just eight remaining Apostles. Stop at all the vantage points, follow the various trails at **Loch Ard Gorge**, and make the most of the new visitor centre.

Beyond Peterborough and the dramatic **Bay of Islands** lies **Warrnambool** ❻, once a busy port and now a holiday centre. People flock here in winter to see the southern right whales off Logans Beach. Around the lighthouse is the **Flagstaff Hill Maritime Village**, a re-created 19th-century port with its chandlers, shipwrights and sailmakers (tel: 03-5559 4600; www.flagstaffhill.com; daily 9am–5pm). The spectacular *Shipwrecked* sound-and-laser show runs nightly at dusk (see website for precise times). **Warrnambool Art Gallery** (tel: 03-5559 4949; Mon–Fri 10am–5pm, Sat–Sun noon–5pm; free) has a large collection of Australiana.

Beyond Warrnambool is **Tower Hill State Game Reserve**, a volcanic crater containing smaller cones where ducks nest, emus share your picnic and there's a good chance of seeing koalas. At dusk the 'roos come out as well.

Port Fairy

Along the coast is the fishing-village charm of **Port Fairy** ❼, where brightly painted boats tie up at the jetty with their catches of crayfish and crab. Port Fairy was named by Captain James Wishart who brought his tiny cutter, the *Fairy*, into the Moyne River to find shelter during a sealing expedition in 1810. Sealers and, later, whalers built stone cottages that still nestle under the tall Norfolk Island pines shading the streets. You can drink at the **Caledonian Inn**, which opened in 1844 and has been in business ever since.

Griffiths Island, at the mouth of the river, was a whaling station, but is now a rookery for thousands of mutton birds that return in September from the north Pacific. The young hatch in January, and every evening until they leave in April, you can watch the adult birds swoop in from the sea

An innkeeper in Flagstaff.

Coastline near Loch Ard Gorge.

TIP

With the desert on one side and the sea on the other, Victoria is notorious for its changeable and unpredictable weather. Be prepared to face cold winds, rain and searing heat all in the same day.

Cattle graze in the shadow of a mountain.

to feed their chicks, if you can see them – it can get very dark by the time they arrive and you simply hear a low whirring as they cruise past your head.

Portland ❽ – big wharves on a broad bay and solid 19th-century bluestone buildings – was a whaling station when Edward Henty arrived in 1834 and ploughed the first furrow in Victorian soil. Take the cliff walks at **Cape Nelson** and view the moonscape bluff of **Cape Bridgewater**, where wind and water have fashioned a petrified forest from scrub.

The coast road to South Australia skirts **Mount Richmond**, a sandcovered volcano ablaze with wild flowers in spring. It borders **Discovery Bay Coastal Park**, with its vast rolling sand dunes and stretches of unspoilt beach, and runs along the southern margin of **Lower Glenelg National Park** ❾, known for its gorge and delicate cave formations. You can drive or take a boat tour from **Nelson** up the gorge to the caves. The park is rich with 700 species of native plants, but most of it can be explored only by river or on rough, sandy tracks.

The Grampians

Pass through the wool town of **Hamilton** – see the **Big Wool Bales** – towards **Halls Gap**, where the ranges of the **Grampians National Park** ❿ rise abruptly to dominate the surrounding plains. These craggy mountains are a series of rocky ranges thrown up by the folding of a sandstone mass into an uncommon cuesta formation – spectacular escarpments on the east side and gentle slopes to the west. Erosion has shaped bizarre rock sculptures, and waterfalls cascade over the sheer face.

Many scenic points are accessible by car, but there is wilderness aplenty for the more adventurous and walking tracks to suit all grades of hiker. You can drive past **Lake Bellfield**, where koalas feed in the manna gums, to the highest peak in the ranges, **Mount William** (1,367 metres/3,829ft). A 1.5km (1-mile) walk takes you to the summit. Return to Halls Gap via the Silverband Road to take in some of the highlights of the **Wonderland Range**.

On Mount Victory Road, short detours lead to **Reid Lookout**, high over the Victoria Valley, and home to

kangaroos and emus. A 15-minute walk along the cliff top brings you to **The Balconies**, outcrops of sandstone that hang like giant jaws over the precipice.

As the road winds through the forest, stop at the viewpoint for the **McKenzie Falls** or take the walking track to the falls along the river, before going on to **Zumstein**. Walter Zumstein, a beekeeper and bush-lover who was a pioneer in this valley in the early 20th century, befriended the kangaroos, and each afternoon their descendants still leave the forest to be fed.

The Wimmera

The Western Highway travels through the heart of **The Wimmera**, the granary of Victoria. This sweep of golden wheat fields in an area the size of Wales stretches west to the South Australia border and north to the sand dunes and dry lake beds of **Wyperfeld National Park ⓫**. It is dotted with small townships and soaring silos, and is populated by more sheep than people.

Horsham ⓬ is a small town, with the excellent **Horsham Regional Art Gallery** (tel: 03-5362 2888; www.

horshamartgallery.com.au; Tue–Fri 10am–5pm, Sat–Sun 1–4.30pm; donation); the **Botanic Gardens** are a nice contribution to the town.

Return east along the Western Highway towards **Ararat**. The town's first settler named a nearby peak Mount Ararat "for like the Ark, we rested there." Two French settlers, who saw that the soil and climate between Ararat and Stawell resembled that of France, planted the first vines in 1863, and wines, both red and sparkling white, have been produced at **Great Western** ever since. The road continues past forested hills to **Beaufort**, notable for its iron-lacework band rotunda topped with a clock tower.

The Eureka Stockade

Ballarat ⓭ is within an hour's drive of Melbourne, a far cry from the jolting day-long journey along potholed tracks that faced the miners bound for the gold-diggings in the 1850s.

On the southern side of the city, the **Eureka Centre** is being remodeled as the Museum of Australian **Democracy at Eureka** (daily 9am–5pm; tel:

Koalas are wild animals and should only be picked up or petted under the supervision of a trained professional.

Climbing in Grampians National Park.

ABORIGINAL ART

More than 40 Aboriginal art sites have been found in caves and rock shelters in the Grampians. Some of the more accessible are in the **Victoria Range**, where you can see hand stencils in red ochre in the **Cave of Hands**, and a variety of paintings including animals, human figures and a kangaroo hunt in the **Glenisla Shelter**. Many of the geographical features of the region are woven into the Dreamtime legends, including the splitting of one of the Grampian ranges by Tchingal, a giant emu, to create **Roses Gap**. You can learn more about the area's traditional inhabitants at the **Brambuk Aboriginal Cultural Centre**, a striking building 2km (1.2 miles) south of Halls Gap (tel: 03-5361 4000; www.brambuk.com.au; daily 9am–5pm; free).

Carman's Tunnel Goldmine, Maldon.

Sovereign Hill, Ballarat.

1800-287-113; www.eurekaballarat.com). At the site, a diorama brings to life the day in December 1854 when the name Eureka was etched into Australian history.

The rumbustious life of those times is re-created in the mocked-up gold-mining town of **Sovereign Hill** (tel: 03-5337 1199; www.sovereignhill.com.au; daily 10am–5pm). In the main street, resembling Ballarat in the 1850s with its old-fashioned wooden shops, apothecary and confectioners, you can watch blacksmiths, tinsmiths and potters at work; sample a digger's lunch at the New York Bakery; or have a drink at the United States Hotel next to the Victoria Theatre where Lola Montez danced her famous and risqué spider dance. Take a ride on a Cobb & Co. coach and pan for gold in the creek. After a look around the Red Hill gully diggings, slake your thirst at the "lemonade" tent – the sly-grog shop where diggers celebrated their luck or drowned their sorrows. Then walk along the underground tunnel of the Quartz Mine, typical of the company mines where, in later years, the real

money was made. It is a ridiculously enjoyable day out and can be topped off with the *Blood on the Southern Cross* sound-and-light show that re-creates the drama of the Eureka Stockade.

Ballarat was born in the boom time, and its wide streets, verandahs and iron lace, towers and colonnades give it grace and distinction. **Ballarat Fine Art Gallery** (40 Lydiard Street; tel: 03-5320 5858; www.artgalleryofballarat.com.au; daily 9am–5pm) is renowned for its Australian paintings, while the **Botanic Gardens** beside **Lake Wendouree** sport Italian statues and a blaze of begonias.

Gold towns

Other gold towns lurk to the north of Ballarat, where thousands of men dug their 12ft by 12ft (13.4sq-metre) claims with ant-like ardour. **Clunes**, the scene of the first gold strike on 1 July 1851, has an ornate town hall, and elegant banks and bluestone churches. **Daylesford** a picturesque town on Wombat Hill, is known (along with its neighbour Hepburn Springs) as the spa centre of Australia. Nowadays, it's also a thriving weekend retreat for Melburnians, including a strong gay and lesbian contingent.

In **Castlemaine** the Greek temple-style market building and other fine edifices date from an era of promise never quite fulfilled. A short ride on one of the steam trains of the **Victorian Goldfields Railway** (tel: 03-5470 6658; www.vgr.com.au; Sun, Wed, some Sat) will take you to **Maldon**, the National Trust's first "notable town in Australia". Its gold-rush era streetscapes are terrific, as much for their tranquillity as their remarkable state of preservation.

In **Bendigo** , some of the richest quartz reefs in the world created a Victorian extravaganza. The scarlet **Joss House** is an interesting reminder of the thousands of Chinese who came to the "Big Gold Mountain", bringing with them temples, teahouses and festivals. The colourful Chinese dragon, Sun Loong, is 100 metres (330ft) long and

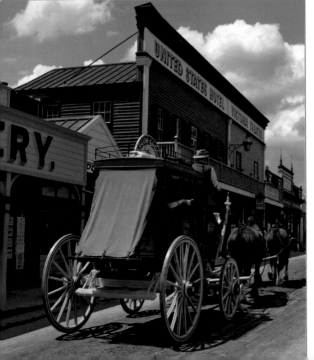

the star of the Bendigo Easter Fair. It is to be found in the **Golden Dragon Museum** (1–11 Bridge Street; www.goldendragonmuseum.org; daily 9.30am–5pm). Elsewhere there are extravagant hotels, another good art gallery (Bendigo; 42 View Street; tel: 03-5434 6088; www.bendigoartgallery.com.au; daily 10am–5pm; donation) and the **Central Deborah Goldmine** (76 Violet Street; tel: 03-5443 8255; www.central-deborah.com; daily 9am–5pm), where you can take an underground tour.

The Murray

Echuca ⓯, 88km (55 miles) north of Bendigo, was an important port on the **Murray River** and its magnificent old timber wharf is now a major draw for visitors. You need a ticket to get in (tel: 03-5481 0500; www.portofechuca.org.au; daily 9am–5pm) but it allows access to displays in two historic pubs and can be boosted to include a cruise on one of the historic paddle steamers. A cruise is *de rigueur* and allows you to relive the days when these mighty vessels, laden with cargo and passengers, made the river a busy thoroughfare, before the railways

made them obsolete. Think about renting a houseboat and making the river, lined with tall red gums, your home for a few days. Back on land, **Sharps Magic Movie House and Penny Arcade** (tel: 03-5482 2361; daily 9am–5pm), in the historic precinct behind the wharf, lets you relive the simple pleasures of pre-electronic entertainment.

The Murray Valley Highway loosely tracks the river as it heads northwest and rejoins it at **Swan Hill** ⓰ where the principal pull is the **Pioneer Settlement** (tel: 03-5036 2410; www.pioneersettlement.com.au; daily 9.30am–4pm), a collection of original historic buildings transplanted to this site to create a typical township of the 19th century. Time rushes by as you stroll in and out of shops and houses. You can cruise on a paddle steamer and, at dusk, take in a sound-and-light show.

It is another 196km (122 miles) to the city of **Mildura** ⓱. While many Australian centres claim the biggest of something, Mildura aims for the longest bar in the world – 91 metres (298ft) long, at the **Workingman's Club**; the largest fruit-juice factory; and the

The clock tower in Bendigo peers out from what was once the post office; the building has now been renovated as a museum.

Paddle boats still ply the river.

FACT

The Murray River once supported many native fish such as the Murray cod and the silver perch. But the introduction of other species, particularly carp, destroyed aquatic plants and became a threat to the native fish, many of which have consequently become threatened species.

largest deckchair ever built (in front of a main-street motel).

Mildura is an exceptionally pleasant and friendly city, with its great climate and water pastimes of fishing, swimming and boating. The town, and the irrigation system that drew settlers to the area, were established by two American brothers, George and William Chaffey. William's imposing homestead, **Rio Vista** (199 Cureton Avenue; tel: 03-5018 8330; www.milduraartscentre.com.au; Wed–Mon 11am–4pm), can be seen at **Mildura Arts Centre**. His other legacy is that, in US style, Mildura has streets with numbers rather than names.

The Murray River, of course, is the dominant attraction, and you can take to it and its series of locks with two-hour trips on the steam-driven *Melbourne* and dinner cruises on the *Rothbury* or *Mundoo*. There is also a wide range of houseboats for hire. From here the Calder Highway runs back to Melbourne.

The Dandenongs

The Ned Kelly statue at Glenrowan.

Approximately 50km (31 miles) east of Melbourne lie the **Dandenong**

Ranges ⓲. Here, the mountain bluffs are riddled with both fern gullies and art galleries, while small towns like **Belgrave** and **Olinda** make lovely destinations for day trips, offering browsing opportunities in antique shops and cafés serving cream teas.

Attractions include the **William Ricketts Sanctuary** (tel: 131 963; www.parkweb.vic.gov.au; daily 10am–4.30pm; free), where romantically idealised Aboriginal spirit figures have been carved from wood by an elderly white sculptor and placed in a forest setting, and **Puffing Billy**, a narrow-gauge steam train that plies a 24km (15-mile) track from Belgrave to Gembrook (tel: 03-9757 0700; www.puffing billy.com.au; daily).

The **National Rhododendron Gardens** at Olinda (tel: 131 963; www.park web.vic.gov.au; daily 10am–5pm; free) are at their spectacular best in October and November but are well worth a visit all year.

Directly north of the Dandenongs, the **Yarra Valley** ⓳ now claims 55 wineries in its gently rolling countryside. Organised wine-tasting tours can

THE KELLY TRIAL

Glenrowan Inn, 16km (10 miles) south-west of Wangaratta, was the site of Ned Kelly's last stand. Kelly's comrades were killed in a shoot-out with police as the inn burned to the ground, and Ned himself was brought to trial in Melbourne, subsequently to be hanged in the gaol there in November 1880.

Glenrowan has rather gone to town on its role in all this. **Kellyland** features computerised mannequins judderingly re-enacting the last stand at regular intervals throughout the day. Outside, a gigantic, technicolour Ned Kelly, in full armour and clutching his gun, looms over a block of tacky shops pushing Kelly kitsch. Many heinous crimes have been linked to Australia's most infamous bushranger, and there's no sign of it ending any time soon.

be arranged or you can dip into the odd cellar door as you pass through. One to look out for is **Yering Station** (38 Melba Highway; tel: 03-9730 0100; www.yering.com; Mon–Fri 10am–5pm, Sat–Sun 10am–6pm), Victoria's first vineyard but now a sparkling modern enterprise with a dramatic architect-designed centre and stunning views. Having the sumptuous **Chateau Yering** hotel with its excellent restaurants next door only adds to its appeal.

Yarra Glen is a relaxed centre to the area and a stop at the historic **Grand Hotel** is recommended. Take the road towards Healesville and pause at the **TarraWarra Museum of Art** (tel: 03-5957 3100; www.twma.com.au; Tue–Sun 11am–5pm), which has changing exhibitions in its sleek, airy, award-winning space.

Only 61km (38 miles) from Melbourne is **Healesville** ⑳, best known for the **Healesville Sanctuary** (tel: 1300-966 784; www.zoo.org.au; daily 9am–5pm). This renowned open-air zoo was established in 1934 to study and breed native fauna and has played a key role in helping to replenish Australia's endangered wildlife.

Travel north on the Maroondah Highway and after 24km (15 miles) turn off to **Marysville**. Once the base for Melbourne's closest ski field, the cross-country resort of **Lake Mountain**, it was razed by the Black Saturday bushfires. A winding road through **Yarra Ranges National Park** leads to the pretty village of **Warburton**.

For downhill skiing, return to the Maroondah Highway and work round to the northeast towards **Mansfield**, an important grazing and timber centre and the gateway to **Mount Buller** (1,808 metres/5,932ft), Victoria's largest ski resort. It lies just 3km (2 miles) from **Lake Eildon**, a 130-sq-km (50-sq-mile) body of water formed from the damming of five rivers to irrigate thousands of square kilometres of farmland. Today the lake is a paradise for water-skiers and fishermen angling for trout, perch and Murray cod.

Kelly Country

Take the Midland Highway north and join the Hume Highway eastward. This is the heart of Kelly Country, the stamping grounds of the legendary Ned Kelly. Today, travellers on the Hume Highway through **Glenrowan** ㉑ can't miss his presence.

Benalla calls itself the "Rose City" after the thousands of bushes that bloom from October to April. These add colour to the unusual **Benalla Art Gallery** (Bridge Street; tel: 03-5760 2619; www.benallaartgallery.com; daily 10am–5pm; free) overlooking the Broken River.

Wangaratta ㉒ is a skilfully planned agricultural centre with a population of 17,000 on the Ovens River. Today it is noted for its wool mills, two interesting 19th-century churches, and the Wangaratta Jazz Festival, which draws crowds every spring.

All towns here have one thing in common – a history linked to gold. In 1853, when gold was discovered in the valley of the Ovens River, dozens of prosperous mining settlements sprang into life almost overnight. By 1870,

The Puffing Billy makes its way through the winding Dandenongs.

BLACK SATURDAY

On Saturday 7 February 2009, some of the worst bushfires on record roared through great swathes of Victoria and took the lives of 173 people. Years of drought, combined with a baking-hot summer, turned much of the country to tinder that was just waiting for the right spark.

As temperatures headed above 47°C (116°F), winds whipped up, some gusting over 120kph (75mph). Several dangerous, but to that point manageable, bushfires began to run out of control. Blazes jumped control lines and embers were blown hundreds of metres, setting off more spot fires which soon combined to create unstoppable fire fronts roaring across thousands of hectares. Houses, farmland and forests were razed and entire settlements were destroyed.

The Kilmore fire, as it became known, devastated Kinglake, Strathewen, Flowerdale and other townships to the north of Melbourne. When it combined with the Murrindindi blaze to the east, it virtually wiped out Marysville, where 34 people perished. Further east, in Gippsland, vast areas of forest were destroyed and much of Wilson's Promontory was affected. Over 1,200 homes were lost across the state and, as well as the human toll, wildlife was decimated and millions of hectares of forest and bushland were destroyed.

FACT

Rutherglen exported wine to England and France in the 19th century, but few vineyards survived an invasion of the phylloxera mite at the turn of the 20th century. Some vintners stubbornly persisted, finding the soil and climate ideal for sherries and dessert wines – they discovered they could ripen their grapes late in the season to a high sugar level.

most of them had folded as the precious mineral became harder to find, but some of the towns survive as vital reminders of a thrilling history in a valley better known today for its wines.

Chiltern was originally established in the 1850s as Black Dog Creek. With its wide streets flanked by shops with Old West-style facades, the town has proved a popular film set. Today its main claim to fame is **Lake View Homestead** (tel: 03-5726 1317; www. nattrust.com.au; Sun 1–4pm), the childhood home of novelist Ethel Richardson, who, as Henry Handel Richardson, wrote some of Australia's classic works, including *The Getting of Wisdom*.

Some 16km (10 miles) northwest of Chiltern is **Rutherglen**, centre of Australia's oldest vine-growing district and still the foremost producer of fortified wines.

The northeast border

Wodonga is the Victorian half of Australia's fastest-growing inland metropolis. Its big brother, **Albury**, across the Murray River in New South Wales, gives the twin cities a combined population of more than 90,000. Hub of the Riverina district, which produces prodigious quantities of grain, fruit and livestock, Albury marks the site where the explorers Hume and Hovell discovered the Murray in 1824 after trekking south from Sydney.

The Murray Valley Highway passes through **Tallangatta**, at the eastern tip of **Lake Hume**. It is a new town, built in 1956 to replace the former community flooded by the damming of the Murray River. Traces of the old township – lines of trees, streets, even some buildings – eerily reappear at times of low water. The lake, four times the size of Sydney Harbour, is now a playground for swimmers, water-skiers, anglers and birdwatchers.

Corryong ㉓, the last town before the border with New South Wales, features the **Man From Snowy River Folk Museum** (103 Hanson Street; tel: 02-6076 2600; www.manfromsnowy rivermuseum.com; daily, Sept–May 10am–4pm, June–Aug 11am–3pm); its varied collection includes what has been enticingly described as "the most recognised snow-ski collection in Australia".

To the south is the village of **Nariel Creek**, where folk-music festivals are held on an old Aboriginal corroboree ground on New Year holidays and Victorian Labour Day weekend. Northwest of Corryong (access from Cudgewa) is **Burrowa Pine Mountain National Park** with rugged walks and views of the Snowy Mountains.

Beechworth

Return west, where the entire township of **Yackandandah** has been classified by the National Trust. Miners who came from California and the Klondike in the 1860s helped to give the place a lingering air of the American West. Today it is the centre of Victoria's largest strawberry industry.

Nestled in the midst of rolling hill country is northeast Victoria's best-preserved gold town, **Beechworth** ㉔. No fewer than 32 of its buildings have

The wine barrels of Coldstream Hill Estate.

been classified by the National Trust, including the towered **Post Office** (1867) with its Victorian stone construction, **Tanswell's Commercial Hotel** (1873) with its handsome facade and wrought-iron verandah, and the **Robert O'Hara Burke Memorial Museum** (1856; tel: 03-5728 8067; www.burkemuseum.com.au; daily 10am–5pm), part of the historic precinct on Loch Street. This museum exhibits relics of the gold-rush era – when 3 million ounces of gold were garnered in just 14 years. There is even a life-sized re-creation of a section of Beechworth's former main street. During its heyday the town had 61 hotels and a theatre that hosted international acts.

Mount Buffalo

South from Beechworth is a region of considerable natural beauty, the beginning of Victoria's high country. **Myrtleford** is the thriving centre of a walnut, tobacco and hop-growing region. **Mount Buffalo National Park** ㉕, a vast plateau at 1,370 metres (4,495ft), becomes a huge snowfield in winter, a carpet of wild flowers in

spring, and a popular spot for bush-walking in the summer and autumn.

Bright, a town of over 2,000 famed for its autumn colours, is a short distance away. Oaks, maples and other hardwoods promote a serenity which belies its violent gold-rush days, including the notorious 1857 Buckland riots when white prospectors brutally ousted Chinese miners from their claims.

Mount Beauty is the gateway to the largest of the alpine resorts at smart **Falls Creek** ㉖ in **Alpine National Park**, where the après ski is as important as what happens on the slopes. Working south along the Great Alpine Road, **Mount Hotham** has downhill and cross-country runs, while **Dinner Plain** is an arresting 1980s resort.

Continue for 160km (100 miles) of attractive high-country motoring until the road joins the Princes Highway.

Gippsland Lakes

Bairnsdale, the commercial centre of **East Gippsland**, lies 285km (177 miles) east of Melbourne. A sheep, dairy and timber centre, it is best

FACT

The Man from Snowy River started life in 1890 as a poem by bush poet Banjo Paterson. It became a silent film in 1920, and a popular modern version in 1982 spawned a sequel in 1988, a TV series in the 1990s and a stage musical. The poem was celebrated in the opening sequence of Sydney's Olympic Games.

Old Farmhouse in the Victorian Goldfields, Castlemaine.

A gazebo decorates the main street of Bairnsdale.

Watch the birdy.

known for its fine **Botanic Gardens** and the "Sistine Chapel" murals in **St Mary's Catholic Church**. Nearby **Paynesville**, a boating resort, features the bizarre yet interesting **Church of St Peter**: a sailors' house of worship, it has a spire like a lighthouse, a pulpit shaped like the bow of a boat, and a sanctuary lighting fixture that was once a ship's riding lamp.

The Princes Highway eastwards runs all the way to Sydney but the only time it touches the coast in Victoria is at **Lakes Entrance** ㉗. This resort is situated at the narrow man-made inlet to the **Gippsland Lakes**, a long string of interconnected lagoons stretching west along the inner shore of the Bass Strait for some 80km (50 miles). They are separated from the sea only by a narrow band of dunes and hummocks called **Ninety Mile Beach**.

The normal population of Lakes Entrance increases by a factor of six in summer as holiday-makers pack the motels and caravan parks. Up-market accommodation is on offer at quiet **Metung**, a few kilometres to the west.

Fishing, boating and swimming are the main draws, while cruise boats offer regular sightseeing tours of the lakes. Sometimes called the Victorian Riviera, the area has consistent temperatures of about 20°C (68°F) in winter. The **Gippsland Lakes Coastal Park**, a reserve of dunes and heath along the lakes' seaward edge, and the **Lakes National Park**, a bird-filled woodland on a sandy peninsula between Lake Reeve and Lake Victoria, help protect natural features.

Snowy River National Park

Logging trucks seem to congregate at **Orbost**, a prosperous town of about 3,000 people near the banks of the lower Snowy River.

Snowy River National Park ㉘, in the mountains above, is popular with whitewater canoeists, who relish the challenge of riding the water through the deep gorges that contribute to the spectacular scenery of this often overlooked area. The Princes Highway then winds through its most remote stretch, 208km (129 miles) of mountains and rainforest, to reach the state border.

At Nowa Nowa, 22km (13 miles) from Lakes Entrance, a winding road will take you to **Buchan** ㉙. It hosts a rodeo over Easter, and a lumberjacks' contest in May, but its main attraction is its limestone caves, unquestionably the finest in Victoria. There are 350 here, but only three are open to the public, including the **Fairy Cave**, whose numerous honeycombed chambers are embedded with ancient marsupial bones (tel: 131 963; www.parkweb.vic.gov.au; tours daily).

The southeast

At the hamlet of Genoa near the NSW border, a sealed side road turns south towards **Mallacoota**. This tiny resort town, much beloved by anglers and nature-lovers, is at the end of a 24km (15-mile) journey off the Princes Highway at Victoria's southeasternmost tip. It is surrounded by **Croajingolong National Park** ㉚, 86,000 hectares (212,500 acres) of rocky cliffs and open beaches, rainforest, open woodland and heath, stretching some 100km (60 miles) from the NSW border to Sydenham Inlet. Numerous nocturnal mammals (including possums and gliders) and many snakes – some venomous – make their homes in the park; hundreds of bird species include lyrebirds, oystercatchers, sea eagles and kingfishers. The pub at the charming village at **Gipsy Point** overlooks the inlet between Mallacoota and Genoa.

It's time for the long trek back towards Melbourne. The string of small cities along the Princes Highway from **Sale** comprises the **Latrobe Valley** ㉛, whose coal produces about 90 percent of the electricity for Melbourne and Victoria. The valley sits upon the world's largest deposit of brown coal, and open-cut mines and the steaming towers of power stations are everywhere.

Moe, the valley's largest and most modern city, is the site of **Old Gippstown** (tel: 03-5127 3082; www.gippsland heritagepark.com.au; daily 10am–4pm), an 1850s heritage park, where industrial and agricultural structures and machinery have been transplanted to a garden setting. To see the real thing, and with a more dramatic backdrop,

FACT

In some of the limestone caves near Buchan, such as Cloggs Cave and New Guinea II cave (which are not open to visitors), explorers have found tools and rock engravings dating back 17,000 years. These are now thought to have been intermittently occupied hunting sites.

Little penguins.

PENGUINS ON PARADE

Every day at sunset at **Summerland Beach** on Phillip Island, hundreds of little penguins – we're not to call them fairy penguins any more – waddle from the waters of the Bass Strait to their protected burrows in the sand. Wings outstretched, they strut in small groups up a concrete ramp past throngs of curious human onlookers. This has developed into a serious, packaged tourist spectacle: there can be days when humans outnumber the penguins. In response to this there are now elite ticketing options, involving a "penguin sky box" or a small-group "more personalised intimate wildlife experience", which sees richer tourists led to a quiet beach by their own ranger. (Tel: 03-5951 2800; www.penguins.org.au; daily dusk; bookings 10am–5pm).

TIP

Just off the north coast of Phillip Island and accessed by a causeway, Churchill Island Heritage Farm has a very well-preserved homestead built in 1872 by Samuel Amess, formerly Mayor of Melbourne (tel: 03-5951 2800; www.penguins.org.au; daily 10am–5pm). A walk around the island is recommended too.

make your way to the tiny mountain community of **Walhalla** ㉜, where what was once Victoria's richest gold mine sits in a beautiful valley, now almost deserted.

Long Tunnel Extended Gold Mine is open for tours (tel: 03-5165 6259; daily) and there's plenty more to keep you in this lovely spot.

Mount Baw Baw ㉝, the nearest downhill ski resort to Melbourne and a National Park, is a short distance to the northwest on the map, but to actually get there is a long and complicated drive down towards Moe and up again.

The Prom

The final swathe of goodies is to be found along the coast. **Wilson's Promontory** ㉞, a huge granite peninsula that represents mainland Australia's furthest thrust towards Antarctica, is the most popular national park in Victoria. The Prom, as it is affectionately called by regular visitors, features more than 80km (50 miles) of walking tracks to long sandy beaches, forested mountain slopes, and heath and

marshes packed with bird, animal and plant life. An estimated 100,000 people visit the park each year; access is managed carefully, and even the hot spots of **Tidal River**, **Squeaky Beach** and **Picnic Bay** rarely feel crowded. Just don't expect to find a camping spot in peak season without booking months ahead (tel: 131963; www.parkweb.vic.gov.au).

The historic township of **Port Albert** to the east is worth a look for the old timber jetty – at which eager 19th-century Chinese gold miners once disembarked. The Port Albert Hotel (1842) was destroyed by fire in 2014.The **Gippsland Regional Maritime Museum** (Sept–May daily, June–Aug Sat–Sun, 10.30am–4pm; tel: 03-5183 2520) is housed in the old Bank of Victoria.

Penguin Island

For many travellers, the most interesting stop in this final stretch to Melbourne is **Phillip Island** ㉟. It is connected to the mainland fishing community of **San Remo** by a bridge under which a flock of pelicans gathers

Speleothem formations in Royal Cave, Buchan.

daily for a feed. In an area of about 104 sq km (40 sq miles), there is a bewildering array of tourist attractions.

Phillip Island was the site of Australia's first motor-racing circuit (1928), and it still attracts crowds today when it hosts the Australian 500cc Motorcycle Grand Prix in October and the V8 touring car championship shortly afterwards. Among other attractions are koala and bird sanctuaries, scenic offshore rock formations, historic homesteads, pottery shops, and sports – from surfing, diving, sailing and fishing to golf, tennis, bowling and croquet. The relaxed north-coast summer resort town of **Cowes** is the tourist centre.

However, unquestionably the biggest regular attraction for Phillip Island visitors is the **Penguin Parade**. About 1.5km (1 mile) off the western tip of the island are the **Seal Rocks**, the breeding ground for Australia's largest colony of fur seals. Early December – the peak of the breeding season – is the best time to watch thousands of seals through coin-operated telescopes in the kiosk on the clifftop at Point Grant.

The Mornington Peninsula

The most popular weekend destination for Melburnians is the **Mornington Peninsula ㊱**, which stretches down the eastern side of Port Phillip Bay. The Nepean Highway follows the bayside coast through a whole series of small resorts, all with beaches, some with bathing huts (although not as photogenic as the ones at **Sandringham**, closer to the city, that make it on to all the postcards). **Sorrento**, towards the tip of the peninsula, is the most attractive settlement and proudly offers a bayside beach as well as the more rigorous waters of the ocean. A ferry makes the short trip across the mouth of the bay to Queenscliff.

Further up on the eastern side of the peninsula sits **French Island ㊲**. It used to be a prison farm and retains some of the old buildings. Most of the land is given over to a national park, with farming taking up the remainder, and it's one of the most peaceful places in the state, with hardly any cars. Visitors travel around by bike. Ferries to the island leave from Stony Point, or Cowes on Phillip Island.

Walking on the beach on the Mornington Peninsula near Sorrento.

Sorrento Back Beach in Victoria.

Iconic sign on Eyre Highway, Nullarbor Plain, warning motorists to look out for camels, wombats and kangaroos.

88 km

Pine trees at Lady Bay, just outside Normanville.

SOUTH AUSTRALIA

South Australia is renowned for food, wine and festivals. It is also blessed with a Mediterranean coastal climate, great beaches and awesome stretches of Outback.

F or a state that covers the gamut of Australian landscapes and culture, from the pastures of the coast, with its easy-going capital city, to the endless vineyards of the Barossa Valley, the barren beauty of the Coorong, the harsh grandeur of **the Nullarbor Plain** and the shifting colours of the Flinders Ranges, South Australia, is surprisingly neglected by visitors, whether from overseas or interstate. It's a puzzle. No other Australian state has such a high proportion of classic Outback desert and arable land. This vast hinterland has seen some strange sights, including the secretive rocket and defence system test site at Woomera.

If you love the outdoors, then getting out in the timeless landscapes of the Outback is really something special. You could find yourself enjoying a desert sunset as you bathe in the warm springs at Dalhousie in the far north, sleeping underground in subterranean Coober Pedy, or dealing with feelings of insignificance when you're the only person for kilometres on end. The vast landscapes of South Australia's Outback are steeped in Aboriginal history and culture and are pretty much untouched by the modern world. This is where you can experience the quintessential Australia that you may have seen in popular films such as *Rabbit-Proof Fence* or *The Adventures of Priscilla, Queen of the Desert*.

Glenelg pier at sunset.

Adelaide

Both visitors and locals often refer to Adelaide ❶ as a big country town. Maybe it's the clean air, the friendly locals who smile at you on the street, the views of the green Adelaide Hills from the central business district (CBD), or maybe it's the space; the roads are wide, there are plenty of parks and the suburbs don't suffer from dense high-rise living. Combine this with a cheaper cost of living than the major cities on Australia's east coast, and you've got one very livable city.

Main Attractions

Adelaide
The Barossa Valley
The Flinders Ranges
Lake Eyre
Coober Pedy
The Fleurieu Peninsula
Kangaroo Island
The Yorke Peninsula
Nullarbor National Park

TIP

The City Loop Bus (route 99A and 99C, and 98A and 98C) is a convenient way to see the sights of Adelaide's CBD, and it's free. It operates daily at regular intervals both clockwise and anti-clockwise and takes in many of the city's attractions, including the Central Market and North Terrace. Visit the Adelaide Metro InfoCentre (corner of King William and Currie streets) for timetables.

Situated roughly one-third of the way from Sydney to Perth, this city of 1.32 million people is ideally placed to ignore the rest of the world – which, for most of its history, it did quite happily. Among Australians, Adelaide used to epitomise conservatism with a small 'c'. In the 1970s the city went through a cultural revival under the premiership of Don Dunstan, and for a while Adelaide led Australia on social and cultural reforms. While a legacy of world-class festivals and food and wine still remains, other parts of the Adelaide scene have not quite kept up.

Adelaide is a city that should be savoured slowly. It is possible to rock around the clock in Adelaide, if you know where to go, but it can be done better elsewhere (except at festival time, when no other Australian city can compare). For most of the year, to get the most out of Adelaide you should shift down a gear or two, move at a leisurely pace and meet the City of Churches on its own terms.

One's first impression of Adelaide is its sheer prettiness. This isn't an accident of nature. The city was laid out in a choice location according to the grand design of a British Army engineer, Colonel William Light, who founded the city in 1836. He came with a bevy of free settlers who had the express idea of founding a Utopia in the Antipodes. Sadly, Light – who was suffering from tuberculosis – was given a breakneck two-month deadline to choose a location and survey it. He managed the feat, choosing an inland site that was controversial at first, but his health collapsed; he had to retire, and died soon after.

The City of Light still follows the colonel's original design. From the air, the original city resembles a lopsided figure eight, with residential North Adelaide on one side of the Torrens River and the central business district on the other.

North Adelaide has some of Australia's grandest homes. It was intended as an exclusive enclave for the transplanted English gentry, who shipped out grand pianos and chandeliers from England to put in their colonial salons. Despite the prevailing local opinion that many were the "idiot sons" for

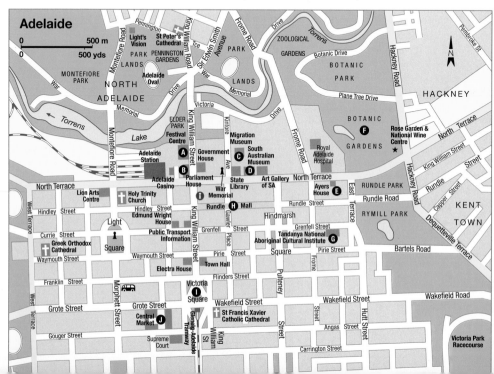

whom there was no room in the old country, the gentry more or less thrived, in spite of itself, on the mineral and agricultural wealth of South Australia.

Also on the north side of the Torrens is historic **Adelaide Oval,** arguably the most beautiful cricket ground in all of Australia, and well worth a visit during the summer cricket season. At the northern end of the Oval stands the neo-Gothic **St Peter's Cathedral,** which has an ornate rose window above the door that depicts stories from South Australia.

South of the river, the central business district was designed for walking; it measures one imperial square mile and is surrounded by extensive parklands, studded with majestic gumtrees, which act as a scenic buffer between the city centre and the suburbs. This leafy moat means it is quite impossible to enter or leave the city without passing through restful greenery. The two halves are connected by King William Street, at 42 metres (138ft) wide, the broadest main street of any Australian capital city – one reason for the lack of traffic jams.

The main intersection in Adelaide is where North Terrace crosses King William Street. Most major attractions are within a few minutes' walk of this intersection.

The **Adelaide Festival Centre** ❶ (tel: 08-8216 8600; www.adelaidefestival centre.com.au) is the oldest multi-purpose performing arts centre in Australia. Its four performance spaces host a variety of events and one-off shows including the nation's premier arts festival. Backstage tours run Tuesdays and Thursdays at 11am. The centre overlooks **Elder Park** by the River Torrens – once a rather unimpressive trickle, but dammed to form an artificial lake. Visitors can choose to take a two-person pedal boat out on the river or cruise to the zoo on board a Popeye cruise boat, an Adelaide tradition that dates back to 1935; a 40km (25-mile) cycle and walking track also runs along the river.

Back on North Terrace is the monumental **Parliament House** ❷, completed in 1939, which is open to visitors (tel: 08-8237 9100; www.parlia ment.sa.gov.au; guided tours Mon–Fri

Adelaide's Festival Centre.

10am and 2pm, when parliament is not sitting; free). Across the road is **Government House** (closed to visitors), the official residence of the governor of South Australia.

The eastern wing of **North Terrace** is the cultural heart of Adelaide, with museums and galleries situated within easy walking distance of one another. Just behind the **State Library**, which houses a tribute to Australian cricket legend Sir Donald Bradman, the **Migration Museum** Ⓒ (tel: 08-8207 7580; www.migration.history.sa.gov.au; Mon–Fri 10am–5pm, Sat–Sun 1–5pm; free) is an excellent place to explore South Australia's cultural diversity.

The **University of Adelaide** could have been transplanted from Oxford, with its ivy-covered walls and dreaming spires. The **South Australian Museum** Ⓓ (tel: 08-8207 7500; www.samuseum.sa.gov.au; daily 10am–5pm; free) houses the world's largest collection of Aboriginal artefacts, as well as an extensive Pacific exhibit and a broad survey of regional natural history (the building can be identified by the huge whale skeletons displayed behind glass

walls). The **Art Gallery of South Australia** (tel: 08-8207 7000; www.artgallery.sa.gov.au; daily 10am–5pm; free) has a renowned collection of 35,000 works. It displays a comprehensive collection of Australian art, including landscapes by Sir Hans Heysen and Aboriginal Western Desert dot paintings, along with tasteful pieces by overseas artists.

North Terrace was once lined with houses like **Ayers House** Ⓔ, the home of Sir Henry Ayers, who contrived to be premier of South Australia seven times – an Australian record – and after whom Ayers Rock (Uluru) was named. The house is now a restaurant and living museum protected by the National Trust (tel: 08-8223 1234; www.ayershousemuseum.org.au; admittance only with tour, every 30 minutes Tue–Fri 10am–4pm, Sat–Sun 1–4pm). The elegant bluestone mansion contains 40 rooms dating from 1846 to the 1870s, and the hand-painted ceilings and ornate chandeliers of the dining room and ballroom are particularly remarkable.

To the north of Ayers House lie the **Botanic Gardens** Ⓕ (tel 08-8222

The Art Gallery of South Australia.

9311; www.botanicgardens.sa.gov.au; daily; guided walks daily 10.30am; free), 16 hectares (40 acres) of manicured lawns, trees, shrubs and lakes, with an impressive rose garden and some exceptional botanical buildings as well, from the old Palm House brought from Germany in 1875 to the extraordinary Bicentennial Conservatory of 1988.

South of Ayers House, in Grenfell Street, is the **Tandanya National Aboriginal Cultural Institute** (tel: 08-8224 3200; www.tandanya.com.au; daily 10am–5pm; free), the city's venue for theatre, dance, talks, demonstrations and constantly changing exhibitions of arts and crafts, representing all aspects of contemporary Aboriginal culture. The Institute has a shop selling native arts and crafts, and a café where visitors can try bush tucker.

The lively, busker-filled **Rundle Mall** ❶ was the country's first traffic-free shopping mall, an idea of former state premier Don Dunstan, who in the 1960s turned Adelaide from a musty provincial centre into "the Athens of the South". He also originated the Festival Centre and introduced some of the most progressive state laws in Australia – laws to recognise Aboriginal land rights, decriminalise homosexuality and guarantee equal opportunity. Dunstan shocked staid old Adelaide, and much of Australia besides (on one occasion, he caused a media frenzy when he wore what were described as "pink hot-pants" to parliament).

In the centre of the city's square mile, King William Street opens out into **Victoria Square** ❶, which is where you can catch the tram to the beach-side suburb of Glenelg. Just to the west is Adelaide's **Central Market** ❶ (tel: 08-8203 7494; www.adelaidecentralmarket.com.au; Tue 7am–5.30pm, Wed–Thu 9am–5.30pm, Fri 7am–9pm, Sat 7am–3pm) – easily one of the most colourful in Australia. A giant covered area packed with more than 200 shops and stalls, it sells cheap fruit, vegetables, cheeses, meats, spices and a variety of esoteric imported foods. But the main attraction is the wealth of local produce that South Australia is famed for, from Maggie Beer's pâtés and Adelaide Hills cheeses, to gourmet delights from the Barossa Valley and fresh local fish such as the delicately sweet King George whiting. There are plenty of tastings to be had as well. It's no wonder this is one of Adelaide's most popular attractions for both locals and visitors. There are also stalls selling books, crafts, jewellery and clothing, alongside cafés and inexpensive eateries.

The market encompasses Adelaide's **Chinatown,** which spills out into Gouger Street, one of the city's main restaurant strips. The others include O'Connell Street (North Adelaide), Rundle Street (East End) and Hindley Street (West End). Between them, they provide a fine choice of Chinese, Indian, Turkish, Italian, Malaysian, Japanese, Greek, African, Vietnamese, Russian, Lebanese, Thai and Australian eateries. Adelaide reputedly has more restaurants per capita than any other Australian city; it would be a shame not to visit as many as possible during your trip.

> **FACT**
>
> The Victorian cast-iron fountain outside Adelaide Arcade used to sit at the intersection of Rundle Mall and Gawler Place. When state Premier Don Dunstan opened the mall in 1976 the fountain flowed with champagne, much to the delight of 10,000 onlookers. It was moved to its current location in 1996.

Fresh blooms at the Adelaide Botanic Gardens.

Festival Frenzy

Sydney, Melbourne and Perth all have their arts festivals, but none compares in size, prestige or sheer excitement to Adelaide's.

The Adelaide Festival of Arts is held in March on even-numbered years and trades on the city's natural advantages. Few places in the world have such an extraordinary range of performance spaces, from the gleaming Festival Centre to the many outdoor amphitheatres and numerous intimate loft spaces. The weather is nigh perfect, with dry, hot days and clear, star-studded nights – and you can walk to every venue within about 15 minutes.

The festival operates on several levels. The official festival lures the high-profile international acts, and kicks off with free weekend concerts in Rundle Park, followed by firework displays. Tickets to the official shows are very reasonable compared with the prices charged in Sydney and Melbourne, and there is usually a string of free events.

At the same time, the Adelaide Fringe is for lesser-known performers and artists. It is second

Adelaide Fringe Festival.

in size only to Edinburgh's annual shindig: literally thousands of acts arrive from all over Australia, Europe and North America. Its popularity has seen it become an annual event. The chaotic, organic nature of the Fringe is what gives Adelaide its buzz. The focus tends to be around the bars and restaurants of Rundle Street East, where the festivities continue until dawn at the Fringe Club, while buskers and performers spread throughout the city.

With nearly 500 events in the programme, every spare corner of indoor space is devoted to some art exhibition, and every stretch outdoors to a site-specific installation. By any standards, it's a remarkable event.

At the same time as the Festival of Arts, Adelaide's Writers' Week lures the literary elite from around the globe. It is entirely free, with readings by famous authors and book launches held in the Pioneer Women's Memorial Gardens on King William Street, across from the Festival Centre.

Although nothing quite matches the festival for action, things are not too quiet in South Australia for the rest of the time. Every March, Adelaide hosts an enormous World Music Festival, known as Womadelaide, in Botanical Park. Tasting Australia is a huge biennial food and wine festival held in the city every odd-numbered year in October.

The Adelaide Festival of Ideas is a recent addition, taking place every odd-numbered year during the winter. It attracts some of the world's leading writers and thinkers such as ex-prime ministers, journalists, political commentators and university professors. A typical festival could touch on such varied topics as the Middle East, globalisation, cloning, theology or even the existence of extraterrestrials.

The Barossa Valley hosts a music festival every October. Most of the concerts are classical and held in Lutheran churches – although the accompanying indulgent meals and fine wines might well have appalled the region's founding fathers.

In early April in odd-numbered years, the Barossa Vintage Festival is a thanksgiving celebration for the region's grape harvest. The seven-day event, based in Tanunda, includes lavish tastings, grape picking and treading contests, and a vintage fair.

Between May and October most wine-producing areas hold food, wine and music festivals, the most notable being the Clare Valley Gourmet Weekend in May; McLaren Vale holds several, including the Sea and Vines festival in June.

Hills and beaches

Cosmopolitan though it can be, Adelaide has never lost that country-town feeling. You can drive across the city in half an hour, and you can be in beautiful countryside in a fraction of the time it takes to leave the other major cities in Australia. Take any one of a dozen roads up into the **Adelaide Hills** and you can happily get lost in leafy, winding laneways. The hills are littered with small commuter suburbs such as **Blackwood, Aldgate** and **Crafers,** some of which are strikingly pretty. There are pubs with hilltop views and restaurants like Windy Point, where you can dine overlooking the expanse of the city's twinkling lights.

Adelaide Hills offers something for most tastes, with bushwalks, markets, wineries, award-winning restaurants, wildlife parks and Birdwood's **National Motor Museum** (tel: 08-8568 4000; http://history.sa.gov.au; daily 10am–5pm), which is the largest of its kind in Australia. You can easily spend a day lapping up the pretty German town of **Hahndorf** and its surroundings, a favourite weekend excursion for Adelaideans.

Another Adelaide ritual is to take the Glenelg tram from the city centre to the beach. The ride takes about 20 minutes and, while **Glenelg** has seen better times and now suffers from overdevelopment, the beach is wide, the sand is white and the site is wonderful.

If Glenelg is too crowded for your liking, Adelaide is blessed with a coastline border fringed by spacious, clean beaches that stretch for many kilometres. **Henley Beach** is a popular, more low-key option, and after a dip or a walk you can dine on some fish and chips at the grassy, beach-side square.

If you like to feel the warm sun all over your skin, drive down Main South Road (A13) for 20km (12 miles) until you see the turn-off on the right to **Maslin Beach.** It's an official nudist beach and its backdrop of sandstone cliffs makes it one of the most beautiful seaside settings in the state. Maslin is friendly and family-oriented, but be warned: the gulf waters are fed by the Southern Ocean and the water can be brisk.

The Barossa Valley

Adelaide sits amid the country's greatest wine regions, of which the **Barossa Valley ❷** is easily the most famous. It was named in 1837 by Colonel William Light, Adelaide's far-sighted planner, because it reminded him of the countryside in Spain where he fought against Napoleon's army in the Battle of Barossa. The valley was settled in the 1840s by Germans seeking freedom to worship in the Lutheran Church. They brought the first vine cuttings with them, and, more than 150 years later, wine drinkers worldwide thank them for their forethought.

The Barossa is accessible either via the direct route from Adelaide through Gawler, or you can choose the scenic route via the Adelaide Hills, which takes you through Cudlee Creek, onto Williamstown and then **Lyndoch**, which is the first major town in the valley. The enjoyable drive takes you past some of the city's reservoirs. Just

FACT

Among the 400 vehicles in the National Motor Museum is an 1899 Shearer, built in Mannum, South Australia: the steam-powered car is the oldest Australian-built vehicle still running. Also on display is a Talbot which completed an epic 51-day journey from Adelaide to Darwin in 1908.

The covered market in Adelaide is great for shopping regardless of the weather.

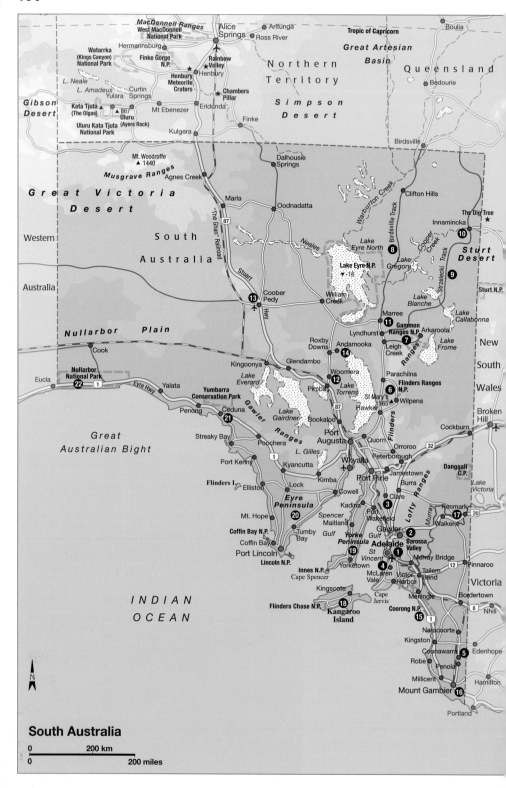

South Australia

0   200 km

0   200 miles

beyond Williamstown, stop at the **Whispering Wall**, which is not only an engineering feat but an acoustic phenomenon. The wall is curved in such a way that whisperings at one end can be clearly heard at the other, which is 140 metres (460ft) away.

From Lyndoch in its forest setting, the Barossa Way continues on to **Tanunda**, the most distinctly German town in the region, which is renowned for its fine butchers and bakeries. Following the road to Nuriootpa, you can take a detour to the left down Samuel Road to visit **Maggie Beer's Farm Shop** (tel: 08-8562 4477; www.maggiebeer.com.au; daily 10.30am–5pm). Maggie is one of Australia's leading celebrity cooks and a Barossa icon – at her farm shop you can catch a daily cooking demonstration at 2pm or pick up some picnic supplies.

Back on the road it's not far to **Nuriootpa**, the commercial centre of the Barossa Valley. Keep following the road to Angaston, where the popular Barossa Farmers' Market takes place each Saturday morning.

Clare

Although the Barossa is the best-known wine-producing area in Australia, it is only one of five major wine regions within easy driving distance of Adelaide. **Clare ❸** is the centre of the wine area of the Clare Valley/Watervale region about 130km (80 miles) north of Adelaide. Jesuit priests fleeing persecution in Silesia settled in the Clare Valley in 1848 and began making sacramental wines at Sevenhill Cellars. Today there are more than 20 wineries and 40 cellar doors in a 25km (15-mile) strip. The region is famed for its Rieslings, but you will also find some fine Shiraz and Cabernet Sauvignon. Many are boutique wineries whose labels are taking their place on some of the world's finest wine lists.

Some of the more renowned names in the business include Neil Paulett, Jeffrey Grosset, David O'Leary, Neil Pike and Mount Horrocks.

More than 60 cellar doors are dotted throughout **McLaren Vale ❹**, 42km (26 miles) south of Adelaide. Cartographers battle to fit all the vineyards on the map; they read like a wine-lover's roll of honour: Geoff Merrill, Hardy's Tintara and Wirra Wirra. This region is renowned for its reds, although there is plenty on offer to please lovers of white wine, including some fine Sauvignon Blanc and Viognier.

In the southeast of the state, on the way between Adelaide and Melbourne, the vineyards of the **Coonawarra ❺** area are justly famed for their reds. Vineyards at **Keppoch** and **Padthaway** are becoming equally well known. **Padthaway Estate Homestead,** now an exclusive hotel, is an imposing stone mansion in an oasis of green English-style gardens. The property was taken up as a sheep run in 1847, and the homestead was built in 1882. Today a number of vineyards spread over the acres where sheep once grazed.

The orchards of the **Riverland**, on the Murray River, produce nearly half of the state's wine grapes. The specialities of the region are brandies and

The wet weather of 2011 caused problems with the harvest.

The Barossa Valley wine region.

TIP

Bundaleer Forest Weekend, held in March, is a music festival where artists perform outdoors in the forest. Hearing the Adelaide Symphony Orchestra while sitting on hay bales at sunset is a memorable experience. The forest is 10km (6 miles) south of James-town and about 2.5 hours' drive from Adelaide. www.bundaleer festival.com.au.

fortified dessert wines. **Berri Estates** is the largest winery in the country, while smaller wineries include Bon-neyview Wines at Barmera.

The most famous is **Banrock Station** near Kingston-on-Murray, which is well worth a visit. Their eco-friendly philosophy is reflected in the design of the visitor centre, which has information on how the winery helps to fund environmental programmes. The winery overlooks restored wetlands.

North from Adelaide

If you're not too keen on driving the vast distances of the Outback on your own, then you could choose to watch the scenery glide past you from the comfort of the **Ghan**, one of the world's great rail journeys. It links Adelaide to the Red Centre, before continuing on to the tropical Top End. The Ghan gets its name from the Afghan camel traders who pioneered travel from Adelaide to the Red Centre.

The Flinders Ranges

The **Flinders Ranges** extend from near Port Pirie, where Mount Remarkable

(975 metres/3,150ft) is the first major peak, to past Mount Painter in the desert and salt lakes to the north. At the top of the **Spencer Gulf**, the road turns away from the ocean and heads into the arid heart of the continent. Here lies **Port Augusta** which, with Port Pirie and Whyalla, forms the basis of South Australia's industrial heart, known as the Iron Triangle. From Port Augusta, the road runs northeast through **Quorn,** then on to **Hawker,** the nearest township to the northern Flinders Ranges. You can travel between Port Augusta and Quorn on the steam locomotive of the historic **Pichi Richi Railway**, which operates on the oldest section of the Ghan track.

By a fortunate coincidence, the most spectacular feature of the Flinders Ranges is also the most accessible. **Wilpena Pound** at the southern end of the **Flinders Ranges National Park ❻** is a raised valley surrounded by quartzite hills. St Mary's Peak is the highest point in the ranges at 1,165 metres (3,758ft).

The only way into Wilpena Pound is on foot: there are a number of hikes that begin at the visitor centre. By comparison with the thin, rocky soil and arid landscape outside, the pound floor is richly vegetated. In fact, Wilpena Pound attracts considerably more rainfall than neighbouring regions. Although the exterior walls of the pound are steep, the inside slopes are relatively gentle. The six-hour return hike up St Mary's Peak rewards you with breathtaking views. Although Wilpena Pound looks like a crater, it is the result of folding rocks, not the impact of a celestial object.

If Wilpena is your only destination in the Flinders, it is worth your while taking the time to detour north past the natural rock feature known as the Great Wall of China, then through **Parachilna Pass** to join the main Leigh Creek Road before heading south. Coming out of the pass, you emerge onto plains that typify central Australia; from here, as you look back,

VALE OF CHEERS

It takes just over an hour to drive to the Barossa Valley, which lies 60km (35 miles) northeast of Adelaide. Along the way you will pass the actual Jacob's Creek, where the famous winery gets its name from, and then row after row of vines belonging to one of the more than 60 local wineries which produce more top-of-the-range wines than anywhere else in Australia, and include some of the most famous names in the business – **Peter Lehmann**, **Yalumba**, **Grant Burge**, **Penfolds** and **Wolf Blass**.

Alongside these giants can be found numerous boutique producers who grow, not for quantity, but to make the highest-quality wine possible from their venerable vines. Nearly all the wineries have tasting and sale rooms, and many have barbecue and picnic areas as well as restaurants and cafés. Like a well-stocked cellar built up over many years, the wineries are spread the length of the Barossa Valley Way, which links most of the main towns in the region. Many Barossa wineries not only produce excellent vintages but also have magnificent grounds and buildings, like the palm groves at **Seppeltsfield**, picturesque **Chateau Yaldara**, and the two-storey historic blue-marble buildings at **Yalumba**. **Bethany Winery** has panoramic views of the valley, while **Rockford Wines** is one of the last bastions of traditional basket-press wine-making.

the open lip of Wilpena Pound clearly shows its strikingly symmetrical form.

The northern end of the Flinders Ranges more closely resembles the other mountains of central Australia than any other features in the south. The base for exploring the **Gammon Ranges National Park** ⑦ is **Arkaroola**, a small settlement geared to the needs of tourists. Gorges and valleys filled with wild flowers and endless variations on the recurrent themes of rock, eucalyptus and folded hills prevail.

Desert tracks

The rugged wilderness and abundant wildlife of the northern Flinders can be easily explored by either foot or four-wheel-drive vehicle. There are several good vantage points where you can see the Flinders Ranges stretching south for many kilometres.

The roads north into the Outback – the **Birdsville Track** ⑧ or the **Strzelecki Track** ⑨ – are rough adventures, aiming towards the distant Queensland border. Not everyone likes the desert, but those who do will find the continual but almost imperceptible changes in scenery endlessly fascinating.

Along the Strzelecki Track, the last stop in South Australia is **Innamincka** ⑩, a settlement with a population of fewer than 200 people where the only two buildings of note are the general store and the pub. Locals will be able to direct you to the Dig Tree, a few kilometres to the east on the border with Queensland, which marks the spot where a supply of food was left for starving members of the ill-fated transcontinental expedition led by Burke and Wills. Camping by Coopers Creek after a few beers at the pub is now the embodiment of the Outback.

The Birdsville Track is deeply entrenched in the Australian psyche. It was developed as a route for driving cattle from western Queensland to Marree, SA, where they could be loaded onto railcars heading south. **Marree** ⑪ itself was a trading depot for the Afghan camel drivers who opened up much of central Australia. The Oodnadatta Track northwest from Marree follows part of the original route that these Afghan traders took.

FACT

In Aboriginal Dreamtime (mythology) the encircling walls of Wilpena Pound (Ikara) were created by two snakes who came to rest here after eating so many participants at an initiation ceremony that they couldn't move. St Mary's Peak is seen as the head of one of them, and the local Aboriginal people prefer visitors not to climb it.

Chateau Tanunda.

TIP

You should not attempt the Strzelecki, Oodnadatta or Birdsville tracks without extensive Outback driving experience, a four-wheel-drive vehicle and a lot of preparation. The Strzelecki Track has no petrol, water or supply station for 500km (300 miles) between Lyndhurst and Innamincka. All the tracks are liable to close after heavy rain.

The track skirts around the southern end of **Lake Eyre**, which is Australia's largest lake when there is water in it – a relatively rare event, although the last few years have seen several metres of water in it at various times.

At 15 metres (50ft) below sea level, Lake Eyre is the lowest part of the continent, a bowl that collects the monsoon rains of northern Australia. The lake can be accessed at William Creek, whose pub bursts with character.

Dalhousie Springs is an Outback oasis and is worth a 180km (112-mile) detour (one-way) off the track north of Oodnadatta.

Driving this far north into the Outback of South Australia you will eventually cross the **Dingo Fence**, which was completed in 1885 to keep dingoes to the north and out of the fertile sheep country of southeast Australia. It is the world's longest fence, stretching 5,320km (3,300 miles) from the Great Australian Bight in South Australia to southeast Queensland. It's questionable whether it has been successful – dingoes can still be found in the southern states – while

it is thought feral animal populations in the south are booming due to lack of competition from native predators.

On the sealed Stuart Highway, which stretches 1,370km (850 miles) from Port Augusta to Alice Springs, the tiny settlement of **Pimba** marks the turn-off to **Woomera** ⓬, the rocket and research base that was only opened to the public in 1982. A visitor centre (tel: 1300-761 620; daily, Mar–Nov 9am–5pm, Dec–Feb 10am–2pm; free) has displays detailing the early days of rocketry. (Woomera is the Aboriginal term for spear launcher.) The Woomera Prohibited Area is adjacent to the town and spans 127,000 sq km (49,000 sq miles) – about the size of England. British nuclear tests took place at Maralinga, at the western reaches of the area, during the 1950s.

Coober Pedy

Coober Pedy ⓭, halfway to Northern Territory on the Stuart Highway, is the best-known town in Outback South Australia. This is the world's largest opal field (for white opals), where the relentlessly hot climate (sometimes

Mine tunnel in Coober Pedy.

soaring to 50°C/122°F or more) has forced the inhabitants to live underground in dugouts.

At first glance, the town looks like a hard-hit battlefield. The almost treeless terrain consists of hundreds of mounds of upturned earth and abandoned mines, where noodlers or fossickers have rummaged through the landscape in search of precious gems. If you should arrive during one of the area's regular dust storms, you could be excused for believing the apocalypse was nigh. But beneath the surface there are homes, shops, restaurants and even churches. There is an underground hotel, too, though suitable only for non-claustrophobics. Visitors should note the beautiful natural patterns in the bare clay walls (and the lack of windows, compensated for by good air conditioning).

Unfortunately, the rapid increase in traffic aiming for the centre has rubbed off some of Coober Pedy's rough edges. For a more unique experience of an Outback opal town, venture off the beaten track to **Andamooka** ⓮, due north from Woomera, where fewer than 500 people dwell, but be aware that any rainfall can quickly leave you stranded. The striking ochre-coloured hills of the **Breakaways** lie 33km (20 miles) north of Coober Pedy. This arid landscape was an inland sea 70 million years ago.

Coorong and beyond

To the southeast of Adelaide, around the mouth of the Murray River, lies an indefinable maze of sandbanks and estuaries. This is the **Coorong National Park** ⓯, a haven for numerous species of waterfowl. The main features are the sand dunes of the **Younghusband Peninsula**, which separates the shallow waters of the **Coorong** from the Southern Ocean, and the Coorong itself (*karangh* or "*narrow neck*" to the Aborigines), a long, thin neck of water stretching 120km (75 miles) from Lake Alexandrina and Lake Albert at the mouth of the Murray River to the saltpans and marshy ponds at the southern end.

If you lack a four-wheel-drive vehicle, it's a half-hour walk across the dunes to the ocean beach, an endless area of golden sand left mostly to the seagulls, oystercatchers, pelicans and only the occasional angler. A great number and variety of waterfowl feed on the water plants in the lagoons and drink at the freshwater soaks. For thousands of years Ngarrindjeri Aboriginal people lived here, netting fish in the lagoons, collecting cockles on the beach and fashioning reeds into rafts and baskets. You may come across their ancient shell middens in the sand dunes – you should not interfere with them in any way, out of respect for the Aboriginal culture.

To explore the Coorong fully, you need time, preferably a boat and, in the heat of summer near the drying salt flats, a strong nose. The spirit of the Coorong was well captured in the 1976 film *Storm Boy*.

South of the Coorong is a series of seaside holiday resorts, with this part of the coast renowned for its shellfish. At **Kingston** you can buy delicious fresh lobster at the jetty. In **Robe,** once

TIP

If you decide to explore the Outback, make sure you are thoroughly prepared and do your research, because once out there you are quite often on your own. Permits are required to visit most desert national parks and you can purchase these at major Outback towns.

Australia produces 97 percent of the world's opal, from the common, milky opal to the rare and valuable black opal.

TIP

There are several paddlewheel vessels (the *Proud Mary, Murray Princess* and *Murray River Queen*) running five- and six-day cruises along the Murray River. Houseboats can be hired at Renmark, Loxton, Berri and Waikerie – you just have to be over 18 and hold a driver's licence. More details: www.murrayriver.com.au.

an important port and retaining much of its early character, the Caledonian Inn, licensed in 1858, still caters to weary travellers.

A stone near the harbour commemorates the thousands of Chinese who disembarked here in the 1850s and tramped hundreds of kilometres through the bush to the Victorian gold diggings, to avoid the £10 arrival tax imposed at Victorian ports. Robe tends to be full in school holidays and overflows at Christmas and on New Year's Eve, but is a lovely, peaceful spot for the rest of the year.

Mount Gambier ⑯ nestles on the side of a 5,000-year-old extinct volcano. Within its rim lie three craters, four lakes, and the mystery of why the largest, **Blue Lake,** turns from winter grey to brilliant azure from November through to March. Outside the city are the Tantanoola limestone caves.

Further north, the **Naracoorte Caves** (tel: 08-8760 1210; www.naracoortecaves. sa.gov.au; various tours daily between 9am and 5pm) contain not only beautiful limestone formations but also a fossil cave where the traces of many extinct animals are being unearthed. They include giant kangaroos, a wombat the size of a hippopotamus and a marsupial lion.

The Riverland

Renmark ⑰, northeast of Adelaide near the Victorian border, was the birthplace of the Murray River irrigation area in 1887. The drive along the **Sturt Highway** roughly follows the river through extensive orchards and vineyards supported by the Murray's waters. Half of South Australia's grapes and 90 percent of the state's stone fruit and citrus are grown in the Riverland. River transport is prominent here, too, with the paddleboat days remembered in the old steamer moored as a floating museum.

Barmera and nearby **Lake Bonney** are the recreational heart of the Riverland. Lake Bonney attracts a wide variety of watercraft: mainly windsurfers and sailing boats. In 1964, the pace increased considerably when Sir Donald Campbell used the lake for an (unsuccessful) attempt on the world water-speed record.

The Remarkable Rocks are a granite formation in Flinders Chase National Park.

The air currents from the plains around **Waikerie** have made it one of the world's leading soaring centres. In summer, when sun-heated air rises in powerful thermals, gliders can be seen throughout the region. For flights, check with the Waikerie International Soaring Centre (tel: 0429-413 570; www.waikeriaglidingclub.com.au). Waikerie's Aboriginal name means *many wings*, after the giant moth *wei kari*. It could easily refer to the abundant birdlife in the nearby Hart Lagoon.

Kangaroo Island

The deeply indented coastline of South Australia has made a set of natural divisions, each with its own appeal. The **Fleurieu Peninsula**, south of Adelaide beyond McLaren Vale, is a popular holiday area for South Australians. **Victor Harbour** is the main resort – its hotels, motels and guesthouses are often full during school holidays. Among Victor's attractions are the little penguin colony on **Granite Island** (connected to the mainland by a causeway with a horse-drawn tram), an adventure park and winter whale-watching trips.

Cape Jervis, at the end of the peninsula, is the stepping-off point for **Kangaroo Island** ⓲. Until the end of the last ice age, 9,000 years ago, the island (Australia's third largest, after Tasmania and Melville) wasn't separated from the mainland. Even now, the finger of the Dudley Peninsula on the island appears to be reaching towards Cape Jervis. The island's main towns are **Kingscote, American River** and **Penneshaw.** Fishing, exploring the scenery and observing wildlife are the main activities for visitors. Seals, sea lions, penguins, echidnas, kangaroos, emus and koalas all live here in abundance. Nightly processions of penguins can be seen on the beaches around Kingscote and Penneshaw, and you can walk among one of Australia's largest colonies of sea lions at Seal Bay. At the large **Flinders Chase National Park,** the only enclosures are to keep the persistent wildlife away from picnickers.

From the gentle sandy beaches of the **Dudley Peninsula** to the pounding surf on the headland of **Cape du Couedic, Kangaroo Island** has a wide range of terrains. The lighthouse at the cape was built in 1906 as an essential navigation aid for coastal shipping. Near it lie two unusual features: **Remarkable Rocks,** a collection of granite boulders worn by the sea into fantastical shapes, some resembling animals and birds, others akin to Henry Moore sculptures; and **Admirals Arch,** a 20-metre (64ft) maw rimmed with fang-like blackened stalactites, framing a maelstrom of surging waves. These are primeval sites at odds with the placid nature of other parts of the island.

Yorke Peninsula

A loop of picturesque towns, **Yorke Peninsula** ⓳ takes in the east-coast port of **Ardrossan** with its attractive water access and, down the coast, **Edithburgh** with its splendid clifftop views and its famous old pub, the Troubridge Hotel. The town's cemetery includes the graves of the 34 victims of the 1909 wreck of the *Clan Ranald*. The scenic route south

Kangaroo Island is full of playful creatures, large and small.

FACT

One transport firm made the Guinness Book of Records in 1999 by hauling 45 trailers, weighing more than 600 tonnes, for 8km (5 miles) using one truck. In real life, few road trains haul more than six trailers in the Outback, and these will be transferred to individual trucks before they reach an urban destination.

Playful seals on the beach.

to Yorketown is a magical drive offering great coastal views of offshore reefs popular with local scuba divers. **Yorketown** is a small farming town surrounded by a series of salt lakes.

Towards the southwestern extremity of the peninsula is the great horseshoe-shaped sweep of **Pondalowie Bay**. Located in a national park, the bay is a fishing, diving and surfing paradise made even more appealing by its remoteness. A full seven hours' drive from Adelaide, it is a great place to camp and enjoy the beauty of the Southern Ocean coastline.

The ports of the Yorke Peninsula's west coast indicate its importance as a grain-growing area. It was from places such as **Port Victoria** that great windjammers left to race back to Britain and Europe with their cargoes of grain. Farming and fishing still play important parts in the peninsula's modest economy, but mineral wealth contributed a colourful chapter to the area's history. The discovery of copper at **Kadina** and **Moonta** led to the mass migration of Cornish miners and their families from southwest England.

Along with the port town of **Wallaroo,** the two hamlets grew as solid Cornish communities with strong Methodist influences, catering to about 30,000 people. The boom period has long passed, but the contribution of the Cornish Cousin Jacks and Cousin Jills, as they were known, remains an indelible part of the peninsula's heritage.

The long road west

Of all the great Australian highway routes, the 2,000km (1,240-mile)-plus stretch from Adelaide to Perth is the one most frequently flaunted, with "We crossed the Nullarbor" stickers displayed on car and van windows. However, the road itself is no longer the challenge – rather it's the cost of fuel to propel a vehicle across several thousand kilometres of nothingness.

On the drive west towards Perth, the **Eyre Peninsula** ⑳ and the attractive township of Port Lincoln exert strong pressure to detour. Explorer John Eyre ploughed through the area in 1841 and, although burnt almost to a frazzle by the harshness of the hinterland, he was impressed by the spectacular coastline. The peninsula has its own historical charm in places like **Coffin Bay,** famous for its delicious oysters, and **Anxious Bay. Port Lincoln** itself has a large tuna-fishing fleet, cruises, and great white shark diving tours. Some of the shark scenes from the film *Jaws* were filmed here.

At **Point Labatt,** on the Flinders Highway, is the only seal colony on mainland Australia. If you would like to get a little closer, dolphin and sealion swimming tours depart from Baird Bay in the warmer months.

Ceduna ㉑ is the centre of a large pastoral industry, but surfers from both east and west coasts know it as a favoured stopping-off place in their pursuit of waves. It's blessed with golden beaches; Cactus is the break surfers speak of with the greatest reverence. But be warned, great white sharks prowl this coastline and shark attacks have occurred. The navigator Matthew Flinders named

nearby **Denial Bay** when he realised it was not the access to the elusive inland sea that was rumoured to exist in central Australia.

Inland from Ceduna is the 106,000-hectare (262,000-acre) tract of **Yumbarra Conservation Park.** Its sandy ridges and granite outcrops appear inhospitable, but the local wildlife (particularly emus and kangaroos) find it ideal. In winter the top of the bight is also a favourite spot for whale-watching. Head of the Bight whale-watching centre (tel: 08-8625 6201; www.headof bight.com.au; whale season June–Oct daily 8am–5pm), 25km (15 miles) east of Nullarbor, offers a great opportunity to get out of the car and stretch your legs. Southern right whales are regularly seen from the spectacular cliffs here during the winter.

Ceduna is South Australia's most westerly town. From here to Norseman in Western Australia it is 1,232km (765 miles), and any other point shown on a map along the way is nothing more than a water storage base or a fuel station. That's what makes crossing the Nullarbor Plain such an intimidating prospect. There are no trees on the plain (nullarbor is Latin for *no tree*), as the limestone is unable to hold rainwater.

The Nullarbor Plain

The **Eyre Highway** hugs the coastline on its long route to Western Australia, passing through **Nullarbor National Park ㉒** during the last stretch of South Australia. For the earlier pioneers, the coastal route was much harsher than the alternative of the interior. While vast stretches of the coastline are devoid of fresh water, limestone sinkholes in the plain might have provided ready supplies.

The desert is also traversed by the Trans-Australian railway, one of the world's great rail journeys, with one straight section that stretches 479km (298 miles), making it the world's longest. It is part of the Indian–Pacific passenger rail service that links Sydney to Perth.

A lasting impression of the coastline of the **Great Australian Bight** is the sheer cliff formations that make the coastal strip near the Western Australian border so spectacular.

TIP

Overtaking a road train requires strong nerves, and you shouldn't even try on dirt roads. Courteous truckers will blink their right-turn indicator to show that the road ahead is clear.

Limestone bunda cliffs, Nullarbor National Park.

Aerial view of Hardy Reef.

Mossman Gorge.

QUEENSLAND

This is Australia's holiday state and the most visited destination after Sydney. Its major attractions include magnificent beaches, the Great Barrier Reef and unique rainforest.

Queensland represents a sizeable chunk of Australia. At more than 2,000km (1,240 miles) from top to bottom and 1,450km (900 miles) at its widest point, its 1.73 million sq km (667,000 sq mile) area could happily contain an assortment of European countries or a few hefty American states. It is unsurprising then that within its confines can be found such a range of terrain: unsullied tropical rainforest, broad expanses of dusty cattle-grazing country – indistinguishable from desert at times – the ragged peaks of the Great Dividing Range, rolling hills and, to cap it all, some great beaches. Plus, tethered along the eastern shoreline, just beyond a scattering of achingly beautiful desert islands, is one of the world's natural wonders, the Great Barrier Reef.

Inward migration

Queensland's proud claim to be the Sunshine State has been readily accepted not just by overseas visitors but also by other Australians, who have been flocking to the state for their holidays for years. When winter arrives many dwellers in the cooler southern states hanker for a spot on one of the endless golden beaches on Queensland's vast coastline. And once they've tasted paradise it's a short step to opt for the sea change – the exchange of the perceived drab

urban existence for the Technicolor joys of perpetual summer. Some move at once, others wait for retirement. Either way, a pattern of migration has long been established. However, it has accelerated to the point where more than 200 people a day are now resettling in the sun, although house prices may slow that down.

Incomers can be found all along the coast, but the clearest concrete (in every sense of the word) evidence is to be found in the developments to the north and south of Brisbane,

Main Attractions

Brisbane
Sunshine Coast
Fraser Island
Carnarvon Gorge
Cairns
The Atherton Tableland
Cape York Peninsula
Lawn Hill Gorge
Mount Isa
Longreach

The Eternal Flame of Remembrance burns for all fallen ANZAC soldiers.

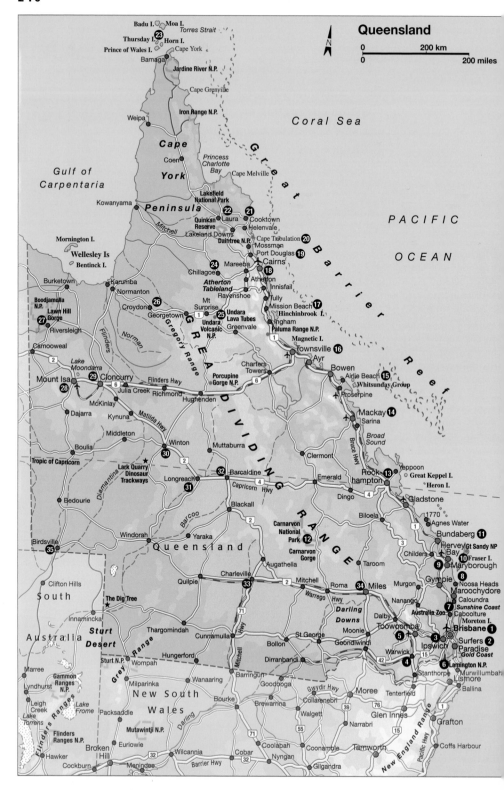

Queensland

0   200 km
0   200 miles

Badu I.   Moa I.
Torres Strait
(23)
Thursday I.   Horn I.
Prince of Wales I.   Cape York
Bamaga
Jardine River N.P.

Cape Grenville

Weipa
Iron Range N.P.

Coral Sea

Cape
Coen
Princess
Charlotte
Bay   Cape Melville
York
Lakefield
National Park
Kowanyama
Peninsula   (22)   (21)
Quinkan   Laura   Cooktown
Reserve   Helenvale
Lakeland Downs
Daintree N.P.   Cape Tribulation   (20)
Mossman
Port Douglas   (19)
Chillagoe   (24)   Mareeba   Cairns   (18)
Atherton   Atherton
Tableland
Mt   Innisfail
Surprise   Ravenshoe
(25)   Tully
Undara   Mission Beach   (17)
Undara   Lava Tubes   Hinchinbrook I.
Volcanic   Greenvale   Ingham
N.P.   Paluma Range N.P.
Magnetic I.
Townsville   (16)
Ayr

PACIFIC

OCEAN

Gulf of
Carpentaria

Mornington I.
Wellesley Is
Bentinck I.

Burketown   Karumba
Normanton
Boodjamulla
N.P.
Lawn Hill
Gorge
(27)
Riversleigh
Camooweal
Lake
Moondarra
Mount Isa   (29)   Cloncurry   Flinders Hwy
(28)   Julia Creek
McKinlay   Richmond   Hughenden
Dajarra
Kynuna   Matilda Hwy
Middleton
Boulia   Winton   Muttaburra
Tropic of Capricorn
Lark Quarry
Dinosaur   (30)
Trackways   Longreach   (32)   Barcaldine
(31)   Capricorn   Hwy
Bedourie   Emerald
Blackall
Birdsville   Windorah   Yaraka
(35)
Queensland   Augathella
Charleville
Clifton Hills   Quilpie   (33)   Mitchell   Roma   (34)   Miles
South   The Dig Tree   Warrego   Hwy
Innamincka
Australia   Sturt   Thargomindah   Cunnamulla   St George
Desert   Range
Hungerford   Bollon   Goondiwindi
Marree   Sturt N.P.   Wompah   Dirranbandi
Gammon   Milparinka   Wanaaring   Barringun
Lyndhurst   Ranges   Goodooga   Gwydir Hwy   Moree
N.P.   New South
Leigh   Lake   Bourke   Brewarrina   Collarenebri
Creek   Frome   Packsaddle   Wales   Walgett
Lake   Darling
Torrens   Flinders
Ranges N.P.   Mutawintji N.P.   (71)   (55)   Narrabri
Euriowie   Coolabah   Coonamble
Broken   Wilcannia   Cobar
Hawker   Hill   (32)   (32)   Nyngan
Cockburn   Menindee   Barrier Hwy   Gilgandra

Great
Barrier
Reef

Charters
Towers   Bowen
Porcupine   (6)   Airlie Beach   (15)
Gorge N.P.   Whitsunday Group
Proserpine
Mackay   (14)
Sarina
Broad
Sound
Clermont
Bruce   Hwy
Emerald   Rock-   (13)
hampton   Great Keppel I.
Dingo   (4)   Yeppoon
Heron I.
Gladstone
1770
Biloela   Agnes Water
Bundaberg   (11)
Carnarvon   Hervey   Gt Sandy NP
National   (12)   Childers   Bay   (10)   Fraser I.
Park   Carnarvon   (9)   Maryborough
Gorge   Taroom   Gympie   (8)
Murgon   Noosa Heads
Nanango   Maroochydore
Darling   Caloundra
Dalby   Australia Zoo   (7)   Sunshine Coast
Downs   Caboolture
Moonie   Toowoomba   Moreton I.
(5)   (3)   Brisbane   (1)
Warwick   15   Surfers   (2)
(4)   Ipswich   Paradise
42   Gold Coast
Stanthorpe   (6)   Lamington N.P.
Murwillumbah
Tenterfield   Lismore
Ballina
39   76
Glen Innes
15   Grafton
New England   Range
Tamworth   Coffs Harbour

Mitchell
Flinders
Norman
Gregory Range
GREAT
DIVIDING
RANGE
Diamantina
Barcoo
Grey   Range
Mitchell
Darling
Pacific   Hwy

on the Sunshine and Gold coasts. Queenslanders tend to take a laconic approach to the arrival of so many incomers from the southern states, seeing it as an affirmation of what they've always known about the superiority of life in the tropics.

Queensland is a gorgeous place, but sometimes great beauty comes with a price. Although the state was inundated with flood waters in the beginning of 2011, the tough Queenslander spirit has enabled people to bounce back. Recovery has been swift for the most part, but it would be wise to check the details of your trip before traveling.

Brisbane

The state capital, **Brisbane** ❶ (or *Brissie* as it's known to the locals), is Australia's third-largest city and has been transformed over the past few years. Close to half of the state's 4.5 million people are to be found within its ambit, scattered over a series of low hills with the Brisbane River at its heart. Until quite recently there was much in the claim that it was "the world's biggest country town", but visitors today will find an urbane and cosmopolitan city, where café culture has colonised the once musty streets.

Like Sydney and Hobart, this easygoing city emerged from nightmarish beginnings. A convict settlement was established at nearby Moreton Bay in September 1824, when the first party of prisoners – the hardest cases, convicted of further crimes since arriving in Australia – arrived from Sydney. Many of the convicts died, victims of the tyrannies of the guards, hunger, tropical disease and an indifference towards prolonging their own miserable lives.

The first convict establishment was at Redcliffe, but due to a shortage of water the penal settlement moved upriver to the site of today's city centre. It was named after Sir Thomas Brisbane (then Governor of New South

Wales). The present government and shopping precincts overlie the original settlement.

Today's central business district (CBD), in an area cupped by the river, is a mixture of stately colonial buildings and eye-catching modern architecture, with greenery provided by the City Botanic Gardens at one end and Roma Street Parkland at the other.

The visitor information centre (Queen Street Mall between Albert and Edward streets; tel: 07-3006 6290; www.visitbrisbane.com.au; Mon–Thu 9am–5.30pm, Fri 9am–7pm, Sat 9am–5pm, Sun 10am–5pm) can help with the usual brochures.

One of the city's more prominent landmarks, **Brisbane City Hall** ❹ makes a good starting point. It's an overbearing structure on King George Square with layered stone and concrete, broken up by entranceways to the transport hub underneath, which has struggled to become the great civic space its architects intended. The **Brisbane Museum** (tel: 07-3339 0800; www.museumofbrisbane.com.au; daily 10am–5pm; free), hosts short-term,

The Brisbane Botanic Gardens lie at the foot of Mount Coot-tha.

Brisbane City Hall.

FACT

Pictures of a flooded Brisbane flashed around the world in January 2011, but within months the city was back to normal, the council having removed 400,000 tonnes of flood waste and 200,000 damaged vehicles. The replacement of the washed-away riverside walkways was the only major outstanding task.

locally themed exhibitions and work by contemporary artists.

The historic centre

Anzac Square ⓑ further up Ann Street is a place for reflection. A perpetual flame commemorating the city's war dead is aligned directly between the clock tower of the Central Railway Station and the **General Post Office** (**GPO**). The latter, with its Corinthian colonnades, can be accessed through tranquil Post Office Square. Follow the narrow lane flanking the building to Elizabeth Street and **St Stephen's Cathedral ⓒ**. Within this precinct you will find the gracefully weathered Pugin's Chapel, also known as old St Stephen's Church, completed in 1850 to a design by celebrated Victorian (the era, not the state) Gothic architect Augustus Welby Pugin. Beside it reposes the more substantial cathedral that replaced it as Brisbane's seat of Catholicism in 1874.

Returning to the GPO and heading west, the shopping hub of **Queen Street Mall** stretches towards the river. The foyer of the former Regent Theatre is an unmissable paean to kitsch medievalism, which has survived virtually unchanged since 1929, although for now it is only visible through glass doors at the back of a café occupying the old ticket office. Another slice of history remains in the refined Edwardian-style **Brisbane Arcade,** built in 1924 and now the city's oldest surviving shopping arcade.

Architectural historians acclaim the **Treasury Building ⓓ** as the finest example of Italian renaissance style in the country. Walk south along George Street to **The Mansions,** a group of 1890 terraced houses with handsome red-brick facades and pale sandstone arcading, now occupied by classy shops and restaurants.

Further down George Street is Queensland's **Parliament House ⓔ** (tel: 1800-197 809; www.parliament.qld. gov.au; Mon–Fri 9am–4.15pm; free), begun in 1865. To the frustration of the architect, Charles Tiffin, who won a nationwide contest with his design on French renaissance lines, it took 24 years to see the work completed. There are conducted tours, or, when

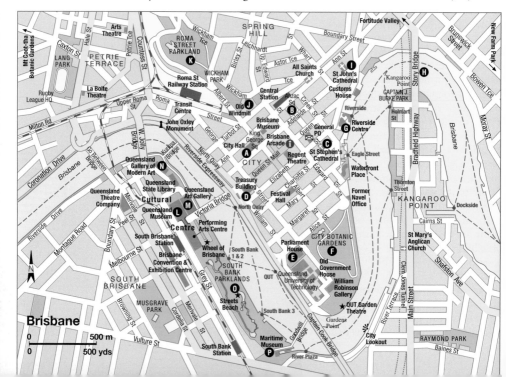

Brisbane

0 ___ 500 m
0 ___ 500 yds

Parliament is sitting (usually May–Oct), a gallery pass enables you to sit in on debates which, given the abrasive nature of the state's politics, can be riveting. Another Tiffin design, **Old Government House,** is now part of Queensland University of Technology and can be found down the road.

Dropping away to the left is the inviting green expanse of the **City Botanic Gardens ⑤**. Originally a vegetable garden for the penal settlement, its 20 hectares (50 acres) of formal lawns and flora now provides respite from the city's bustle for hordes of office workers, students and tourists. Highlights include an avenue of weeping willows planted over 150 years ago, and a boardwalk through mangroves growing on the river bank.

The Brisbane River

Leaving the gardens at the northeastern corner, pass the Former Naval Offices, follow the riverside pathway and take in the views. Eagle Street Pier is the starting point for various sightseeing cruises. Then comes the acclaimed modernist construction that is Harry Seidler's **Riverside Centre ⑥**. It houses some fine eateries. A short distance on lies the Customs House – now a function centre – opened in 1889 and crowned by a distinctive copper dome.

Looming ahead is Brisbane's most distinctive structure, the **Story Bridge ⑧** joining Kangaroo Point with the CBD. Tram tracks were removed in 1959 but otherwise it stands unchanged since its opening on 6 July 1940. At the time, it symbolised progress in an era of political and economic uncertainty, and even now, it radiates pride and permanence. Test its sturdiness and your fortitude by booking a bridge climb (tel: 07-3514 6900; www.storybridge adventures.com.au).

Walking across the bridge is rewarded with fine views back across the city, but the easier way to **Kangaroo Point** is to hop on to one of the buzzing water ferries, the River Cats.

Once across, there are plenty of adventure activities on offer at the old **Brisbane Naval Stores,** or you can just enjoy a pleasant stroll through the parkland, where sculptures of varying degrees of accomplishment are lurking. Climb up the cliff steps for spectacular views and a glimpse of the historic **St Mary's Anglican Church**.

City-centre completists, however, will defer such delights and follow the road north behind the Riverside Centre, turn left up Wharf Street, and investigate **St John's Cathedral ①** in Ann Street. This probably qualifies as Australia's newest Gothic cathedral; although work started in 1901, the final touches to the facade were only completed in 2009.

Just down Ann Street, **All Saints Church** (1862) is the oldest Anglican church in Brisbane. Cross into Wickham Terrace, nod in a knowing manner at Wickham Terrace Car Park, which won architect James Birrell awards for his innovative use of concrete, and amble along to the **Old Windmill ②**. Built in 1829 and one of only two convict buildings

The George Street mansions.

Brisbane's Treasure Casino.

TIP

Eagle Street Pier is the departure point for paddlewheeler cruises on board the Kookaburra River Queens I and II. Lunch cruises depart Thu–Sun at noon and last around 2 hours; dinner cruises are 2.5–3 hours and leave Thu–Sat at 6.30pm (tel: 07-3221 1300; www.kookaburra riverqueens.com). You can also book a cruise without a meal.

surviving from the first wave of construction, it is small and unprepossessing. A design flaw meant it never worked as a windmill, so to grind corn for the settlement convicts were put to work turning a treadmill. It soon earned a soubriquet as the "tower of torture".

Continue along Wickham Terrace for 300 metres/yds or so and take a path into **Roma Street Parkland K**. Here the Roma Street railway shunting yards have been converted into a splendidly diverse area of waterfalls, lakes, misty crannies of tropical vegetation, and cultivated floral displays that attract their own ecosystem of insects and birds.

The nearby old residential area of **Spring Hill** is an attractive maze of early houses, some of them old Queenslanders – distinctive, shady, wooden homes built on stilts to maximise the circulation of cooling air. Worth seeking out are the Spring Hill Baths in Torrington Street, the first public baths in the state and sufficiently atmospheric to feature heavily in the film *Swimming Upstream*.

South Bank

Across the river to the west of the CBD is one of Brisbane's most vibrant areas, the rapidly evolving South Bank, with its impressive complex, the **Queensland Cultural Centre,** and the sprawling pleasure gardens of South Bank Parklands. Cross over from the CBD by the Victoria Bridge and on the right can be found four key attractions. The **Queensland Museum L** (tel: 07-3840 7555; www.qm.qld.gov.au; daily 9.30am–5pm) has several million items including everything from Muttaburrasaurus, the most complete dinosaur skeleton found in Australia, to the tiny aeroplane Bert Hinkler flew from England to Australia in 1928. The museum also contains the **Dandiiri Maiwar Centre** devoted to Aboriginal and Torres Strait Islander cultures.

At the **Queensland Art Gallery M** (tel: 07-3840 7303; www.qagoma.qld.gov.au; Mon–Fri 10am–5pm, Sat–Sun 9am–5pm; free), core exhibitions are supplemented by touring art shows. A second gallery, the **Queensland Gallery of Modern Art N** (hours and details as above), or GoMA as

The storied Story Bridge.

It is known, has an impressive presence with exhibitions of modern contemporary works in a sparkling, purpose-built structure. Just behind it, a dramatic new footbridge links the precinct with the CBD. This is one of two new river crossings in the city, the other being the new Go Between Bridge upstream, named, following a public vote, after Brisbane's quirkily perfect rock band, the Go-Betweens. (Somewhere in the process the bridge lost the hyphen.)

The **State Library** holds important historical archives. To the left after crossing Victoria Bridge is a fine **Performing Arts Centre** and behind it the Convention and Exhibition Centre. On the river bank is the Wheel of Brisbane (tel: 07-3844 3464; www.thewheelofbrisbane.com.au; Mon–Thu 10am–10pm, Fri–Sat 9am–midnight, Sun 9am–10pm), a giant Ferris wheel offering superb views over the surrounding country.

South Bank Parklands

The site of the 1988 World Expo, **South Bank Parklands** Ⓞ, has put many of the former Expo pavilions to innovative use. Attractions in the 16 hectares (40 acres) of riverside parkland include a diverse array of restaurants that take maximum advantage of the city's weather. Brisbane, once a culinary desert, now enjoys a reputation for chefs who take advantage of the state's natural resources: giant mud crabs, macadamia nuts, coral trout, oysters, mangoes and other delicacies.

South Bank even has a large swimming lagoon at Streets Beach, complete with imported sand.

Stick with the promenade by the river and at the end of the striking Goodwill Bridge, which takes pedestrian traffic across to the CBD, you will find the **Queensland Maritime Museum** Ⓟ (tel: 07-3844 5361; www.maritimemuseum.com.au; daily 9.30am–4.30pm) with its collection of all things nautical, including a handful of vessels moored by the bank.

Outside Brisbane

Urban Brisbane gives way quickly to rural. Just 8km (5 miles) west of the centre, the **Mount Coot-tha Botanic Gardens** consist of over 57 hectares (141 acres) of ponds and parkland, where thousands of plant species thrive. Further west, rainforest-cloaked mountains shelter the city and offer a generous choice of picnic spots, bush walks and wilderness areas, all within half an hour's drive of the city centre.

To the east, downstream along the Brisbane River, you can reach the various beaches of **Moreton Bay** and the islands (some unpopulated) that make this a vast fishing and sailing paradise. Moreton Island is home to Mount Tempest, at 285 metres (935ft) the world's highest stabilised coastal dune.

The Gold Coast

South of Brisbane, the 32km (20-mile) stretch of coast from South Beach, just above Surfers Paradise, down to Coolangatta – which was pure bushland just two generations ago – is the fastest-growing tourist and residential area in Australia. The beaches, particularly

> **FACT**
>
> The wry nickname "Brisvegas" is often applied to Brisbane. Rather than it being an allusion to the flurry of high-rises in the CBD or sarcastic reference to the absence of any glitzy nightlife, it apparently derives from an Elvis tribute CD released as recently as 1994.

FORTITUDE VALLEY

Many of Brisbane's suburbs will clamour for your attention, but none more brazenly than Fortitude Valley to the north of the CBD. Once Brisbane's premier commercial and retail hub – with some grand old buildings to match – it has been reborn as a cosmopolitan precinct of cool bars, funky eateries, pounding clubs, sweaty music venues and residential apartments. Street action radiates around the pavement cafés in **Brunswick Street Mall,** though new bars have begun surfacing in some of the surrounding blocks. Either way, the precinct pumps it up at weekends when the bohemian and fashionable let their well-coiffeured hair down.

Family (MacLachlan Street) claims a 33,000-watt sound system and runs at weekends; the **Press Club** on Brunswick Street sees itself as cooler; on Ann Street **The Zoo** is the live band venue; and the **Wickham Hotel** is the gay HQ, although many other venues cater to the market.

Chinatown Mall in Duncan Street provides a range of Asian gastronomical possibilities including Thai, Malaysian, Korean and Japanese…but not so much Chinese. Excellent Chinese restaurants do operate within Chinatown but, in general, Chinese restaurateurs and shopkeepers have gravitated to Sunnybank, a well-to-do fringe suburb with a large expatriate Chinese community.

TIP

Descendants of the Kombumerri people, who once inhabited the area around Burleigh Heads, run various guided tours that explain the significance of rock formations and middens (ancient feasting grounds, not rubbish tips). Contact Kalwun Paradise Dreaming (tel: 07-5578 3044; www.kalwun.com.au).

The wheel of Brisbane.

Burleigh Heads set in a national park, are strikingly gorgeous, and from a heady apartment or hotel room on the umpteenth floor of a high-rise at **Surfers Paradise** ❷ the sight of sands stretching away to the north and south can be breathtaking. Down below, though, it's somewhat different. On the beach you can feel crowded in by towers thrown up with little evident architectural merit; height is the only yardstick, and the current leader is the Q1 building, which offers visitors the chance to scare themselves silly by climbing around the building's exterior on the SkyPoint Climb (tel: 07-5680-7700; www.skypoint.com.au). Its claim to capture "the aura of modernity evident in world-famous buildings by architects such as Renzo Piano and Frank Lloyd Wright" seems to be the height of folly. Which, incidentally, is 323 metres (1,060ft).

Comparisons between Surfers Paradise and Ipanema, Miami and Cannes also seem wide of the mark. There's little sense of the style or class that such parallels might suggest. Stores are functional at best, tacky souvenir

shops abound and patches of ground are purloined for haphazard collections of glorified fairground attractions, such as the Vomatron or the Sling Shot, both to be found on the corner of Gold Coast Highway and Cypress Avenue.

Night time is when the place really comes alive, possibly because you can't see it so well. Party-goers take over the streets, casinos and restaurants and the clubs start buzzing. Unsurprisingly, the beaches can be pretty quiet in the morning; that's when families are out in force.

Away from Surfers, the super-rich are indulged at **South Beach** in the six-star (sic) resort, Palazzo Versace. Further south, numbers of international visitors diminish and domestic tourists and hard-core surfies dominate.

Theme parks

The Gold Coast scores strong popularity points among the locals with its family-oriented theme parks. Performing dolphins and a dynamic water-ski show are the main pulls at **Sea World** (tel: 07-5519 6200; www.seaworld.com.au; daily 10am–5.30pm); **Dreamworld,** a large amusement park with a reassuringly Australian atmosphere, combines laid-back fun with adrenaline-pumping rides as well as a section devoted completely to the Wiggles (tel: 07-5588 2222; www.dreamworld.com.au; daily 10am–5pm); **Wet 'n' Wild** is a huge aquatic park with a mind-boggling variety of rides and adventures (www.wetnwild.com.au; daily May–Aug 10am–4pm, Sept–Apr 10am–5pm).

Surpassing them all as a tourist attraction is **Warner Brothers' Movie World,** where startling rides such as Superman Adventure and the Wild West Falls Adventure are augmented by stunt shows and special-effects displays (www.movieworld.com.au; daily 10am–5.30pm). **Whitewaterworld,** the latest addition to the list, is a sister operation to Dreamworld and will make you soggy in ever-more

imaginative ways (tel: 07-5588 1111; www.whitewaterworld.com.au; daily 10am–4pm). Unfortunately none of these theme parks is cheap, but you can easily spend a day in each of them. The best plan is to arrive early and get the best value for your money.

Finally, the **Australian Outback Spectacular** packages up "a genuine Aussie Outback experience", which is, of course, nothing of the kind (tel: 133 386; www.outbackspectacular.com.au; Tue–Sun 7.30pm).

For an antidote to excess, the **Currumbin Wildlife Sanctuary** (28 Tomewin Street, Currumbin; tel: 07-5534 1266; www.cws.org.au; daily 8am–5pm) offers every variety of indigenous fauna, as well as the chance to act as a perch for flocks of lorikeets at feeding time.

The Darling Downs

Inland from Brisbane, the countryside is almost entirely ignored by tourists. Here, the tablelands give way to the Darling Downs, a vast area of beautiful, rolling plains and rich soil. **Ipswich ❸**, now an easy commute from Brisbane, is an old railway town whose history is well displayed at the Workshops Rail Museum (North Street; tel: 07-3432 5100; www.thework shops.qm.qld.gov.au; daily 9.30am–4pm), but there are plenty of other interesting features on its heritage trail.

The pleasant city of **Warwick ❹** serves as a livestock industry hub. The second-oldest town in Queensland retains a good deal of historical character, much of it linked to prosperity deriving from the discovery of gold nearby. There are some beautiful buildings, but its most famous feature is the month-long Rose and Rodeo Festival, which attracts the country's best cowboys every October.

Hilly **Toowoomba ❺** is not just Queensland's largest inland conurbation but also a garden city of some note. Situated on the rim of the Great Dividing Range, with the Darling Downs laid out before it, Toowoomba is colourful all year but sensational when spring flowers bloom.

Lamington National Park ❻, in the McPherson Ranges directly behind the Gold Coast, is vast and offers some

Enjoying the sun on the Gold Coast.

TIP

If you like a thrill you can explore the Sunshine Coast on a Harley-Davidson or in a souped-up trike. **Freedom Wheels** (tel: 07-5485 3513; www.free domwheels.com.au) offers excursions lasting from an hour to a full day, as well as extended tours over several days into Outback Queensland.

Feeding the birds at Currumbin Wildlife Sanctuary.

fabulous bushwalking through dramatic rainforest. Occupying part of the rim of an ancient volcano, Lamington has a wide range of ferns and hundreds of species of orchid.

The Glass House Mountains

North of Brisbane there are more of the contrasts between the sublime and the kitsch that characterise the Gold Coast, but with the Sunshine Coast the balance is very different. The beaches are just as glorious, but the resorts are less brash.

Follow the Bruce Highway out of Brisbane, and as the suburbs are left behind look out for the unique geological formations of the **Glass House Mountains** looming up on your left, which dominate the landscape for several kilometres. Walks up them or drives between them are recommended. And it's the Glass House Mountains Road you'll want anyway for the **Australia Zoo ❼** (tel: 07-5436 2000; www.australiazoo.com; daily 9am– 5pm), near Beerwah. The organisation has adjusted to life after "crocodile hunter" Steve Irwin – killed by a

stingray barb in 2006 – by shifting the focus to his children Bindi and Robert, but otherwise continues virtually unchanged as both a tribute to Irwin and as a focus for the environmental work that he so assiduously promoted.

Back on the highway, a cartoon Aussie boozer, the **Ettamogah Pub,** reacquaints us with the trashy, while **Aussie World** (tel: 07-5494 5444; www. aussieworld.com.au; daily 9am–5pm), next door, is really a glorified fairground. Stay inland and take the Nambour Tourist Drive. Six kilometres (4 miles) south of Nambour, marvel at an enormous fibreglass fruit: The Big Pineapple. Buy local fruit, tour a pineapple farm, and learn about the pineapple industry in a theatrette inside the structure. This is but one of dozens of "Big Things" that litter eastern Australia, and, in its attention to detail, it's one of the less tacky. Really.

The Sunshine Coast

All this can distract visitors from what is one of the most gorgeous stretches of Queensland's coastline. The action begins at **Caloundra,** where Bribie

Island lies just across the Pumicestone Channel, but, more importantly, where the serious surf beaches begin. Caloundra is now a blossoming family resort. Further up, Mooloolaba is also seeing a spate of high-rise development. Beaches all along this stretch are gems. Try seeking out the unspoilt Marcoola Beach at Coolum, a relaxed and up-market settlement.

Many visitors stick with the Sunshine Highway all the way to **Noosa Heads** ❽. Noosa has been called the Cannes of Australia, a heady blend of beauty, sophistication and wealth. Nestling beside the tranquil waters of Laguna Bay, Noosa comes close to distilling the essence of the Australian Dream. Today Noosa is a collection of townships strung along the coast. The perfect waves that wrap around the points of Noosa's National Park rank among the world's finest, and surfers were the first to populate the area.

Publicity soon lured a different clique – the wealthy early retirees of Sydney, Melbourne and Adelaide. From the moment they saw Noosa Heads, these refugees from colder climes began buying up large tracts of the best land. Today, the village of Noosa is lined with glitzy restaurants and boutiques, although it can't seem to entirely shake off the raffish charm of old. Only a few metres from Hastings Street, Noosa's main business thoroughfare, swimmers still float lazily in a sea so clear you can see whiting and flathead scud across the bottom. Sheltering Noosa from the prevailing southeasterly winds is the headland, gateway to the 334-hectare (825-acre) Noosa National Park, an area of woodland and marshes on the south bank of the Noosa River.

Travelling north on Highway 1

Highway 1, the main coastal route from Brisbane to Cairns, stretches for 1,703km (1,058 miles), and, although it is being continually improved, don't think of it as a highway in the American or European sense; much of it is just a good-quality undivided two-lane road. Distances between coastal centres can be vast and, by comparison with more populated areas in the south of Australia, rural Queensland remains something of a diamond in the rough. Still, small diversions from the route north will reveal magnificent and uncrowded beaches, pristine rainforests, tropical islands, authentic country pubs, splendid fishing and diving, and the most mouth-watering local tucker.

Highway 1 runs through Gympie, a one-time gold-mining town which hosts a week-long Gold Rush Festival every October, then to atmospheric **Maryborough** ❾ which has a railway museum and some fine old Victorian buildings. From nearby Hervey Bay, a barge will carry you and your vehicle over to **Fraser Island** ❿.

Childers, on the highway to the north, is a National Trust-listed town surrounded by rolling hills covered in sugar cane. The town encapsulates the region's early architecture. A turn-off to Woodgate Beach and Woodgate National Park, about 40km (25 miles) down the side road, pays dividends.

TIP

The sleek new Noosa Visitor Information Centre (Hastings Street, Noosa Heads; tel: 1300-066 672) provides information about accommodation as well as events like the Noosa Long Weekend in June, the Celebration of Food and Wine in May and Noosa Jazz Festival in September.

The Glasshouse Mountains.

The next major town north is **Bun-daberg** ⓫ on the coast, 45km (28 miles) from Highway 1. For millions of Australians, Bundy is synonymous with rum. Here, in the heart of sugar country, is the distillery that put the town on the map. An inexpensive tour provides an insight into the production process, a visit to a museum and a taste of the product (Whittred Street; tel: 07-4131 2999; www.bundabergrum.com.au; tours run on the hour Mon–Fri 10am–5pm, Sat–Sun 10am–4pm). There is much else to see around town, including a selection of museums and a turtle hatchery. From Bundaberg, cruises and flights operate to **Lady Elliot Island,** 85km (53 miles) away, on the southern end of the Great Barrier Reef.

The twin coastal resorts of **Agnes Water** and **Town of 1770** have become popular fishing and boating centres as well as being the departure point for visits to Eurimbula and Deepwater national parks, with their pristine coastal landscapes.

Pass up the next detour, to the surprisingly attractive industrial centre of

Waiting for the lunch boat to arrive.

Gladstone, unless you happen to be interested in the world's largest aluminium plant (A\$355 million to construct) or you are one of the fortunate heading out by ferry or helicopter to Heron Island.

Carnarvon Gorge

The Dawson Highway, heading west from Gladstone, is the route to one of Queensland's most outstanding national parks at **Carnarvon Gorge** ⓬. This 30km (16-mile) sandstone gorge has a profusion of palm trees, cycads, ferns and mosses as well as fine examples of Aboriginal rock paintings.

Rockhampton

Back on Highway 1, and north of the Tropic of Capricorn (marked by a roadside spire), **Rockhampton** ⓭ made headlines around the world when it was the first city hit by the massive floods that inundated Queensland in January 2011. Normally it hums quietly as the commercial heart of central Queensland. A colourful former mayor, Rex Pilbeam, had a Brahman bull cast

THE GEM FIELDS

Fortune hunters should head 270km (170 miles) inland from the town of Rockhampton to **Emerald**, a centre for the farming of cotton, citrus fruits, grapes and fodder crops. It is also a gateway to the famous central Queensland gem fields, where scores of latter-day pioneers fossick for precious stones. There's nothing fancy about the gem fields; in tents, caravans and tumbledown tin shacks the miners have traded traditional comforts for the freedom and excitement of their own frontier, their rewards being sapphire, topaz, amethyst and jasper. These are the largest sapphire-producing fields in the world, and some fossickers have struck it rich in their first week, but most haven't. Various fossicking parks give visitors a chance to try their hand.

in concrete and erected at the northern entrance to the city (the Brahman is the breed favoured by cattlemen to the north), and a similar sculpture of a Hereford (the breed favoured in the south) at the southern end. When the beasts were made, Pilbeam – anticipating playfulness by locals – had several spare sets of testicles placed in storage. Hooligans struck the Brahman almost immediately. They were dumbfounded when workmen bolted on a replacement appendage the same day.

Rockhampton has a population of about 85,000, with modern pubs and office blocks interspersed among older buildings – and what buildings! The National Estate lists Quay Street in its entirety on its heritage register, and superb colonial homes are found in Agnes Street. Look out for the excellent collection of Australian art at **Rockhampton Art Gallery** (62 Victoria Parade; tel: 07-4936 8248; daily 10am–4pm; free), and the outstanding Botanic Gardens. Pick up a heritage guide from the visitor information centre in the old Customs House on Quay Street.

The starting point for **Mackay** ⓮, 333km (207 miles) to the north, is the large tourist information centre set in a replica of the Richmond Sugar Mill, the first in the area. Fanned by tropical breezes and surrounded by a rustling sea of sugar cane, Mackay is a pleasant city of wide streets and elegant old hotels. A stroll through the centre reveals an assortment of Victorian buildings interspersed with several displaying the sleek lines of 1930s Art Deco. North of the centre there are fine beaches and the new Marina Village.

Airlie Beach ⓯ and neighbouring **Shute Harbour,** 135km (84 miles) to the north, act as the gateway to the Whitsunday Islands, see page 238. There are fine eateries and accommodation from backpackers' hostels to four-star resorts. This is the place to find a berth on one of the many island-hopping yachts.

Townsville

Eyebrows used to be raised at the idea of visiting **Townsville** ⓰, but these days the state's second-biggest city is a

The Ettamogah Pub tilts in all directions.

GOLD TOWNS

Head west from Townsville to gold country, and the vistas along the Flinders Highway rapidly turn from lush green to the parched semi-arid savannah of Australian myth. **Charters Towers**, 135km (84 miles) inland, owes its heyday to an Aboriginal boy who found gold in 1872 while on an expedition with prospector Hugh Mossman. A tiny town suddenly boomed. Of the splendid architecture that resulted, the restored Stock Exchange in the historic Royal Arcade is one of the city's 19th-century highlights. Gold is still produced locally, with companies reworking old sites. One is in **Ravenswood**, 38km (24 miles) south of the Flinders Highway, where among deserted shacks and derelict equipment two ancient pubs still function and there's a small museum.

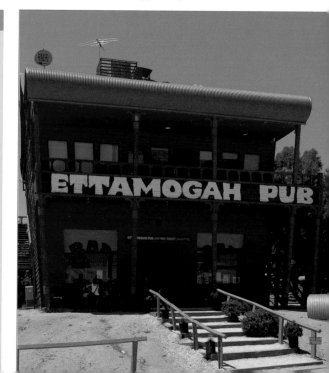

FACT

The old British Leyland Mini Moke is enjoying a last hurrah on Magnetic Island. This distinctive vehicle of the 1960s doesn't go particularly fast but you're sitting so close to the ground, have so much wind blowing through your hair and are feeling so many bumps in the road through the rudimentary suspension that it feels as if you're hurtling along.

All kinds of boards are welcome on the beach.

relaxed and graceful place with plenty to attract the casual visitor. This is due in part to two destructive cyclones that ripped the foreshore apart in 1997 and 1998, prompting a A$29-million restoration along The Strand. The resultant 2.2km (1.5-mile) stretch of white sand, swaying palms, water parks, play areas and casual restaurants redefined Townsville as a tropical resort city of considerable appeal. Townsville's residents congregate here to sunbathe, barbecue, browse and birdwatch.

Flinders Street, the main thoroughfare, has notable late 19th-century architecture, including many of the city's 58 National Trust-listed buildings. At its northern end the **Museum of Tropical Queensland** (tel: 07-4726 0600; www.mtq.qm.qld.gov.au; daily 9.30am–5pm), its atrium dominated by a huge cross-section of an 18th-century naval frigate, provides a good child-friendly introduction to the history, peoples and geology of the area.

Next door, **Reef HQ** (tel: 07-4750 0800; www.reefhq.com.au; daily 9.30am–5pm) has a huge coral-reef aquarium as its centrepiece.

Overlooking everything is the craggy Castle Hill. In a typical display of civic pride, an early resident worked out that if Castle Hill were just a few metres higher, it could officially be called a mountain. He began carting soil up the hill and dumping it on top. The town never got its mountain, but the project became a kind of monument to obscure endeavour everywhere. Climb, or more likely drive, to the top for a different perspective of the city and look out to sea, where **Magnetic Island** can be seen offshore.

It's only a 20-minute ferry ride from Townsville, but Magnetic Island feels worlds away. Hire a Mini Moke and hop from one bay to another, follow one of the many trails into the forest, or maybe stumble over an old wartime lookout post. There are plenty of places to stay at all budgets.

Townsville's relatively green hinterland strip is bordered by rocky mountain ranges that eventually give way to the inland savannah. About 10km (6 miles) north of Ingham, as you reach the top of a steep hill, you are suddenly treated to one of the most breathtaking

sights of the whole coastal trip. Be ready to stop and admire the view of **Hinchinbrook Island** across the narrow mangrove-lined channel.

Mission Beach and Innisfail

From Cardwell northward the highway sticks pretty close to the coast, offering plenty of diversions to peaceful little spots for picnics, fishing and water sports. A trip up **Tully Gorge** offers dramatic scenery and the opportunity to take in some whitewater rafting.

Mission Beach ⓱, an 18km (11-mile) detour off the highway, is a relaxed, low-rise destination. The beach is perfect, the restaurants are good and there's always the option of a quick trip across to Dunk Island if you crave a spell on a westward-facing strand for a change.

This stretch of coastline bore the brunt of Cyclone Yasi in February 2011. Rebuilding was swift and even devastated Dunk and Bedarra islands reopened within the year. Yasi followed Cyclone Larry of 2006, when the brunt of the damage was inflicted on **Innisfail**, 49km (30 miles) to the north. Even before that, locals' claims that this would be the next happening place in the region aroused some scepticism, but it's a nice enough town and its Art Deco architecture and Chinese temple are worth a look.

Cairns

And so on to **Cairns** ⓲, pulsating visitor centre of tropical north Queensland. Until the 1980s, this was a sleepy provincial backwater wallowing in a swamp. Not terribly much had changed since it was founded just over a century before, on some not very picturesque mangrove flats, to service the gold and tin fields further inland. Then the tourism boom hit. There's still a core of old-style tropical charm in the languid pubs and distinctively Queensland-style porches, but today Cairns, with a population of 164,000, has a modern international airport, bustling shopping malls and a vast variety of restaurants. Almost any sporting activity – diving trips to the Reef, bungy jumping, whitewater rafting, tandem parachuting, hiking the Atherton Tableland – can be arranged.

Palm Cove has been designed around the 500-year-old Melaleuca trees that dot the town and beaches.

Diving at the Great Barrier Reef.

Fraser Island

Fraser is the world's largest sand island; its ecology is unlike any other – a fact that put it on the UN's World Heritage list in 1992.

Instead of barren desert, which you might expect from a sand island, the entire interior is covered with a rich patchwork of forests, whose muscular vegetation manages to survive on the nutrients in only the top 15cm (6ins) of soil.

The island's landscape changes every few hundred metres, from classic Aussie scrub and reed-filled swamps surrounded by 60-metre (200ft) satinay trees, to expanses of lush rainforest, with plants so dense that they almost block out the sunlight. Amid the forests are some 40 freshwater lakes, including both perched (above sea level) and window lakes (at or below sea level). Some of them have water the colour of tea, while others are perfect blue with blinding white sands – **Lake Mackenzie**, for example, could be in the Caribbean.

The beaches of Fraser Island are made up of sand that has been accumulating for 750,000 years.

This magnificent island has been reshaping itself over thousands of years. Enormous sand dunes creep like silent yellow glaciers, consuming entire forests then leaving them behind, petrified and ghostly. But plant life always revives; there are more independent dune systems on Fraser, showing sand and vegetation in different stages of interaction, than anywhere else on earth. The island entered the history books in the 1830s, when a British ship was wrecked here. The lone survivor, Eliza Fraser, spent many months living with the local people before being "rescued" by an escaped convict. British settlers then used the island as a sort of natural prison camp for Aborigines. When fine wood was discovered soon after, the British herded the Aborigines off, killing many, it is said, by driving them into the sea.

Visiting Fraser Island

There are arguments about how to manage the booming number of annual visitors – from 10,000 in the early 1970s to 350,000 today. There can be few other World Heritage sites so readily available to the public, and the island's four ranger stations are kept busy managing the place in such a way that visitor pressures don't cause more damage.

Anglers head for **Waddy Point**, while nature-lovers seek out the soft sands of the deserted beaches (swimwear optional). The **Great Sandy National Park**, covering 840 sq km (325 sq miles), is a jigsaw of lakes, dunes, forest and beach.

For a small fee, anyone can bring a four-wheel-drive vehicle from the mainland, bounce along the island's trails, rip up and down **Seventy-Five Mile Beach** on the east coast and camp in designated areas. (Note that a four-wheel-drive is essential; tyre pressure should be reduced for beach travel, which should be attempted only at low tide. Count on getting bogged at least once during your visit.) There are plenty of organised tours for those daunted by off-road driving.

Non-tented sleeping options include Kingfisher Bay Resort, shrewdly conceived to repose so lightly amid scrub and natural lagoons as to be barely noticeable from the beach or from passing yachts. Even with 1,000 guests, it maintains an uncrowded sense of serenity and is the accommodation of choice for affluent guests.

The focus of Cairns remains the **Esplanade**. The waterfront is lined by high-rise hotels and backpacker accommodation, and there's always an array of picnicking locals beneath the Moreton Bay figs and palms. Its centrepiece is a huge landscaped swimming lagoon, classic red-and-yellow-garbed lifeguards in attendance, its lawns carpeted with minimally clad sunbathers. A leisure and shopping centre, the Pier is still struggling to impose itself, but weekend markets, and a marina for the region's marlin fishing fleet and pleasure boats, give verve to the waterfront.

The **Cairns Historical Museum** (corner Lake and Shields streets; tel: 07-4051 5582; www.cairnsmuseum.org.au; Mon–Sat 10am–5pm) has exhibits on the more rough-and-ready past of the area, while the elegant **Regional Art Gallery** (corner Abbot and Shields streets; tel: 07-4046 4800; www.cairns regionalgallery.com.au; Mon–Fri 9am–5pm, Sat 10am–5pm, Sun 10am–2pm) has local artists' work on display as well as visiting exhibitions.

But the real attractions of Cairns lie beyond the town limits; either out to sea for the **Great Barrier Reef** or inland where the lush, cool plateau of the **Atherton Tableland** deserves extensive exploration. Like the rest of the region, it was opened up by prospectors in the 1870s. It is now a major dairy farm area, with a range of B&Bs and farm-stay accommodation with faintly chi-chi names.

However, for many tourists there is only time for a day-trip package. This means taking the pleasant 64km (44-mile) return trip from Cairns to the village of **Kuranda;** one way by train, with vintage coaches climbing tortuously through spectacular scenery, tunnels and past impressive waterfalls; the other half of the journey by Skyrail, a cable car that almost brushes the rainforest tree tops. Kuranda is one big shopping opportunity, with a daily craft market, galleries, didgeridoo outlets and a host of restaurants and cafés. Beyond that, the station is charming and there's a butterfly sanctuary and aviary.

The far north

North of Cairns, the Cook Highway runs through one of the most

TIP

Drop in at the century-old Cairns Yacht Club to meet barnacled locals while washing down prawns with beer. Hemmed in on all sides by high-rises, the club has been assured that its two-storey weatherboard headquarters will remain unmolested by developers – for now. Its verandah is a fine place to sip a beer.

A well-lit walkway along the water in Cairns.

TIP

Heading north from Port Douglas, you pass cane farms and exotic fruit plantations to Miallo, famous as the place where actress Diane Cilento established her 500-seat Karnak Playhouse (tel: 07-4098 8194; www.karnakplay house.com.au) with her late husband, the playwright Anthony Shaffer. It's worth a look just for the setting.

Quay Street is noted for its history and most of the buildings in it are beautiful examples of Australia's early architecture.

classically gorgeous parts of Australia. Strings of uncrowded, palm-fringed beaches (including those of the beach-side suburbs of Trinity, Kewarra and exclusive Palm Cove) look as Hawaii must have done before the developers arrived. Having said that, construction is moving apace and for Palm Cove in particular it's worth checking in advance on the likely impact that the latest building works may have on your holiday haven.

The Great Barrier Reef comes within 15km (9 miles) of the shore-line, and from various ports diving boats head out to the sand cays and coral reefs. One of the most popular starting points lies some 80km (50 miles) north of Cairns. **Port Douglas** ⑲, like most of the coastal settlements, was founded after a gold rush in the 1870s, when the Gugu-Yalangi Aborigines were forced from their land. For a time it was more important than Cairns, but its popularity faded when the gold ran out. For the next century, Port Douglas boasted little more than two pubs and a pie shop. Today, the pubs and pie shop are still

there, but they've been joined by glitzy new resorts like the Sheraton Mirage, which continues to attract world leaders and household names from the entertainment industry. There are also some fine restaurants and chic boutiques on Macrossan Street, and you can find nightly cane-toad races in one of the bars; the palm-fringed village atmosphere that could still be enjoyed in the 1990s has long gone.

However, Four Mile Beach is among the region's most beautiful, while every morning dozens of boats head out from the marina for day trips on the Reef. Just offshore are the immensely popular Low Isles, and a string of excellent snorkelling spots is only an hour away. Passages are available on everything from tiny yachts catering for only a dozen passengers right up to the massive Quicksilver catamarans that can shuttle hundreds of people at a time.

Cape Tribulation rainforest
Returning to the highway, just north of the Port Douglas turn-off, is Moss-man and the road to **Mossman**

Gorge. The brand-new $20 million Mossman Gorge Centre (tel: 07-4099 7000; www.mossmangorge.com.au) is the starting point for self-guided walks or insightful Dreamtime walks, led by the gorge's traditional owners, the Kuku Yalanji. Slightly further north, past rich sugar-cane country, the village of **Daintree** is the starting point for river trips. Just after dawn, the bird-life is extraordinary (parrots, ospreys, great white herons). Later in the day, you'll see saltwater crocodiles lounging in sunny bliss.

Cross the Daintree River by ferry (6am–midnight) and drive for 36km (23 miles) to **Cape Tribulation ㉓**. It's an incongruous name for one of Australia's most serene corners, but then Captain Cook was in a poor mood after his ship, the Endeavour, ran onto a reef in 1770. "This was where our troubles began," he noted in his log, and his subsequent naming of Mount Misery, Cape Sorrow and the like indicate a man who hadn't perked up.

Troubles returned in the early 1980s, when the Queensland government decided to push a road through the rainforest to improve access for tourists and remote Aboriginal communities. Hundreds of eco-activists descended on Cape Trib to throw themselves in front of the bulldozers. Ironically, this focused so much attention on the area that Cape Trib became a household name in Australia, and is now firmly on the tourist map. The road was eventually completed, but the outcry prompted a United Nations World Heritage listing for the Daintree area, which is now part of a national park.

Today, the isolated, otherworldly atmosphere of Cape Trib appears to have barely changed. There is a scattered community with a few grocery stores and, except for a couple of hours in the middle of the day, when tour buses arrive from Cairns, there are usually few people on the beaches. Meanwhile, a cluster of new high-quality eco-lodges nestles in rainforest-covered hills. There are also coral reefs quite close to the shore, a very unusual phenomenon.

The contentious coastal road to Cooktown is now a reality – although barely. You need a four-wheel-drive vehicle to bounce through tunnels of virgin forest, plough across shallow rivers and up 45-degree inclines. Although you glimpse the sea rarely, the views and sense of isolation are worth it. The road is open all year with extreme caution – watch the tide at Bloomfield River unless you'd like to contribute to the crocodiles' diet. Otherwise, in a conventional vehicle, you can make the journey from Cairns on the inland Cape York Development Road, which was only fully sealed in 2006. Call in at the Lion's Den pub, just off the highway at Helenvale – it's one of the oldest in north Queensland, with the original wooden bar, piano and a vast array of pickled snakes.

Cooktown

At the end of the line is **Cooktown ㉑**, a place that has always had a Wild West reputation as an isolated tropical

TIP

Lizard Island, 27km (19 miles) off the coast and about 100km (60 miles) north of Cooktown, is a dry, rocky, mountainous island with superb beaches for swimming and pristine reef which makes for great snorkelling and diving. Charter flights operate from Cairns and Cooktown.

THE ATHERTON TABLELAND

The hill country inland from Cairns offers respite from the tropical heat of the coast; with its sprinkling of attractive townships, inviting lakes, picturesque waterfalls and towering forests, it is deserving of proper investigation over a few days. With its elevation and associated rainfall, this fertile plateau at the northern end of the Great Dividing Range is prime dairy country. In the early days of colonial settlement, great areas of forest were cleared of valuable timber, leaving today's rolling pastureland.

It was the Chinese, originally drawn by tin and gold mining in the region, who led the way in agriculture, and evidence of their presence is manifest in **Atherton**, the main town in the area. The 1903 Hou Wang Temple (Herberton Road; www.houwang.org.au; Wed–Sun 11am–4pm) was the focal point of Chinatown.

Yungaburra, a few kilometres to the east, is dotted with heritage buildings and has a famed 500-year-old curtain fig tree, as well as being a good spot to see platypus – by the bridge. **Malanda** is worth a look, and **Millaa Millaa** is a pretty place to join a waterfalls circuit taking in four examples, with Millaa Millaa Falls being the highlight.

Millstream Falls are the widest in the country and can be found outside **Ravenshoe,** if you're not detained by the town's steam train.

The World's Oldest Rainforest

The rainforest is at least 100 million years old (compared with the Amazon's 10 million) and is a vital component of Queensland.

All the Earth's rainforests are thought to have begun around present-day Melbourne some 120 million years ago, when Australia was a part of the great continent of Gondwanaland. When Oceania broke away, 50 million years ago, the drier land began to replace tropical conditions. The rainforests that once covered Australia retreated to less than 1 percent of the continent; logging has reduced that by more than half.

North Queensland's rainforest – now protected as part of the Wet Tropics World Heritage area and a patchwork of national parks – has the highest diversity of local endemic species in the world. Fully one-fifth of Australia's bird species, a quarter of its reptiles, a third of its marsupials, a third of its frogs

Be careful not to venture off the path when visiting the rainforests of Queensland.

and two-fifths of its plants are here in a tiny fraction of the Australian landmass.

Conservationists waged battles with the timber industry and the Queensland government throughout the 1980s. Ultimately, the eco-activists triumphed over the bulldozers; today most North Queenslanders accept the importance of the wet zones. With its capacity to attract visitors, it doesn't do the local economy any harm either.

Dangerous wildlife

As for the seething tangle of vines and ferns itself, the rainforest has always deployed a wide array of defences against intruders. First off, there's the taipan snake, whose bite is 300 times more toxic than a cobra's. Some other native snakes are nearly as dangerous. However, death by snakebite is rarer than death by lightning strike.

The local (non-venomous) python is hardly worth a mention, although the largest recorded scrub python, found in the Tully area, measured 8.5 metres (28ft) long. The saltwater crocodiles that lurk in the remoter rivers here only grow up to about 6 metres (20ft) – but that's still enough to grab the unwary by the legs and spoil their day with the death-roll they use to disable and eventually kill their victims.

If you see a tree goanna – a giant speckled lizard with enormous claws – don't startle it: it may confuse you with a tree, climb up your leg and disembowel you. (Why it would attack a tree in the first place isn't entirely clear.) A kick from a frightened cassowary – a 2-metre (6ft) -tall flightless bird with a bony crown – can tear open your ribcage so, if you meet one in the bush, give it plenty of room.

The barking or bird-eating spider, with a leg span up to 15cm (6 inches), may be found in areas bordering on rainforest and can deal you a nasty bite.

Even some plants are armed and dangerous. The heart-shaped leaves of the Gympie vine, for example, inject silica spines into any skin unlucky enough to brush it. It's "like a blow-torch being applied to your flesh", apparently.

The chances of encountering any of these horrors are minimal. Access for visitors is tightly controlled and any sightseeing is likely to be from defined paths or boardwalks, where the route is well marked.

You can take it a step further by visiting the **Daintree Discovery Centre**, where the whole rainforest experience is packed into a fenced compound and enjoyed from either the raised boardwalk on the forest floor or an aerial walkway.

refuge which you could escape to when nowhere else would have you. It is located on the mangrove estuary where Captain Cook spent seven weeks repairing the *Endeavour*. The local Gugu-Yalangi people were friendly, and it was the most significant contact between Aborigines and Europeans to that date. The time ashore gave Sir Joseph Banks the opportunity to make more detailed studies of local wildlife than he had been allowed at Botany Bay.

When an Irish prospector struck gold at Palmer River in 1873, Cooktown became one of Australia's busiest ports, with 94 pubs (many little more than shacks) and 35,000 miners working on the claims. There's a mural in the Middle Pub depicting those days, when miners blew thousands of pounds' worth of gold dust in a single night, chased women such as the legendary Palmer Kate, passed out on drugged whisky and then woke up penniless in the swamps.

Cooktown still thrives on those memories, and it has maintained a languid charm. Poking between palm trees on the wide main street are many late 19th-century buildings, including the three surviving watering holes (to avoid confusion, known as the Top, Middle and Bottom pubs).

The **James Cook Historical Museum** (corner of Helen and Furneaux streets; tel: 07-4069 5386; daily 9.30am– 4pm) is one of the best in Australia and is located in the former convent of St Mary; exhibits include the original anchor of the *Endeavour*, retrieved from the Reef. The Cooktown cemetery, just north of town, is full of its own stories of the old pioneers.

The Cape Yorke Peninsula

Beyond Cooktown sprawls the **Cape York Peninsula,** a popular destination for four-wheel-drive expeditions in the dry season. The red-dust road runs from one lonely bush pub to the next, past ant hills, forests full of screaming cockatoos, and vast sandstone bluffs

rich in Aboriginal rock art. It can take several days to get to Australia's northernmost point, the tip of Cape York, and it's essential that you travel with someone who has serious off-roading experience. It's best to go in convoy with at least one other vehicle.

The tiny township of **Laura** ㉒ at the southern tip of the Lakefield National Park (an expanse of marshland, lagoons, mangrove swamps and rainforest that is rich in flora and fauna) is one of the last accessible spots without a four-wheel-drive vehicle as long as you stay outside the park. It's worth the trip to see some fabulous Aboriginal rock art. Split Rock can be explored on your own, while other sites can be enjoyed in the company of Aboriginal guides booked through the Quinkan Regional Cultural Centre (tel: 07-4060 3457; www. quinkancc.com.au).

Heading north, the journey passes the bauxite-mining town of Weipa and the Jardine River Crossing (which has a ferry). Torres Strait is the end of the line, where there are campgrounds; 6km (4 miles) to the northeast, at

TIP

For a scenic overview of Mount Isa, head for the **City Lookout** (a short drive off Hilary Street), preferably at dusk when the mine lights up. You can see the whole city sprawled out across a flat valley, backed by low hills, and all dominated by the mine.

Zip-lining above the trees.

Balancing Rock is not a trick of the eye, but rather a matter of physics.

Road train on a dirt road to Chillagoe.

Punsand Bay, is the closest population to the continent's northernmost tip.

Boats run from Red Island Point (Bamaga) to Thursday Island, the administrative centre of the Torres Strait Islands, many of which were named by Captain Bligh when he passed through on an open longboat after the *Bounty* mutiny. From June to September, the ferry also operates from Punsand Bay. **Thursday Island ㉓** (pop. 2,600) was once one of the world's great pearling stations. Although there are no tourist traps or beaches of note, T.I. is a pleasant enough place to lay up after the rigours of the road. Its cosmopolitan mix of inhabitants is a carefree and friendly crowd who like to party. There are four old pubs, the more modern Jardine Motel, and a Japanese cemetery from pearling days.

A special way to take a close look at the far north Queensland coastline and the Torres Strait is a five-day return voyage from Cairns on the MV *Trinity Bay*, a working cargo ship supplying the remote Cape York communities all the way up to Thursday Island. It's air-conditioned and comfortable, and dress and conversation are informal. (Tel: 07-4035 1234; www.seaswift.com.au).

The Queensland Outback

Most of Queensland's key destinations (and by far the majority of the population) are on the coast, and yet much that is most fascinating about the place is to be found inland. It's impossible to get a real handle on the state until you've headed off into the Outback. There are countless ways to do it, but with the idea of describing a circuit (which needs a good parcel of time) let's look at a journey moving inland from Cairns. This is the starting point of the Savannah Way, which eventually winds up in Broome in northern Western Australia. The land is vast and there may be hundreds of kilometres between destinations, so keep a keen eye on the fuel gauge and consider keeping a can of spare fuel in the trunk.

Chillagoe ㉔, 215km (134 miles) west of Cairns, is not actually on the Savannah Way but is worth a visit. It's a mining town with plenty of detritus from the industry to provide character. Limestone bluffs around the town add drama to the harsh terrain, while spectacular caves in the **Chillagoe-Mungana National Park** can be explored on your own or with guided tours. Book at the Hub (21–3 Queen Street; tel: 07-4094 7111; www.nprsr.qld.gov.au).

More subterranean wonders are to be found at the **Undara Lava Tubes ㉕** a few kilometres south of the Savannah Way, one of the best examples of lava-tube formation anywhere on the planet. These are created when lava follows the line of river beds, the lava surface cools but the molten material within flows out, leaving a tube behind. Some of the tubes are 15–20 metres (50–65ft) in diameter. Full resort accommodation is offered in beautifully restored vintage rail carriages relocated there for the purpose. (tel: 07-4097 1900; www.undara.com.au; various times). It's also a Savannah Guide Station.

The Savannah Way continues on through **Georgetown,** where there are a few significant buildings and the **Terrestrial Centre** in Low Street (tel: 07-4062 1485; Apr–Sept daily 8am–5pm, Oct–Mar Mon–Fri 8.30am–4.30pm) which highlights the importance of minerals to the area. It's another 148km (92 miles) to **Croydon 26,** a friendly township with a well-preserved timber pub and an interesting historic precinct. From here there's an old railway service, the Gulflander, which runs through to **Normanton,** just a short distance from the **Gulf of Carpentaria.**

Towards the border with the Northern Territory, where the terrain is becoming drier and less hospitable, **Lawn Hill Gorge 27** provides a green oasis and stakes a claim to be one of the most spectacularly beautiful locations in the state. Not many people get out this far, but, for those who do, there are kayaks to paddle down between sheer red sandstone cliffs, and easy hikes through the surrounding Boodjamulla National Park. A half-hour drive away is the World Heritage-listed Riversleigh Fossils site.

Mining towns

Track south down dirt roads to **Mount Isa 28** and discover the full significance of the finds at the **Riversleigh Fossil Display & Interpretive Centre** attached to the Outback at Isa complex (tel: 07-4749 1555; www.outback atisa.com.au). Mount Isa is a mining city truly in the middle of nowhere. A rich lode of lead, silver, copper and zinc was discovered here in 1923, and a tiny tent settlement rapidly developed into Australia's largest company town, dominated by the looming presence of the mine and its tailings. Working mine tours are no longer available, but you can take a two-hour underground tour of the ersatz Hard Times Mine, through the Outback at Isa operation.

The municipal boundaries of the Isa extend for 41,000 sq km (15,830 sq miles) – an area the size of Switzerland. Away from the mines, people relax at the artificial Lake Moondarra or socialise in any of the numerous licensed clubs, which welcome visitors. In August, Mount Isa hosts a three-day rodeo, the largest and richest in Australia.   *Xxxxxx*

The School of the Air, first established in Cloncurry, now operates from here, providing children on remote properties with direct radio and internet contact with a teacher. Its premises adjoin the Kalkadoon High School on Abel Smith Parade and can be toured (Abel Smith Parade; tours Mon–Fri 9am and 10am in term time; tel: 07-4743 2788).

Cloncurry ㉙ is also a mining town, but in this case the main employer, the vast open-cut **Ernest Henry Mine**, is a bus ride away from the centre. Conducted tours are comprehensive and informative (tel: 07-4769 4500). Among the attractions in town, John Flynn Place (corner Daintree and King streets; tel: 07-4742 4100; Mon–Fri 8.30am–4.30pm all year, Sat–Sun 9am–3pm May–Sept) contains a museum devoted to the Royal Flying Doctor Service and its founder.

The Matilda Highway

The Matilda Highway heads southeast through **McKinlay**, home of the pub used in the Crocodile Dundee films and now called the Walkabout Creek Hotel. Some 241km (150 miles) further on

sits **Winton** ㉚, a town full of character and home to the Waltzing Matilda Centre (tel: 07-4657 1466; www.matilda centre.com.au; 50 Elderslie Street; Nov–Mar, Mon–Fri 9am–5pm, Sat–Sun 9am–3pm, Apr–Oct daily 9am–5pm), which celebrates the song, its composer "Banjo" Paterson and all aspects of Outback life. This is also dinosaur country.

From Winton, the Matilda Highway continues to **Longreach** ㉛, where two major attractions await. A local manufacturer helped develop the **Australian Stockman's Hall of Fame** (Landsborough Highway; tel: 07-4658 2166; www.outbackheritage.com.au; daily 9am–4pm) as a fascinating tribute to the cattle drovers, shearers, jackaroos and entrepreneurs who opened up Australia to settlement.

Longreach was where Qantas set up its first operational base in 1922, and its original hangar, with the old sign still on it, has become part of the multimillion-dollar **Qantas Founders Outback Museum** (Landsborough Highway; tel: 07-4658 3737; www. qfom.com.au; daily 9am–4pm), which displays a retired Qantas Boeing 747

The Ernest Henry Mine.

DINOSAUR DISTRICT

Detour south from Winton to **Lark Quarry Dinosaur Trackways** (tel: 07-4657 1466; www.dinosaurtrackways.com. au; tours at 10am, noon, 2pm), where petrified footprints denote a dinosaur encounter millions of years ago. The theme is maintained in two towns to the north: **Richmond** has Kronosaurus Korner (91–93 Goldring Street; tel: 07-4741 3429; www.kronosauruskorner.com. au; daily 8.30am–4pm), a marine fossil museum, while **Hughenden** is home to the Flinders Discovery Centre (37 Gray Street; tel: 07-4741 2970; daily 9am–5pm), with a replica of a dinosaur skeleton found locally. A concrete dinosaur in the middle of town presses the point home. Nearby is the majestic **Porcupine Gorge** with its 120-metre (400ft) -high walls.

jumbo jet (still in flying condition), replicas of its early fleet of biplanes, and a comprehensive record of the national airline's growth.

Barcaldine ㉜, to the east, is notable for a collection of vintage hotels and pubs, and as home to the Workers' Heritage Centre (Ash Street; tel: 07-4651 2422; www.australianworkersheritagecentre. com.au; Mon–Sat 9am–5pm, Sun 10am–4pm), where a collection of historic structures house displays commemorating the role played by workers in the development of Australia.

The Matilda Highway continues south all the way to Charleville ㉝. The usual assortment of historic buildings is worth a look, but the points of difference are the Cosmos Centre (Qantas Drive; tel: 07-4654 7771; www. cosmoscentre.com; Apr–Oct daily 10am–4pm, Nov–March closed Sun, evening sessions available), an observatory and museum which host astral viewing sessions; and the Steiger Gun, a bizarre device designed in 1902 to fire hot air into the sky in order to create rain.

Heading east through Roma and then Miles ㉞, with its charming

Historical Village (Murilla Street; tel: 07-4627 1492; www.mhv.org.au; daily 8am–5pm), would eventually lead back to the east coast.

Queensland's far west

But that would be to ignore two of Queensland's iconic sites. **The Dig Tree,** on the border with South Australia, is where the famous base camp of the Burke and Wills expedition just missed a rendezvous with the men who could have rescued them from starvation and death.

Finally, there is **Birdsville** ㉟. This isolated far western settlement has a population of 120, but each September it grows by five or six thousand for the Birdsville Races, when 300 light aircraft cram the airport, with their pilots camped under the wings. The 1884 Birdsville Hotel is a legendary watering hole. West of here are only the sand dunes of the Simpson Desert. A huge sandhill called **Big Red**, 36km (22 miles) to the west, marks the beginning of the famous Birdsville Track and is a popular spot for sunset parties.

Café proprietor in Wyandra, 100km (60 miles) south of Charleville.

The Big Red.

THE RAINFOREST

Tropical or temperate, the rainforest is one of Queensland's defining characteristics, as well as a key tourist attraction.

High rainfall – at least 2 metres (6.5ft) – is a prerequisite for rainforest, and then it's generally a matter of latitude and proximity to the ocean which defines it as either tropical or temperate. The Australian state of Queensland is big enough to meet both of these requirements.

Rainforests are nature in *extremis*. Two-thirds of all the Earth's plant and animal species can be found within them, and in north Queensland the highest diversity of local endemic species in the world is present. It is the last bastion for many of these animals, while others are still being discovered, particularly in the upper regions under the canopy, an area only recently appreciated for the richness of its various flora and fauna.

It is estimated that the tropical rainforest stretching from just north of Cairns to Cape Tribulation and on to Cooktown is in the region of 110 million years old, and constitutes the last remnant of the forest that used to cover all of Australia and, before that, Gondwanaland. Now protected as an element of the Wet Tropics World Heritage Area, it is a key attraction for tourists. The economic rationale that has seen the destruction of forests elsewhere in Australia and round the world will probably now protect it.

There are more than 520 species of lizards found in Australia. The five main families of lizards are geckos, legless lizards, dragon lizards, monitor lizards (or Goannas), and skinks.

The orange-thighed frog (Litoria xanthomera) is a tree frog native to a small area in tropical northern Queensland. The call of the frog is a long "aaa-rk", followed by a soft trill. They call after heavy monsoon rain, and often congregate around ponds, or at the edge of any standing body of water.

When the platypus was first discovered in Australia, many European naturalists were convinced it must be an elaborate hoax. It is the only living member of its family (Ornithorhynchidae) and genus (Ornithorhynchus), and is one of the few monotremes.

Gigantic trees in Daintree National Park.

THE DAINTREE

Some of the most easily accessible rainforest, and therefore most visited, is in the Daintree National Park. There's a well-worn route from Cairns or Port Douglas up to Cape Tribulation, and every tour bus or expedition will stop at least once for a walk in the woods. In several places there are short boardwalk circuits from handy parking spots, and the way is marked by a series of interpretive boards. This makes it easy for the visitor to explore, and also helps in managing the forest by keeping tourists away from more pristine areas.

The complete packaged rainforest experience can be enjoyed at the Daintree Discovery Centre (tel: 07-4098 9171; www.discoverthedaintree.com; daily 8.30am–5pm), a short distance north of the Daintree ferry. Boardwalks wend along the forest floor, and a steel walkway through the canopy allows an entirely different perspective on life as the birds see it. Audio guides are available and there are more of the ubiquitous interpretive boards. The cassowaries here seem used to visitors.

The red-necked pademelon (Thylogale thetis) is a small, forest-dwelling marsupial. The animal is very shy, and typically hides in the forest during the day, only emerging to look for food at night. The pademelon was nearly hunted to extinction by imported foxes on the mainland, but can be found throughout Tasmania.

The cassowary (Casuarius casuarius) is the third-largest flightless bird, after the ostrich and the emu. Its claws are particularly sharp, and cassowaries have been known to strike out at humans, although the legend that a human can be disembowelled with a single kick by the cassowary's strong legs has never been proven.

To see the rainforest from a different perspective, take a zip-line tour that stops at several platforms perched among the tree tops.

THE GREAT BARRIER REEF AND THE ISLANDS

The Reef is not only Queensland's major attraction, it is one of the natural wonders of the world. It is both the largest coral reef on Earth and one of the most accessible, and also has a selection of stunning islands.

The Great Barrier Reef.

The world's largest coral reef consists of more than 2,500 separate, interconnected reefs, stretching more than 2,300km (1,430 miles) from just above the tip of the Cape York Peninsula in the north to just north of Bundaberg in the south.

In the nomination that saw the Reef given a World Heritage listing, one of the supporting arguments was that, "Biologically, the Great Barrier Reef supports the most diverse ecosystem known to man. Its enormous diversity is thought to reflect the maturity of an ecosystem which has evolved over millions of years…" At the heart of that ecosystem is the polyp, a tiny animal consisting of little more than a mouth and surrounding tentacles to feed it – plus a limestone carapace into which it withdraws during the day. It is the skeletal remains of these creatures that form the basis of the reef. Individual polyps are linked by body tissue, thereby sharing the colony's food, but the main nutrient for a photosynthetic coral's food is algae cells within its tissue called zooxanthellae, which convert the sun's energy into nutrients.

The fragile coral

Over millions of years the reef has grown into the largest living entity in the world. This structure is fragile, however, and it only takes small environmental changes to disrupt its delicate balance. Coral bleaching is the major threat. If the water temperature rises by just a degree or two over a sustained period, the corals expel their zooxanthellae, lose their capacity for photosynthesis and become colourless. The process is not irreversible, but if the water does not cool within a month or so the coral will die.

Severe damage was caused by extended hot spells in 1997–8 and again in 2002, and most marine scientists believe that global warming not only exists but has a direct bearing on these incidents. The Australian government finally signed the Kyoto Protocol in December 2007 after the long-serving coalition government of John Howard was defeated at the ballot box. Then in December 2015, at a UN conference in Paris, over 190 countries signed an agreement to limit global warming.

There are other dangers, too. Human traffic can cause significant damage to coral, whether through chains and anchors from boats, or by snorkellers and divers who brush against polyps and damage or kill them. The Reef is also under pressure from the effects of poor water quality, which is often caused by soil and fertiliser runoff from the shore, and is not helped by the wash from cyclones. The Great Barrier Reef Marine Park was established in the 1970s to protect this magnificent resource; the Great Barrier Reef Marine Park Authority monitors the effects of tourism and fishing with research.

The islands

While only a few are literally coral islands, the 20 or so resort islands inside the Great Barrier Reef Marine Park offer many attractions. Lodging varies from five-star resorts to backpacker hostels and campsites. Some islands are dry, barren and windy; others are lush and covered with rainforest.

The South

Lady Elliot Island ❶: dubbed an "Eco Island", this is a quiet and beautiful 42-hectare (103-acre) coral cay, with bungalow accommodation and some permanent tents. It is 80km (50 miles) from Bundaberg and reached by air. Its coral setting ensures easy access to good diving and snorkelling.

Lady Musgrave Island ❷: a tiny uninhabited cay available only for daytrippers or campers (with a National Parks permit). Access is by boat from Bundaberg. It offers diving and snorkelling within a brilliant blue lagoon.

Heron Island ❸: only 1km (0.5 miles) long, this is the Reef's most famous coral cay and is number one for diving (along with Lizard at the northern fringe of the Reef). The Reef is certainly at its most accessible:

Exploring the reef.

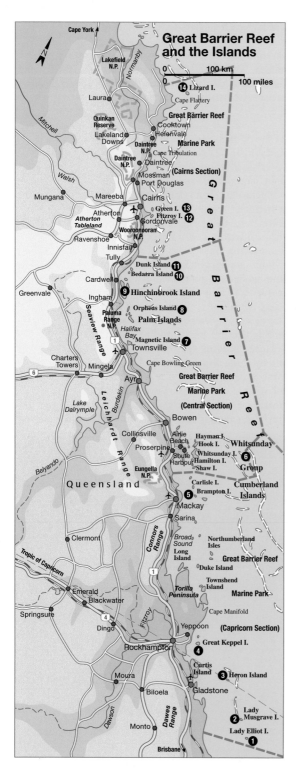

Great Barrier Reef and the Islands

where the beach ends, the coral begins, with its abundant marine life.

Great Keppel Island ❹: there are excellent white sandy beaches, long hiking trails, views of the mainland, and plenty of social activities. Great Keppel is not directly on the Reef; short cruises run out for divers. Access is by air from Rockhampton or by sea from Rosslyn Bay.

Brampton Island ❺: a mountain-ous island 32km (20 miles) from Mac-kay, Brampton has one resort set in a tropical garden. Sailing, water sports, beaches and rainforest walks are the attractions. Access is from Mac-kay and Shute Harbour but not for day-trippers.

The Whitsundays

At the southern end of **The Whit-sundays ❻** archipelago, **Lindeman Island**'s resort is Australia's first Club Med, and beyond the buildings it has retained the beauty of its natu-ral setting. There is tennis, swimming and fishing, and 20km (12 miles) of bushwalking trails through 500 hec-tares (1,230 acres) of national park. Access is from Mackay, Hamilton Island and Proserpine.

Three very different resorts co-exist on **Long Island,** and it is only a short boat trip from Shute Harbour. Long Island Resort is for all ages, and is particularly popular with the young. Peppers Palm Bay is ideal for a back-to-nature holiday with lovely beaches, clear water and coral, and solitude. The self-catering Paradise Bay Eco Resort provides waterside cabins.

The largest, most aggressively mar-keted Whitsunday resort on **Ham-ilton Island** has a high-rise hotel, a floating marina, an airstrip with direct flights to major cities and a full sports complex. With a pseudo-South Seas main street once described as "Daiquiri Disneyland", Hamilton Island is not the place for a quiet island sojourn, although its five-star qualia resort is the Reef's most luxu-rious hideaway.

The largest of the group, **Whitsunday Island** covers 109 sq km (42 sq miles) and has no resort, but does offer the fabulous Whitehaven Beach – a great option for campers (with permits).

A self-contained resort on a large, hilly island, **South Molle Island** is popular with families, and diving, swimming, sailing, golf, fishing and shopping are all offered. Travel is from Shute Harbour or Hamilton Island.

Daydream Island is a popular family resort with all the necessities for a good time at a reasonable all-inclusive tariff. Great beaches and a wide range of activities are just 15 minutes from Shute Harbour or Hamilton Island.

As the second-largest island in the Whitsundays, **Hook Island** provides budget camping and cabins as well as services for visiting yachts. There is an underwater observatory here and Aboriginal cave painting at Nara Inlet.

Hayman Island is an exclusive five-star resort set in a coral-trimmed lagoon, close to the outer Reef and a favourite with honeymooners. Access is from Hamilton Island, Proserpine, Shute Harbour and Townsville.

The Centre to the North

Magnetic Island ❼ is a large (5,000-hectare/12,400-acre) island and a national park; this pleasant, populated (2,300) haven is almost an outer suburb of mainland Townsville. There are plenty of walks in the rainforest, or up to the 500-metre (1,640ft) Mount Cook. Horseshoe Bay has a koala and wildlife park. Bikes, scooters and Mini Mokes can be rented.

Orpheus Island ❽ is in the Palm group northeast of Townsville and is very close to the outer Reef. An exclusive resort hidden among the trees has good accommodation and entertainment. Seaplane access from Townsville.

Hinchinbrook Island ❾ is accessible from Cardwell by boat. The jagged peaks, golden beaches and luxuriant rainforests of Hinchinbrook National Park can be fully explored by experienced hikers. The island's signature east-coast trail has limits on walker numbers so book in advance.

FACT

Not all of the Reef's islands are made of coral. In fact, nearly all of the popular resort islands are continental in nature – the tips of offshore mountain ranges. The true coral cays of the real Reef are more numerous but tend to be smaller and more fragile.

Diving and snorkelling are the islands' principal businesses.

Visiting the Reef

Every morning dozens of boats head out to various pre-selected sites. About an hour later, you'll be moored by the gorgeous coral.

The easiest way to visit the Reef is not to stay on an offshore island but to take a day trip from **Cairns** or **Port Douglas**. You can also take Reef trips from **Cape Tribulation**. Trips from some of the island resorts or coastal towns further south, such as Townsville, tend to be less commercialised and sophisticated and, indeed, less frenetic.

Because the water is so shallow, snorkelling is perfectly satisfactory for seeing the marine life (in fact, many people prefer it to scuba diving; even so, most boats offer tanks for experienced divers and resort dives for people who have never dived before). Above the waves, the turquoise void might be broken only by a sand cay crowded with sea birds, but as soon as you poke your mask underwater, the world erupts. It's almost sensory overload: there are vast forests of staghorn coral,

An aerial view of Green Island, where a luxury resort will cater to your every need.

whose tips glow purple like electric Christmas-tree lights; brilliant blue clumps of mushroom coral; layers of pink plate coral; bulbous green brain coral.

Tropical fish with exotic names slip about as if showing off their fluorescent patterns: painted flutemouth, long-finned batfish, crimson squirrelfish, hump-headed Maori wrasse, cornflower sergeant major.

Thrown into the mix are scarlet starfish and black sea cucumbers. You definitely don't pick up the sleek conus textile shells – they shoot darts into anything that touches them, each with enough venom to kill 300 people. There are 21 darts in each shell and so, as one captain notes, "if they don't get you the first time, they'll get another try".

When to go

Almost all Reef trips follow a similar format. There's a morning dive or snorkel, followed by a buffet lunch; then, assuming you haven't eaten too much or had too much free beer, an afternoon dive. There should be a marine biologist on board to explain the Reef's ecology. Before you book, ask how many passengers the boat takes: they vary from several hundred on the Quicksilver fleet of catamarans to fewer than a dozen on smaller craft.

The Reef is at its best from late April through to October, the clear skies and moderate breezes offering perfect conditions for coral viewing, diving, swimming, fishing and sunning. In November the first signs of the approaching "Wet" appear: variable winds, increasing cloud and showers. By January it rains at least once most days. And when the winds are up and the waters are stirred, visibility under the water diminishes. Furthermore, in rough seas excursion boats have fewer places to anchor and may be restricted to areas which have been over-visited and where, consequently, the coral has been damaged. Pick the time of your visit carefully.

In general, the further out the boat heads, the more pristine the diving (the Low Isles, for example, near Port Douglas, have suffered). But don't be conned by hype about the "Outer Reef"; although, as the edge of the continental shelf, it may be the "real" Reef, it looks exactly the same as other parts.

Even in the winter months, the water here is never cold, but it is worth paying a bit extra to hire a wet suit anyway; most people find it hard not to go on snorkelling for hours on end in this extraordinary environment.

A small fragment of the Family Islands, **Bedarra Island** ⑩ has an exclusive resort set in rich rainforest with pure beaches and tranquil coves. Go via **Dunk Island** ⑪, where the recluse E.J. Banfield lived for 26 years at the turn of the 20th century, writing his *Confessions of a Beachcomber*. The island is a rainforested national park with a large resort nestled in one corner and a camping ground alongside it. Access is from Townsville, Cairns and Mission Beach.

Surrounded by coral reef, **Fitzroy Island** ⑫ is a great place for diving and fishing. **Green Island** ⑬ is a tiny coral cay just off Cairns with a good underwater observatory, but it's mostly for day-trippers. The most northerly island, **Lizard Island** ⑭ is home to the marlin boats. Lizard allows access directly from the beach to the Reef and has stunning diving. Fly from Cairns.

The diving

With more than 2,000km (1,240 miles) of reef to choose from and numerous departure points, it is useful to have a grasp of the diving that awaits you.

Cod Hole, just off Lizard Island, is one of the best-known dive destinations because this one isn't just about coral gardens. You also get the chance to encounter potato cod, giant (up to 100kg/220lbs) man-sized fish that will nuzzle up to you in the hope of the food that most expeditions take along.

The SS **Yongala** passenger ship sank in 1911, but the wreck was only discovered 100km (60 miles) east of Townsville in 1958. The remains of the 110-metre (360ft) -long vessel are still intact and attract thousands of divers every year. Expeditions run from Townsville. **Wheeler Reef** is also accessed from Townsville and has a reputation for being one of the finest night dive sites, although, with its range of coral, eels, sharks and countless other fish, it's good at any time of day.

Lady Elliot Island has several outstanding dive sites, including the **Blow Hole**, a cave dive accessible via

Electric buggies are the popular way for tourists to get around Hamilton Island.

Lizard Island.

FACT

The washout from Queensland's massive floods at the beginning of 2011 is likely to have a major impact on the Great Barrier Reef, particularly off the coast of southern Queensland. Fertilisers in the water stimulate the growth of seaweed, which chokes the coral, while sediment blocks the sunlight. The effects are likely to be felt for years.

two openings 25 metres (82ft) down on the eastern side of the Island. Lion fish and gnome fish are among the company likely to greet you. The **Anchor Bommies** nearby also has rays and the added interest of two coral-encrusted naval anchors sitting on the sea bed.

Agincourt Reef is the destination of the substantial Quicksilver operation. You can't miss their massive silver catamarans, which transport visitors in their hundreds from pick-up points in Cairns, Palm Cove and Port Douglas out to their two-storey floating pontoon on the outer reef. Despite the numbers, the reef is well stocked with coral and associated marine life and ideal for beginners wanting a trial dive.

Heron Island has numerous attractions, including the Heron **Bommie**, one of the most famous dive sites on the reef. It is a nesting ground for green turtles between October and March. **Osprey Reef** is spectacular for its colony of white-tip reef sharks and some of the finest coral to be seen anywhere. Grey reef sharks, potato

cod and dogtooth tuna are amongst the other inhabitants. Cairns and Port Douglas are the departure points.

Bait Reef is in the Whitsundays so boats run out of Airlie Beach to this wonderland of tropical marine life. Much of what interests is close to the surface, so snorkellers are well catered for, along with novice divers who are comfortable up to 10 metres (32ft) down. **Hardy Reef**, also in the Whitsundays, is notable for a 70-metre (230ft) reef wall where numerous species of fish drift around both hard and soft coral.

Wolf Rock's four submerged volcanic peaks have swim-throughs and ledges along with a rich selection of subaquatic life. It's to be found on the Sunshine Coast off Double Island Point.

Ex-HMAS *Brisbane*, a former Royal Australian Navy destroyer, was scuttled off Mooloolaba on the Sunshine Coast as a wreck site. It's now 28 metres (92ft) down and experienced divers can look around parts of the ship's interior, helped by access holes.

Moore Reef.

Ex-HMAS Brisbane.

PROTECTING THE GREAT BARRIER REEF

The world's largest living entity is top of the list on many tourist itineraries, but its fragility means it's important to minimise visitor impact.

The Great Barrier Reef may be the largest collection of living organisms on Earth, but it is also extremely fragile. Rising sea temperatures have added to the already considerable risk posed by tourism, pollution and natural enemies such as the crown-of-thorns starfish. Protecting the reef from its natural and mad-made enemies has become more important than ever, as we learn about the biodiversity under the waves. The reef's astonishingly complex and diverse ecosystem will disappear forever if precautions aren't taken immediately.

The appeal of the Great Barrier Reef to visitors is undeniable, and tourism is big business. But should you decide to visit the park, there are a number of things you can do to limit your environmental impact. Scuba diving is one of the main tourist draws to the reef, but it can take an average of 25 years for coral to recover from an accidental knock and scrape from an inexperienced diver. The main way to avoid causing damage to the reef is to take scuba lessons before you travel, and then to make sure you choose a recognised dive operator to take you to the site. Smaller groups of divers are also preferable as they are less likely to cause disturbance to the coral and its inhabitants.

If you fish, make sure you use the Marine Park Authority's zoning maps, which will let you know of any restrictions in the area. Be sure to return any unwanted or undersized fish to the water as quickly as possible. Use official campsites and take all litter, including fishing lines, with you when you leave.

A giant potato cod.

Clownfish live at the bottom of the sea in sheltered reefs or in shallow lagoons, usually in pairs. In the wild, they live in a symbiotic relationship with the sea anemone.

A diver contemplates a sea fan, or gorgonian. A colony can be several metres high and across but only a few centimetres thic There are more than 500 species of gorgonians in the ocean.

A crown-of-thorns starfish.

THE REEF'S GREATEST ENEMY?

For years, the worst threat to the Reef was thought to be the crown-of-thorns starfish (above), an ugly creature that clamps on to coral and effectively spits its stomach out. Its digestive juices dissolve the polyps and leave great expanses of coral bleached and dead. The crown-of-thorns is poisonous to other fish and is almost indestructible: it can regenerate to full size from only a single leg and small piece of intestine.

With only a few around, it was easy to ignore its depradations on the reef, but in the early 1960s the pattern changed. Instead of a few crown-of-thorns starfish, suddenly there were millions. Green Island was the first to see the plague in 1962. From there it spread southwards, reaching the reefs around Bowen by 1988. Surveys between 1985 and 1988 established that about 31 percent of the reefs examined had been affected. Even after millions of dollars' worth of research, no one knows what caused the proliferation of the starfish. Furthermore, no economic way to get rid of the pest has presented itself.

Recently, however, marine biologists have decided to let the crown-of-thorns infestation run its destructive course. The latest wisdom posits that it is a natural, if poorly understood, part of the reef's life cycle and that the reef can return to pre-outbreak levels of coral in 10–15 years. Only time will tell if this scientific theory is correct.

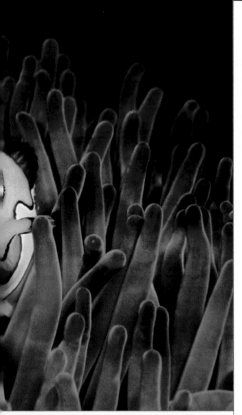

yellow crinoid (phylum Echinodermata) waves in the waters the Great Barrier Reef. The name crinoid comes from the eek word for lily, although this is an animal, not a plant.

sea slug.

Six species of sea turtle call the Great Barrier Reef home, while there are two distinct genetic groups of the green sea turtle: one at the north end of the reef, and one at the south.

Uluru at sunset.

Simpson's Gap, near Alice Springs.

NORTHERN TERRITORY

Fewer than one in 100 Australians live in the vast Northern Territory, an untamed region with a climate, a landscape and a history all of its own.

The Northern Territory, or just "NT", is Australia in epic mode. Things here are larger than life – the sky, the distances, people's dreams and visions, the Earth itself. An area of 1.35 million sq km (521,240 sq miles) – more than double the size of France, yet inhabited by just 244,000 people – provides plenty of room to move.

The locals are a breed apart: tough, laconic, beholden to no one. Like the inhabitants of any inhospitable environment, they possess friendliness by the bucketful, a truly egalitarian spirit, and a wicked sense of humour.

Many urban Australians visiting NT's Outback feel as though they have entered a foreign land. They find a kind of detachment, a floating feeling of insubstantiality inspired by the uncomfortable knowledge that nothing human beings do here can ever touch the soul or the brute power of this ancient land.

Long distances

Despite its size, the Northern Territory fits neatly into a travel itinerary. There is the Red Centre – Alice Springs and the stunning hinterland in the Territory's south; various points along "The Track" (the Stuart Highway) heading north; and the Top End of Darwin, Kakadu and surroundings.

The distance between points of interest can be intimidating – roughly 1,600km (1,000 miles) from Alice to Darwin – but only by driving through NT do you get a true sense of its grand and ancient terrain.

Apart from the Top End, which is swamped by tropical monsoons from February to March each year, most of the Territory is an arid zone. Rainfall is minimal, averaging about 250mm (9.8ins) a year. But, when rain does come, it comes Outback-style: no half measures.

Main Attractions
Alice Springs
Uluru and Kata Tjuta
Tennant Creek
Kakadu National Park
Darwin
Tiwi Islands

The Rim Walk in Kings Canyon.

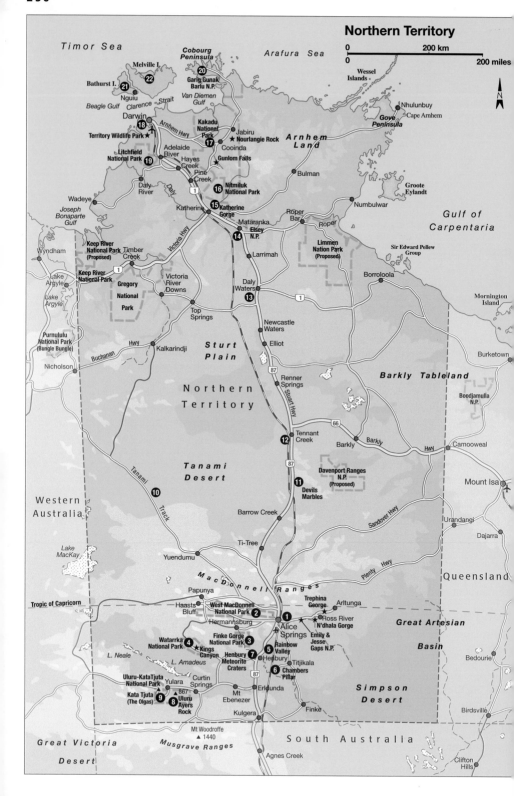

Northern Territory

0   200 km
0   200 miles

Timor Sea

Arafura Sea

Cobourg
Peninsula

Melville I.

20 Garig Gunak
Barlu N.P.

Bathurst I. 21

22

Van Diemen
Gulf

Wessel
Islands

Nguiu

Beagle Gulf Clarence   Strait

Nhulunbuy
Cape Arnhem

Darwin

18

Arnhem Hwy

Kakadu
National
Park

Jabiru

Nourlangie Rock

Arnhem
Land

Gove
Peninsula

Territory Wildlife Park

Litchfield
National Park 19

Adelaide
River

Hayes
Creek

Cooinda

17

Gunlom Falls

Daly
River

Pine
Creek

16

Nitmiluk
National Park

Bulman

Groote
Eylandt

Wadeye

Joseph
Bonaparte
Gulf

Daly

Katherine 15 Katherine
Gorge

Numbulwar

Gulf of
Carpentaria

Wyndham

Keep River
National Park
(Proposed) Timber
Creek

Mataranka
Elsey
N.P.

14

Roper
Bar

Roper

Sir Edward Pellew
Group

Lake
Argyle

Lake
Argyle

Keep River
National Park

Gregory

Victoria
River
Downs

Larrimah

Limmen
Nation Park
(Proposed)

Borroloola

Mornington
Island

Purnululu
National Park
(Bungle Bungle)

National

Park

Top
Springs

Daly
Waters

13

Hwy

Buchanan

Kalkarindji

Sturt
Plain

Newcastle
Waters

Elliot

Burketown

Nicholson

Northern
Territory

Renner
Springs

Barkly Tableland

Boodjamulla
N.P.

Victoria Hwy

Stuart Hwy

Tanami
Desert

Tanami

Track

10

66

12

Tennant
Creek

Barkly Barkly

Hwy

Camooweal

Mount Isa

87

Davenport Ranges
N.P.
(Proposed)

11

Devils
Marbles

Sandover Hwy

Urandangi

Western
Australia

Barrow Creek

87

Dajarra

Lake
MacKay

Ti-Tree

Yuendumu

Plenty Hwy

Queensland

Tropic of Capricorn

MacDonnell Ranges

Papunya

Haasts
Bluff

West MacDonnell
National Park

2

Trephina
George

Arltunga

Great Artesian

Hermannsburg

1

Alice
Springs

Ross River

N'dhala Gorge

Watarrka
National Park 4

Finke Gorge
National Park

3

Emily &
Jesse
Gaps N.P.

Basin

Kings
Canyon

Henbury

7 Rainbow
Valley

5

Bedourie

Meteorite
Craters

Henbury

Titjikala

Uluru-KataTjuta
National Park

Yulara

867

Curtin
Springs

6

Chambers
Pillar

Simpson
Desert

Birdsville

L. Neale

L. Amadeus

Kata Tjuta
(The Olgas) 9

8 Uluru
Ayers
Rock

Mt
Ebenezer

Erldunda

Finke

Kulgera

Clifton
Hills

Great Victoria

Mt Woodroffe
▲ 1440

South Australia

Desert

Musgrave Ranges

Agnes Creek

The Red Centre

Australia's Red Centre is the heart of the country in more ways than one. For many visitors, Australia is primarily a nature trip, and it is here in central Australia that the continent's greatest natural feature stands – **Uluru**, or **Ayers Rock**. But just as two-thirds of the Rock's awesome mass lies hidden beneath the ground, so Uluru and the other main tourist sights represent the mere tip of the great iceberg that is the Outback.

Incidentally, the Red Centre isn't just a cute name. The sand and rock around here are red because of iron oxides found in the sandstone. The sun is red when it drops, and red scars mark the flow of mineral-rich, ultra-healthy water. Even some of the kangaroos are red.

Alice Springs

Alice Springs ❶ – or the Alice – is the natural base for exploring the Red Centre. It is a grid-pattern, sunscorched town of squat, mostly modern buildings, which crouches in one of many gaps (or Outback oases) in the rugged **MacDonnell Ranges**. These hills – which turn an intense blue at sunset, as if lit internally – act like a wagon train, a protective ring that might just keep the expanse of the Outback at bay.

Alice has enjoyed a tourist boom, based on Uluru and Aboriginal art and culture. Its present population of over 28,000, one-tenth of which is Aboriginal, represents the greatest demographic concentration for 1,500km (900 miles) in any direction.

By no means a picture-postcard town, Alice has strange powers of attraction: visitors find themselves drawn again and again to this incongruous outpost, and many who come here for short-term work wake up 10 years later and wonder what happened. It's not necessarily easy to meet someone who was actually born in Alice.

Settlement began here in 1871 in the form of a repeater station on the Overland Telegraph Line, constructed beside the permanent freshwater springs. Lying 4km (2.5 miles) north of the present township, the **Telegraph Station** (tel: 08-8952 3993; www.alicespringstelegraph-station.com.au; Mon–Sat 8.30am–5pm;

View towards the West MacDonnell Ranges, Alice Springs.

The Royal Flying Doctor service operates more than 50 aircraft and has around 500 full-time staff. It can make over 160 landings and deal with more than 600 patients each day, nearly 100 of whom will need an aerial evacuation.

Sun 9am–5pm) and **Springs** form a popular tourist site. Then, as now, water dictated all human movement and settlement, and the line, running from Adelaide through Alice and up to Darwin, followed virtually the same route as The Track does now. The line linked the cities of Australia's south and southeast with the rest of the world, as it continued from Darwin through Indonesia to Singapore, Burma, British India and across Asia and Europe to colonial headquarters in London. Keeping the line open was a full-time job, and it is still possible to see some of the original telegraph posts, now disused, rising from the hard earth.

Alice developed slowly; in 1925, it had just 200 residents. Four years later, the coming of the Ghan train – which at that time ran from Adelaide via Oodnadatta to Alice and is named after Afghan camel drivers who pioneered transport in these parts – saw things pick up, but the trip was fraught with hazards. In the mistaken belief that the Outback never flooded, the track was routed across low-lying terrain; consequently, the train was often stranded, with additional supplies having to be parachuted in to the hapless passengers. A new, flood-proof route was completed in 1980, and the Ghan remains one of Australia's great rail journeys. In February 2004 Alice Springs ceased to be the end of the line, when the Alice–Darwin 1,420km (880-mile) extension was completed. The event fulfilled a century-old promise of a key economic and tourism link.

The Flying Doctor

In Alice, spend your first sunset on **Anzac Hill** to get the lie of the land. One of the town's most popular attractions is the **Royal Flying Doctor Service Visitors' Centre** (tel: 08-8238 3333; www.flyingdoctor.org.au; tours Mon–Sat 9am–4pm, Sun 1–4pm). The service, established in 1928 by the Rev. John Flynn – who now graces the A\$20 bill – provides essential medical treatment to many isolated communities and cattle stations the length and breadth of the Outback. Flynn's grave is 7km (4 miles) west of Alice on Larapinta Drive – he is pinned down in perpetuity by one of the Devil's Marbles, poor chap.

Another popular spot is the **Alice Springs School of the Air** on Head Street, which services the educational needs of far-flung children. The school, unique in the world, conducts primary-level classes via radio, and the most notable of its 26 bases across the Outback is in Alice, covering an area of 1.3 million sq km (500,000 sq miles). It is the world's biggest classroom, and visitors can listen to lessons being taught there.

The **Alice Springs Desert Park**, situated just outside Alice at the base of the MacDonnell Ranges, is a must-see primer for anyone about to explore the desert. Its 35 hectares (86 acres) contain 320 arid-zone plant species and more than 400 desert-dwelling animals. The birds of prey nature theatre, where wild birds interact with park rangers in an astonishing way, is unforgettable.

The **Araluen Cultural Precinct** (tel: 08-8951 1122; https://artsandmuseums.

ABORIGINAL FESTIVALS

Many tourists want to experience life in remote Aboriginal communities. This is not always possible with the permit system for travel into the communities, but a number of communities celebrate annual festivals at which visitors are welcome. If you want to enjoy one of these opportunities to get an insight into Aboriginal life, you will need to rough it a little: camping is usually the only accommodation option.

The **Barunga Festival** (www.jawoyn.org), held on the Queen's Birthday long weekend in early June, is a celebration of sports and culture, particularly music. More than 20 communities come together at the festival, a four-hour drive from Darwin. The program includes a battle of the bands and the sports program, there are performances of traditional dance, arts and crafts. Beswick Falls (djilpinarts.org.au), south of Katherine, hosts the Walking with Spirits festival every July. In a spectacular lakeside setting, guests can enjoy not just traditional corroboree, but also songs and stories told in dance, music, puppetry, fire and film.

August is the time for Stone Country Festival (www.travelnt.com) in the Arnhem land community of Gunbalanya. From rock art tours to spear throwing, live bands and art sales, painting demonstrations and the ubiquitous football and basketball competitions, there's a packed program.

nt.gov.au; Mon–Fri 10am–4pm, Sat–Sun 11am–4pm) on Larapinta Drive contains the Strehlow Research Centre, the Museum of Central Australia, the Memorial Cemetery, the Central Australian Aviation Museum and the Araluen Centre, including the Namatjira Gallery.

The **Strehlow Research Centre** chronicles the life and work of Ted Strehlow, who was born at Hermannsburg, the Lutheran mission established in 1877. He became a patrol officer and researcher among the Arrernte people, winning their trust, and artefacts from his comprehensively documented collection that are not culturally sensitive are on display at the centre.

For non-aviators, the **Aviation Museum** is uninspiring; the cemetery is more interesting because the famous Aboriginal landscape painter Albert Namatjira and the legendary gold seeker Harold Lasseter (whose lives form a pretty comprehensive recent history of the region) are buried there, as are a number of Afghans, in a separate section at the back, facing Mecca.

If you find yourself in Alice in September, don't miss the **Henley-on-Todd Regatta** (www.henleyontodd.com. au). This grandly named event is a boat race unlike any other. The "boats" are bottomless wraparounds, and teams of about eight runners inside each one race along the dry bed of the Todd River. Much merriment is had by all.

Around Alice

Alice's immediate surroundings offer numerous attractions. To the east, in the **Eastern MacDonnell Ranges**, **Emily Gap**, **Jesse Gap**, **Trephina Gorge**, **N'dhala Gorge** and the old gold town of **Arltunga** are interesting excursions.

Stretching west from Alice is the **West MacDonnell National Park ❷**, incorporating many of the gaps in the ranges. These include **Simpson's Gap**, accessible via an excellent cycle path from Alice; **Standley Chasm**, whose steep walls become alive with colour an hour either side of midday; **Serpentine Gorge**; the **Ochre Pits**, used by Aborigines for centuries; **Ormiston Gorge and Pound**, with some fine walking trails; **Glen Helen Gorge**, with a comfortable lodge nearby; and

FACT

Alice Springs gained fame through Neville Shute's 1950 novel A Town Like Alice, filmed in 1956 with Peter Finch and in 1981 as a TV series with Bryan Brown. Its title echoes the longings of an Aussie prisoner of war in Malaya in World War II. Shute (1899–1960), a prolific London-born novelist, emigrated to Australia after the war.

Alice Springs at night.

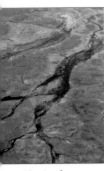

The view from an aircraft provides a unique perspective on the arid land around Alice Springs.

A painting on display at the Northern Territory Aviation Museum.

Redbank Gorge. A 223km (138-mile) walking track, the **Larapinta Trail**, constructed by local prisoners, connects many of the attractions of the MacDonnells. Guided treks along the whole track can be arranged in Alice.

To the south is **Finke Gorge National Park ❸**, featuring the picturesque Palm Valley, with its distinctive red cabbage palms, and the Finke River, whose watercourse is one of the oldest in the world at 350 million years in some areas. This park is accessed via Hermannsburg, by four-wheel-drive only.

Due west of here is one of Central Australia's star attractions – spectacular **Kings Canyon** and **Watarrka National Park ❹**. The 350-million-year-old canyon shelters a permanent rockpool, aptly named the Garden of Eden and visited during the magnificent four-hour **Canyon Rim Walk**. The nearby Kings Canyon Resort offers a range of accommodation. There is also accommodation 36km (22 miles) from the Canyon Rim Walk at Kings Creek Station, which offers basic cabins and a camping ground.

The **Mereenie Loop Road** is a dirt road that connects Watarrka National Park with Namatjira Drive and attractions like Glen Helen Gorge. The track skirts the desert's eastern edge and should not be tackled by a conventional vehicle without local advice. Beware of crossing camels. The road crosses Aboriginal land so you will need a permit; these are readily available at tourist centres in the area but can only be issued on the day of travel.

Rock formations south of Alice

South of Alice lies **Pine Gap**, off-limits to visitors but notable as the largest US communications and surveillance base in the Asia-Pacific region. Most of the 400-odd Americans employed here live in Alice; they hold weekend barbecues and baseball games in town parks.

The Aboriginal rock carvings at **Ewaninga**, of undetermined age, remain cryptic and alluring. Kaleidoscopic **Rainbow Valley ❺** is a stunning rock formation (with primitive camping conditions), as is **Chambers Pillar ❻**, a solitary upstanding red ochre outcrop inscribed with the names and dates of early explorers, who used it as a convenient landmark.

The **Henbury Meteorite Craters ❼**, just off the highway, consist of 12 indentations, about 5,000 years old, the biggest of which (180 metres/590ft wide by 15 metres/49ft deep) was caused by four meteors, each the size of a 200-litre (44-gallon) drum. The craters have become occasional pools, sprouting plants and attracting a variety of animal life.

En route to Uluru is **Curtin Springs**, a sprawling cattle station established in 1930 to breed horses for the British Indian Army. The roadside pub is a bit of a showroom for weird and wonderful tourist paraphernalia.

Dominating the horizon is **Mount Conner**, a table-top monolith that many people initially mistake for Uluru. Conner, at 700 million years old, is 150 million years older than Uluru and Kata Tjuta and just 4 metres (13ft)

lower than Uluru. You can visit Mount Conner by helicopter or with Discovery Ecotours (tel: 08-8956 2563; www.tours.net.au) both based in Yulara, or on a day tour from Ayers Rock Resort.

Uluru and Kata Tjuta

From here, the road leads to Australia's great Outback icon, **Uluru** ❽ (**Ayers Rock**; charge for a three-day pass), whose surrounding Uluru-Kata Tjuta National Park was World Heritage-listed for its natural significance in 1987, and for its cultural significance in 1994. It was first sighted by a European in 1872 when explorer Ernest Giles noted a prominent hill in the distance. The following year, William Gosse discovered that the hill was in fact "one immense rock rising abruptly from the plain". After climbing it barefoot and soaking up its mystical aura, he enthused: "This rock appears more wonderful every time I look at it."

Uluru means "meeting place", and many Aboriginal Dreaming tracks or songlines intersect here. Spirituality is often grounded in common sense, and Uluru, with its permanent waterhole,

abundant animal life, shelter and firewood, has been saving lives for millennia. The rock is sacred to the local Anangu people, who resumed ownership of the lands inside the national park in 1985, in a historic handover ceremony. The Anangu have a controlling interest on the park's board of management; the chairperson is Anangu, and the meetings are bilingual (Pitjantjatjara and English). No park policy or development occurs without consultation. The Anangu receive more than A$2 million in revenue under the terms of the handback, but there is a caveat: tourists are allowed to climb over the rock on a defined path, although Anangu sacred places are still out of bounds.

Climbing Uluru is a major attraction for many visitors, but is considered by resident park rangers and rescue teams to be a dangerous activity. More than a dozen climbers have been killed, and every few days someone has to be rescued. The Anangu would prefer that no one climbed, but at the same time they respect tourists' urge to do so. In one local language,

FACT

Over 500kg (1,100lbs) of metal have been found at the Henbury Meteorite Craters, mainly iron and nickel. There is not much left now, but fragments of the meteorite can be seen at the Museum of Central Australia in Alice Springs.

The Henley-on-Todd Regatta.

Uluru is the world's largest monolith. It stands 348 metres (1,142ft) tall and its circumference at the base is almost 9km (5.5 miles). Its elevation is 867m (2,844ft) above sea level.

Walking around the rim of Kings Canyon.

the word for the ubiquitous tiny black ant is *minga* – it is also the word for tourist. This cutting-edge ecotourism is about as happy as this sort of cross-cultural marriage of convenience gets.

Recognising that the climb cannot be closed until more alternative activities are in place, the board of management opened a cultural centre in 1995 to mark the 10th anniversary of handback. An alternative to climbing is the 9.4km (5.8-mile) "base walk" around the rock, which is well marked. A self-guiding brochure is available from the cultural centre and numerous interpretive signs are displayed.

While more walks in the rock's vicinity are scheduled, **Kata Tjuta ❾** or **The Olgas** has a number of excellent trails, including the three-hour **Valley of the Winds** circuit. No climbing of Kata Tjuta (which means "many heads", referring to the 36 domes) is permitted and, just in case you get the urge to take home any souvenir rocks or sand, bear in mind that it is disrespectful to Aboriginal sentiments and that park authorities receive, on average, two letters a week from visitors

returning rocks they had taken, claiming that their luck has been bad ever since their stay in Uluru.

The 380,000-odd annual visitors to the national park are serviced by the award-winning **Yulara Resort**, which has been given a major refurbishment. There is a wide range of tours and activities available, and the sight of a sunset traffic jam has to be seen to be believed. Uluru, like the entire Red Centre, will humble you with its scale and overwhelm you with its beauty.

The first attempt at luxury tented accommodation on the edge of the Uluru-Kata Tjuta National Park burnt down when an official bush burn got out of control. **Longitude 131** is now back in business, with 15 air-conditioned tents.

The Track to Tennant Creek

Anyone seeking the old-style Outback experience of endless long, hot, dirt roads may like to leave the highway 21km (13 miles) north of Alice Springs and head northwest along the **Tanami Track ❿** to rejoin civilisation 1,050km (660 miles) away at Halls Creek in the Kimberley. But, for most tastes, the 1,500km (930-mile) route along a good paved road to Darwin will suffice.

Heading north from Alice, one passes through the tiny community of **Barrow Creek**, before reaching the **Devil's Marbles Conservation Reserve ⓫** (403km/250 miles from Alice), a series of granite boulders that litter either side of the highway for several kilometres. Some of the larger ones stand precariously balanced on tiny bases. It's thought they were once part of one solid block, broken and gradually rounded by wind and water erosion. The local Aboriginal people believe them to be the eggs of the rainbow serpent.

Tennant Creek ⓬ (504km/313 miles from Alice) is a gold town, although only one major mine is still in production. Gold was discovered in 1932 but the rush was short-lived, and the place seemed destined to become a

ghost town until the discovery of copper in the 1950s brought new prosperity. The town is 12km (7 miles) from the creek; the story goes that a cart carrying timber to build the first pub for the miners became bogged here. It was too much trouble to continue, so the hotel was erected on the spot. With a tree-lined double highway and a population of over 3,500, the town bears few signs of such a haphazard beginning.

To explore the remote **Barkly Tableland**, take the Barkly Highway east for 185km (115 miles), then turn north onto the Tablelands Highway and towards the remote township of **Borroloola** (pop. 900), just inland from the Gulf of Carpentaria and famous for its barramundi fishing. Like any journey that involves driving into the true Outback, this route requires ample preparation, including fuel, emergency rations and water. The last leg to Borroloola is on the Carpentaria Highway, an excellent sealed road.

Into the Top End

North of Tennant Creek, the tiny township of **Renner Springs** marks a geographical and climatic end to the long, dry journey through the Red Centre: this is the southern extremity of the monsoon-affected plains of the Top End. But the changes between the desert and the plans are slow and subtle. Termite mounds are fascinating features of this scrubby country. They are usually about 3 metres (11ft) high and point north–south, a position that allows termites the maximum benefit of both heat and shade. This orientation inevitably led to them being called "magnetic anthills"; at first glance it does look as if they are built on compass bearings.

At **Elliott**, golfers can enjoy the far-out experience of playing nine holes on a desert course with well-kept greens.

Newcastle Waters is a historic stock-route junction town established as a telegraph station. In 1872 at **Frew's Ironside Ponds**, some 50km (31 miles) north of Newcastle Waters, the respective ends of the telegraph

wire were joined to establish the overland communication link.

The **Daly Waters Pub** ⓭ is worth a pause for a drink and rest. Built in the 1930s as a staging post for Qantas crew and passengers on multi-hop international flights, it is full of related memorabilia. **Mataranka** ⓮ is a small town that was really put on the map only when an earlier rail track from Darwin was laid in 1928. Before that, it was part of the huge Elsey farming property (in 1916 Mataranka Station was established as an experimental sheep run, a project doomed to failure in this classic cattle country). Today, the surprise attraction is the **Mataranka Homestead Tourist Resort**, a 4-hectare (10-acre) section of tropical forest, including palms and paperbark trees adjoining the **Elsey National Park**. The nearby sparkling **Mataranka Thermal Pool**, with a water temperature of 34°C (93°F), is a real oasis amid the north's arid surrounds. Also adjacent to the tourist park is a replica of the Elsey Station homestead, made for the 1981 film *We of the Never Never*.

Katherine, 103km (63 miles) to the

The Yulara Resort has seven different tiers of accommodation, ranging from a camping ground to a luxury resort. Its water supply is drawn from underground rivers.

Walking around Uluru.

TIP

Visitors to Tennant Creek can tour the underground gold mine at Battery Hill Mining Centre, about 1.5km (1 mile) east of the town centre. There's an enormous ore crusher plus two museum buildings, and you can try your hand at noodling for your own gold (tel: 08-8962 1281; www.barklytourism.com.au; daily 9am–5pm).

Kata Tjuta.

north, is the Top End's second most important town after Darwin. It has a population of 10,500 and a well-developed infrastructure of shops, camping grounds, hotels and motels. Since colonial days, Katherine has been an important telegraph station and cattle centre.

Katherine Gorge

To the east of the township, **Katherine Gorge ⑮** is one of the best-known features of the Territory. It's a massive stretch of sandstone cliffs rising to more than 100 metres (330ft) above the Katherine River, with 13 main canyons. The gorge is best explored by water. Tour boats operate mostly on the lower two canyons, but the more inquisitive traveller can explore the other 11 gorges upstream – by hiring a canoe– for a total of 12km (7 miles) before the river widens out again. (The small crocodiles looking on are freshwater and don't attack humans, although they can be unnerving.) In recent years "saltie" crocs have been found; this has led to a ban on swimming. Check current recommendations before getting into the water.

The gorge system is part of the 1,800-sq-km (695-sq-mile) **Nitmiluk National Park ⑯**, which deserves at least a couple of days. There are also several walking trails in the park that follow the top of the escarpment, looking down into the gorge. Katherine is also home to a Savannah Guide Station. These eco-accredited specialist guides focus on heritage, culture, and the preservation of the natural environment.

From Katherine, the Victoria Highway strikes west towards the Kimberley region of Western Australia. Just before the WA border, there is a turnoff to **Keep River National Park**. Like the better-known formations across the border in the Purnululu National Park, Keep River features a series of fascinating banded sandstone towers that shelter a wide range of vegetation and animal life.

The richness of Kakadu

One of the brightest jewels in the whole array of Australian wilderness lies to the north of Katherine, at **Kakadu National Park ⑰**. The park's prime accommodation and

commercial centre is Jabiru, 250km (155 miles) southeast of Darwin. The richness of Kakadu defies description. Here, where the Arnhem Land escarpment meets the coastal floodplains, scenic splendour, ancient Aboriginal culture and paintings and an incredible array of flora and fauna come together in a brilliant, coherent whole.

The statistics of Kakadu – which is now on the World Heritage list – give some indication of what this area has to offer. The park covers 19,804 sq km (7,200 sq miles), with further extension likely. It is home to a quarter of all Australian freshwater fish, more than 1,000 plant species, 300 types of birds, 75 species of reptiles, many mammals and innumerable insects. Its world-famous galleries of Aboriginal art – particularly at Nourlangie and Ubirr rocks – give a significant insight into early man more than 20,000 years ago. In Kakadu the oldest evidence for the technology of edge-ground stone axes has been found.

Coming into Kakadu from the south, via the road from **Pine Creek**, one should detour into **Gunlom**, with its magical combination of waterfall and plunge pool. This oasis featured in the 1986 film *Crocodile Dundee* and is even more beautiful than its celluloid image.

Most visitors approach Kakadu along the sealed **Arnhem Highway** from Darwin. This road terminates at **Jabiru**, a service town for the Ranger Uranium Mine; the mine operates in an enclave surrounded by the national park and near to **Arnhem Land**, a great expanse of Aboriginal land that is closed to tourists. The juxtaposition of national park and uranium mine has provided ongoing controversy in Australian politics for years.

A good introduction to Kakadu is a boat tour on **Yellow Water**, at Cooinda, which offers the finest natural wildlife viewing anywhere in Australia. You are likely to see saltwater crocodiles, Jabiru storks, brolga cranes and a host of water birds, resident and migratory – but only during the dry season (May–Sept). During The Wet, when water is plentiful, the

animals disperse across the region, and successful viewing is more haphazard.

Other easily accessible sights within the park are the paintings of **Ubirr Rock** and the towering faces of **Nourlangie Rock**. The splendid **Bowali Visitor Centre** has a permanent display setting out the features of the park. The **Marrawuddi Gallery** features displays of Aboriginal art, books and gifts.

To see what makes Kakadu special, however, head out to one or more of the water holes nestled at the base of the escarpment.

The most popular conjunction of swimming hole and waterfall is **Jim Jim Falls**. The deep, cool pool and the nearby sandy beach are remarkably attractive and have the distinct benefit of being easy to visit, at least when the access road is open (June–Nov). Effort is well rewarded for those who decide to walk into nearby **Twin Falls**, where the two strands of water drop right onto the end of a palm-shaded beach. However, don't swim there because large and possibly hungry crocodiles have been known to move in. Both Jim Jim and Twin Falls turn into seething

FACT

Jeannie Gunn, the author of the 1908 Outback novel We of the Never Never, was the wife of the manager of Elsey Station, and the first white woman to set foot in this area. The saying goes that those who live in the region can "never never" leave.

A boat trip through the Katherine Gorge.

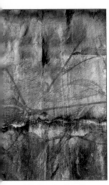

Rock paintings in Kakadu National Park.

Kakadu National Park.

maelstroms during wet-season flooding, at which time they are inaccessible to anyone without a helicopter. In the dry season, they are tranquil places of exquisite beauty, but you will need a four-wheel-drive vehicle.

The Adelaide River

On the Arnhem Highway to Darwin you cross the **Adelaide River**, and at that point you'll find the *Adelaide River Queen* (tel: 08-8988 8144; www.jumpingcrocodilecruises.com.au), which can take you on a short (90-minute) river cruise to see the "jumping crocodiles", which leap almost clear of the water when offered a slice of steak, just as they do when catching birds and bats in midair. There are more croc cruises just down the river.

Darwin

Darwin ⓲, capital of the Northern Territory, was founded in 1869, after more than four decades of failed settlements in the north – abandoned one after another because of malaria outbreaks, cyclones, and supply failure due to the sheer distance from the other settlements. Named after the naturalist Charles Darwin, one of whose shipmates on the *Beagle* discovered the bay in 1839, it drifted on in a tropical stupor for decades, punctuated only by the discovery of gold at Pine Creek in 1870 and a minor revolution in 1919. Some 243 people were killed and another 300 injured in the first savage surprise Japanese bombing attack in February 1942, and Darwin suffered repeated raids over the following 18 months.

Today's Darwin has a pace that might – almost – be described as brisk, at least by Northern Territory standards. Once the neurotic front line of colonial Australia, the city's populace now reflects its proximity to Asia: the mix of some 50 cultures, including Aborigines, Vietnamese, Filipinos, Malays, New Guineans, Pacific Islanders, Japanese and Indonesians – and Greeks and other Australians – provides a strong cosmopolitan flavour. That mix might have become more predominantly Asian had the Japanese advance in World War II not been stalled at New Guinea. When the Japanese bombed Darwin's port, there was mass panic, desertions,

.he evacuation of the civilian popula-
ion, and the looting of homes by some
of the army marshals who remained.
The desperate dash for safety in the
south became known derisively as the
Adelaide River Stakes.

Discoveries of oil and gas in the
Timor Sea have led to an influx of
mining engineers, refinery workers
and skilled tradesmen, feeding an economic boom. In turn, this has led to a
housing boom, with apartment blocks
proliferating and real estate prices
rocketing. Many locals have cashed in
on the housing boom, while doomsay-
ers predict that the levels of economic
and housing activity are not sustainable
in the long term, and that the downturn will surely come. Meanwhile, the
defence forces give another boost to the
economy, with army, navy and airforce
personnel spending at least two years
in Darwin as part of their service.

Everywhere there is a spirit of opti-
mism, although population mobility
remains an important factor. Many
people leave the Territory on retirement to head south, where health and
aged care facilities are better.

Darwin sights

The focal point of the city's defence
was the **Old Navy Headquarters A**.
This simple stone building, dating
from 1884, was a police station and
courthouse. It and other historical
buildings, such as **Fannie Bay Gaol**
(1883) and **Brown's Mart** (built in
1885, and the oldest in the city centre),
contrast with Darwin's new cyclone-
proof architecture, represented by the
city's high-rise hotels, **Sky City Casino**
and **Parliament House**.

Despite the changes, it is Darwin's
natural charm and the relaxed Top End
lifestyle that give the new city its appeal.
The town is flanked by great expanses
of golden sandy beaches and in the dry
season – April to October – the vision of
sand, clear blue skies and tropical flora
makes Darwin immensely attractive.

For six months of the year **Darwin
Harbour B** becomes the playground
of the area's boating populace. Many
people swim here, even though huge
saltwater crocodiles are regularly
pulled from the water. It may be more
relaxing to swim on the Fannie Bay side
at nearby **Mindil Beach** or **Vestey's**

FACT

The walls at Ubirr Rock
have been painted and
repainted over millennia.
The earliest paintings
may be up to 23,000
years old – which would
place them among the
oldest artworks known
anywhere on Earth – but
most of the paintings in
the main gallery are in
the familiar x-ray style
that is less than 1,500
years old.

CYCLONE TRACY

In four furious hours on Christmas Eve
1974, Cyclone Tracy swept in from the
north and flattened the city of Darwin.
With gusts up to 280kph (175mph),
the hurricane destroyed more than
5,000 homes – 80 percent of the city.
The dead and missing totalled 66 in
one of the most dramatic natural disasters in Australian history. With massive government funding, the city was
rebuilt in the knowledge that the character and ambience of the old Darwin
had been blown away forever.

Most of the old-style Darwin was
levelled, to be replaced by a modern,
more commercialised city. But of the
over 30,000 residents evacuated in
the nation's fastest-ever mass population shift, the majority returned. Today
the city has 120,000 inhabitants.

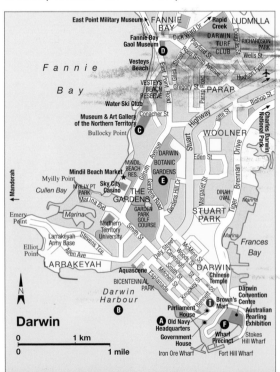

Darwin

TIP

As an alternative to walking, explore Darwin on the Tour Tub (www.tourtub.com.au), an open-topped minibus that allows you to get on and off anywhere on its circular route. It can often be unbearably hot in the middle of the day. If exploring the city on foot, take your tour in the early morning or late afternoon.

(named after the cattle company that once employed most Darwinians). Mindil Beach is the scene of a popular sunset market every Thursday (5pm–10pm) and Sunday (4pm–9pm) April to October only (www.mindil.com.au). The Asian food stalls are marvellous.

Other markets are in **Parap** on Saturday morning (8am–2pm; www.parapvillage.com.au), in **Rapid Creek** on Sunday (6.30am–1.30pm) and in **Nightcliff** on Sundays (8am–2pm; www.nightcliffmarkets.com).

When the tides are right in early August at **Fannie Bay**, about 4km (2.5 miles) from the city centre, Darwin conducts its famous **Beer Can Regatta**. Thousands of beer cans are used to build a fleet of wildly imaginative, semi-seaworthy craft. The whole city turns out to watch them race or wallow in the bay. This event is in keeping with Darwin's reputation as the world's beer-drinking capital.

In 1981 the ambitious **Museum and Art Gallery of the Northern Territory ⊙** (tel: 08-8999 8264; www.magnt.net.au; daily 10am–3pm; free) was opened. Its five galleries include one of the world's best collections of Aboriginal art and cultural artefacts, and archaeological finds from the Pacific region. Don't miss the fine collection of Aboriginal contemporary art, the Tiwi Pukumani burial poles and "Sweetheart", a stuffed saltwater crocodile 5 metres (17ft) long.

The **Fannie Bay Gaol Museum ⊙** (tel: 08-8999 8264; https://artsandmuseums.nt.gov.au; daily 9am–5pm; free) displays old cells and gallows from the prison's grim past.

Darwin's tropical nature makes a visit to the 34-hectare (84-acre) **Botanic Gardens ⊕** worthwhile, and fish-feeding at the **Aquascene** (tel: 08-8981 7837; http://aquascene.com.au) in Doctor's Gully Road, near the corner of Daly Street and the Esplanade, is lots of fun, especially with children. Fish can be hand-fed at high tide every day; check website for times.

Finally, the **Wharf Precinct ⊖** has undergone a major renovation: on any balmy afternoon, head out to the end of the pier, where dozens of restaurants have set up outdoor tables. It's the perfect place to drink in the tropical air, or drop a line to catch a passing Spanish mackerel. In 2010 the waterfront expanded to include a convention centre, high-rise apartments, offices, two major hotels and a wave pool for surfers. The total cost of the project was A$1 billion.

Exploring the Top End

About 60km (40 miles) south of Darwin on the Cox Peninsula Road, the **Territory Wildlife Park** (tel: 08-8988 7200; www.territorywildlifepark.com.au; daily 8.30–6pm) provides a potted display of the Top End's varied bird, marine, and bush wildlife, and an aquarium representing an entire Top End river system, viewed from a shuttle train that potters around the 400-hectare (988-acre) property.

A two-hour drive to the southwest of Darwin is **Litchfield National Park ⊕**, 153 sq km (59 sq miles) of sandstone plateau with pockets of rainforest. It is

Children of the Tiwi Islands.

one of the best areas in the Top End for bushwalking, but is even more popular for its waterfalls and clear pools, which provide excellent swimming.

Darwin is the ideal base for exploring the remote, mangrove-filled north. Easily reached by light plane is the **Cobourg Peninsula ㉔**. Because it is on Aboriginal land, permission is required before visiting, but that can be arranged by tour operators. Cobourg was the site of one of the earliest attempts to establish a British base in northern Australia. Through a series of misadventures and bungles, Port Essington failed, but the bay in which it was built is a place of extravagant beauty in one of the most remote corners of the continent. **Seven Spirit Bay** (www.sevenspiritbay.com.au; closed for renovation, due to reopen in 2017) is perhaps the most out-of-the-way five-star resort in the world.

The Tiwi Islands

Splaying out to the north of Darwin like a giant ink blot, the two Tiwi Aboriginal islands, **Bathurst ㉑** and **Melville ㉒** are among Australia's most isolated outposts. Although the mainland is only 80km (50 miles) away, dugout canoes rarely survived the journey, so the Tiwi culture and language developed separately from that of other Aboriginal groups. Early Dutch explorers met with hostility. When the British set up an outpost on Melville in 1824 it lasted less than five years, owing to Tiwi sieges and tropical disease. As a result, the Tiwis largely escaped the scorched-earth period of Australia's colonisation.

Control of their own affairs was returned to the Tiwis in the 1970s; most crucially, since they have never been moved, their land rights have never been disputed. This confident sense of possession may be why they are so outgoing; despite their once-fearsome reputation, they now bill their lands as the Friendly Islands.

Visiting the Tiwi Islanders requires a permit, organised by the Tiwi-owned tour company. It's worth the journey: this remote coastline alternates between croc-infested mangrove swamps and blinding-white beaches where you can walk for many kilometres without seeing another person.

TIP

However tempting the water might seem, it is unwise to swim off the coast of the Northern Territory between October and May. Box jellyfish, whose sting can be fatal, are usually present in significant numbers. Always observe the warning signs.

Termite mounds in the Northern Territory.

VISITING THE ISLANDS

The best time to visit the Tiwi Islands is in late March or early April, during the Aussie Rules Tiwi Islands Football League Grand Final. This is the only day you can visit the islands by yourself without a permit. On the same Sunday there is also the Tiwi Islands Annual Art Sale, where local jewellery, paintings and crafts are sold. The rest of the year, visitors can only go on organised tours. The catamaran Arafura Pearl takes day-trippers to Nguiu on Bathurst Island for a visit to the art centre during the dry season. A charter plane allows visits to the three art centres on Bathurst and Melville Island (A$500 for a day trip). Call **Tiwi Art Network** on 08-8941 3593, or visit www.tiwiart.com. Two-night plane charter visits to the islands are also available from **Aussie Adventure Tours** (tel: 1300-721 365; www.aussieadventure.com.au).

ULURU AND KATA TJUTA

Held sacred and owned by the Anangu Aboriginal people, natural rock formations Uluru and Kata Tjuta are two of the Northern Territory's largest and most iconic sites.

In the southern part of the Northern Territory stands the colossal Uluru, a giant, sandstone rock which rises up 348 metres (1,160ft) above sea level from the flat desert floor. Also known by its colonial name, Ayers Rock, the title changed to Uluru when ownership was transferred back to the Anangu (the indigenous traditional owners) in 1985.

Uluru measures 5km (3.25 miles) in length and 9.4km (5.75 miles) around. The rock changes colour depending on the light and atmospheric conditions, and never remains the same hue. For the best experience, visit at sunrise and watch from the new viewing area, Talinguru Nyakunytjaku (which means "look from the sand dunes"). Uluru is a sacred site for the Anangu. From a distance, Uluru looks smooth and featureless. But up close its face is weather-beaten, pitted with holes and gashes, ribs, valleys and caves. In the "Tjukurpa" or Creation Time (the traditional Anangu law that explains how the world was created) these features are related to the journeys and actions of ancestral beings across the landscape. It is hard to come away from Uluru without feeling enriched by its calm spirituality.

Climbing Uluru has become a controversial activity. The climbing path is about 1.6km (1 mile) long and can be a treacherous and strenuous climb. Being an Aboriginal sacred site, the owners ask you to respect their law and not to climb; the route is a sacred path of spiritual significance that is only taken by a few Aboriginal men on special occasions.

When visiting Uluru, be mindful of the fact that the site is sacred.

The area that would later become the Uluru–Kata Tjuta National Park was separated from the Petermann Reserve in 1958; it was placed under the management of the Northern Territory Reserves Board and originally named the Ayers Rock Mount Olga National Park.

Aboriginal pictograms, or rock art, can be seen in several caves near Uluru; these typically represent Dreamtime stories.

A view of Kata Tjuta.

KATA TJUTA

Kata Tjuta, also known as Mount Olga (or colloquially as The Olgas), means "many heads" and is a group of more than 30 rounded red rock domes rising from the desert floor. The product of 550 million years of pressure from water and wind erosion, the natural phenomenon is under the protection of its Aboriginal owners in the Uluru-Katja Tjuta National Park and is inscribed on the World Heritage List.

Thirty kilometres (19 miles) west of Uluru, Kata Tjuta is a sacred Aboriginal men's place relating to knowledge that is considered powerful and dangerous. Most of this sacred knowledge has never been revealed to outsiders.

There are three walking trails: the Walpa Gorge, The Valley of the Winds and the Kata Tjuta dune viewing area. As you walk these peaceful trails, you may hear the sounds of birds such as Port Lincoln parrots and grey-headed honey-eaters piercing the silence.

e first dirt roads to the area now recognized as the Uluru-
ta Tjuta National Park were developed in 1948. The first
rists arrived by bus in the 1950s, but it wasn't until the
rly 1970s that the decision was made to remove all tourist
omodations to an area outside the park. By the year 2000
re were more than 400,000 annual visitors to the park,
ich is now jointly managed by the local Pitjantjatjara
origines and the National Parks and Wildlife Agency.

*Camels were originally
brought to Australia as an
alternative to the horse; they
have since become feral and
are considered a minor
agricultural pest.*

The Perth skyline.

WESTERN AUSTRALIA

Three-quarters of the population of WA live in its attractive capital, Perth; the vast emptiness beyond includes barren desert, lush forests, rugged canyons and gold-mining towns.

Western Australia is, quite simply, enormous. Covering more than 2.5 million sq km (960,000 sq miles), it is much larger than the states of Alaska and Texas combined. In fact, if WA were a separate country, it would be the ninth largest in the world – and the emptiest. India is about the same size, with a population of 700 million, whereas the whole vast, dry expanse of Western Australia is inhabited by just 2.5 million people, about 75 per cent of whom live in Perth.

Being so far from the main Australian population centres on the east coast, WA conveys a feeling of utter isolation. **Perth** is the world's remotest state capital city, closer to Bali than it is to Sydney. Most of the state is parched and barren, but the north is lushly tropical and the southwest is temperate. In springtime, between September and November, many visitors travel from the eastern states just to see the profusion of wild flowers that turn the south into a riot of colour. Western Australia's vastness, small population and rugged scenery give this state a strong sense of being a new frontier, an impression which is heightened when you're only a few hours way from remote Outback scenery.

When planning a trip in WA, it's a good idea to keep an eye on the map scale and distances. It's all too easy to outline a weekend tour through an apparently tiny proportion of the state – only to add up the distances and find this would mean driving some 1,600km (1,000 miles). If you are based in Perth, with limited time to spare, consider joining an organised tour group or excursion. Several Perth tour operators run day, overnight and longer tours to WA's scenic highlights, such as the Margaret River region, Albany, Kalbarri National Park and the Pinnacles.

Main Attractions
Perth City
Swan River
His Majesty's Theatre
Rottnest Island
The Pinnacles
Monkey Mia

Enjoying a coffee.

The first arrivals

Western Australia was the arrival point for the first Australians. It is thought that, more than 50,000 years ago, the forebears of today's Australian Aborigines sailed across on bamboo rafts from what is now Indonesia, arriving in waves over many centuries. From the northwest, they gradually spread out to occupy the whole continent.

The first recorded European view of the west Australian coast occurred in 1616, when Dirk Hartog, a Dutch captain, sailed to what is now Dirk Hartog Island near Carnarvon. The first English explorer known to have visited Australia was William Dampier, who was on the *Cygnet* in 1688 when it was repaired at what is now Cygnet Bay in the Kimberley. He was unimpressed with what he saw, finding the land useless and the Aborigines the "miserablest people in the world".

In 1827, amid fears that the French might seize the coast, Captain James Stirling was despatched from Sydney to find a potential site for a western settlement. In 1829 the first colonists arrived to set up shop on a site he had spotted 16km (10 miles) upstream on the Swan River. Surrounded by black swans, a village of some 300 residents was founded and named Perth.

Inducing other colonists to head west was no easy matter. An acute labour shortage led to convicts being imported in 1850; by 1858, the population of Perth was still barely 3,000. But gold changed all that.

When news of the great finds of the 1890s at fields at Kalgoorlie to the east reached the outside world, Perth became the leaping-off point for one of the last great gold rushes. Still, many parts of the northeast of the region were among the last to be settled in Australia, when some of the world's largest cattle stations were opened in the Kimberley. Throughout the 20th century, the discovery of mineral deposits throughout the state provided the main basis of its wealth – from uranium to gas and oil on the northwest shelf.

Perth

As in the gold-rush days, almost all visits to the wild west still start in **Perth** ❶, whose population now stands at

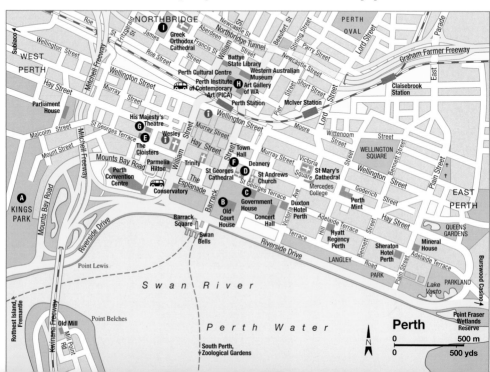

about 2 million. Set on the west coast, a high-tech counterweight to the older, heavily populated eastern cities, the city has become a symbol of Australian confidence.

Perth's current, resource-driven boom is its biggest since the roaring 1980s, when it was the base of a posse of high-profile multimillionaires, exemplified by Alan Bond, who worked so closely with the Labor politicians of the time that the state was referred to as "WA Inc". But the powerful alliance collapsed in the wake of the 1987 Wall Street crash, when one tycoon after another was implicated in corrupt dealings, charged and jailed. Today, Perth is booming again, and well worth a visit.

The city takes full advantage of its setting on the serpentine Swan River. The dominant view is over **Perth City,** where the **Swan River** widens into a broad bay about 1km (0.5 miles) across. On the edge of the business district, set high on an escarpment, is **Kings Park** Ⓐ (www.bgpa.wa.gov. au), a 400-hectare (988-acre) reserve of botanical gardens and bushland

offering panoramic views over the city and the river. Dominating the jetty on Riverside Drive are the sail-shaped copper wings of the tower containing the **Swan Bells** (swanbells.com. au; daily from 10am, closing times vary seasonally; charge to ascend the tower), a gift from the church of St Martin-in-the-Fields, Trafalgar Square, London, to mark Australia's bicentenary in 1988.

Perth's early buildings

Successive mining booms since the 1970s have led large multinational and West Australia-based companies to build high-rise office blocks in Perth. Their presence has dramatically changed the city skyline, causing older residents to complain that the city has lost its intimate country-town feel. But the odd architectural gem can still be found. Tucked into the back of **Stirling Gardens** is **Old Court House** Ⓑ (1837), Perth's first brick building, which has a modest facade of Doric columns. On the whole, however, buildings predating the state's 1890s gold rush are rare. **Government**

TIP

City-centre buses in Perth are free. The free service applies to all regular buses while they're in the central zone, as well as CATs (Central Area Transit), distinctive buses – red, blue or yellow, depending on the route – linking main tourist sights and running from early morning until early evening.

Perth's riverfront along Kings Park.

Leafy, laid-back Northbridge.

Perth's Town Hall is the only convict-built Town Hall in Australia.

House **C** (also in Stirling Gardens; www.govhouse.wa.gov.au) stands as a true reflection of the beginning of the state. Constructed in the 1860s by convict labour, it placed a regal stamp of authority on the new settlement. Some say the emerging Australian "larrikin" characteristic shows through in the upstairs windows, which are in the shape of a broad arrow – the motif on the uniforms of the convict builders.

Other early buildings include the **Deanery D**, on the corner of Pier Street, opposite Stirling Gardens, built by paroled convicts in 1859, and the Elizabethan-style **Cloisters** building **E**, at the western end of St George's Terrace, established in 1858 as the first public school for boys. The old **Town Hall F** (Hay Street Mall) was the last building in Perth to be built by convict labour (commenced in 1867). It has been the site of various entertainments as well as formal civic ceremonies and political meetings. It was a rallying point for conscription during both World Wars.

The city architecture of the 1890s gold rush includes **His Majesty's**

Theatre **G** (www.hismajestystheatre.com. au), also known as His Maj, at the west end of Hay Street. To discover more about the gold rush and its pivotal role in the city's development, visit the 1899 **Perth Mint** (eastern end of Hay Street; www.perthmint.com.au; daily 9am–5pm; guided tour every hour), among the world's oldest operating mints. Try picking up a block of gold worth A$250,000, minting your own medallion, or watch gold being smelted.

Two sections of town with contrasting histories are **London Court** (www. londoncourt.com.au) and **East Murray Street Precinct**. London Court dates back to 1937, a monument to mock-Tudor kitsch, whose curiosities include a clock tower at each end: one a replica of London's Big Ben, the other of the Gros Horloge in Rouen, France. East Murray Street is the genuine colonial item. It appears on the original town plans of 1838 and now stands lined by early 20th-century buildings.

Cultural centre

On the northern side of the railway station, across the lovely **Horseshoe Bridge**, lies the **Perth Cultural Centre H** (www.perthculturalcentre.com.au), comprising the **Art Gallery of Western Australia** (www.artgallery.wa.gov.au; Wed–Mon 10am–5pm; free entrance and guided tours) and the Western Australian Museum. The art gallery displays more than 1,000 works of art, including one of the continent's best collections of Aboriginal art. One painting that is almost always included in a guided tour is *The Foundation of Perth* by George Pitt, depicting the wife of an early dignitary ceremoniously felling a tree to mark the city's founding. A copy of this painting was given to every WA school to mark the state's centenary celebrations in 1929.

The **Western Australian Museum** (www.museum.wa.gov.au; Thu–Tue 9.30am–5pm; free) traces the history of the state from the formation of the Australian continent 120 million years ago to the present day. Don't miss the fascinating natural history section or the illuminating Katta Dijinoong Gallery, devoted to Aboriginal history and culture. The museum will be temporarily closed from June 2016 until 2020.

In the museum's beautifully preserved **Old Gaol** (1856), life in the early days of the colony has been recreated in a collection of period interiors, including a 1917 pharmacy and an original court room. There is also a good little courtyard café here.

Just along from the Art Gallery of WA, and also forming part of the cultural centre, is the **Perth Institute of Contemporary Art** (www.pica.org.au; Tue–Sun 10am–5pm; free), which offers a lively programme of exhibitions, installations and events, as well as a great café-bar.

The cultural centre stands on the doorstep of **Northbridge ❶**, where Perth's ethnic diversity is displayed on a plate, as it were. You can walk past tanks of live mud crabs and crayfish, smell the sharp tang of lemongrass, chew on chickens' feet or dim sum at eight in the morning, or have a beer on the balcony of a pub, watching all the action on the streets below. Northbridge also has nightclubs and discos as lively as any in Sydney.

Another fruitful neighbourhood for restaurants and bars is **Subiaco**, a fashionable suburb on the western side of town (direct access on the Perth–Fremantle railway). Come here for brunch on Friday or Saturday, perhaps after a walk in nearby Kings Park.

Fremantle

Fremantle ❷, just 19km (12 miles) from Perth's city centre but deemed a city in its own right, was brushed up for the America's Cup race in 1987 and has since become one of Western Australia's most popular attractions. Unlike glittering Perth, the old port's colonial charms remain intact, including the **Round House** (www.fremantle roundhouse.com.au), which actually has 12 sides; WA's oldest public building

(1830); and its first jail, built where Captain Fremantle landed to claim Western Australia for the Crown.

If you arrive by ferry, you will disembark at Victoria Quay, at the far end of which you will notice the sail-like roof of the excellent **Maritime Museum** (http://museum.wa.gov.au; daily 9.30am–5pm), exploring all aspects of Fremantle's seafaring heritage from whaling and pearling to its role in World War II and as the place of disembarkation for thousands of post-war immigrants. The **Shipwreck Galleries** (same hours as the Maritime Museum, but free) on Cliff Street, is devoted to marine archaeology. It has relics from some of the many ships wrecked off WA's coast over the centuries, including original timber (partially reconstructed) and treasures from the Dutch ship *Batavia*.

Fremantle Prison (www.fremantle prison.com.au; daily 10am–5pm), a maximum security prison until 1991, offers a variety of tours including a torchlight tour. Ghost sightings are not guaranteed, but the tours include the gallows yard and hellish cell blocks built by convict labour in 1855.

TIP

Fremantle is a 30-minute train ride from Perth railway station, and Transperth buses to Fremantle leave from St George's Terrace. But try to arrive by boat along the Swan if you can. The ferry from Barrack Street Jetty takes about an hour.

'The Caller', a sculpture by Gerhard Marks outside the Art Gallery of Western Australia.

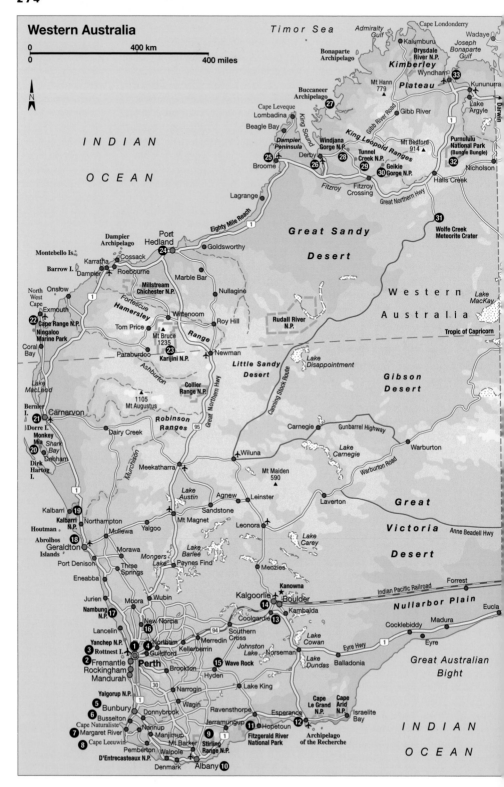

Western Australia

0 _____ 400 km
0 _____ 400 miles

N

Timor Sea

INDIAN

OCEAN

Admiralty Gulf
Cape Londonderry
Kalumburu
Wadaye
Kimberley
Drysdale River N.P.
Joseph Bonaparte Gulf
Bonaparte Archipelago
Mt Hann 779
Plateau
Wyndham
33
Kununurra
Darwin
Buccaneer Archipelago
27
Gibb River Road
Gibb River
Lake Argyle
Cape Leveque
Lombadina
Beagle Bay
King Sound
King Leopold Ranges
Mt Bedford 914
Purnululu National Park (Bungle Bungle)
Dampier Peninsula
Windjana Gorge N.P.
Tunnel Creek N.P.
32
Nicholson
Broome
25
Derby
26
28
29
Geikie Gorge N.P.
30
Halls Creek
Lagrange
Fitzroy
Fitzroy Crossing
Great Northern Hwy

Great Sandy
Desert

31
Wolfe Creek Meteorite Crater

Eighty Mile Beach
Goldsworthy

Western
Australia
Lake MacKay

Dampier Archipelago
Port Hedland
24
Montebello Is.
Karratha
Cossack
Roebourne
Marble Bar
Barrow I.
Dampier
Nullagine
Millstream Chichester N.P.
North West Cape
Onslow
Fortescue
Wittenoom
Roy Hill
Rudall River N.P.
Tropic of Capricorn
Exmouth
22
Cape Range N.P.
Ningaloo Marine Park
Hamersley
Tom Price
Mt Bruce 1235
Range
Newman
Coral Bay
Paraburdoo
23
Karijini N.P.
Little Sandy
Desert
Lake Disappointment
Gibson
Desert
Lake MacLeod
Ashburton
1105 Mt Augustus
Collier Range N.P.
Bernier I.
21
Carnarvon
Robinson
Ranges
Carnegie
Gunbarrel Highway
Dorre I.
Monkey Mia
Shark Bay
Denham
Dairy Creek
95
Great Northern Hwy
Camping Stock Route
Lake Carnegie
Warburton
Warburton Road
Dirk Hartog I.
20
Murchison
Meekatharra
Wiluna
Mt Maiden 590
Kalbarri
19
Lake Austin
Agnew
Leinster
Laverton
Great
Kalbarri N.P.
Northampton
Mullewa
Yalgoo
Sandstone
Mt Magnet
Leonora
Houtman
Abrolhos Islands
Geraldton
18
Morawa
Lake Barlee
Victoria
Anne Beadell Hwy
Port Denison
Mongers Lake
Paynes Find
Lake Carey
Desert
Three Springs
Eneabba
Menzies
Forrest
Jurien
Moora
Wubin
Kanowna
Indian Pacific Railroad
Nambung N.P.
17
New Norcia
Kalgoorlie
Boulder
Nullarbor Plain
Eucla
Lancelin
16
Coolgardie
14
Kambalda
Cocklebiddy
Madura
Yanchep N.P.
1
4
Northam
Merredin
13
Southern Cross
Lake Cowan
Eyre Hwy
Eyre
3
Rottnest I.
Guildford
Kellerberrin
Johnston Lake
Norseman
1
2
Perth
Brookton
15
Wave Rock
Lake Dundas
Balladonia
Great Australian
Fremantle
Rockingham
Mandurah
Hyden
Lake King
Bight
30
Narrogin
Yalgorup N.P.
5
Bunbury
Wagin
Ravensthorpe
Esperance
Israelite Bay
6
Busselton
Donnybrook
Jerramungup
11
Hopetoun
12
INDIAN
Cape Naturaliste
7
Margaret River
Nannup
Manjimup
Fitzgerald River National Park
Cape Le Grand N.P.
Cape Arid N.P.
Archipelago of the Recherche
8
Cape Leeuwin
Pemberton
Mt Barker
Stirling Range N.P.
1
OCEAN
D'Entrecasteaux N.P.
Walpole
Denham
Albany
10

One pleasure of Fremantle is to wander at random, soaking up the laid-back atmosphere and admiring the frilly ironwork of the gold-rush architecture. It has no shortage of restaurants and coffee shops (explore South Terrace, aka Cappuccino Strip), and plenty of interesting shops. On Fridays and weekends dip into the splendidly restored **Fremantle Markets** (corner of South Terrace and Henderson Street; fremantlemarkets.com. au) for interesting crafts and souvenirs.

Perth's beaches

From Fremantle a string of soft, sandy beaches stretches all the way to Hillary's Boat Harbour, 50km (30 miles) north. Development, though continuous, is almost without exception low-rise and low-key, set well back from the shore. Each of the beaches has its fans. For surfing, head for **Scarborough** or **Trigg**; for a lively après-beach scene, choose **Indiana Cottesloe Beach**, which offers good food, cocktails and fabulous sunset views.

For family-friendly attractions, head for **Hillary's Boat Harbour**, where

the AQWA (Aquarium of Western Australia; www.aqwa.com.au; daily 10am–5pm) re-creates WA's five coastal environments. The highlight is the walk-through aquarium, representing the shipwreck coast where sharks, loggerhead turtles and stingrays glide smoothly overhead within centimetres of upturned faces. Other highlights include a touch pool, saltwater crocodiles of the far north coast and tropical fish of the coral coast.

Rottnest Island

Hillary's Boat Harbour is, along with Barrack Street Jetty in Perth and Fremantle one of the springboards for **Rottnest Island ❸** (www.rottnestisland. com), an idyllic getaway just 19km (13 miles) offshore. First settled as a natural prison for West Australian Aborigines, Rotto (as it is known locally) is now a favourite holiday spot. Private motor vehicles aren't allowed on the island, so visitors tend to wobble along on bicycles, which can be brought on the ferry or rented on the island.

Visitors can spend their time boating, golfing, playing tennis or just

The Round House.

A perfect white-sand beach.

lazing on a quiet beach. In summer, divers come here to explore the world's southernmost coral reef. The island's pub, the Hotel Rottnest, originally served as the official residence of the Australian state governor; it now has live music on summer evenings. Facilities have recently been upgraded with a A$6.5 million makeover. Accommodation is limited to the Hotel Rottnest and Rottnest Lodge, and at peak times is allocated by public ballot, as demand is so high. If you want to stay overnight or longer, book well in advance.

The Swan Valley

If you have limited time during your stay in Perth, and can manage only one out-of-town trip, it is worth venturing into the **Swan Valley**. A major wine-producing area, it offers vineyard tours and elegant towns such as **Guildford ❹**, one of the earliest settlements in Western Australia, and is only 30 minutes by train or road from Perth's CBD. To follow the Swan Valley food and wine trail, a 32km (20-mile) loop linking some of the best vineyards and microbreweries, as well

as the Margaret River Chocolate Company, leave the town via the West Swan Road and return by the Great Northern Highway. Also along the route is **Caversham Wildlife Park** (www. cavershamwildlife.com.au), the best place in the region for kangaroo-spotting for visitors too short of time to go into the bush. Caversham forms part of Whiteman Park, packed with family attractions, including an excellent **Motor Museum** (www.motormuseumof wa.asn.au; daily 10am–4pm).

Down the coast from Perth

Head south of Perth for the region's top wineries and dense karri and jarrah forests, but be careful not to miss things along the way. The Perth-to-Bunbury Highway is a direct and efficient way to get to Bunbury and Margaret River, but you'll have to take the old coast road if you don't want to miss the bits in between.

Immediately south of Fremantle the landscape is fairly industrial apart from **Rockingham** (47km/30 miles south of Perth), a springboard for Penguin Island, named after its colony of 1,100 penguins, and **Mandurah** (74km/40 miles from Perth), a fast-growing but nonetheless delightful town on the Peel Estuary. In high season the towns and campsites around Mandurah are busy with holidaymakers, but for the rest of the year they can be enjoyed in relative peace.

Further down the coast (140km/75 miles from Perth) is the dairy town of **Harvey**, dating back to 1890. The nearby **Yalgorup National Park** can be reached by the old coast road. It is a sanctuary for water birds and wildlife, though it is the colony of living, rock-like creatures known as thrombolites (the earliest-known life on Earth and very rare) that makes it special. The only access point is via the coast road, 25km (15 miles) south of Mandurah, indicated by a large brown sign for the Lake Clifton platform, an observation walkway built across the shallows containing the thrombolites.

GETTING TO ROTTNEST ISLAND

Rottnest's proximity to the mainland makes it an easy day trip by ferry from Perth. Rottnest Express (tel: 1300-467 688; www.rottnest express.com.au) operates from Rous Head Harbour in Northport, the B Shed at Fremantle, and from the Barrack Street Jetty in Perth (the last option includes a Swan River cruise with commentary). **Rottnest Fast Ferries** tel: 08-9246 1039; www.rottnestfastferries.com.au) operates from Hillary's Boat Harbour.

It takes approximately 25 minutes to get to the island from Fremantle, around 45 minutes from Hillary's and 90 minutes from Perth. The cost of the ferry crossing includes the entrance charge to the island. The ferry crossing to Rottnest can get choppy. If you're prone to seasickness, or have children with you, take tablets beforehand.

The beauty of the island is perhaps best appreciated from the air, so you may want to consider taking the **Rottnest Air Taxi** (tel: 0411-264 547; www.rottnest.de) instead of the ferry. You will also get there a lot quicker – taxis spend just 12 minutes in the air. Flights leave from Jandakot Airport in Perth for Rottnest Aerodrome at times arranged to suit you (planes take either three or five passengers; prices start from A$96 same-day return per person, based on five people sharing a six-seater).

The city of **Bunbury** ❺ (180km/110 miles south of Perth) is a busy port that owes its existence to Lt Henry St Pierre Bunbury, who travelled overland to the coast from Pinjarra in 1836. At **Koombana Beach**, just north of town, visitors can feed a community of bottlenose dolphins that visit the beach daily at the Dolphin Discovery Centre (www.dolphindiscovery.com.au; daily 9am–2pm in winter, 8am–4pm in summer).

Forests and vineyards

It was logging of the nearby forests that brought prosperity to the region; jarrah and blackbutt hardwoods abound here, and can be seen in much of the early architecture. Bunbury sits at the northern end of **Geographe Bay**, a large, sheltered waterway that has **Cape Naturaliste** as its northern spur. From here a cape-to-cape hiking trail leads south to Cape Leeuwin, 135km (84 miles) away.

On the southern coast of the bay, the resort town of **Busselton** ❻ has a fine setting on the Vasse River. Its 2km (1.2-mile) jetty, the longest in the southern hemisphere, has an interpretive centre and a multimillion-dollar underwater observatory (www.busselton jetty.com.au; daily Sept–Apr 8.30am–6pm, May–Aug 9am–5pm) that takes visitors 8 metres (26ft) below sea level for amazing views of fish and coral.

Margaret River ❼, 280km (173 miles) from Perth, is internationally famous for estate-grown and bottled wines. Names like Leeuwin, Xanadu, Moss Wood, Devil's Lair, Howard Park and dozens more rival the world's best. This is crafted wine and a far cry from the mass production of Australia's eastern states. Margaret River's success sparked a Western Australian wine revolution that has encouraged quality production from Swan Valley down to the Great Southern region. Not only do many of these vineyards offer fantastic wine, but their restaurants represent better value for money than most establishments in Perth.

Surfing the big waves and swimming are two popular reasons locals visit the region. Yallingup, Injidup, Smiths Beach, Bunker Bay and Three Bears (only accessible by 4WD) are

Goode Beach, near Albany.

Drive carefully at dusk and at night, when wildlife is most active. If a kangaroo jumps in front of your car, don't swerve. Most fatal road accidents involving wildlife occur when drivers swerve, hit loose gravel on the side of the road and lose control.

The busy port of Bunbury.

among the many surf breaks, but if you plan to tan, they are equally as inviting to lie on the sand and have a quick dip when the time comes to cool off.

Margaret River is also renowned for its cheese (www.mrdc.com.au), chocolate (www.chocolatefactory.com.au) and local microbrews. Check out the Duckstein (www.duckstein.com.au) for a cleansing ale.

Visits to spectacular caves such as **Mammoth**, **Lake** and **Jewel**, and browsing in arts and crafts shops, are alternatives to wine (and beer) sampling.

Cape Leeuwin ❽ marks the southwest extremity of Australia and the junction of the Indian and Southern oceans. This point marked the start of Matthew Flinders' odyssey when he set out to circumnavigate and chart the Australian coastline in 1790.

Inland lies **Pemberton**, surrounded by three national parks – a region of giant karri and jarrah trees. Some of the trees are over 50 metres (160ft) tall – the world's tallest hardwoods. The adventurous can climb the **Gloucester Tree** to the fire tower, 60 metres (190ft) above the ground.

The south coast

Travelling east along the coast road towards Denmark and Albany, stop at **Walpole** to view the ancient Tingle Forest from the Treetop Walk (daily 9am–5pm; wheelchair access), a lofty ramp looping over the Valley of the Giants.

Further east is the **Stirling Range National Park** ❾, its conical hills and jagged peaks rising to 1,000 metres (3,300ft), presenting challenging walks. A seasonal centre for wild flowers, including native orchids, it receives Western Australia's only snowfall.

To the south, **Albany** ❿ is where European settlement was first established in the western half of Australia. On Christmas Day 1826, Major Lockyer arrived from Sydney in the brig *Amity*, attracted by the splendid expanses of **King George Sound**, an enclosed waterway twice as large as Sydney Harbour. Today tourists flock here from July to November to spot whales – an ironic attraction for a town that (until 1978) was the last operating whaling station in the southern hemisphere. A museum, **Whaleworld** (www.whaleworld.org; daily 9am–5pm; guided tours every hour from 10am to 3pm), tells the story.

Albany is also one of Australia's most picturesque towns, with a wonderful bay-side location and well-preserved 19th-century streetscapes. At nearby **Strawberry Hill** stands the state's oldest house, built in 1836 for the first government resident, Sir Richard Spencer. There is plenty of exploring to be done here. The post office, with its shingled tower, is the oldest in Western Australia, and the **Church of St John the Evangelist**, built in 1848, is the earliest house of worship in the state. Overlooking King George Sound is a memorial to the **Australian Light Horse** that served in Egypt and Gallipoli in World War I. It was moved here from Port Said, Egypt, after the 1956 Suez War. Nearby Mount Adelaide, a military history precinct, looks down on the waters where the ANZAC Dardanelles invasion fleet assembled in 1914.

Perhaps the most spectacular park in the region is **Fitzgerald River National Park** ⓫, 185km (115 miles) northeast of Albany. It includes an impressive stretch of coastal landscape and also contains a group of mountains known as the **Barren Range**, with dramatic views of the Southern Ocean.

The easternmost town of **Esperance** ⓬ is 750km (465 miles) from Perth. Local attractions include the salt-rich **Pink Lake** and the grave of Tommy Windich, an Aboriginal guide who accompanied explorer John Forrest on his two overland treks to Adelaide in 1870 and 1874.

Cape Le Grand and **Cape Arid** national parks offer superb beaches, an abundance of birdlife and some terrific campsites. Offshore lies a maze of beautiful islands called the **Recherche Archipelago**. On the road from Albany to the capes, opportunities for camping, fishing and surfing present themselves at almost every turn.

The goldfields

Around 200km (125 miles) north of Esperance is the crossroads town of **Norseman**, from where the Eyre Highway heads east across the vast Nullarbor Plain to eastern Australia, crossing the border into South Australia after 725km (450 miles). Alternatively, the route north heads to Kalgoorlie and the goldfields.

The birthplace of the West Australian goldfields was **Coolgardie** ⓭, 190km (118 miles) north of Norseman. In September 1892 it was the site of Australia's richest strike – producing 85kg (200lbs) of gold in a single month. By 1900, it was a town of 15,000 people with a score of hotels, half a dozen banks, three breweries, two stock exchanges and seven newspapers. By 1905, however, the lode was running out. Today Coolgardie is an attractive, historic township with elegant buildings.

Kalgoorlie ⓮, 40km (25 miles) away, started off as Coolgardie's twin city, but it has survived as a thriving mining town of over 30,000, the hub in a region full of boom and bust. When Irishman Paddy Hannan discovered gold here in 1893, it was soon realised that the wealth of the Kalgoorlie find far exceeded anything else ever found in Australia. Kalgoorlie's Golden Mile became the richest piece of real estate in the world.

However, water in the area was in short supply, so the celebrated engineer C.Y. O'Connor built a pipeline from Mundaring Weir near Perth, more than 500km (300 miles) away. Today, the area continues to yield 241 million grams (850,000oz) of gold per year.

Kalgoorlie's architecture retains much of its early charm, with the **Palace Hotel** (www.palacehotel.com.au) being a fabulous example of Edwardian excess. The business district of Kalgoorlie is a leafy refuge from the moonscape of the mines; the continuing trade in beer, prostitution and minerals still reflects much of the town's earlier freebooting ways. For miners who gamble on the Earth's riches every day, other (less legitimate) forms of gambling thrive – especially "two-up", a uniquely Australian game based on the toss of two pennies.

Emus are a fairly common sight in the road-side bush.

The Valley of the Giants Treetop Walk, Walpole.

TIP

The best time to view
Wave Rock is Aug–Dec
when wild flowers are in
bloom. Other interesting
rock formations in the
immediate area are
Hippo's Yawn, a
20-minute walk away,
and the Humps and the
Breakers. For details on
how to get to these
rocks, check with the
tourist office at the Wave
Rock Wild Flower Shop
and Visitor Centre (tel:
08-9880 5182).

When the Burswood Casino was about to open in Perth, the manager visited Kalgoorlie to see how Australia's most famous two-up school operated.

The main reason for visiting Kalgoorlie is to see the **Super Pit** (www.superpit.com.au), a working goldmine of awe-inspiring proportions. It runs tours on the third Sunday of every month, departing from the Super Pit shop in Kalgoorlie. Those whose visit does not coincide with the guided tours should head for the Super Pit lookout (daily 7am–9pm; free), just off the Goldfields Highway. It is best to come at night when the pit is lit up by high-voltage lights.

Many towns haven't fared as well as Kalgoorlie. Ghost towns such as **Gwalia** and **Kanowna** dot the area, while many outposts have seen their populations dwindle so much that they, too, will soon be deserted. In many of these centres stand the imposing relics of Australia's Wild West era.

Wave Rock

The Super Pit at Kalgoorlie.

The most famous inland attraction of the southwest is **Wave Rock** ⓑ,

approximately 350km (250 miles) from Perth. This natural feature appears on almost every tourist brochure of Western Australia. The rock, a few kilometres east of **Hyden**, is at once exciting and disappointing to visit. From below, this 15-metre (50ft) -high lip of solid granite looks set to curl over and crush bystanders. But, taking a wider perspective, one sees that the wave is just one wall of a huge granite dome, underscored by erosion; and a walk along the top rather shatters the illusion.

While you are in the area of Wave Rock, you may like to take time to visit other interesting rock formations in the immediate area. **Hippo's Yawn** is a 20-minute walk away, and the **Humps** and the **Breakers** are also nearby. For details on how to get to these rocks, pop into the tourist office at the Wave Rock Wild Flower Shop and Visitor Centre (tel: 08-9880 5182; www.waverock.com.au/wildflower_shoppe.htm).

Due west of the goldfields, farmers harvest the state's other golden bounty: wheat. **Merredin** is a busy town at the heart of one of the world's great grain belts. It was founded in 1891 around

a water hole on the way to the gold-fields, and has since become a research centre for improving the wheat yield of the area. Merredin's annual agricultural show is one of the most prestigious in the state. The town's tree-lined main street is best in November, when the jacarandas bloom.

Situated on the Avon River, **Northam** is the central hub of the western wheat fields, and also the scene of a hell-for-leather river race each August, when hundreds of canoeists and power-boaters dash madly downstream in the Avon River Descent.

It wasn't until Robert Dale led an expedition over the Darling Range and into this 150km (90-mile) stretch of fertile valley that the early settlers could be certain that the west held land capable of sustaining livestock and crops. The valley's towns were settled soon after Perth. For an insight into the pioneering history, **York**, with its extravagantly designed town hall, **Toodyay** and **Mahogany Creek** are well worth exploring.

North of Perth

The Perth to Darwin route is Australia's longest capital-to-capital haul. At 4,027km (2,502 miles), it is the most desolate trek.

A major attraction of taking the Great Northern Highway inland route rather than the coastal Brand Highway is **New Norcia** ⑯, 130km (80 miles) from Perth. The settlement was established by Benedictine monks in 1846 as an Aboriginal mission. The monastery is still operating, although many of the town's more impressive buildings are closed to the public. However, the Spanish architectural influence is interesting and the museum and art gallery (www.newnorcia.wa.edu.au; daily 9am–4.30pm) provide fascinating insights into pioneer life. Guided tours of the settlement are available, or visitors can take a self-guided 2km (1.2-mile) walk linking the major sites, including the Abbey Church. This is decorated with locally inspired

sgraffito and an image of Our Lady of Good Counsel, said to have been held up to repel a bushfire in 1847. Be sure to come away with some of the delectable treats, such as New Norcia nut cake and Dom Salvado Pan Chocolatti, produced by the monastery's bakery.

Heading up the coastal Brand Highway, the tiny town of **Gingin** – 82km (51 miles) north of Perth – is a good first stop. There are excellent fishing grounds off the coast, 48km (30 miles) to the west: estuaries such as the mouth of the Moore River at **Guilderton** are ideal for casting a line. Just to the south of Guilderton is the **Yanchep National Park** (vehicle charge), offering wetlands, woodlands, bushwalks, caves and an Aboriginal heritage trail.

Further north along the coast road is **Lancelin**, 127km (79 miles) north of Perth, protected by two large rock islands and surrounded by towering sand dunes. Gutsy winds off the Indian Ocean make it ideal for windsurfing and surfing. It attracts top international surfers, but also caters to novices keen to learn.

FACT

Western Australia has 10,000 species of wild flowers, 6,000 of them native to the state. Make sure you travel in spring (July–Nov) if you want to see the state in all its floral glory. The heart of Western Australia's wildflower country is the inland area roughly between Moora and Geraldton.

The Exchange Hotel, a pub in Kalgoorlie.

TIP

Virgin Australia flies to
Geraldton daily,
departing from Perth
domestic terminal. In
Geraldton, hire a car
from Avis, Budget or
Hertz, which all have
offices at the airport, and
drive to Greenough and
surrounding areas.

The Pinnacles

The only way of proceeding north of Lancelin is to follow the Brand Highway. Though considered the coastal route, it is quite a distance inland, and you must turn off it in order to see the ocean.

Nambung National Park , 29km (18 miles) south of the coastal town of Cervantes and 245km (153 miles) from Perth, shouldn't be missed. The **Pinnacles Desert** within the park (see opposite) is a bizarre sight: a world of limestone spires all rising from smooth sand dunes. When Dutch explorers first saw the Pinnacles from their vessels, they thought they had found the ruins of a long-deserted city. In fact, they are entirely natural. A circular track leads around the spires (vehicle charge).

A short distance up the coast is **Jurien**, a lobster-fishing centre set on the shores of an attractive sheltered bay, framed by spectacular sand dunes. **Port Denison** (now referred to as Dongara-Denison), 170km (105 miles) further up the coast, has Australia's biggest rock lobster grounds; more than 400 fishing boats work the area.

Maritime Geraldton

From the Pinnacles, continue north along Brand Highway towards Geraldton. About 25km (13 miles) south of the city, look out for **Greenough Historical Hamlet** (daily 9am–5pm), a collection of 19th-century colonial buildings, restored by the National Trust, that presents a vivid picture of life for the early settlers.

Geraldton ⓲, 425km (265 miles) north of Perth, supports a population of about 35,000 and is the administrative centre for West Australia's mid-coast region. It has a near-perfect climate, superb fishing conditions and fine sandy beaches that stretch north and south of Champion Bay. This stretch of coast saw many shipwrecks when early Dutch mariners heading for the East Indies were swept too far south.

The **Abrolhos Islands**, 64km (40 miles) offshore, have claimed many ships over the years, including the Dutch East Indiaman *Batavia*, which ran aground in 1629. Survivors waited behind while the captain and a few crew headed off for Java in an open boat. While the survivors were awaiting rescue, a mutiny broke out, driving loyal crewmen to a separate island. When the captain finally returned from his epic journey, many of the mutineers were hanged; two others were cast ashore to fend for themselves.

The Abrolhos sit on one of the finest reefs on the west coast, and divers can visit various wrecks. Many relics rescued from the deep are on view in the **Western Australian Museum** (http://museum.wa.gov.au; daily 9.30am–4pm; donation) in Geraldton and at Fremantle's Shipwreck Gallery, where the hull of the *Batavia* is on display.

For panoramic views of the area surrounding Geraldton, head for **Waverley Heights**. **Ellendale Bluffs** are notable for their sheer cliffs, at the base of which is a permanent water hole. Locals will advise you to visit **Chapman Valley**, at its most spectacular in spring (Sept–Nov) when the wild flowers are in bloom.

New Norcia's St Gertrude's College.

A century ago, **Northampton**, 48km (30 miles) north of Geraldton, was an important rural outpost. Recently it has been spruced up by residents to create an unusually pretty Outback town. Buildings such as **Chiverton House Museum** (Fri–Mon, Wed 10am–noon, 2–4pm; free) were built by convict labour; the cemetery in the grounds of Gwalia Church records the passing of the convicts and free settlers who first came to the area.

About 20km (12 miles) away is **Horrock Beach**, with fine sand expanses and bays. When there is water in it, don't be surprised to see **Lake Hutt**, near Port Gregory, turn pink in the midday sun – a bizarre phenomenon caused by light refraction and naturally occurring beta carotene in the water.

Kalbarri National Park

Comprising 186,000 hectares (460,000 acres), **Kalbarri National Park ⓳** (tel: 08-9937 1140) features a combination of stunning river gorges and towering sea cliffs. The park is set around the lower reaches of the Murchison River, which weaves its way to the Indian Ocean past the multi-hued sandstone formations of Red Bluff.

South of Carnarvon is the great system of peninsulas and inlets of **Hamelin Pool** and **Denham Sound**. These two huge expanses of water are protected in the northwest by **Dirk Hartog Island**. A pewter plate, nailed in 1616 to a post on Cape Inscription by the Dutch explorer Hartog, marked the first known landing of Europeans on Australia's west coast. A replica of this plate is in the **Shark Bay Shire Office** (the original is in Amsterdam).

Shark Bay

Despite its name, **Shark Bay** is one place where every visitor ventures into the water. That's because this is the site of **Monkey Mia ⓴**, perhaps one of Australia's most delightful tourist attractions. In the small bay near Denham township, wild dolphins come to shore to be fed and mingle with visitors. This came about when local fishermen started tossing fish scraps overboard to following dolphins – by 1964, they were coming in to be hand-fed. This unique interaction between

TIP

To discover more about Western Australia's history and heritage, visit the Greenough Historical Hamlet (daily 9am–5pm) on Brand Highway, a 20-minute drive south of Geraldton. Its collection of 19th-century colonial buildings, restored by the National Trust, includes a church and a schoolhouse.

The Pinnacles.

THE PINNACLES

Most organised tours north of Perth include a stop at the Pinnacles in Nambung National Park. These strange limestone formations are believed to have been shaped around 30,000 years ago by winter rain leaching into the sand dunes and turning the lower levels of the lime-rich sand into a soft limestone. Plants then grew upon the surface of the dunes, accelerating the leaching process and causing a hard cap to form around the roots of the plants. Wind erosion eventually removed the surrounding sand, leaving the hard rock exposed and moulding it into weird and wonderful shapes. The process continues to this day: submerged sections of the Pinnacles are thought to be as least as deep as the exposed sections are high.

The Kalbarri Wild Flower Centre provides a nature trail or a guided walk through Kalbarri's Native Botanic Garden.

Feeding a dolphin at Monkey Mia.

humans and dolphins is still very delicate, so follow the rangers' instructions.

Monkey Mia is only the best-known corner of Shark Bay, which was declared a World Heritage area in 1991. Covering 2.3 million hectares (5.7 million acres), it comprises a series of cliff-lined peninsulas and islands with some 145 species of plants (28 endemic to the region, having developed in isolation). The extraordinary salinity of the southern parts of Shark Bay has allowed the growth of stromatolites at Hamelin Pool – giant masses of algae that are considered the oldest form of life on Earth (they probably first formed 3 billion years ago). Somewhat more exciting to observe are the many dugongs, humpback whales and green and loggerhead turtles that roam the splendid arc-shaped bays.

On Shark Bay's slender land prongs, scientists are reintroducing furry marsupials with quaint names like burrowing bettongs and western barred bandicoots. These native species, almost eaten to extinction by introduced foxes and cats, now live behind predator-proof fences.

The tropical north

Carnarvon ㉑ is 1,000km (600 miles) north of Perth on the beautiful **Gascoyne River**. Sitting just below the Tropic of Capricorn, Carnarvon has warm winters and tropical summers that encourage vibrant tropical wildlife, and yield a huge banana crop and boatloads of prawns. The town was established in 1883, though Dutch explorer Willem de Vlamingh first landed nearby in 1697. Picturesque **Pelican Point** is good for swimming. **Miaboolya Beach** is worth a look, as is the **Bibbawarra artesian bore**, where water surface temperatures are 70°C (158°F).

Further north, a spectacular coastline unfolds, with blowholes, sheltered beaches and wild seascapes. The landlocked **Lake MacLeod** is famous for salt production. Inland, southwest of **Exmouth** is the **Cape Range National Park ㉒**, based along a rugged, dry limestone ridge. Boat trips through Yardie Creek Gorge are good, with predictable sightings of rock wallabies.

Offshore, **Ningaloo Reef** in its protected marine park stretches 260km

EXPLORING KALBARRI

To get the most out of Kalbarri National Park and the multitude of adventure activities on offer, especially when time is limited, you may want to sign up with a specialist tour operator.

Kalbarri Safari Tours. For a quad bike tour, tel: 08-9937 1011; http://kalbarri quadsafaris.com.au.

Kalbarri Boat Hire. For a canoe safari, tel: 08-9937 1245; www.kalbarriboathire. com.

Kalbarri Sand-Boarding. Like surfing, but on sand, tel: 08-9937 1104; www. sandboardingaustralia.com.au.

Kalbarri Reefwalker Tours. Coastal Cruises, tel: 08-9937 1356; www.reef walker.com.au.

Kalbarri Aquarium (tel: 08-9937 2027; www.kalbarriexplorer.com.au/oceanarium; daily 10am–4pm) provides a good overview of the local marine life.

(160 miles) from Amherst Point around North West Cape into the Exmouth Gulf. Western Australia's largest coral reef, with 250 species of coral and more than 500 fish types, Ningaloo is an unspoilt delight for divers. Coral outcrops can be reached just 20 metres (65ft) from the beach, though they extend 7km (12 miles) into the ocean. Dolphins, dugongs, manta rays, giant cod and sharks abound. Whale sharks visit the reef from March to June.

Coral Bay, 1,132km (703 miles) from Perth, is renowned for fishing and diving. Snorkelling tours go out from here or Exmouth.

The Pilbara

To the east of Exmouth lies the region called **The Pilbara**, focal point of the state's mineral wealth and one of the world's richest series of holes in the ground. Here, iron ore is king, and company towns seem to appear overnight amid the spinifex. Ore mined at such places as Tom Price and Mount Newman is freighted by rail systems to the coastline, where it is shipped off for national or overseas processing.

The northwest was first explored by the English pirate and explorer William Dampier in 1688 and 1699, so names based on *Buccaneer*, *Cygnet* and *Roebuck* (his vessels) litter the coast. The **Dampier Archipelago** includes **Barrow Island**, the centre for the North West Shelf oil and gas fields. Far from being an environmentally threatened area, it is classified as a wildlife sanctuary and has some unusual animal, bird and plant life.

Roebourne is the oldest town in the northwest, but in recent years its importance has waned because of the clout of the newly established mining towns. The ghost town of **Cossack** is a reminder of the one-time might of the local pearling industry (before it moved north to Broome and beyond), while a jaunt up the **Fortescue River** reveals the lush area around the Millstream, a bountiful supply of fresh water for many Pilbara towns. The **Millstream-Chichester National Park** is a fine outing for naturalists or hikers.

The magnificent **Karijini National Park ㉓** (previously Hamersley Range National Park), with spectacular gorges and bluffs, can be reached from **Tom Price**. Karijini's visitor centre (tel: 08-9189 8121; daily 9am–4pm; closed late Dec–late Feb) is worth a look. Designed to withstand bushfires, the centre is shaped like a goanna (an animal sacred to the local Banyjima Aboriginal people) and contains information on the natural and cultural history of the area. Karratha, 40km (25 miles) from the port of Dampier, has been developed as the work base for the mighty Hamersley Iron concern.

For an indication of just how much ore might be coming out of the ground, take a look at the loading facilities at **Port Hedland ㉔**. This seaside town, which copes with more tonnage than any other port in Australia, is almost exclusively geared to handle the iron ore from the huge open-cut and strip mining centres of the Pilbara. Port Hedland is built on an

FACT

The Pilbara was the setting for Australia's longest strike, which lasted from May 1946 until August 1949. Aboriginal pastoral workers, claiming they were treated like slaves, demanded fair wages and better working conditions. Even after most of the demands were met, many did not return to the stations but pooled their meagre resources to set up cooperatives.

Driving through the Outback in Pilbara.

FACT

The Outback town of Marble Bar is renowned as the hottest place in Australia. Daytime temperatures can regularly soar past 38°C (100°F), even in winter. In Dec–Jan, temperatures higher than 45°C (113°F) are common.

island linked to the mainland by three long causeways. Visitors can view the loading from the wharves, where some of the world's largest ore carriers dock. The Port Hedland visitor centre offers daily tours of the BHP-Billiton Nelson Point and Port Authority workings, and half-day tours of Dampier Salt and BHP's Boodarie Iron.

Port Hedland has no shortage of drawbacks. Its tropical setting makes it prone to cyclones; its seas are considered unsafe for swimming, thanks to sharks and stonefish; and its industrial and mineral landscape might not be to everyone's liking. But the local fishing is excellent, there are nearby Aboriginal carvings, bird life is abundant, and you can cool off in the town swimming pool or at Pretty Pool inlet.

To sample a real Western Australian Outback town, detour 193km (120 miles) southeast to **Marble Bar**. With a population of less than 400, it owes its existence to the discovery of gold in 1891 and 1931. The disused **Comet Gold Mine**, 10km (6 miles) south of town, has a museum and visitor centre.

Snorkelling from a catamaran.

Broome

Coming from the south, along the vast monotony of the road between Port Hedland and Broome, the highway describes a gentle arc along a stretch of coastline known aptly as the **Eighty Mile Reach**.

During the 1920s, **Broome** ㉕ was the capital of the world's pearling industry, with more than 300 luggers (pearling vessels) competing for finds off the northwest coast of Australia. For the mostly Japanese divers, the real wealth lay in the mother-of-pearl shell, which was used in jewellery and for buttons; a pearl was an unexpected bonus. But it was a dangerous job, as the Japanese Cemetery testifies. Broome went into the doldrums when plastic buttons flooded the market after World War II. The recent development of cultured pearls has revitalised the industry (although the harvesting now occurs in remote aquatic farms), and several Broome jewellery shops, including one owned by the dominant pearling operator, Paspaley Pearls, sell fine pearls in a variety of settings. A stroll through the timber dwellings of Chinatown, with its multilingual street signs, provides an insight into what the town was like in the pearling days.

With a large Asian population, Broome has retained enough character to be one of Australia's most fascinating communities. Aboriginal culture thrives here, with an Aboriginal radio and TV station (Goolari, known as GTV), which broadcasts partly in local dialect. The town comes alive each August when fishermen, farmers, miners, drovers and tourists swell the population tenfold for the Shinju Matsuri – Festival of the Pearl.

Residents will point out such exotic attractions as the "Golden Staircase to the Moon", an optical illusion created when moonlight reflects on the ocean bed at low-water spring tides. At **Gantheaume Point**, when the tide is low, giant dinosaur tracks thought to be 130 million years old can be viewed.

The 22km (14-mile) **Cable Beach** was named after the underwater communication link between Broome and Java (and on to London), which was established in the 19th century. Today it is the core of Broome's tourist industry, with an up-market resort and crocodile farm complementing the glorious ocean beach. A ride on a camel train along the beach at sunset is a great experience.

The Kimberley

For Australians, the **Kimberley** region is the final frontier. About half the size of Texas but with only 26,000 inhabitants, encompassing 0.5-million-hectare (1.2-million-acre) cattle ranches and enormous Aboriginal tribal lands, it was first explored in the 1890s but has opened to travellers only over the past 20 years. The landscapes here are awe-inspiring, even by antipodean standards. The blood-red desert is sliced by lush, forest-filled gorges, where freshwater crocodiles and stingrays swim; the coastline is torn by tropical fjords with tidal waterfalls that flow horizontally. Everything is on a gargantuan scale: vast meteor craters, petrified coral reefs and desert rivers that swell from 100 metres (330ft) wide in the dry season to 13km (8 miles) wide in the wet.

Generations of isolation have left the Kimberley region the most Aboriginal part of Australia, with some immense tracts of tribal land. Remote communities have their own language, newspapers and radio stations; Aboriginal guides work at the national parks and conduct tours of ancient cave paintings; and it has one of Australia's few Aboriginal-owned resorts (at Cape Leveque).

This independence was hard-won. White ranchers arrived here in the 1890s after the world's longest – and most gruelling – cattle drive across central Australia. Soon the Kimberley was the scene of a little-known Aboriginal uprising and of several massacres of indigenous peoples by settlers. Aboriginal bushrangers roamed the Kimberley, easily evading mounted police in the rugged terrain.

Derby ㉖, 216km (134 miles) along the highway northeast from Broome,

TIP

The only sensible time to visit the Kimberley, whose landscapes are hallucinatory even by antipodean standards, is Apr–Sept. At other times it is unbearably hot and humid, with a good chance of being isolated by flash floods.

Karajini National Park.

Sunset at Cape Leveque.

A dry river bed in Bungle Bungle National Park.

is the administrative centre for the huge cattle-producing region of West Kimberley. Unlike bustling Broome, with a population of 10,000, Derby is a sleepy town where little seems to have changed over the decades. From here, sightseeing is mostly done by light plane: taking a flight from Derby over **King Sound** and the **Buccaneer Archipelago** ❷ beyond will unfold one of the world's most spectacularly beautiful coastlines, a maze of islands, red cliffs and white beaches – uninhabited except for the mining communities of **Cockatoo Island** and **Koolan Islands**.

From Derby, you can either follow the main all-weather **Great Northern Highway** or turn off onto the "Beef Road", which cuts through the heart of the Kimberley. Some 7km (4.5 miles) outside Derby is a huge boab tree that is reputed to have been used as an overnight prison when transporting prisoners in colonial times. The boab (a close relation of the southern African baobab tree) is often known as the "bottle tree" and can have a circumference greater than its height – the girth frequently exceeds 10 metres (33ft).

Windjana Gorge National Park ❷ (tel: 08-9195 5500), 145km (90 miles), to the east, is worth a visit for its eerie Windjana figures in Aboriginal rock paintings, and its huge flocks of spooky, screeching white cockatoos. **Tunnel Creek National Park** ❷, 35km (22 miles) further on, allows you to walk through an underground stream course populated by bats. Only recently has this part of the Kimberley become accessible to people other than the toughest pioneers, cattlemen or prospectors. The roads are constantly being improved.

East of Derby, on the Fitzroy River near the township of Fitzroy Crossing, is **Geikie Gorge** ❸, 14km (9 miles) long, with limestone cliffs up to 30 metres (100ft) high. This is one of the most spectacular gorges in the northwest and a pleasant camping spot. Interesting tours conducted by Aboriginal rangers can be taken along the river, where freshwater crocodiles sunbake at the water's edge; down below, you can see sawfish and stingrays that

have adapted to life in fresh water. On the eastern side lies **Fossil Downs**, a huge private cattle station (over 405,000 hectares/1 million acres), founded in 1886. It is the only Kimberley cattle station still owned by descendants of the original pioneers, the MacDonalds.

East Kimberley and the Bungle Bungles

The Great Northern Highway cuts along the southern perimeter of the Kimberley before entering the new township of **Halls Creek,** which, with its comfortable hotels and air-conditioned supermarkets, serves as a base for the regional pastoral industry. At Old Halls Creek, remnants of the 1884 gold rush can be seen. The rush made a few prospectors rich, but the harsh environment and shortage of water ruined a good many more.

South of Halls Creek, 130km (80 miles) away, is the meteorite crater at **Wolfe Creek ❸**, the second largest in the world – although it really comes into perspective when seen from the air.

The turn-off 110km (68 miles) north of Halls Creek leads to a 4WD track to one of the most astonishing natural features in the world: the **Bungle Bungle Range**. The Bungles cover some 640 sq km (247 sq miles) of the Ord River Valley with a labyrinth of orange and black (caused by the black lichen and orange silica) horizontally tiger-striped, domed mountains. Within the canyons and gorges of the **Purnululu National Park ❷** are palm-filled grottoes, enormous caves and white-sand beaches. The rough track from the highway deters many, so a thriving industry has arisen in **Kununurra** to fly tourists over (and, more recently, into) the Bungle Bungles.

A true gem of the Kimberley lies to the north of Purnululu: **Argyle Diamond Mine** is the world's largest, extracting some 1,000kg (6.5 tons) of diamonds each year. The Argyle Diamond Pipe was discovered in 1979 and remains the only source of deep-pink diamonds. Air tours to the mine are available from Kununurra.

Wyndham ❸ is the most northerly port in Western Australia, a small scattered community that has changed little since the days of the gold rush. You can see large crocodiles lying on the mudflats below the Wyndham wharf. Cattle that miss their footing when being loaded onto ships provide an occasional meal.

The Ord River was dammed in 1971 to harness the monsoon runoff for irrigation; in recent years, this has opened up the East Kimberley to the cultivation of tropical crops. To the south, Lake Argyle in the **Carr Boyd Range** is the main reservoir (boat tours are available). The damming of the Ord River would have submerged **Argyle Downs Homestead**, home of one of the northwest's great pioneering families, the Duracks, so it was moved to a new location to escape the rising waters. It is now a museum about life for the early settlers of the Kimberley.with changing artworks from all around Australia.

FACT

The Kimberley is such an isolated region that the extraordinary "Bungles" were unknown to all but a few locals until 1983, when a photographer came upon them by chance.

THE DAMPIER PENINSULA

For those with a sense of adventure, a road trip from Broome to Cape Leveque traverses the whole Dampier Peninsula. Most people drive or fly straight through to Kooljaman Resort (www.kooljaman.com. au). But there are several Aboriginal communities who welcome visitors and offer accommodation and tours, and who are happy to share their traditional knowledge. Parts of the Cape Leveque Road are still unsealed, very sandy, and can be badly corrugated, so it is a good idea to hire a 4WD; the journey takes about two-and-a-half hours. Destinations include **Beagle Bay**. There is no accommodation but check out the famous Sacred Heart Church and its beautiful altar decorated with mother-of-pearl shell. **Middle Lagoon** (www.middle lagoon.com.au) offers great fishing, a lagoon safe for swimming, camping, beach shelters and self-contained log cabins. **Lombadina** (tel: 08-9192 4936; www.lombadina.com) is another Aboriginal community further north. Their accommodation and tours are well established and their beach one of the most stunning. **One Arm Point** (also known as Ardyaloon; tel: 08-9192 4932) is a few kilometres beyond Kooljaman. You can tour the aquaculture hatchery that is breeding juvenile trochus shells. When travelling across Aboriginal land, respect for the culture, privacy and people is paramount, so if you see a sign that says "no entry", abide by it.

THE WILDFLOWERS OF WESTERN AUSTRALIA

In spring, the bush is ablaze with wild flowers, from bold and brilliant banksias to delicate ice daisies.

Western Australia is known for its beautiful wild flowers. People travel from all around the country – and the world – to view the impressive display. The flowering is most spectacular during spring (August through to November), though at almost any time of year you will find some flowers brightening the olive- and sage-greens of the bush. Banksias, for example, often bloom in autumn or winter.

It might seem strange that such a dry landscape should produce so many wild flowers; there are various reasons for this success. For millions of years western Australia has avoided the sort of landmass upheaval that has caused species in other parts of the continent to die out. The flowers have also benefited from the lack of shade-casting trees and have enjoyed the protection of less engulfing plants and shrubs.

The state has some 10,000 species of wild flowers, 6,000 of which are native. Some areas are particularly well endowed: Kalbarri National Park, the karri forests around Pemberton, and the Stirling Ranges north of Albany. The southwest is known for its delicate flowers such as orchid, kangaroo paw and mountain bell.

Closer to Perth, John Forrest National Park is another rich area, or you could simply visit Kings Park Botanic Garden. We recommend you pack a picnic and a camera and take your time enjoying the rich palette of the blooms. The Western Australian Visitor Centre in Perth has maps to ensure you make the most of the wild-flower season.

In spring, daisies of many types and colours carpet forest clearings, heathlands and fields.

A display of spring wildflowers. If you have a special interest wild flowers it is worth taking an escorted wild-flower tour, a option offered by most of the day-tour operators in Perth.

Albany bottlebrush. Bottlebrush is more commonly associated with the eastern states (it was one of the plants the naturalis Joseph Banks collected on Cook's voyage of 1770), but you w also find it in WA, especially in damp habitats.

Succulents, such as these in a forest near Karridale, also flourish in the south. Succulents survive in hot, arid areas. Their characteristic fleshy leaves, stems and roots store water and their compact shape reduces dehydration. The best-known type of succulent is the cactus, but there are many other forms.

…ksias have large cone-shaped …vers comprising hundreds of … individual flowers. The …perate southwest corner of WA …ports some 60 different species, …ny of which flower in winter. …ksias are named after Joseph …ks, Captain Cook's botanist, … were celebrated in the …gglepot and Cuddlepie book … bushbaby drawings of the …dren's author and illustrator … Gibbs (1877–1969).

GRASS TREES

Even if you are not in Western Australia during the wildflower season, the bush is a fascinating landscape with a rich biodiversity that is at last being championed by conservationists after well over a century of indiscriminate land clearance for agriculture.

Among the many types of eucalyptus (gumtrees), paper bark and banksias, the tree that perhaps stands out above all others is the grass tree *(Xanthorrhoea)*, with its distinctive fire-blackened trunk surmounted by a mop of spiky grass and spear-like flower shaft.

Grass trees are very slow-growing (about 1 metre/3ft every 100 years) but can live for hundreds of years, and their ability to survive in tough conditions has made them a symbol of the Australian Outback. Like many other bush plants, they have evolved to withstand bushfires; germination is actually assisted by fire. The distinctive flower shaft will often shoot up in the year following a bushfire, providing valuable food for wildlife in an otherwise charred, barren landscape. In contrast to the slow-growing trunk, the flowering stalk grows rapidly after germination, at a rate of 2–3cm (1in) a day.

The grass trees are known as balga (black boys) to the Aborigines, who traditionally used a waterproof resin produced from the base of the plant to make glue. The shafts could also be used as spear heads, and the dried flower shafts could be rubbed together to create fire. The tender shoots could be eaten, and the nectar from the flowers of the plant was used to make a sweet drink. Today the grass trees are prized by horticulturalists – plants saved from the developers' bulldozers can, with great skill and care, be transplanted and coaxed into life.

Grass tree (Xanthorrhoea), with its distinctive fire-blackened trunk surmounted by a mop of spiky grass and spear-like flower shaft.

The distinctive flower shaft of the grass tree will often shoot up in the year following a bushfire, providing valuable food for wildlife in an otherwise charred, barren landscape. In contrast to the slow-growing trunk, the flowering stalk grows rapidly after germination, at a rate of 2–3cm (1 inch) a day.

Dove Lake, Cradle Mountain and Lake St Clair National Park.

The bridge at Richmond.

TASMANIA

Australia's smallest and remotest state is also the most temperate. It has no arid Outback, but there's an abundance of cool forests, rugged mountains, highland lakes, lush pasture and fruitful orchards.

Perth
Sydney

"How beautiful is the whole region, for form, and grouping, and opulence, and freshness of foliage, and variety of color, and grace and shapeliness of the hills, the capes, the promontories; and then, the splendor of the sunlight, the dim rich distances, the charm of the water-glimpses!" Such was the view of inveterate traveller Mark Twain, commenting on his voyage to Tasmania in the 1890s.

However, he then went on to point out the irony behind this observation: "And it was in this paradise that the yellow-liveried convicts were landed, and the Corps-bandits quartered, and the wanton slaughter of the kangaroo-chasing black innocents consummated on that autumn day in May, in the brutish old time. It was all out of keeping with the place, a sort of bringing of heaven and hell together."

This is the paradox of Tasmania, nowhere more so than at the Port Arthur Penal Settlement, the most popular of the state's myriad tourist attractions. It sits in a jaw-droppingly gorgeous setting: an amphitheatre of rolling green meadow leading down to the tranquil blue waters of Mason Cove, dotted with picturesque sandstone ruins glowing golden yellow in the watery sunlight. Even without the sun, there is something magisterial and uplifting about the setting. Yet this must be reconciled with its original

role as a setting for a prison regime, which was considered by many to be the harshest in the British Empire.

Van Diemen's Land

That was in the days when the island was called Van Diemen's Land (after being so named by Abel Tasman in 1642) and when British colonists were establishing their second toehold on the Australian continent. It was a struggle to tame the inhospitable land and establish viable agriculture. Today there are still vast stretches of Tasmania that

Main Attractions
Hobart
Richmond
Port Arthur
Freycinet National Park
Bay of Fires
Cradle Mountain

Hobart and Mount Wellington.

The Salamanca Market is the perfect place to browse for used books.

are only accessible by tough walking tracks. Even in populated regions, there is a sense of space. It's to be expected in an island the size of Ireland but with a tenth of the latter's 6.4 million people.

Tasmania's appeal resides in the range and beauty of its landscapes and natural features, from the lakes and mountains of the central highlands, culminating in the iconic Cradle Mountain, to the deserted beaches of the east coast, where the aquamarine of the sea is offset by the vibrant orange lichen on the rocks. And if this isn't enough, try the islands in the Bass Strait, where, such is the sparseness of the population, every motorist acknowledges every other.

Few venture to such far-flung outposts on their first visit, though. There are no international flights to Tasmania and just the odd cruise ship, so most visitors come via the mainland, either on the *Spirit of Tasmania* ferries from Melbourne to Devonport or by air into Hobart or Launceston.

Hobart

If you follow Twain's lead and make **Hobart ❶** your first port of call,

you'll find a small, distinguished city nestling between the waters of the Derwent and the brooding bulk of Mount Wellington. These features have prevented the urban sprawl that affects many mainland cities, while a spell in the economic doldrums in the 1960s and 1970s meant that much of the old colonial architecture was spared from development. Today there are numerous well-preserved Georgian and Victorian buildings to give character and a nod back to old England.

Hobart's waterfront is a magnet. There are the classic views across to Mount Wellington and plenty of remnants of the thriving 19th-century port. At **Victoria Dock ❹**, the beautifully restored ixl **Jam Factory** is on the site of the first wharf and now contains the remarkable, award-winning **Henry Jones Art Hotel**, and the University of Tasmania's **Centre for the Arts**.

Visit both, then wander across to the adjoining **Constitution Dock**. Consider fish and chips from one of the floating stalls, then head to **Salamanca Place ❸**. This is the site of a pulsating Saturday-morning market, but even without that, the old stone warehouses are atmospheric and appealing. They house a lively arts centre as well as the usual selection of galleries, bars and cafés. Behind them is the pedestrianised **Salamanca Square**, a modern development that successfully latches on to the original buildings.

East along Salamanca Place, turn up Kelly's Steps to the eyrie of **Battery Point ❻**, where a pristine collection of the city's earliest dwellings is to be found. At its centre is Arthur's Circus, doing a fine impression of a village green, while Hampden Road's range of eateries includes the peerless **Jackman & McRoss** bakery/café. The **Narryna Heritage Museum** (tel: 03-6165 7000; www.narryna.com.au; Tue–Sun 10am–4pm) preserves a merchant's house in Victorian splendour.

Westwards along Salamanca Place brings you to the administrative centre

Map: Hobart

QUEENS

Brooker Avenue

Letitia Street

DOMAIN

Lower Domain Road

Berriedale, Museum of Old & New Art (MONA)

Tasman Bridge

Royal Botanical Gardens

Government House **K**

Hobart

0   500 m
0   500 yds

N

Burnett St

GLEBE

Aberdeen St

Tasman Highway

NORTH HOBART

Tasma St

Warwick St

Argyle Street

Campbell St

Brooker Avenue

Elizabeth Street

Patrick St

Murray St

Liverpool St

Penitentiary Chapel & Criminal Courts **I**

Cenotaph

Davey St

Theatre Royal **H**

HOBART

Freight Terminal

Elizabeth St Mall

Tasmanian Museum & Art Gallery **G**

Evans St

Centre for the Arts **A**

Brisbane St

Melville

St David's Cathedral **D**

Town Hall **E**

F

Hunter St

Victoria Dock

Bathurst

Collins

Maritime Museum of Tasmania

Constitution Dock

Harrington

Parliament House

Goulburn

Barrack St

Salamanca

B

Salamanca Steps

Kelly's Steps

Molle St

Sandy Bay Rd

Narryna Heritage Museum

BATTERY **C** POINT

Liverpool

Macquarie St

Davey

Hampden

Rd

Anglesea Barracks

Wrest Point Casino

Derwent

Kangaroo Bay

of the state. The discreet sandstone-clad modernism of the **Supreme Court** on the left is balanced by the more conventional Victorian bulk of **Parliament House** on the right (tours when houses not sitting; tel: 03-6233 2200; www.parliament.tas.gov.au; Mon–Fri or daily 10am and 2pm; free).

Macquarie Street

A block further back, Macquarie Street has **St David's Cathedral** ⓓ – the Georgian-style seat of the local Anglican bishop; the **Treasury Building** facing onto the formal gardens of Franklin Square; the **General Post Office**, built with the grandeur that characterises these buildings; the **Town Hall** ⓔ; the Art Deco sleekness of the **Mercury Newspaper Building**; and the **Tasmanian Museum and Art Gallery** ⓕ (tel: 03-6165 7000; www.tmag.tas.gov.au; Tue–Sun 10am–4pm; free).

The museum is a repository for colonial and contemporary art, local fauna, a collection of Chinese antiquities, and material illustrating early polar exploration. The **Maritime**

Museum of Tasmania (tel: 03-6234 1427; www.maritimetas.org; daily 9am–5pm) is small but worthwhile for its collection of photos, models, navigational instruments and relics exploring Tasmania's link with the sea.

Another block back from the water, the main downtown shopping area centres on **Elizabeth Street Mall** ⓖ.

North, beyond the mass of the Royal Hobart Hospital, the old **Theatre Royal** ⓗ on Campbell Street is a blushing star. Its plush auditorium can usually be inspected if you employ a touch of charm at the box office, and it is well worth a look to appreciate the set-builder's art. The auditorium was completely rebuilt in 1984 after a fire.

A few blocks up Campbell Street the **Penitentiary Chapel and Criminal Courts** ⓘ (tel: 03-6231 0911; www.penitentiarychapel.com; tours Sun–Fri 10am, 11.30am, 1pm, 2.30pm, Sat 1pm and 2.30pm; ghost tour Mon and Fri nights) are all that remain of the original vast Hobart Gaol. Splendid tours are run by knowledgeable National Trust volunteers.

An exhibit at the Maritime Museum of Tasmania.

Hobart harbour.

An African figure made from beads at the Museum of Antiquities, part of Moorilla Estate Winery.

Sir John Franklin's statue in Franklin Square.

The Queens Domain

If you head northeast and can manage to cross some busy highways, **Queens Domain** has, since the early days, been a place of recreation, remembrance and, for the occupant of Government House, residence. The **Cenotaph** ❿ is flanked by a couple of interesting modern glass and stone pyramids that incorporate audio tributes to those lost in combat. The **Royal Botanical Gardens** ⓚ were established in 1828 and are faithful to the early vision of the founders by collecting every conceivable variety of flora.

Outer Hobart

North Hobart has a plethora of cosmopolitan bars, restaurants and entertainment venues. Further north still, **Runnymede** in New Town is an early 1830s homestead maintained by the National Trust (61 Bay Road, New Town; tel: 03-6278 1269; www.nationaltrusttas.org.au; Sept–June Tue–Fri 10am–4pm, Sun noon–4pm; guided tours available Tue–Thu, booking essential) and worth a stop on the way to the **Moorilla Estate**.

This winery not only claims one of Tasmania's leading restaurants but also houses arguably the most significant addition to Tasmania's cultural infrastructure in years: the **Museum of Old and New Art**. MONA (Main Road, Berriedale; tel: 03-6277 9900; www.mona.net.au; Wed–Mon 10am–6pm; free) was built from scratch by entrepreneur David Walsh to house a wide-ranging and esoteric collection ranging from historical artefacts from the great civilisations through to challenging modern work, all loosely linked by the concept of sex and death as the driving forces of creativity. Its dramatic galleries opened at the beginning of 2011.

West of the city centre, Mount Wellington provides superb views of the city; make sure that you visit the **Cascade Brewery** (Cascade Road, South Hobart; tel: 03-6224 1117; www.cascade breweryco.com.au; daily, tours between 11am and 2.15pm; booking essential). Relish the picturesque setting, a choice of tours, and the opportunity to drink your way through the sampling room. The brewery is also the starting

point for *Louisa's Walk*, a promenade through the **Female Factory** in which professional actors enact a gripping chapter in history (tel: 03-6233 6656; www.livehistoryhobart.com.au; daily 1–2pm; booking essential). You can visit the site on your own, too.

On the other side of the Derwent, the suburb of **Bellerive** fans out from **Kangaroo Bluff Battery**, an emplacement designed to guard the city from attack. The **Tasmanian Cricket Museum** (tel: 03-6282 0433; Tue–Thu 10am–3pm, Fri 10am–noon) is located at **Blundstone Arena**, where state and international cricket is played in a village-green atmosphere.

Leaving Hobart via the **Tasman Bridge** is the first step towards the Tasman Peninsula, where so much colonial history was forged.

Richmond

The direct route goes across Sorell Causeway, but that would be to neglect the wonderful colonial township of **Richmond** ❷. It sits in the Coal River Valley, its convict-built stone bridge offset by the English village-style church on the hill beyond. This is the kind of setting that led Mark Twain to observe that "wherever the exiled Englishman can find in his new home resemblances to his old one, he is touched to the marrow of his being; the love that is in his heart inspires his imagination, and these allied forces transfigure those resemblances into authentic duplicates of the revered originals". Most of the town was built between 1824 and 1840, and it is the consistency in style that gives Richmond its charm. There's the obligatory gaol for this staging post on the Hobart to Port Arthur road, as well as a couple of churches. More recent attractions include a maze and the **Old Hobart Town Model Village** (21 Bridge Street; tel: 03-6260 2502; www.oldhobarttown.com; daily 9am–5pm).

Pass through Sorell and pause, if you must, at the Colonial and Convict Collection (self-proclaimed as junk) at **Copping** before continuing to **Eaglehawk Neck**. This isthmus to the Tasman Peninsula is where the infamous Dog Line was set. A team of ferocious fidos was chained to a row of posts so that no convict could cross without coming into range of at least one of them. See the fearsome statue.

There are gentler attractions nearby. The **Tesselated Pavement** suggests that nature has tiled the shoreline, while across the isthmus the **Tasman Arch** and **Devil's Kitchen** are popular stops on the bus tours to Port Arthur.

The **Tasmanian Devil Park** (tel: 1800-641 641; www.tasmaniandevilpark.com; daily 9am–5pm, later in summer) at Taranna is an optional stop, and your chance to see a rare animal facing extinction from a disease epidemic, before the main attraction: the **Port Arthur Penal Settlement** ❸ (tel: 1800-659 101; www.portarthur.org.au; daily 9am–dusk). See page 304.

Don't miss the **Coal Mines Historic Site**. Convicts provided the labour, and the ruins reveal grim evidence of their travails (daily 24 hours; free).

TIP

A joint venture between various agencies has seen the publication of a free booklet, Great Short Walks, which outlines 60 treks in some of the most beautiful areas in the state. There are information boards at the start of each route co-ordinated with the design of the booklet.

Old and new structures at the Cenotaph.

Fishermen can often be seen unloading their catches at harbours all along the east coast.

View of the Freycinet peninsula.

The East Coast

The Tasman Highway runs up the east coast, arriving first at the sleepy resort of **Orford**. Continue to Triabunna, where ferries depart for **Maria Island** ❹ (tel: 03-6234 2999; www.mariaisland ferry.com.au; 4 sailings daily except May–Aug, check online timetable). Originally a penal settlement, it is now a national park and a haven for wildlife and walkers. No traffic is permitted unless you take a bicycle; the only accommodation is in unpowered bunkhouses in the settlement at **Darlington**. Natural wonders abound – **Fossil Cliffs** and the **Painted Cliffs** amongst them. Up the coast the old **Spiky Bridge** and pristine **Spiky Beach** are untrumpeted gems.

Swansea is a low-key resort with lovely views across Great Oyster Bay to the pink granite peaks of the Hazards on the **Freycinet Peninsula**, another of Tasmania's big tickets. It's quite a long drive to get there, but the rewards are worth it. First stop is **Coles Bay** ❺, the service and accommodation centre that happens to have some rather fabulous beaches. However, the main attraction is **Freycinet National Park** ❻ (tel: 03-6256 7000; www.parks.tas.gov. au; daily Nov–Apr 8am–5pm, May–Oct 9am–4pm;) and its headline act, **Wineglass Bay**.

Bicheno, to the north, is a family resort with a pretty fishing boat shelter, the Gulch, and a big blowhole. The **Douglas-Apsley National Park** has a natural water hole and is a popular picnic spot.

The northeast

After a handful of other beach resorts, you wind round into **St Helens** on sheltered George's Bay. With a population around the 2,000 mark, it is the largest town on the east coast. It's a nice enough place, but it's better to follow the road out to **Binalong Bay** at the southern end of one of the world's great coastal stretches, the **Bay of Fires** ❼. It consists of 30km (19 miles) of some of the finest beach in the world and much of it is inaccessible by road. There are four-day guided walks, which include a couple of nights at a stunning modern lodge, but otherwise you have to fend for yourself. Northern

access is via the **Mount William National Park**, where the lighthouse at **Eddystone Point** marks the top of the bay.

The road inland from St Helens climbs steeply into tin country. A turn off to **Pyengana** reveals a cheese factory; the **Pub in the Paddock,** where a pair of beer-drinking pigs dwell; and the less contrived appeal of **St Columba's Falls**. Further inland, **Derby** has its gleaming **Tin Centre** (tel: 03-6354 1062; www.trailofthetindragon.com; daily 10am–4.30pm, winter until 4pm) to provide a glimpse back to the days when the area's prosperity lay beneath the ground.

The road north runs to **Bridport ❽** with its mix of holiday shacks and a tired resort playing host to fans of fishing and beaches. The acclaimed **Barnbougle Dunes Golf Links** is a short distance out of town and appeals to a different breed of pleasure seekers.

Purple people head to **Bridestowe Estate Lavender Farm** (tel: 03-6352 8182; www.bridestowelavender.com. au; daily Jan 9am–6pm, Sept–Apr 9am–5pm, May–Aug 9am–4pm; free except Dec–Jan), a blanket of colour in December and January just before the crop is harvested. **Lilydale**, on the road winding down towards Launceston, has an attractive main street notable for historic **Bardenhagen's General Store**, and the imaginative paint jobs that have been applied to the town's power poles.

Launceston

Tasmania's second city has undergone a revival in recent years due, to some extent, to the advent of cheaper air fares from the mainland and also to some shrewd investments in tourist infrastructure. Of particular note has been the development of the old railway workshops at Inveresk, especially the new site operated by the **Queen Victoria Museum and Art Gallery** (tel: 03-6323 3777; www.qvmag.tas. gov.au; daily 10am–4pm; free). This impressive complex combines art

galleries with museum space marking the industrial history of the area. The Blacksmith Shop, complete with deafening soundscape, gives an impression of the labours of the past.

Launceston ❾ has more than its share of distinguished Victorian architecture on its undulating streets, and much pleasure comes from simply walking around the city centre. Indeed, Cameron Street, with its red-brick terraces replete with filigree ironwork, must be one of the best-preserved streets of the era in Australia. It leads off **Civic Square**, which gathers up the grandiose **Town Hall**, the **Library** and the simple **Macquarie House**, a stone warehouse from 1830.

The main shopping area radiates out from **Brisbane Street Mall** and includes graceful **Quadrant Mall** and hapless modern construct, **Yorktown Square**. The **Old Umbrella Shop** (Mon–Fri 9am–5pm, Sat 9am–noon; free) in George Street has remained unchanged for the best part of a century and is now run by the National Trust.

To the east of the centre **City Park** is laid out Victorian style with original

FACT

George's Bay has plenty of variety on offer for anglers. Estuary and bay fishing offers bream, salmon, flathead and trevally; deep-sea fishing adds trevalla, gemfish, blue grenadier and others; offshore reef options include stripey trumpeter, cod, perch and squid.

FREYCINET NATIONAL PARK

There are few places in the world where the elements of landscape combine so winningly as at Freycinet National Park. The mix of mountains, forest, beaches and achingly blue sea, not to mention the abundant wildlife, is hard to match and impossible to beat. It's best just to surrender to it and allow as much time as possible to take it all in. And the best way to see it is to get out there and walk.

The most popular trek is the fairly stiff climb up to the saddle between two of the Hazards: Mount Amos and Mount Mayson. This houses the **Wineglass Bay** lookout. Even for regulars, the view down can take you by surprise; there's the faultless symmetry of the curve that gives the bay its name and, if you're lucky and the sun's out, the searing azure of the sea. For the first-time visitor, it is just breathtaking. It is not unusual to find groups of people settled on the benches or clumped on nearby rocks, gazing down in silence, lost in contemplation. (Or getting their breath back.) Some turn back now, while others scramble down to the beach, perhaps as part of a longer hike which could take in **Mount Graham** or **Mount Freycinet**, or to return via **Hazards Beach**. There are several shorter walks too, at **Cape Tourville**, **Sleepy Bay** or **Little Gravelly Beach**, for instance. Pick up a map at the visitor centre just inside the park.

Artist at work in the Blacksmith Shop of the Queen Victoria Museum and Art Gallery.

fountains, rotundas and a conservatory. A monkey enclosure contains macaques that have been exciting local children for years. Other highlights around the city include the original **Queen Victoria Museum** (tel: 03-6323 3777; www.qvmag.tas.gov.au; daily 10am–4pm; free), the **Design Centre of Tasmania** (tel: 03-6331 5506; www.designtasmania.com.au; Mon–Fri 9.30am–5.30pm, Sat–Sun 10am–4pm), the **National Automobile Museum of Tasmania** (tel: 03-6334 8888; www.namt.com.au; daily Sept–May 9am–5pm, June–Aug 10am–4pm) and **Boag's Brewery** (tel: 03-6332 6300; www.jamesboag.com.au; Mon–Fri 8.45am–4.30pm; tour times vary; free), where enthusiasts can take a tour and drink beer.

The river front has enjoyed a revival with **Seaport**'s hotel, restaurants and bars making the most of the setting, and a boardwalk eastwards runs past **Ritchies Mill**, home to **Stillwater**, one of several outstanding city eateries.

Few cities have such a remarkable phenomenon as **Cataract Gorge** within walking distance of the centre.

Paths run along its steep walls – the southern one tough, the northern one easy. If walking is out, then pleasure boats sail part of the way up the South Esk River. Walkers can go all the way to the **Cliff Grounds** area, where the gorge opens out into a basin, with gardens and a rotunda on one side, and grassy banks and an open-air swimming pool on the other. A chairlift and suspension bridge link the two sides.

The Tamar Valley

Launceston's playground lies to the north in the **Tamar Valley**, an area best known for its vineyards. Although there is an officially sanctioned **Tamar Valley Wine Route**, with special signage (blue grapes on yellow), just as much fun can be had by following your nose.

Make a stop in **George Town** ❿, where the first settlers on the Tamar pitched up. The **Watch House Museum** (Macquarie Street; Nov–Apr Mon–Fri 10am–4pm, Sat–Sun noon–2pm; May–Oct Mon–Fri 10am–3pm, Sat–Sun noon–2pm) tells the story.

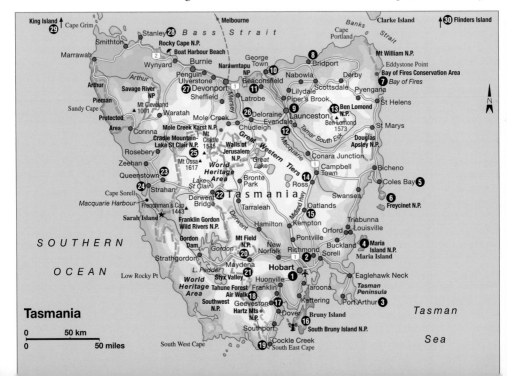

Tasmania

0   50 km

0   50 miles

Low Head at the mouth of the Tamar has the atmospheric **Pilot Station** where whitewashed houses, some for rent, are dotted around a green. There's a **Maritime Museum** (tel: 03-6382 1143; http://museum.lowhead. com; daily 10am–4pm) and the chance to watch a pilot boat at work guiding vessels up the tricky river.

Batman Bridge is the only fixed crossing above Launceston. Turn right for **Beaconsfield** ⓫, a town which gained global notoriety when two miners were trapped in its gold mine in 2006 (they were saved after a nailbiting two-week rescue operation). The impressive **Beaconsfield Mine and Heritage Centre** (tel: 03-6383 1473; www.beaconsfieldheritage.com.au; daily 9.30am–4.30pm) is housed in old mine buildings.

Beauty Point's attractions are on its wharf. **Seahorse World** (tel: 03-6383 4111; www.seahorseworld.com.au; daily Sept–Apr 9.30am–3.30pm, May–Aug 10am–3pm; tours every half-hour) has seahorses, funnily enough. You can guess the main attraction at the neighbouring **Platypus House** (tel: 03-6383

4884; www.platypushouse.com.au; daily 9.30am–3.30pm).

Detours from the road back to Launceston may include **Grindelwald**, a resort hotel for those yearning for a faux Swiss village, and **Tamar Island**, just north of the city, a wetlands reserve with an easily accessible boardwalk.

The Midland Highway

The Midland Highway runs down to Hobart and takes in some of the best of the colonial villages. **Longford** has numerous listed buildings, especially along Wellington Street, and **Brown's Big Store** has grand Victorian style. Close by are two country estates, both open to the public. **Woolmers Estate** has an exuberant mansion and extensive grounds containing a coach house, stables, cottages, and a working woolshed. Also at Woolmers is the **National Rose Garden,** which will eventually feature over 500 varieties (tel: 03-6391 2230; www.woolmers.com.au; daily 10am–4pm; regular guided tours of the house). **Brickendon Estate**'s **Historic Farming Village** has great character (tel:

Cataract Gorge is one of Tasmania's premier attractions.

Victorian facades, Launceston.

The Gulag Peninsula

As the most fearsome prison of the Antipodes, Port Arthur's natural isolation made it the perfect site for the worst criminals.

Port Arthur was designed to be the ultimate prison. Establishments in Hobart, Sarah Island and Maria Island predate it, but all had their problems. The new place had to be secure and remote enough to make escape difficult, if not impossible, but it was also to employ the "enlightened" punishment regime favoured at the time.

In this setting, 110km (68 miles) from Hobart, security was not a problem; if the convicts escaped, the dog line at Eaglehawk Neck would stop them. The rumour that sharks patrolled the sea didn't exactly encourage a swim to freedom either.

With a population of prisoners, soldiers and settlers many kilometres from anywhere, this was not just a prison but a penal settlement, one built on an industrial scale. Convicts were employed in shipbuilding, timber felling, agriculture and

Many of the buildings were destroyed by bushfires which ravaged Port Arthur in 1897.

animal husbandry. The population needed to be self-sufficient, and a thriving village grew up around the prison, with farms, shops and Australia's first railway system (pulled by convicts instead of mules).

Today, tourists are efficiently managed through the site. On buying your ticket you are allocated a time for a boat cruise and another for the guided tour, ensuring that the constant flow of visitors is fed through as comfortably as possible. The quieter times are first thing in the morning before the bus tours arrive from Hobart, and mid-afternoon onwards when most of them have departed.

You are also given a playing card to use in the Lottery of Life exhibition that leads out to the main site. Each card corresponds to an inmate whose history you follow through the display. You may have been transported for stealing bread but worked your way through the system to win the prized ticket of leave. Or you may be a recidivist who meets a sticky end.

After this and the guided tour you can start exploring. The best-known building in Port Arthur is the long, squat sandstone **Penitentiary**, a former flour mill converted in 1848 into a 136-cell prison for the worst offenders, although they were allowed out during the day to work. Two bushfires in the late 1890s gutted this and other edifices.

Take a stroll up the path to the left to the **Commandant's House**, with an extraordinary view over the bay and the site. It was one of the few wooden houses to survive the flames.

The path from the bay runs past the ruined hospital to the **Separate Prison** – built in the 1850s on a radical concept of punishment being developed in Britain. Instead of physical pain, prisoners were subjected to total sensory deprivation: kept in tiny cells for 23 hours a day, they were not allowed to talk or interact with others. Not surprisingly, the treatment led to more derangement than rehabilitation; Port Arthur was used as a mental asylum in later years.

Harbour cruises run out around the **Isle of the Dead** and **Point Puer Boys' Prison**, and twice a day you can land on the former, which became the cemetery for the prison colony. A lone convict once lived on the island to dig the graves.

On the way back to the visitor centre, the shell of the Broad Arrow Café is part of a **Memorial Garden** to the victims of a gunman who massacred 35 people in and around the site in April 1996. Visitors should not broach the subject with staff.

03-6391 1383; www.brickendon.com.au; Tue–Sun 9.30am–5pm).

Evandale ⑫, to the east of the highway, makes much of hosting the National Penny Farthing Championships each February, but there are numerous other pretexts for a visit: the two churches to St Andrew – one Anglican, the other a more extravagant Uniting Church; the interior to **Brown's Village Store**; and the **Clarendon Arms**.

For a break from historic villages, follow the steep, winding C401 from Evandale up towards **Ben Lomond National Park** ⑬. Once you've negotiated the tortuous Jacob's Ladder, you arrive at the **Alpine Village**. In winter this is one of two snowfields in the state (the other is at Mount Field), and during the rest of the year there are some lovely Alpine walks.

Return to the Midland Highway for **Campbell Town**'s **Heritage Highway Museum** (tel: 03-6381 1353; Mon–Fri 10am–3pm; free). Elsewhere the theme is bricks: millions of them in the convict-built **Red Bridge**, and a few thousand set into the pavements

on both sides of the highway as part of a project that will eventually see one brick for each of the 68,000 people transported to Van Diemen's Land.

Ross ⑭ is arguably the most unspoilt of all the historic towns. **Church Street** is unsurpassed in its Georgian structures and includes **Ross Village Bakery**, where you can relax with a sticky cake. Continue down to the stone **bridge** and follow the path behind the Uniting Church to the remains of the **Female Factory**.

Ross benefits from being bypassed by the highway, as does **Oatlands** ⑮, which has dozens of old sandstone buildings and the towering **Callington Mill** (tel: 03-6254 1212; daily 9am–4pm; tours available; free), but, lacking the shady elms that contribute so winningly to Ross's ambience, it attracts fewer visitors. Make the most of this and follow the town's walking trail in peace.

Kempton is the last town worth exploring, and then it's a straight run into Hobart, unless the Romanesque church of St Mark in **Pontville** interests you. ●

Time stands still at the Grove in George Town for a home maid.

The bridge at Ross was constructed in 1836.

The Huon Valley

TIP

Day entry to national parks in Tasmania costs A$24 per vehicle (except for Cradle Mountain – A$16.50 per adult) and can be purchased online, at national park visitor centres and at some state visitor information centres. For multiple visits a two-month pass costs A$60. See www.parks.tas.gov.au for more information.

South from Hobart, the **Huon Valley** is an area that people don't necessarily see on their first visit to the island, but its gentle pleasures reward those who make the effort. For long draped with the orchards that gave the Apple Isle its name, the area is as likely to reveal vineyards or berries in its rolling meadows these days. In fact its providores and gourmet restaurants have made it something of a foodie's haunt.

Sticking to the coast road, check out the **Shot Tower** (tel: 03-6227 8885; taroona.tas.au/shot-tower; daily 9am–5pm) at **Taroona**; perhaps the exhibition in the foyer of the **Australian Antarctic Division HQ** (tel: 03-6232 3209; Mon–Fri 9am–5pm; free) outside Kingston; and the novel snorkel trail at **Tinderbox**, where you swim out and read a series of information boards on plates on the sea bed.

Kettering has a sparkling cove, but most people are there for the ferry to **Bruny Island** ⑯. It could be viewed as two islands joined by a narrow isthmus (The Neck) and locals refer to North Bruny and South Bruny. Either

The beach on the Neck has protected areas for penguins and mutton birds.

way, it's a lengthy 63km (39 miles) from top to bottom. **Adventure Bay** on the more rugged South Bruny is the main holiday centre, if you can call it that. Most activity involves walking or fishing, and maybe visiting **Cape Bruny Lighthouse** or **Fluted Cape**. A boat excursion will reveal seals, dolphins and any other aquatic life that turns up. **The Neck** has a penguin viewing point and a lookout reached by a steep flight of steps.

On the mainland, make your way to **Huonville**, the area's commercial centre, where visitor interest focuses on the river. There are easy walks or rigorous tests of your capacity to withstand intense G-forces on the **Huon Jet** boat.

Continuing south, **Franklin** is but a street along the river bank. However, the **Wooden Boat Centre** (tel: 03-6266 3586; www.woodenboatcentre. com; Mon–Fri 10.30am–4.30pm, weekends to 4pm) is an interesting stop. For a small fee, you can follow the progress of students on an 18-month boatbuilding course. At the end of their studies they will have jointly built a complete vessel.

Forests of the south

Geeveston **⓱** is a timber town. The clues are easy to spot: the two huge trunks either side of the road as you drive in, the life-size carved wooden figures placed along the streets, and the **Forest and Heritage Centre** that doubles as the visitor centre in the middle of town. Geeveston is on the edge of a huge area of managed forest, and beyond that there's only the uninhabited wilderness of **Southwest National Park**, a World Heritage Area.

The spectacular **Tahune Forest Air Walk ⓲** (tel: 1300-720 507; www.adventureforests.com.au; daily Oct–Mar 9am–5pm, Apr–Sept 10am–4pm), a 28km (17-mile) drive west, is a 600-metre (1,970ft) steel walkway high in the canopy, which gives a new perspective on life in the forest. Part of it is cantilevered out over the banks of the Huon River. Quieter, and just as alluring, is the **Hartz Mountains National Park**, where trails take a few minutes or several hours.

Pass through somnolent **Dover** and then turn inland to the **Hastings Caves and Thermal Springs**

(tel: 1300-827 727; www.parks.tas.gov.au; daily Dec–Jan 9am–5pm, Feb–mid-Apr 10am–4pm, mid-Apr–Sept 10.30am–3.30pm). Bask in one and enjoy a guided tour of the other.

A dirt road leads to **Cockle Creek ⓳**, the most southerly point you can drive to in Australia. Consecutive settlements failed at whaling, logging and mining; now it just attracts tourists. Walkers can take on the multi-day **South Coast Track**. Many just walk the two hours each way to **South Cape Bay** and back. And everyone else does the stroll to the bronze whale by the bay.

The Gordon River Road

Visitors can penetrate furthest into the World Heritage Area along the Gordon River Road to Strathgordon.

Follow the course of the Derwent north from Hobart and dawdle for a while in **New Norfolk**, a town with a lumpen paper mill but also scenic stretches of hop gardens and their associated oast houses. Look out for a pair of sturdy old inns and, in **St Matthews**, traces of the oldest church in

A carved statue in Geeveston, where the principal industry is timber.

The Tahune Forest Airwalk.

The playground in Mount Field National Park has a wooden wombat.

Hiking the Overland Track.

the state, buried beneath all the subsequent renovations.

It's just a few kilometres to the blissful tranquillity of the **Salmon Ponds Heritage Hatchery and Garden** (tel: 03-6261 5663; www.salmonponds.com.au; daily 9am–4pm). Its history as a breeding ground of early introduced species is interesting, but the main pleasure is in just strolling in the glorious gardens.

Not far along the Gordon River Road, **Mount Field National Park** ❷⓿ can get busy with day-trippers from Hobart, so be prepared to share the boardwalks to the most accessible sights including **Russell Falls** and, above it, **Horseshoe Falls**. The **Tall Trees** trail provides a first taste of the giants of the forest, and another hour's walk brings **Lady Barron Falls** into range. Go deeper into the park for Alpine uplands and the snow fields.

Junee Cave, in Maydena, is the entrance to an extensive karst system. Just beyond the village, after a bridge, take a track on the right which winds round to the **Styx Valley** ❷❶. At **Big Tree Reserve**, a boardwalk loop skirts through some of the highest trees in the country, all *Eucalyptus regnans* or swamp gum. There have been long battles by conservationists to save these and others like them from the loggers; the evidence is in scrawled rebuttals to the propaganda on the information boards erected by Forestry Tasmania.

Enjoy the long drive through wild mountain scenery to **Strathgordon**, perched at the end of **Lake Pedder**, and on for a final few kilometres to the engineering marvel of the **Gordon Dam** in all its grey concrete glory.

The Lyell Highway

As the Lyell Highway from New Norfolk climbs up to the Central Plateau, look for hydroelectric activity, with power stations and old workers' camps at **Tarraleah** and **Bronte Park**. Fishing fans should turn right down the Marlborough Highway for **Great Lake**. It has amazing trout and a remarkable collection of shack communities. Otherwise continue to **Derwent Bridge** ❷❷.

This is where hikers finish the Overland Track at the visitor centre at the

end of **Lake St Clair**. Casual visitors can embark on shorter walks, take a cruise up the lake, or combine the two by chugging to the far end and walking back. Make time to inspect **The Wall**, a long-term project by sculptor Greg Duncan to carve a 100-metre (330ft) -long relief depicting the life and history of the Central Highlands (tel: 03-6289 1134; www.thewalltasmania. com; daily Sept–Apr 9am–5pm, May–Aug 9am–4pm).

The drive continues past access points to the **Franklin River** for kayakers and whitewater rafters, until the landscape changes from lush green hills to bleak brown and grey. Gold, and then copper, was discovered here in the late 1800s. Trees were lopped to fuel the smelters, and sulphurous outpourings put paid to any remaining vegetation. The land is now entirely denuded. It's bleak but also strangely compelling.

In the midst of all this sits **Queenstown** ㉓, a rough-and-ready mining town, which now receives a daily influx of tourists who arrive on the steam-drawn (at least for the last few kilometres) **West Coast Wilderness Railway** from Strahan on the west coast. They may take in the old-fashioned **Galley Museum** (1 Driffield Street; tel: 03-6471 1483; Oct–Apr Mon–Fri 9.30am–5.30pm, Sat–Sun 12.30–4.30pm, May–Sept Mon–Fri 9.30am–4.30pm, Sat–Sun 12.30–4.30pm) and the **Miners Siding** public sculpture, or maybe just have a drink in the historic **Empire Hotel**.

The Miners Siding, a sculpture in Queenstown.

Macquarie Harbour

Strahan ㉔ (pronounced *strawn*) began life as a timber town, thrived on the copper that passed through and always supported a small fishing fleet. Now, however, it's driven by tourism; this is down to its position on **Macquarie Harbour.**

It's almost obligatory for visitors to take a cruise (World Heritage Cruises daily 9am; tel: 03-6471 7174; www.worldheritagecruises.com.au; or Gordon River Cruises, daily 8.30am; tel: 03-6471 4300; www.gordonrivercruises.com.au), which includes a swing through **Hell's Gates** at the mouth of the harbour, a look at a fish farm and then a tramp around the ruins on **Sarah Island**.

The West Coast Wilderness Railway.

FACT

As something of a labour of love, a team of volunteers spent several years restoring Queenstown's Paragon Theatre. This Art Deco classic was built in 1932 and reopened as a 60-seat luxury cinema in 2009, one of the few remaining of its kind in Australia. Unfortunately, however, due to financial problems and the dwindling population in the area, the theatre was up for sale at the time of going to print.

Walls of Jerusalem National Park.

Probably the toughest penal establishment in the colony, Sarah Island was for the worst recidivists. From 1822 they were put to work fashioning ships from the local Huon pine and had to suffer appalling living conditions for the 11 years the establishment existed before all convicts were transferred to Port Arthur.

The cruise continues on to the **Gordon River** and a stop for a walk through the rainforest. Back at Strahan look into the visitor centre, where, in a small theatre, the play *The Ship That Never Was* tells the story of Sarah Island (tel: 03-6471 7700; daily Sept–May 5.30pm).

The road north from Strahan passes the extensive **Henty Dunes**, which stretch for many kilometres behind Ocean Beach, and then turns inland to more mining towns. **Zeehan** is the most significant, having boomed in the 1900s on the back of silver. In those days the magnificent **Gaiety Theatre**, looking beautiful after an extensive restoration, could fill its 1,000 seats nightly with the biggest names of the era. The stimulating **West Coast Pioneers Museum** (Main Street; tel: 03-6471 6225; daily 9am–5pm) has extensive displays on mining, minerals and local history.

Cradle Mountain and Mole Creek

Continue through Rosebery and Tullah before making for Cradle Valley. The first sighting of **Cradle Mountain ㉕** looming up across Dove Lake must rate alongside the first view of the Opera House in Sydney in the chart of magical travel moments; you've got a pretty good idea what it should look like but are still blown away by the real thing. Drink it in, then it's a matter of picking your walk. Most choose the **Dove Lake** circuit, which takes up to two hours, but there are plenty of other options, all outlined on the maps available at the visitor centre. Hardy hikers will tackle the 80km (50-mile) **Overland Track**.

If the weather closes in – and it often does – look around Waldheim, the lodge occupied by Gustav Weindorfer, who first campaigned to designate the area a national park.

Continuing eastwards along the edge of the Great Western Tiers, there is hiking to be done in the vehicle-free **Walls of Jerusalem National Park**, but it is not to be undertaken lightly.

Detour north for **Sheffield**, which has put itself on the tourist map by commissioning murals to cover every available wall; and maybe have a look at the wilfully eccentric **Tazmazia** and the associated **Village of Lower Crackpot** (500 Staverton Road; tel: 03-6491 1934; www.tasmazia.com.au; daily Nov–Apr 9am–5pm, May–Oct 10am–4pm), with its comical model houses.

Mole Creek Karst National Park is abundant with caves. Tours go into **Marakoopa Cave** (tel: 03-6363 5182; www.parks.tas.gov.au; daily 10am–4pm; call for tour times), which contains glowworms, underground rivers and the superb Great Cathedral; and the smaller **King Solomon's Cave** (same details).

Chudleigh has an acclaimed honey farm, and once you've stopped for your sweet tooth you'll be in to **Delo-raine ㉖**. It's a pretty town on the banks of the Meander River, and a rewarding way of exploring it is to follow the trail of sculptures that winds along the main street and down by the river banks.

The north

The Bass Highway snakes its way north, but detour to **Latrobe** for its Victorian high street, and the **Australian Axeman's Hall of Fame** (tel: 03-6426 2099; www.axemanscomplex.com. au; daily 9am–5pm), where proprietor and legend, David Foster, may be on hand to explain wood-chopping.

Devonport ㉗ is the home port for the *Spirit of Tasmania* ferries that traverse the Bass Strait. The centre need not detain you, but the recently upgraded **Bass Strait Maritime Centre** (tel: 03-6424 7100; Tue–Sun 10am–4pm), formerly the Devonport Maritime Museum, is worth a visit.

The Bass Highway continues along the north coast to **Ulverstone**, a comfortable family destination with nice parks, and a smattering of Victoriana.

Industry hits you with a thud at **Burnie**, where the shell of a massive paper mill and the state's biggest container port dominate. The **Burnie Regional Museum, formerly the Pioneer Village Museum** (tel: 03-6430 5746; Mon–Fri 10am–3pm), with its reconstituted 1900 street scene, is impressive, as are some of the works in the **Burnie Regional Art Gallery** (tel: 03-6430 5875; www.burniearts.net; Mon–Fri 10am–4.30pm, Sat–Sun 1.30–4.30pm; free). And a short ride inland to **Fern Glade** provides a good chance of spotting platypus in the wild.

Wynyard has discreet appeal and **Table Cape** demands a visit in spring, when the tulip farm is in full flower, but the lighthouse and the views from it are worth a look at any time.

Possibly the finest bay is at **Boat Harbour Beach**, and its lovely relaxed atmosphere has remained despite the arrival of more and more beach houses and summer visitors.

Visitor favourite **Stanley ㉘** is dominated by the Nut, a huge plug of volcanic rock at the end of a spit. You can walk or take the chairlift to

Cradle Mountain Lodge offers luxury accommodation on the edge of the National Park.

Village of Lower Crackpot.

the top if you don't mind the wind. Down below, Alexander Terrace has well-kept cottages, one of which was the original home of Joe Lyons, the first Tasmanian prime minister.

The Van Diemen's Land Company (VDL) was crucial to Stanley. The old company store can be found near the wharf, while the clifftop-situated **Highfield** (tel: 03-6458 1100; www. historic-highfield.com.au; daily 9.30am–4.30pm) was company HQ.

An incarnation of VDL still manages the **Woolnorth** estate that covers the state's northwestern tip. The only way to visit is on a tour (tel: 03-6452 1493; www.woolnorthtours.com.au; daily if enough interest; booking essential), taking in a wind farm placed to take full advantage of the Roaring Forties, and dramatic **Cape Grim**.

The Bass Strait Islands

King Island ㉙ is best known for cheese from **King Island Dairy**; there's a shop to visit but no tours, so try **Currie**, the main town (if a handful of streets warrants the term), with its quaint harbour where giant crabs and crayfish are landed. There's a small museum, too, just below the lighthouse (Lighthouse Street; tel: 03-6462 1512; daily 2–4pm).

Ships have often come to grief here, but **Cape Wickham Lighthouse**, on the northern tip, has played its part in keeping the numbers down. At **Yellow Rock Beach**, wreckage from a paddle steamer can still be seen in the surf.

In the south there's the intriguing **Calcified Forest**, while the **Kelp Industries Centre** explains why tons of the stuff is hanging out to dry.

King Island is relatively flat and windswept, whereas **Flinders Island** ㉚ has some serious hills, culminating in **Mount Strzelecki**. The southern corner also has the immaculate sands of **Trousers Point** and **Fotheringate Beach**. The main town is **Whitemark**, but the important **Furneaux Museum** (Sat–Sun spring 1–5pm, winter 1–4pm 1–4pm; tel: 03-6359 8434 to confirm opening hours) is up at **Emita**. Many of the exhibits stem from the time of the forced exile of Tasmania's Aboriginal population in 1838, and the chapel at nearby **Wybalenna** is on the site of their settlement.

Strahan harbour with one of the Gordon River excursion boats.

The Overland Track

Tasmania's most famous hiking trail threads its way through the fabulous landscapes between Cradle Mountain and Lake St. Clair.

First blazed in the 1830s by surveyors, gold prospectors and fur-trappers, the Overland Track is Australia's most famous walk – a six-day traverse of Tasmania's central plateau through an ancient glacial landscape. About 9,000 hikers undertake the 65km (40-mile) journey from Cradle Mountain to Lake St Clair each year, carrying all their equipment and supplies both in and out.

The hike is not easy, but the rewards are spectacular and accessible to anybody reasonably fit and well prepared. For most local bushwalkers (and an increasing number are travelling here from overseas) completing the track is a rite of passage, an unforgettable expedition among stunted buttongrass moorlands, craggy snow-capped peaks, myrtle and sassafras forests, and crystalline cold-water tarns. Such is its popularity that a new online booking system and a A$200 high-season (Oct–May) charge on top of park entry fees, restricted numbers to 60 hikers per day. All hikers are required to start at Cradle Valley in the National Park's north, and finish at Cynthia Bay on Lake St Clair. This one-way traffic eases the congestion on the route and ensures that every hiker experiences the best of the Overland Track.

Lodgings and equipment

Huts line the trail – seven on the main track; distances between each vary from 6.5km (4 miles) to 11km (7 miles) – although carrying a tent is essential in this World Heritage Area, with exposed escarpments subject to bitter weather. Hikers need equipment for all four seasons, regardless of when they are travelling – from sunglasses, sunblock and shirt collars, to thermals, waterproofs and a woollen beanie. Warm socks, gaiters and a good sleeping bag are also must-haves. A hiking fuel stove, medical kit and 1:100,000 map are essential. Thongs (flip-flops) are suggested for foot relief around the huts after a long day in heavy boots.

What to carry is a delicate balance between distance, time and weight. Most walkers spend five nights on the trail. It's essential to pack light, to pick each item of clothing carefully and take only what's necessary. Be sure to carry enough food and water for an extra day in case of unexpected delays. A tip for hiking dinners is to add fresh ingredients to basic carbohydrate (pasta, rice or couscous) dishes, such as a squeeze of lemon juice. Salt, pepper, curry powders and chilli are ideal – experienced trekkers often say that food cannot be flavoured spicy enough after a long walk through a cold and unforgiving climate.

One of the walk's highlights (apart from a side-trip up Mount Ossa, at 1,617 metres/5,305ft the island's highest peak) is the camaraderie to be found around the huts each night. Everybody on the walk is considered equal – regardless of age, nationality or occupation – since all share in the rigours and delights of the hike. It's an experience so detached from the daily trivialities of the world outside.

For bookings, see www.overlandtrack.com.au or www.parks.tas.gov.au, tel: 1300-827 727 or visit the Cradle Mountain and Lake St Clair National Park visitor centres. The website also gives details on accommodation, transport and park entry fees. Contact Tasmanian Travel Centres for information on tour operators that offer private guided trips.

View of Barn Bluff from the Overland Track.

FREYCINET NATIONAL PARK

Wineglass Bay is the headline attraction, but there is plenty more to see; keen walkers could easily spend a few days here.

The Freycinet Peninsula is one of the most beautiful places in the world. The combination of mountains, forest, beaches and blisteringly blue sea, not to mention the abundant wildlife, is hard to match and impossible to beat. It's best to surrender to it and allow as much time as possible to take it all in. Pitch a tent just back from the beach and get close to nature (but not too close; secure food from inquisitive wallabies and wombats). Alternatively, follow the path to luxury and book into the Freycinet Lodge, inside the park boundary, for a couple of nights of hedonism. Settle on the balcony of your cabin and watch the scurrying animals in the undergrowth below.

In summer there is good swimming to be had, while anglers are spoilt for choice. Above all, though, this is a place for walking. The Wineglass Bay Track is a must, whether it's just a climb up to the saddle for the view, or perhaps as part of a longer trek, which could take in Mount Graham or Mount Freycinet. People with mobility problems or young children can still take on the shorter walks, some with views of Wineglass Bay. Another option is to join one of the boat trips around the peninsula, which embark from Coles Bay.

The Cape Tourville walk, which affords partial views of Wineglass Bay, is an easy 20-minute stroll around the lighthouse. While you walk, keep your eyes and ears open for unusual birds. Freycinet's avian visitors include yellow-tailed black cockatoos, and the rare white-bellied sea eagle.

The waters around the Freycinet Peninsula are rich in marine life, as well as being incredibly beautiful.

The bright orange deposits on boulders along the shoreline in Freycinet and all along the east coast are in fact a type of rock lichen. They are a complex mixture of fungi and algae which extract nutrients from the rocks they're attached to.

Sunset at Coles Bay.

VISITOR FACILITIES

The visitor centre is just a few hundred metres inside the park on the right-hand side. This is where park permits can be purchased and maps and guides picked up. Even those who have already paid their park fees should find a stop rewarding as there are displays about many aspects of the park's history and geology, as well as useful pointers towards the weather and the state of the various walks.

One of the walks starts immediately behind the visitor centre. The Great Oyster Bay walk is a 5-minute amble down to Richardson's Beach, where the cormorants play and the Hazards loom above.

The Centre is also the place to register for the campsites, which need to be booked in advance at all times. Indeed some, such as those at Honeymoon Bay (open only at Easter and in the summer), are so popular that a ballot system is used to allocate spaces. There are powered sites for caravans and RVs, and unpowered ones for tents. Electric barbecue facilities are provided at various points as all campfires are banned, although portable fuel stoves are allowed.

othing beats that first view of Wineglass Bay which comes as generous reward for the steep climb up to the saddle between Mount Amos and Mount Mason.

can take 20 minutes to walk to the end of Wineglass Bay, and then the choice must be made whether to return via the addle or Hazards Beach.

The 30km (19-mile) Freycinet Peninsula Circuit takes at least two days to complete.

Beachside pool at Bondi Beach.

TRAVEL TIPS
AUSTRALIA

TRANSPORT

GETTING THERE AND GETTING AROUND

GETTING THERE

By Air

Almost all foreign visitors travel to Australia by air. Brisbane, Cairns, Melbourne and Sydney are the major tourism gateways, with daily flights arriving from Asia, Europe and North America. Less frequent flights also arrive directly in Adelaide, Darwin, Cairns and Perth. More than 40 international airlines currently fly to and from Australia (see Major Airlines list).

Getting to Australia can be expensive. Fares vary widely, so seek advice from a knowledgeable travel agent before buying a ticket. A departure tax is included in the cost of your international ticket, so it no longer has to be paid at the airport when you leave.

There may be price advantages in pre-booking your domestic travel along with your flight to Australia, and since the launch of budget carriers Virgin Blue, Jetstar and Tiger Airways (see Domestic Flights), competition has lowered domestic fares considerably. The early birds often secure the best deals. Special pre-booked packages tend to incorporate inexpensive hotel and car rental rates.

Qantas usually offers good deals to Australia (it also operates Qantas Vacations). Tickets can be booked by calling 1800-227 4500 or 1800-227 4795 (in the US and Canada), or 0843 658 0811 (in the UK).

Major Airlines Flying to Australia

Air Canada
Tel: 1300-655 767
www.aircanada.com
Air China
Tel: 02-9232 7277

Flying Times

Sydney–Melbourne, 1 hr 20 mins
Sydney–Perth, 4 hrs 50 mins
Melbourne–Adelaide, 1 hr 20 mins
Melbourne–Canberra, 1 hr
Brisbane–Sydney, 1 hr 25 mins
Brisbane–Melbourne, 2 hrs 20 mins
Adelaide–Alice Springs, 2 hrs
Perth–Adelaide, 3 hrs
Canberra–Sydney, 50 mins

www.airchina.com.au
Air New Zealand
Tel: 132 476
www.airnewzealand.com.au
British Airways
Tel: 1300-767 177
www.britishairways.com
Cathay Pacific Airways
Tel: 131 747
www.cathaypacific.com
Emirates Airlines
Tel: 1300-303 777
www.emirates.com
Gulf Air
Tel: 1300-366 337
www.gulfair.com
Japan Airlines
Sydney-based Tel: 1800-80 2228
www.au.jal.com
Malaysia Airlines
Tel: 132 627
www.malaysiaairlines.com
Qantas
Tel: 131 313
www.qantas.com.au
Singapore Airlines
Tel: 131 011
www.singaporeair.com
South African Airways
Tel: 1300-435 972
www.flysaa.com
Thai Airways International
Tel: 1300-651 960

www.thaiairways.com.au
United Airlines
Tel: 131 777
www.united.com
Virgin Australia
Tel: 13 67 89
www.virginaustralia.com.au

GETTING AROUND

By Air

Australia's national domestic airline is **Qantas,** with competition, on most routes, from **Virgin Australia** (tel: 136 789, www.virginaustralia.com. au). Qantas launched its own budget domestic airline, **Jetstar** (tel: 131 538; www.jetstar.com), and was then joined by **Tiger Air** (tel: 03-9335 3033; www.tigerair.com) on selected routes. Each of these airlines operates regular scheduled flights between all capital cities and regional centres throughout Australia. Both Jetstar and Virgin Australia operate from Australian cities to a number of Asian and Pacific destinations. **Qantas** (tel: 131 313, www.qantas.com.au) also operates regular scheduled flights between all capital cities and regional centres throughout Australia.

Although many domestic flights are often fully booked, cheap flights are regularly to be found by booking in advance. All the airlines offer cheaper deals for the first few seats with the rate increasing as the aircraft fills up. Conditions can be onerous, however, with checked baggage bringing additional fees on some ticket bands (all on Tiger), strict adherence to weight limits with hefty penalty rates for transgressors, and reduced flexibility to change flights with the lower fare bands. Some of the best deals are to be had if you are prepared to fly at off-peak times or book via the internet. Some airlines add a fee for payment by credit cards.

Some of the best deals include both air travel and accommodation outside the main holiday seasons – check with airlines for special offers.

Each state is serviced by regional airlines such as QantasLink, providing access to remote destinations.

From the Airport

Sydney

Situated approximately 8km (5 miles) from the Central Business District (CBD), Sydney Airport is best reached by car, taxi or train. Just 10 minutes to the domestic terminals and 12 minutes to the international, trains run from Central Station up to eight times an hour on weekdays, and four times an hour on weekends. The only bus to the airport from the city is the No. 400, which runs from Bondi Junction and takes 40 minutes. For exact times and information visit www.airportlink.com.au, or tel: 02-8337 8417.

Canberra

Canberra airport is 7km (4 miles) from the city centre. An Airport Express bus charges A\$12 each way; other bus companies run regular services into town too. The taxi fare is about A\$25.

Melbourne

Melbourne's Tullamarine airport is 22km (14 miles) from the city centre. A taxi costs about A\$50–60; for about half that price, the Skybus departs every half-hour (you can pre-book tickets at www.skybus.com.au). Avalon Airport is 55km (34 miles) from the city on the road to Geelong. Bus transfers are available to Southern Cross Station in the city.

Adelaide

The dual international/domestic airport, 8km (5 miles) from the city centre, has a Skylink shuttle bus, which runs about every 30 minutes, stopping at major hotels (tel: 1300-311 108; www.skylink.com). Adelaide Metro (www.adelaidemetro.com) runs buses through the city to the airport

Bargains by Bus

If you plan extensive bus travel in Australia, several discount plans offer unlimited travel within various time frames. There are also set-duration and set-distance fares.

A Queensland taxi cab waits for a fare.

seven days a week from 4.50am to midnight. A taxi into the city centre costs about A\$25.

Brisbane

The domestic and international airport terminals lie 16km (10 miles) from the city centre. At any time when flights are arriving or departing a combination of bus and fast rail transport options provides easy connections between Brisbane Airport, Brisbane city and the Gold Coast. The hub is the city coach/rail terminus, and the "TransLink" service (tel: 131 230) or the information desks at the airport will help you identify the easiest and most convenient way to get from A to B.

Darwin

Darwin airport is 12km (7.5 miles) from the CBD, and a taxi costs around A\$35. An airport shuttle (tel: 08-8981 5066) costs about A\$16.

Perth

Taxis from the domestic and international airports to Perth city cost around A\$40 and A\$35 respectively and to Fremantle A\$75. One shuttle bus meets all flights and runs to accommodation in the city, while another travels between Fremantle and the airport (pick-ups must be pre-arranged by phone, preferably the day before). For the Perth shuttle, tel: 08-9277 4666. One-way trips are A\$20 for adults from the international terminal and A\$15 from the domestic terminals. Bookings for the Fremantle service are on tel: 08-9335 1614. TransPerth (tel: 13 62 13) operates bus services (number 380, 37 and 40) from Perth terminals.

Hobart

The Airporter Bus meets all flights into Hobart International Airport and drops off at hotels in the city centre and inner suburbs. Charges are A\$18

for adults one way or A\$32 return; children and concessions A\$8. A taxi to the city centre will cost over A\$40.

By Bus

Long-Distance Buses

Competition between the major bus companies means many bargains are available when travelling by bus. The biggest company, with the most services, is **Greyhound Australia** (tel: 1300-473 946; www.greyhound.com.au).

The standard of buses is high, with most having reclining seats, seats for the disabled, videos, washrooms and air conditioning. Smoking is prohibited on all buses. Bus terminals are well equipped with toilets, showers and shops, and are generally very clean. However, you should be aware that distances are enormous in Australia, so think twice before hopping, say, onto the Brisbane–Cairns leg, because it takes more than 24 hours. Greyhound has various money-saving passes, including ones that are based on kilometres travelled.

There are many other bus companies in Australia, offering a variety of transport/hotel packages departing regularly from capital cities. Prices are per day inclusive of bus travel, accommodation and various day tours or driver commentary. Some of the more adventurous routes are taken by deluxe four-wheel-drive vehicles, incorporating camping, and are accompanied by a cook.

Sydney

Sydney has an extensive bus service with main termini at Circular Quay, Wynyard and Central Station. For all route information visit the Transport Infoline website: www.131500.com.au, or tel: 131 500. At Circular Quay there is an information kiosk at the centre of the row of bus stops, on

Melbourne Transport

For information on all public transport in Melbourne visit the Public Transport Victoria hub centrally located at Southern Cross Station (open Mon–Fri 7am-7pm, Sat–Sun 9am-6pm; www.ptv.vic. gov.au).

the opposite side of the street (Alfred Street) from the ferry wharfs. Be aware that during peak hour, many buses only accept pre-paid tickets.

City Sightseeing operates two buses along the main tourist routes: the Sydney Explorer, which covers the city, and the Bondi Explorer, which takes in the eastern suburbs. More information is available at http:www. city-sightseeing.com.

Canberra
In Canberra, Action bus services are adequate and modern. Plan your journey online using the trip planner at www.action.act.gov.au or call 131 710. It is possible to purchase daily and off-peak daily bus passes that allow unlimited rides on the buses.

Melbourne
Public Transport Victoria or the PTV, Melbourne's public transport system is one of Australia's best. Trams form the basis of the system. There are about 750 trams venturing as far as 20km (12 miles) out of the city. Buses are the secondary form of public transport, often taking over when trams are out of service. Trains connect an underground city loop to the outer suburbs.

The Public Transport Victoria hub at Southern Cross Station can supply all the information you need about public transport. You can also buy a myki smart travel card or myki visitor pack here, and pick up timetables and maps. A Free Tram Zone was recently introduced in Melbourne CBD. It includes the area from the

iconic Queen Victoria Market, across to Victoria Harbour in Docklands, up to Spring Street and over to Flinders Street Station and Federation Square. The City Circle Tram runs approximately every 12 minutes (Thu–Sat 10am–9pm, Sun–Wed 10am–6pm).

Adelaide
A free City Connector is an easy way to get around the city. The Connector buses travel in both directions within Adelaide City and North Adelaide, and you can hop on and off at various stops. It operates on two loops, an inner city loop and an extended North Adelaide loop. Routes 98A and 98C link the city and North Adelaide and routes 99A and 99C connect the city main destinations, both run every 30 minutes daily.

All information regarding the Adelaide transport system is available from the Adelaide Metro InfoCentre on the corner of King William and Currie streets, tel: 08-8210 1000 or 1300-311 108; www.adelaidemetro.com.au.

Brisbane
For information on city buses in Brisbane, go to the Translink office in the Brisbane Visitor Information Centre, on Queen Street Mall or visit www.translink.com.au. The pre-paid Go Card can be used on buses, trains, CityCats and ferries, and is available from the Translink office. Apart from the regular city buses, there are **Cityxpress** buses, which connect certain suburbs to the city, and **Rockets**, which are peak-hour commuter services. A free City Loop bus connects many of the key sites around the city centre.

Darwin and Alice Springs
Both Darwin and Alice Springs have town bus services that connect accommodation precincts with the CBD. **Darwinbus** (tel: 08-8924 7666) has Flextrip card for $20 for 10 trips, and weekly cards also for

Brisbane Ferries

Brisbane ferries – City Cats – provide river crossings to Kangaroo Point, South Bank Parklands and along the river to other locations. They depart from Eagle Street Pier and Edward Street on the corner of the Botanic Gardens. They are fast, efficient and inexpensive.

$20.. In Alice Springs, there are no bus services on Sundays and public holidays. The Alice Springs Bus Guide is available from Railway Terrace, near the Coles supermarket. Comfortable, frequent and fast buses connect the three central attractions – Darwin, Alice Springs and Uluru.

Greyhound Australia (tel: 1300-3868 0998; www.greyhound.com.au) runs daily between Alice Springs and Yulara (Ayers Rock). It is 460km (286 miles) each way.

Perth
The Free Transit Zone operating in the Perth city area allows free travel on any bus – look for the red FTZ logo at bus stops to identify the travel boundaries. Free CAT (Central Area Transit) buses also operate in Perth, Fremantle and Joondalup city centres. The **"Perth Tram"** (actually a bus) operates a circuit of tourist attractions. For maps and on-the-spot information about all forms of public transport, a Transperth office is in the Plaza Arcade (off the Hay Street Mall), tel: 136 213; www.transperth.wa.gov.au.

High-speed ferries travel from Perth, Fremantle and Hillarys to Rottnest Island.

Tasmania
Metro Tasmania runs an extensive network of bus services in Hobart, and they are an easy way to reach sights that are more than a casual stroll from the town centre, such as Hobart's beaches, the Taroona Shot Tower, the Cadbury Factory and Cascade Brewery. Buses run Monday–Thursday 6.30am to 10.30pm and until midnight on Friday and Saturday. There is a limited service on Sunday and holidays.

By Train

A wide network of modern railways operates from coast to coast. The principal lines follow the east and south coasts, linking the cities of Cairns, Brisbane, Sydney, Melbourne, Adelaide and Alice Springs. The most comprehensive service is operated

Sydney Transport and Passes

The State Transit Authority operates the buses in Sydney, and **CityRail** the trains. Ferries are run by **Sydney Ferries**. For information on buses, trains and ferries from 6am–10pm daily, tel: 131 500, or check www.131500.com.au, www. cityrail.info, www.sydneyferries.info or www.sydneybuses.info. The front of the White Pages phone book also has information on Sydney's transport.

Whether you want to see the sights of Sydney or explore the Blue Mountains, Southern Highlands or Newcastle, it is easy on public transport. To travel on trains, buses, ferries and light rail, all you need is an **Opal card** (www.opal.com.au). You can also buy a My Multi Day Pass in three section-based fare bands. Buy these passes from locations and stores displaying the transport symbol.

by **Countrylink**: reservations are required; tel: 132 232; www.country link.info.

The line between Sydney and Perth via Adelaide is the famous **Indian–Pacific** run (linking the Indian Ocean to the Pacific Ocean). On its 4,352km (2,700-mile) journey, taking 65 hours (three nights), the train crosses the treeless Nullarbor Plain, with the longest stretch of straight track in the world. Comforts include an observation lounge and bar. If money is no object you can travel in the historic Prince of Wales carriage, complete with wood panelling and cathedral glass doors.

Other popular scenic rail journeys run by Great Southern Railway (tel: 1800-703 357; www.greatsouthernrail. com.au) include the **Overland**, an overnight journey between Melbourne and Adelaide, and the **Ghan**, which runs straight through the middle of the country, from Adelaide in South Australia through Alice Springs and on to Darwin. The two-night, 3,000km (1,864-mile) trip can be broken in Katherine for short sightseeing tours by boat or helicopter, and Alice Springs for longer stopovers.

For travel in Western Australia it is possible to take a bus or train to the southern and southwest regions in the area bounded by Kalbarri, Meekathara, Kalgoorlie, Esperance, Albany and Augusta. For more details contact **Transwa**, tel: 08-9326 2600 or 1300-662 205, or visit www. transwa.wa.gov.au.

Tickets

The classes available are first, holiday and economy. First-class passengers have sleeping berths with showers in their cabin, a first-class restaurant and lounge. Other classes get aeroplane-style reclining seats and a buffet car.

A Rail Australia pass entitles international visitors to unlimited travel on **Countrylink**, **Queensland Rail** and **Great Southern Railway** services for a six-month period. Most states have their own passes as well.

The **Countrylink Backpacker Rail Pass** is only available to foreign passport holders and is valid for 14 days to six months of unlimited economy-class travel, plus some metropolitan train travel. Ausrail Flexi Pass provides six months of unlimited travel on CountryLink, Great Southern Railways or Queensland train services. Available for international tourists only. If bought outside Australia – A$890, in Australia – A$990.

Sydney Ferries and Cruises

Weather permitting, which it usually is, ferries are by far the most picturesque way of travelling around Sydney. Departing from the wharfs at Circular Quay, all tickets and timetables can be found at the Sydney ferries office.

The trip to Manly is the longest ferry run, covering 11km (7 miles) in 30 minutes. The alternative **Jetcat** service offers the same trip in half the time for slightly more money. There are currently temporary timetables in place for both services while the east side of Manly Wharf is redeveloped. Visit www.sydneyferries.info for exact times.

Sydney

Trains are the most time-efficient way to navigate Sydney. With a fairly frequent service, most of Sydney's main areas are covered, including the central "City Circle" stations – Central, Town Hall, Wynyard, Circular Quay, St James and Museum. Most do not run between midnight and 4.30am, when a **Nightrider** bus service takes over.

The **Airport link** trains run about every 10 minutes between the city and the domestic and international terminals, and the journey to Sydney's Central Station takes about 15 minutes.

Canberra

There are no train services in Canberra.

Melbourne

The city has an extensive train service, with all lines radiating out from the central Flinders Street Station. The public transport information centre (PTV), Southern Cross Station (tel: 1800-800 007) provides timetables and maps and sells tickets (also valid on city buses and trams). Apart from the underground city loop, stations are above ground. Train services on most lines depart every 15 or 20 minutes on weekdays, and every 20 to 30 minutes on weekends.

Adelaide

Train services are limited and are mostly used by locals to get out to far-flung suburbs. Generally speaking, you will need to rely on other forms of transport in Adelaide. One exception is the tram route linking Victoria Square in the city to the popular beach-side

Ferries are a great way of getting to Taronga Zoo, Kirribilli and Watsons Bay, not to mention a good opportunity to see the harbour, bridge and Opera House from all angles.

The **Rivercat**, a high-speed catamaran, cruises all the way up the Parramatta River.

Harbour cruises are a great way to relax while seeing Sydney off dry land. Daily cruises start at 10.30am and depart from Wharf Four. With comfy seating and unlimited tea and biscuits, these STA cruises are less expensive than private options and the commentary provides an interesting addition to the scenic backdrop.

suburb of Glenelg, which tends to get quite busy in the summer months.

Brisbane

The Queensland Rail City (formerly **Citytrain**) services are very efficient. They all pass through the city stations of Roma Street, Central and Brunswick on their way out to the suburbs. The Translink information on railway services is available at the Visitor Information Centre at the former Regent Cinema in the Queen Street Mall (or call 13 12 30).. There are tickets that enable unlimited travel in one day.

Darwin

There are no city trains serving Darwin.

Perth

Five train lines service the Perth area. Wellington Street is Perth's central station, with an underground terminal for the nearby Mandurah line.

Hobart

Regular passenger rail services ceased in Tasmania in the 1980s, but there are a few tourist/heritage railways operating in the state. Visit www.puretasmania.com.au and www. donriverrailway.com.au for more information.

By Sea

After arriving in Australia, a number of the international cruise lines continue around the coastline at a leisurely pace.

Day-trips and cruises operate between the mainland and the Great Barrier Reef. Six-day cruises run from Cairns to Cape York. The coral-fringed

Whitsunday Islands are one of the best cruising and yachting locations in Australia (rent yachts from operators at Airlie Beach – the motto is, if you can drive a car, you can sail a yacht). River cruises and houseboat rentals are available on major rivers such as the Murray, or the Myall Lakes and the Murray River.

The only regular maritime services are the passenger and car ferries called *Spirit of Tasmania I* and *II*, operating between Melbourne and Devonport. The trip from Victoria can be rough and takes about 11 hours. Tel: 1800-634 906 (in Australia) or see www.spiritoftasmania.com.au.

Taxis

Sydney

All taxis are metered, so do not ride unless the meter is on. There is an initial hiring charge (called "flag fall"), then a set rate per kilometre thereafter. Between 10pm and 6am, this rate increases by 20 percent. A phone booking costs extra. There may be additional charges for road, bridge, ferry, tunnel and airport tolls. For information on taxis in NSW see the Taxi Council of NSW website, www.nswtaxi.org.au.
Premier Cabs: tel: 1300 795 608; www.premiercabs.com.au
Taxis Combined: tel: 133 300; www.taxiscombined.com.au
Legion Cabs: tel: 131 451; www.legioncabs.com.au
RSL Cabs: tel: 02-9581 1111; www.rslcabs.com.au
Silver Service: tel: 133 100; www.silverservice.com.au
In addition, there are companies that operate water taxis on the harbour. The price depends on the distance and time of day. **Water Taxis Combined:** tel: 02-9555 8888; watertaxis.com.au; **Yellow Water Taxis:** tel: 1300-138 840, www.yellowwatertaxis.com.au.

Melbourne

Melbourne's transport system tends to curl up and go to sleep around midnight, after which taxis are the only form of transport available. Try **13 Cabs**, tel: 132 227; www.13cabs.com.au; or **Silver Top Taxis**, tel: 131 008; www.silvertop.com.au.

Canberra

If you're waiting at a Canberra taxi rank with no taxis in sight, call **Canberra Elite Taxis** on tel: 132 227 and they'll send one along. All taxis are metered. Between 9pm and 6am, the

rate goes up. For more information, visit www.canberracabs.com.au.

Adelaide

There are a number of taxi services available. **Adelaide Independent Taxi Service**, tel: 132 211; www.aitaxis.com.au; **Suburban Taxi**, tel: 131 008; www.suburbantaxis.com.au; **Yellow Cabs**, tel: 132 227; www.yellowcab.com.au.

Brisbane

The city's officially recognised services are **Yellow Cabs** (tel: 131 924; www.yellowcab.com.au) and **Black and White Cabs** (tel: 133 222; www.blackandwhitecabs.com.au). Both charge a booking fee, with a standard fixed flag fall weekdays 7am–7pm, and a standard rate per km. After-hours flag fall is higher.

Darwin

Darwin has three major taxi companies: **Darwin Radio Taxi**, tel: 131 008; www.131008.com; **Arafura Shuttle**, tel: 08-8981 3300; and **Blue Taxi Company**, tel: 138 294; www.bluetaxi.com.au.

Perth

Hail taxis on the street, find them at a rank, or phone **Black and White** on tel: 133 222; www.bwtaxi.com.au or **Swan** on tel: 131 330; www.swantaxis.com.au, for up to four passengers. Black and White also have maxicabs (up to 10 passengers) and a service for the disabled (tel: 133 222 for these). Rates are reasonable: a small flag fall charge followed by a rate per kilometre.

Hobart

Taxis can be hired in the street if their vacant sign is lit. All cabs use meters and tipping is not necessary. **United Taxis**, tel: 133 222 , will connect you to taxi companies in most of the major towns in Tasmania, including **City Cabs** in Hobart.

Motorcycles and Bicycles

Both are available for hire throughout Australia. Thoughtfully designed systems of bicycle paths provide good views or access to tourist sites – a pleasant, healthy and environmentally friendly alternative to the city bus tour.

Sydney

Bonza Bike Tours (www.bonzabiketours.com) offers 1- to 5-hour tours of the city from A$29, as well as bike hire. A range of mountain, hybrid and children's bikes, including dragsters, choppers and tandems, is for hire in **Sydney Olympic Park** (www.

sydneyolympicpark.com.au). *Cycling Around Sydney* by Bruce Ashley is a useful guide available from book and bike shops.

Canberra

Cycling is perhaps the most pleasant choice for sightseeing in Canberra, as the terrain is flat and bike paths are extensive. Bicycles can be hired by the hour, by the day or by the week. If you intend hiring a bike, make sure to get a copy of the *Canberra Cycleways* map from the tourist office or bookshops.

Melbourne

Melbourne is fairly flat, which affords the cyclist a number of good long tracks. Bike paths lie along the Yarra River, the Maribyrnong and the Merri Creek. For general cycling information, contact **Bicycle Network Victoria** at 4/246 Bourke Street, tel: 03-8376 8888; www.bicyclenetwork.com.au. **Melbourne Bike Share** has docking stations around the city and, for a small fee, bikes are available for sightseeing. Helmets are compulsory, however, so go equipped or buy a cheap one from a local store.

Adelaide

Running alongside the Torrens River in Adelaide is the 35km (22-mile) -long Linear Park Bike and Walking Track, one of the best in Australia. You can hire bikes from **Linear Park Bike Hire**, tel: 08-7424 7677. You can also get free use of a bike for two hours within the city limits under a scheme run by **Bicycle SA** and **Adelaide City Council** called the City Bike Scheme. Once the two hours are up, an hourly rate applies. For more information see the Adelaide City Council website (www.adelaidecitycouncil.com) or contact the Cycling Information Centre at 46 Hurtle Square (tel: 08-8232 2644). The Adelaide Council provides a free bike hire service daily (tel: 08-8168 9999; www.adelaidecitycouncil.com).

Brisbane

Brisbane City Council has built more than 500km (310 miles) of cycleways across the city. The riverside Bicentennial Bikeway, from the CBD along Coronation Drive to Toowong, is one of the most pleasant. Maps of popular cycleways can be found on the council's website, www.brisbane.qld.gov.au.

Darwin

You can hire scooters along Mitchell Street. Try **Darwin Scooter Hire**, 9 Daly Street (tel: 08-8941 2434). Small

50cc scooters are very popular for running out to the beaches around Darwin. Bicycles can be hired from some of the backpacker hotels, and some five-star hotels offer their guests cycle hire. There are plenty of cycle tracks; especially good is the one to East Point around Fannie Bay. Bicycles can be hired from Darwin Walking and Bicycle Tours (www.darwinwalkingtours.com/bicycle-hire-darwin).

Perth

Cycle paths have been developed all around Perth, alongside the freeway and coast, into the hills and cross-country. The **WA Bicycle Network** (www.transport.wa.gov.au/cycling) is a useful source of information. Maps are available from bike shops, or the **Bicycle Transportation Alliance** (2 Delhi Street, West Perth, tel: 08-9420 7210; http://btawa.org.au). **All About Bikes** (on the corner of Riverside Drive and Plain Street, tel: 08-9221 2665; http://aboutbikehire.com.au) rents bikes, double bikes and quadcycles.

Hobart

Tasmania's longest-dedicated cycleway is the 15km (9-mile) Intercity Cycleway in Hobart. The bike club **Bicycle Tasmania** (www.biketas.org.au) has all the information you'll need.

By Car

Car Hire

By international standards, renting a car in Australia is expensive. The big three rental companies are **Avis**, **Hertz** and **Budget**, whose rates are just about identical. **Thrifty** and **Europcar** are also players in the market. The small outfits are usually much cheaper and offer special deals, but they may not offer all the services of the major companies – which can be useful. These include discounts for pre-booking overseas, and the ability to return the car to another city at no extra charge. Be aware that many rental cars have manual, rather than automatic, gears (the latter are pricier). The big three have offices in almost every town, as well as at airports and rail terminals. They offer unlimited

Basic Motoring Rules

Australians drive on the left. The law requires you to keep your seat belt fastened at all times, whether as driver or passenger. Overseas licences are valid throughout Australia.

kilometre rates in the city, but when travelling in the Outback, rates are usually per kilometre. Compulsory third-party insurance is included in car rentals, but collision damage waiver is an add-on. More comprehensive insurance plans are available for an additional fee, or your travel insurance may cover them. Most companies have 25 as their minimum driver age, or will charge a premium for drivers aged between 21 and 25.

Since driving a conventional vehicle off sealed roads may invalidate your insurance, four-wheel drive (4WD) cars are expensive but worth considering for safe Outback touring. Camper vans are popular, especially in Tasmania; they aren't cheap, however, and it might work out more economical to rent a regular car and stay at budget hotels.

Motoring Advice

If you do opt to explore Australia by car, keep in mind that distances are often huge and towns may be few and far between. Many visitors on short-term trips opt to fly between major cities.

The major highways linking capital cities are all sealed and of a good standard, but you don't have to go far to find yourself on dirt roads. In remote areas such as Cape York and the Kimberley, most 4WDs travel in pairs or teams, to assist one another when bogged.

If you're getting around the Outback independently, you must constantly remind yourself that you're in frontier country. Do plenty of research and planning before you head off. Carrying adequate water, notifying people of your intentions, using reliable vehicles and protecting yourself from sunburn should be high

You'll need a good map.

on your list. Picking up hitchhikers is, in general, a bad idea.

Independent travellers should be aware that significant tracts of the Outback are designated as Aboriginal land, and a permit may be required to enter them.

The speed limit in a built-up area is 60kph (37mph) and sometimes 50kph (31mph) or 40kph (25mph) in suburban residential areas; in the country it is usually 100kph (62mph), unless otherwise signposted. Darwin has the most open roads in the country. Beyond city limits there is a maximum speed limit of 130kph (81mph).

Drink driving is a major problem. There is random breath testing for alcohol in most states. If you exceed 0.05 percent blood-alcohol level (ie more than around three drinks), a hefty fine and loss of licence are automatic.

Fuel comes in super, unleaded, super-unleaded, LPG (gas) and diesel. It is becoming more expensive in remote country areas.

Each state has an Automobile Association that offers excellent maps and literature. For a small membership fee, they also provide a free, highly recommended, nationwide emergency breakdown service.

Automobile Associations

Sydney: National **Roads and Motorists' Association** (NRMA), 74–6 King Street, tel: 132 132 or 02-9292 8292; www.nrma.com.au
Canberra**: National Roads and Motorists Association** (NRMA), ACT Woden, 6/17 Neptune Street, tel: 02-6285 2811 ACT 2600; road assistance 13 1111; www.nrma.com.au
Melbourne: **Royal Automobile Club of Victoria** (RACV), 501 Bourke Street; tel: 131 111 or 03-9944 8888; www.racv.com.au
Adelaide**: Royal Automobile Association of South Australia** (RAA), 41 Hindmarsh Square, Adelaide, tel: 131 111; www.raa.com.au
Brisbane: **Royal Automobile Club of Queensland** (RACQ), 2649 Logan Road, Eight Mile Plains, tel: 1319 05; www.racq.com.au
Darwin: **Automobile Association of the Northern Territory** (AANT), 2/14 Knuckey Street, Darwin, tel: 131 111 or 08-8925 5901; www.aant.com.au
Perth: Royal Automobile Club of Western Australia Inc. (RAC WA), 832 Wellington Street, West Perth, tel: 131 703; www.rac.com.au

A – Z

A HANDY SUMMARY
OF PRACTICAL INFORMATION

A

Accommodation

The standard of accommodation in Australia is high. Note that Sydney's hotels are significantly more expensive than anywhere else in Australia, with the possible exception of Perth. Serviced apartments are popular, especially in the cities, with Quest (www.quest.com.au) and the Oaks Group (www.theoakshotelresorts.com) the reliable leaders in the field.

Australia has been slow off the mark in developing ultra-luxury lodges on the New Zealand model. However, a number of signature properties have sprung up around the country, including Saffire in Tasmania's Freycinet region, Southern Ocean Lodge on Kangaroo Island, and Wolgan Valley in the Blue Mountains near Sydney. Rates are around $1,000 a night.

At the opposite end of the scale, there is an excellent choice of backpacker budget accommodation available (for example, Darwin, NT). Victoria Street in Sydney's Kings Cross has a score of hostels; it's also the place to network with other travellers to arrange lifts, buy cheap flights, or buy a car for an extended road odyssey around Oz. Log onto www.tntmagazine.com.au for more information.

Over the past decade, the choice of accommodation available in wilderness areas has increased significantly. In addition to camping, properties such as Eco Beach outside Broome or Wildman Wilderness Lodge near Kakadu let you experience these pristine areas without sacrificing your creature comforts.

For a holiday with a difference, you can stay as a paying guest with Australian families in a private home or on a working farm.

B&Bs come and go, so the best source of current information is the **Bed and Breakfast and Farmstay Australia** (BBFA); visit www.australianbedandbreakfast.com.au covering more than 1,000 B&Bs and Farmstays. The Farmstays include everything from small dairy farms in the hills to vast grain farming and sheep- and cattle-grazing properties.

Admission Charges

Compared with the UK and USA, admission charges to sights and attractions are fairly low, and often free for museums, though you may find that they charge for entry to temporary exhibitions. The "worlds" – including Dreamworld and Sea World in Queensland, for example – have some of the highest admission charges, but usually offer discounted family tickets, which can help keep a lid on costs if travelling with children. Concession prices are often available on production of a student or senior card.

For more information contact the relevant tourist office (see page 330), while contact information for Australia's National Parks and National Trust offices are listed under Useful Addresses.

B

Budgeting for Your Trip

The cost of living in Australia has traditionally been lower than Europe and the USA (although manufactured goods tend to be more expensive in Australia). However, since the global financial crisis started in 2008, Australia's economy has outperformed most others and the Australian dollar used to be stronger (at time of print it is: A$1= US$0.74). These days, however, Australia feels relatively expensive to visitors from the US and Europe. Mind you, Sydney has always had property prices up there with cities like London and New York, and day-to-day expenses such as public transport and dining out tend to be noticeably higher than in other Australian cities. As you move away from the east coast, where most of Australia's population lives, to cities like Adelaide, Hobart and Darwin, the cost of living is lower again. However, there are exceptions such as Perth, where the mining boom has sent prices skyrocketing, and the isolated towns and settlements of the Outback, where the cost of transporting supplies long distances drives petrol and food prices upwards.

In general accommodation can cost from A$50–60 for a double room in a country pub, A$100 for self-contained cabin-style accommodation in the country, A$120 for a basic hotel room and A$200 upwards per night for five-star hotels.

The variety of climates means Australia grows lots of fresh produce that is of a high quality, although the standard in supermarkets is generally lower than what you will find in markets and fruiterers. A takeaway or dine-in café meal costs anywhere from A$15 to A$25, a main in a restaurant ranges from A$25 to A$35 and a main in a fine dining restaurant costs A$40–50. In major cities, some of the most affordable and best-quality food can be found in Asian restaurants, particularly around Chinatown.

TRANSPORT

Travel tends to be expensive because of the distances involved and high fuel prices. Car hire can start from around A$70 per day including insurance, although significant discounted rates apply for longer rental periods. Budget airlines Virgin Blue, Jetstar and Tiger continue to have price wars and you can pick up flights from Sydney to Cairns, some 2,500km (1,550 miles), for A$149 one way. An airfare between Sydney and Melbourne can cost as little as A$60 if you book a few weeks ahead. The train between Sydney and Melbourne can cost around A$100, but when you take into account the 12 hours' travel time versus only 1.5 hours on a plane, it's easy to see why most people prefer to fly.

C

Climate

The seasons in Australia are the reverse of the northern hemisphere's. September to November is spring, December to February summer, March to May autumn, and June to August winter. Since fine, mild weather occurs during all seasons, any time can be recommended for a visit to Australia – although some months are warmer and drier than others.

About 40 percent of the country lies in the tropical zone north of the Tropic of Capricorn. In the Top End around Darwin (the monsoon belt) and near Cairns, there are only two seasons: the dry (April–November) and the wet (December–March). In the dry, there are warm days, clear blue skies and cool nights. The wet is usually characterised by heavy rain alternating with sunny hot weather. On the Great Barrier Reef most rain falls in January and February.

In the southern temperate zone seasons are more distinct. Winter days in Sydney are usually sunny with a maximum of 15°C (60°F) – chilly enough to require an overcoat – while humid summer temperatures can regularly hit 30°C (90°F) and higher. Snow falls on the southern mountain ranges, but not in the cities (except Hobart). Melbourne is pleasant in spring, summer and autumn, but winter can be grey and miserable, especially in July and August. Tasmania, the island state off the southern tip of the continent, is the coolest: summers are by far the best time to visit here, as winters can be damp and depressing.

South Australia has a Mediterranean climate: summers are hot and dry with temperatures regularly above 30°C (85°F), and highs of 40°C (105°F) and above are not uncommon.

Western Australia also has a Mediterranean climate. There are four distinctive seasons and moderate temperatures in its southern parts, while the north is in the tropical zone, so Top End conditions prevail.

In central Australia, summer temperatures are generally too high for comfort. In winter, the nights may be cool, with clear warm days.

Visitors should also bear in mind the various Australian school holidays; Christmas coincides with the long summer school break, which lasts throughout January. Easter is another big break. If you are travelling during these seasons, book well in advance.

Crime and Safety

When it comes to crime, Australia is a relatively safe country. That being said, you should use the same common sense and precautions as you would elsewhere regarding your possessions and personal security. Issues surrounding prostitution, drugs and drunken behaviour occur in all cities. However, these are unlikely to affect travellers. If an incident occurs, report it to the police or, for urgent attention, call the emergency services by dialling **000**.

When it comes to safety, non-human elements can pose more of a risk in Australia. Bushfires occur regularly each year and it is important to be aware of fire bans or restrictions. If you are out in the bush and notice smoke, it is important to take it seriously and head for the nearest open space.

It is also important you thoroughly prepare if you are bushwalking or exploring the Outback. Take plenty of water and supplies, a good map and let a friend or the local ranger know of your plans in case you get stranded. Daily temperatures can reach the extremes, with searing heat during the day and freezing nights.

In northern Australia saltwater crocodiles are a real danger and have been known to take humans. They can be found in rivers, creeks, waterholes and around the coast. In popular tourist areas, croc-inhabited waterholes are regularly signposted. However, if you are unsure whether a place is croc-free, it is best not to risk swimming at all.

Box jellyfish are another danger in the far north during the wet season (November to May). Their venomous sting is extremely painful and can be fatal. During these months make sure you wear a special "stinger" suit.

Unsuspecting tourists can easily find themselves in trouble when swimming at Australian surf beaches. Lifesavers patrol popular beaches and put up red and yellow flags that swimmers should stay between. If an undertow or "rip" drags you out, raise

A–Z

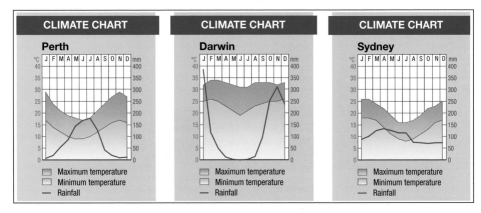

an arm if you need help and a surf lifesaver will come to your aid.

Customs Regulations

There are no customs charges on personal belongings intended for use during your stay. Non-dutiable allowances are 250g (8oz) of tobacco goods and 2.25 litres (2.4 quarts) of alcohol. You may also import dutiable goods to the value of A$1,000 in personal baggage. Visit www.border. gov.au.

Australian produce is of a very high standard because it is free from many insect pests and diseases common to other countries. This is due in part to the strict control on the importation of insects, animal and plant products, fruit, vegetables and seeds.

Laws strictly prohibit the export of protected Australian wildlife and products made from the skins, feathers, bones, shells, corals, or any part of protected species.

Quarantine

Australia is free of rabies, anthrax and foot-and-mouth disease, so all incoming animals are placed in quarantine. Cats and dogs (including guide dogs) are quarantined for up to 6 months, depending on the animal's country of origin – from the UK the period is 30 days. See www.agriculture. gov.au.

D

Disabled Travellers

Most new buildings, public transport and tourist attractions have wheelchair access and other facilities for the disabled. The major rental car companies have a small number of cars with hand controls (reserve

at least seven days in advance). Advance notice with relevant details of your disability will facilitate the best possible assistance from airlines, hotels or railway offices. Taxi fleets in state capitals all have cars that can carry wheelchairs. Tourism Australia has further information on its website (www.australia.com). Also, the National Information Communications Network (NICAN) provides a directory of accessible accommodation, recreation and other facilities. Contact NICAN at: Unit 5, 48 Brookes Street, Mitchell, ACT 2911, tel: 02-6241 1220; freecall: 1800-806 769; www.nican.com.au.

The state automobile associations publish accommodation directories which include information on disabled access.

E

Electricity

The power supply is 220–240 volts AC. Sockets are three-pin flat plugs. You may be able to find adaptors in hardware stores or at some hotels.

Embassies and Consulates

If you need help with matters such as legal advice or a stolen passport while in Australia, most countries have diplomatic representations, with embassies in major cities. A comprehensive list of every country represented in Australia is available on the Australia Department of Foreign Affairs and Trade website www.info.dfat.gov.au.

Canberra
Canada
Commonwealth Avenue, Yarralumla, tel: 02-6270 4000; www.canada international.gc.ca/australia-australie.

Canberra Embassies

Over 60 countries have diplomatic representation in Canberra, and their buildings form a tourist attraction in their own right.

The embassies are mostly south and west of Capital Hill, scattered through the suburbs of Red Hill, Forrest and Yarralumla. Many of the buildings have been designed in the architectural style of the country the mission represents, such as the US Embassy in a red-brick Williamsburg Mission style and the Thai Embassy with its upswept roof corners and gold-coloured roof tiles.

Ireland
20 Arkana Street, Yarralumla, tel: 02-6214 0000; www.embassyof ireland.au.com.
Japan
112–4 Empire Circuit, Yarralumla, tel: 02-6273 3244; www.au.emb-japan. go.jp.
Malaysia
7 Perth Avenue, Yarralumla, tel: 02-6120 0300; www.malaysia. org.au.
New Zealand
Commonwealth Avenue, Yarralumla, tel: 1300- 559 535; www.nzembassy. com/australia.
Singapore
17 Forster Cresent, Yarralumla, tel: 02-6271-2000; www.mfa.gov.sg/ canberra.
UK
Commonwealth Avenue, Yarralumla, tel: 02-6270 6666; ukinaustralia.fco. gov.uk.
USA
21 Moonah Place, Yarralumla, tel: 02-6214 5600; canberra. usembassy.gov.

Sydney
Canada
Consulate-General of Canada Level 5, Quay West, 111 Harrington Street, tel: 02-9364 3000; www.canadainternational.gc.ca/ australia-australie.
China
Consulate General of the P.R. of China/Hong Kong, 39 Dunblane Street, St Camperdown; tel: 02-8595 8002 (9am–12.30pm); http://sydney. china-consulate.org/eng.
France
Consulate-General of France, Level 26, 31 Market Street, St Martin's Tower, tel: 02-9268 2400; www.amba france-au.org.

Australia's distinctive coat of arms.

TRANSPORT

Japan
Consulate-General of Japan, Level 12, 1 O'Connell Street, tel: 02-9250 1000 www.sydney.au.emb-japan.go.jp.
USA
Consulate-General of the United States of America, Level 10, MLC Centre, 19–29 Martin Place, tel: 02-9373 9200; www.usembassy-australia.state.gov/sydney.

Melbourne
Japan
8/570 Bourke Street, tel: 03- 9679 4510; www.melbourne.au.emb-japan.go.jp.
UK
17th Floor, 90 Collins Street, tel: 03-9652 1600; http://ukinaustralia.fco.gov.uk.
USA
553 St Kilda Road, tel: 03-9526 5900; http://melbourne.usconsulate.gov.

Adelaide
Germany
147/809 Pirie Street, tel: 08-8224 0682; http://germany.visahq.com.
Italy
398 Payneham Road, Glynde, tel: 08-8337 0777; www.consadelaide.esteri.it.
UK
444/446 Pulteney Street, tel: 08-8232-9817; http://ukin australia.fco.gov.uk.

Brisbane
China
Level 9, 79 Adelaide Street, tel: 07-3031 6300; http://brisbane.chineseconsulate.org.
Italy
Level 8, 199 George Street, tel: 07-3229 8944; www.consbrisbane.esteri.it.
UK
9/100 Eagle Street, tel: 07-3223 3200; http://ukinaustralia.fco.gov.uk.

Perth
Canada
Third Floor, 267 St George's Terrace, tel: 08-9322 7930; www.canada international.gc.ca/australia-australie.
UK
Adelaide Terrace, tel: 08-9224 4700; http://ukinaustralia.fco.gov.uk.
USA
4th Floor, 16 St George's Terrace, tel: 08-9202 1224; http://perth.usconsulate.gov.

Darwin
British Consulate (emergencies only) 07-3223 3200.

Overseas Missions
Canada – Ottawa
Australian High Commission, Suite 710, 50 O'Conner Street, Ottawa, Ontario, K1P 6L2, tel: 1 613-236 0841; www.canada.embassy.gov.au.
Toronto
Australian Consulate-General, Suite 1100 South Tower, 175 Bloor Street East, Toronto, Ontario, M4W 3R8, tel: 1 416-323 4280; www.dfat.gov.au/missions/countries/cato.html.
Vancouver
Australian Consulate, 1075 West Georgia Street, Vancouver, BC V6E 3C9, tel: 1 604-694 6160; www.dfat.gov.au/missions/countries/cava.
Hong Kong
Australian Consulate-General, 23/F Harbour Centre, 25 Harbour Road, Wan Chai, tel: 852-2827 8881; www.hongkong.china.embassy.gov.au.
Ireland
Australian Embassy, Cumberland Rd, Dublin , tel: 353 1-664 5300; www.ireland.embassy.gov.au.
Japan
Australian Embassy, 2-1-14 Mita, Minato-Ku, Tokyo 108-8361, tel: 81 35232 4111; www.australia.or.jp/en.
New Zealand – Wellington
Australian High Commission, 72 Hobson Street, Thorndon, Wellington, tel: 64 4473 6411; www.newzealand.embassy.gov.au.
Auckland
Australian Consulate-General, Level 7 PricewaterhouseCoopers Tower, 186–194 Quay Street, Auckland, tel: 64 9921 8800; www.newzealand.embassy.gov.au.
Singapore
Australian High Commission, 25 Napier Road, Singapore 258507, tel: 65 6836 4100; www.australia.org.sg.

Painkillers Aussie-style.

UK
Australian High Commission, Australia House, The Strand, London WC2B 4LA, tel: 44 20-7379 4334; www.uk.embassy.gov.au.
USA – Washington DC
Australian Embassy, 1601 Massachusetts Avenue, Washington DC NW 20036-2273, tel: 1 202-797 3000; www.usa.embassy.gov.au.
New York
Australian Consulate-General, 150 East 42nd Street, 33rd floor, New York, NY 10017-5612, tel: 1 212-351 6500; www.newyork.usa.embassy.gov.au.
San Francisco
Australian Consulate-General, 575 Market Street, Suite 1800, San Francisco, CA 94105-2185, tel: 1 415-644 3620; www.usa.embassy.gov.au.
Atlanta
Australian Consulate-General, Atlanta Financial Center, 3353 Peachtree Road, NE, Suite 1140, Atlanta GA 30326, tel: 1 404-364-8560; www.usa.embassy.gov.au.

Emergencies

Call **000** for police, fire and ambulance assistance. This number is toll-free from any phone in Australia and can be made from public phones without a phonecard or coins. **112** is the international standard emergency number that can be dialled from any mobile phone.

G

Gay and Lesbian Travellers

Australia is popular with gay and lesbian travellers, although homophobic attitudes do exist, mostly in areas away from inner cities and popular tourist spots.

One of the main attractions is Sydney's annual gay and lesbian **Mardi Gras** each March, one of the greatest celebrations of its kind in the world. Sydney's Oxford Street is where all the action takes place, and outside Mardi Gras it remains a popular gay and lesbian hub, along with Newtown. **Midsumma** (www.midsumma.org.au), held each January/February, is the major gay and lesbian festival in Melbourne.

Major cities have gay and lesbian newspapers and magazines, available from many inner-city cafés, bars and pubs. Gay and Lesbian Tourism Australia (GALTA) is a network of gay-friendly tourism operators (www.galta.com.au).

H

Health and Medical Care

Australian doctors, dentists and hospitals all have modern equipment, high-level training and extensive facilities. They are also expensive.

New Zealand, Belgium, Finland, Italy, Malta, the Netherlands, Norway, Slovenia, Sweden, the UK and Ireland have reciprocal health-care agreements with Australia, so visitors are entitled to free hospital treatment and Medicare (the Australian national health plan) benefits for GP treatment. Taking out a travel insurance policy that covers your health, before travelling to Australia, is recommended, however.

Vaccinations are not required if you are flying directly to Australia and have not passed through an epidemic zone or a yellow fever, cholera or typhoid-infected area in the six days prior to your arrival.

The sun in Australia has extremely strong ultraviolet rays, so extended exposure is not recommended, especially when the sun is at its fiercest – between 11am and 4pm. A wide-brimmed hat and adequate-strength sunscreen are essential.

I

Internet

Internet cafés are easily found all over Australia, particularly in the larger towns and cities. However, their numbers have probably peaked as smart-phone use accelerates.

M

Maps

Tourist information centres usually have free, quality local maps that also include useful tourism information. If you are travelling by car, many car-hire companies supply GPS devices. You can also pick up Australian road atlases from any good bookshop. Australia is a vast country and it is easy to get lost once you head to the Outback, so it is recommended you purchase maps that detail geography as well as road and track types for Outback travel and long-distance bushwalking.

The Tourism Australia website (www.australia.com) has a wide range of state, city and localised maps that can be useful for planning your itinerary.

Media

Each major city has one daily newspaper and in some cases two. The Sydney Morning Herald (www. smh.com.au) and the Melbourne Age (www.theage.com.au) are the two most important capital-city dailies, and can usually be found around Australia. The only national daily newspapers are The Australian and The Financial Review. Numerous weekly magazines are sold alongside local editions of international publications, such as Newsweek and Time.

The largest-selling papers are the tabloids in Sydney (the *Daily Telegraph*) and Melbourne (the *Herald-Sun*, online at www. heraldsun.com). There are about 120 newspapers catering to Australia's ethnic minorities, which are published in either English or one of 40 other languages.

Australia has a high readership of magazines: in addition to 1,200 magazine titles, airmail copies of overseas newspapers and journals are readily available at specialist newsagents and numerous bookstores in major cities.

The number of free-to-air television stations varies around the country. In some remote areas, the ABC (Australian Broadcasting Corporation) may be the only station. This is the national, advertisement-free, television and radio network – the equivalent of Britain's BBC. The capital cities also offer three commercial stations and the excellent SBS (Special Broadcasting Service) multicultural station, with shows in many languages with subtitles. With the introduction of digital television, there are now 15 free-to-air stations available to suitably equipped households.

On radio, there is always ABC (FM and AM), plus a full spectrum of commercial and public broadcast stations, offering everything from rock to classical music.

Money

Australia's currency is in dollars and cents. The coins come in 5-, 10-, 20- and 50-cent silver pieces and 1- and 2-dollar gold coins. Notes are A$5, 10, 20, 50 and 100. Amounts of

over A$10,000 must be declared on entering and leaving Australia.

The larger hotels will usually exchange cash and well-known traveller's cheques. Nearly all places accept major credit cards such as American Express, Visa, and MasterCard.

Banks The four big banks in Australia are the National (NAB), the Commonwealth, Westpac and ANZ. Trading hours are generally Monday–Thursday 9.30am–4pm, until 5pm on Friday. A few of the smaller banks and credit unions open on Saturday mornings.

Traveller's cheques in any currency can be readily cashed at international airports and banks. Bureaux de change offices are open seven days a week and are located throughout major cities – but usually charge a significant fee, so try to change money at banks when you can, despite limited opening hours.

Credit/Debit Cards and ATMs Carrying a recognised credit or debit card such as Visa, MasterCard or American Express is always a good idea when travelling. A credit card should provide access to EFTPOS (electronic funds transfer at point of sale), which is the easiest and often the cheapest way to exchange money – amounts are automatically debited from the selected account. Many Australian businesses are connected to EFTPOS.

Australian currency cash withdrawals can be made from automatic teller machines (ATMs) that are linked to overseas banks. Since some credit card companies start charging interest on cash withdrawals immediately, it is usually cheaper to withdraw cash using a debit card rather than a credit card. Some UK banks charge a fee for using debit cards overseas, so check this out before travelling to avoid any nasty surprises on your bank statement when you return home.

Some of the islands and the Outback towns have limited banking facilities, so make sure you have plenty of cash before heading into these less populated areas.

Tipping

Australia does not have a tipping tradition, as waiters are given a decent hourly wage. However, in cities especially, it is becoming customary to leave about 10 to 12 percent of the total bill.

Porters at luxury hotels once never received tips, but since many overseas visitors give them a dollar

TRANSPORT

or two, there is an increasing look of expectancy. Porters at airports and taxi drivers do not expect to be tipped, but will hardly throw the money back if you do. "It's up to you" has become the common advice from Australians. In other words: nobody really expects a tip, but it's always appreciated.

O

Opening Hours

General retail trading hours for stores are Monday–Saturday 9am–5pm. Most shops open 10am–4pm on Sunday too. Late-night shopping (until 9pm) takes place at least one night a week in the capital cities – usually a Thursday or Friday.

Restaurants and snack bars, bookshops and local corner stores are open until later in the evening; at times all weekend. Australians still enjoy the tradition of the weekend holiday and most offices are closed on Saturday and Sunday.

Banks open Monday–Thursday 9.30am–4pm and until 5pm on Friday. Some selected branches are open on Saturday morning as well. All banks, post offices, government and private offices, and most shops close on public holidays (see Public Holidays, below).

P

Postal Services

Post offices open Monday–Friday 9am–5pm, and the postal service is reasonably efficient. Post offices also provide fax services at urgent or ordinary rates, the cost depending on the rate selected and the destination.

The front pages of the telephone directory give further information on all postal services, including telephone interpreter service, community service and recorded information service.

Post Restante: post offices will receive and hold mail for visitors. American Express offices will also hold mail for members.

Public Holidays

Public and school holidays affect availability of transport and hotel reservations, which often results in higher prices. The public holidays observed Australia-wide are as follows:
1 January New Year's Day

Phonebox in Melbourne's Chinatown.

26 January Australia Day
mid-March or early October (varies in different states) Labour Day
late March/early April Good Friday, Easter Saturday and Monday
25 April Anzac Day
2nd Monday in June Queen's Birthday
25 December **Christmas Day**
26 December **Boxing Day**

In addition, the states have their own public holidays, such as Victoria's Melbourne Cup Day (first Tuesday in November).

R

Religion

Australia is a secular multicultural society and numerous religions are practised. In the major cities you will find all types of places of worship. Christianity has the most adherents and you won't be hard pushed to find church services for major denominations in cities and towns. The major cities have some magnificent cathedrals.

Buddhism, Islam, Judaism and Hinduism also have large followings in Australia. Muslim communities can be found in the western suburbs of Sydney, concentrating around Lakemba, and the northern suburbs of Melbourne around Broadmeadows. A strong Jewish community exists in Melbourne around St Kilda East.

S

Student Travellers

Australia is popular with international students and backpackers so there is an abundance of budget tourism operators and accommodation providers. STA Travel has offices in every state and offers a range of products and services aimed at

students. Look out for free copies of TNT Magazine for budget travel tips and information (www.downunder. com). Universities also offer a range of services and local advice for international students, including affordable accommodation on campus.

T

Telephones

Emergency numbers: **police, ambulance, fire, tel: 000, or 112 from mobile telephones.**

Australia has several telecommunication operators including Telstra, Optus and AAPT. Rates vary between companies for long distance, but local calls on all networks are untimed.

Toll-free Phone Calls

Toll-free or freecall numbers are common in Australian business. Numbers beginning with 13 (ie Qantas domestic 131 213) can be called from any phone in Australia at local-call rates; numbers starting with 800, 1300 or 1800 are freecall numbers (toll-free) when dialled from within Australia.

Making Calls

Public telephones are located throughout cities and towns. Most public telephones take phonecards, which can be bought at newsagents and stores in various denominations. Dialling from hotel rooms is much more expensive than from a public or private phone.

Subscriber Trunk Dialling (STD) for calling long distance is available on all private and most public telephones. Dial the regional code (say 02 for NSW, 03 for Victoria, etc) followed by the local number. STD calls are cheapest between 7pm and 8am.

A – Z

International Calls

Direct-dialled international calls may be made from any ISD-connected private or public phone. International public phones are located at city GPOs, rail termini and airports. There are off-peak rates to most countries which generally apply all day Saturday and 11pm–6am Sunday to Friday. Dial 0011 followed by the relevant country code.

Time Zones

Australia has three time zones: Eastern Standard Time for the east-coast states (Tasmania, Victoria, New South Wales, Queensland), 10 hours ahead of GMT; Central Standard Time (covering Northern Territory and South Australia), which is 30 minutes behind the east coast, or 9.5 hours ahead of GMT; and Western Standard Time (Western Australia), which is 2 hours behind the east coast, or 8 hours ahead of GMT.

During the summer most states introduce Daylight Saving Time, moving the clock forward by 1 hour. New South Wales and Australian Capital Territory run daylight saving October–March; Victoria, South Australia and Tasmania October–April. Neither Queensland nor Western Australia uses Daylight Saving Time.

Toilets

In their typical no-nonsense fashion, Australians manage without euphemisms for "toilet". "Dunny" or "thunder box" is the Outback slang, but "washroom", "restroom", "Ladies" and "Gents" are all understood. Public toilets are often locked after certain hours, but you can generally use the facilities in any pub or cinema without making a purchase. Toilets are generally clean, even in the Outback.

For those who like to plan their rest stops, the government has produced the Toilet Map, available at www.toiletmap.gov.au, with details of the various public toilets in each of Australia's states.

Tourist Information

Tourist information within Australia is handled principally by state tourist offices. These offices are generally open seven days a week, and will provide brochures, maps, price lists and other information. They can often book accommodation, tours and transport on your behalf. Most towns also have a local tourist information office.

ACT – Australian Capital Territory
Canberra and Region Visitors Centre
330 Northbourne Avenue, Dickson, ACT
Tel: 1300-554 114 or 02-6205 0044
www.visitcanberra.com.au

New South Wales
Sydney Visitor Centre
Corner Playfair and Argyle Streets, The Rocks, Sydney NSW
Tel: 1800-067 676 or 02-8273 0000
Also at Dickson Street, Chinatown
Tel: 02 9265 9333
www.sydneyvisitorcentre.com
www.therocks.com

Victoria
Melbourne Visitors Centre
Federation Square, Melbourne
Tel: 03-9658 9658
www.visitvictoria.com

South Australia
South Australian Visitor and Travel Centre
9 James Place, Adelaide
Tel: 1300-764 227 276 or 1300 588 276
www.southaustralia.com

Queensland
Visitor Information Centre
Queen Street Mall, Brisbane
Tel: 07-3006 6290

www.queenslandholidays.com.au
www.visitbrisbane.com.au

Northern Territory
Tourism Top End
6 Bennett Street, Darwin
Tel: 1300-138 886 or 08-8936 2499
www.travelnt.com

Western Australia
Western Australian Visitor Centre
55 William Street, Perth
Tel: 1800-812 808 351 or 08-9483 1111
www.westernaustralia.com

Tasmania
Tasmanian Visitor Information Centre
22 Davey Street, Hobart
Tel: 03-6238 4222
www.discovertasmania.com.au
www.hobarttravelcentre.com.au

U

Useful Addresses

Tourist Information Abroad

Tourism Australia supplies excellent information for travellers wishing to plan their trip. Their URL is www.tourism.australia.com.

London
Australia House, 6th Floor, The Strand, London, WC2B 4LG
Tel: 020-7438 4600

Los Angeles
2029 Century Park E Ste 3150, Los Angeles, CA 90067
Tel: 310-695 3200

Hong Kong
Suite 6706, Central Plaza, 26 Harbour Road, Wanchai
Tel: 852-2531 3832

Singapore
101 Thompson Road, United Square 08-03, Singapore 307591
Tel: 65-6351 6323

Sydney
Tel: 02-9360 1111

National Trust Offices

The National Trust in Australia owns and preserves more than 180 historic properties. All of them are open to the public and Trust members are entitled to free entry. If you intend to visit a number of Australia's historic buildings it may be worth joining. Annual membership costs A$100 for an individual, A$130 for households. Non-members can pay to see particular properties. To join call toll-free in Australia 1800-246 766 or contact one of the state offices. A reciprocal arrangement exists with similar organisations in other countries, so bring their cards with you to Australia.

The Melbourne Visitors' Centre is next to St Paul's Cathedral.

National
The Australian Council of National Trusts, 14/71 Constitution Avenue, Campbell, ACT 2612
Tel: 02-6247 6766
www.nationaltrust.org.au
New South Wales
Observatory Hill, The Rocks, Sydney, NSW 2001
Tel: 02-9258 0123
www.nsw.nationaltrust.org.au
Australian Capital Territory
1st Floor, North Building, Civic Offices, Civic Square, Canberra, ACT 2608
Tel: 02-6230 0533
www.nationaltrustact.org.au
Victoria
4 Parliament Place, East Melbourne, Vic 3002
Tel: 03-9656 9800
www.nattrust.com.au
South Australia
Beaumont House, 631 Glynburn Road, Beaumont 5066
Tel: 08-8202 9200
www.nationaltrustsa.org.au
Queensland
Ground Floor, 91–95 William Street, Brisbane, Qld 4001
Tel: 07-3223 6666
www.nationaltrustqld.org
Western Australia
The Old Observatory, 4 Havelock Street, West Perth, WA 6005
Tel: 08-9321 6088
www.ntwa.com.au
Tasmania
Franklin House, 413 Hobart Road, Launceston, TAS 7250
Tel: 03-6344 6233
www.nationaltrusttas.org.au

National Parks

Some national parks require you to purchase permits before entry. Visitor centres and regional offices where you can obtain information and permits are located throughout Australia and are often in or close to popular parks. National parks information can also be obtained from these regional offices:
NSW: National Parks and Wildlife Service
Level 14, 59 Goulburn Street, The Rocks, Sydney, NSW 2000
Tel: 1300-072 757 or 02-9995 6500
www.nationalparks.nsw.gov.au
ACT: Territory and Municipal Services
Tel: 13 22 81
www.tams.act.gov.au
Vic: Parks Victoria
Level 10/535 Bourke Street Melbourne, Victoria 3000
Tel: 03-8627 4700; or 131 963
www.parkweb.vic.gov.au
SA: National Parks South Australia

Tel: 08-8204 1910
www.environment.sa.gov.au
Qld: Parks & Wildlife Service
160 Ann Street, Brisbane, Qld 4000
Tel: 137 468
www.nprsr.qld.gov.au
NT: Parks & Wildlife, Northern Territory
Goyder Centre, 25 Chung Wah Terrace, Palmerston, NT 0830
Tel: 08-8999 4555
www.parksandwildlife.nt.gov.au
Tas: Parks and Wildlife Service
134 Macquarie Street, Hobart 7000
Tel: 1300-827 727
www.parks.tas.gov.au

V

Visas and Passports

Visitors to Australia must have a passport valid for the entire period of their stay. All non-Australian citizens also require a visa – except for New Zealand citizens, who are issued with a visa on arrival in Australia. The visa you need depends on what your visit is for and how long you plan to stay.

Visitor visa (subclass 600, free visa) allows you to stay in Australia for up to three months. You are not allowed to work. Electronic Travel Authority ETA (subclass 601) allows you to enter Australia as many times as you want, for up to three months at a time, for up to 12 months. The service fee is A$20. EVisitor (subclass 651, free visa) is for people who hold passports from certain countries. You may enter Australia as many times as you wish, for up to three months, for up to 12 months after the visa is granted. Special category visa (subclass 444) is for citizens of NZ. Working holiday visa (subclass 417) is for young people between 18-31 years of age. You must apply for it outside of Australia. You can only work six months with one employer. For more information about other visa types see www.border.gov.au.

Temporary residence Those seeking temporary residence must apply to an Australian visa office, and in many cases must be sponsored by an appropriate organisation or employer. Study visas are available for people who want to undertake registered courses on a full-time basis.

Entry requirements for Australia are continually updated. Information and applications for visas should be made to the nearest Australian Government representative in your home country well before travelling (see page 327), or visit www.border.

gov.au, which gives information on all the different types of visas, and allows online applications.

W

Weights and Measures

Australia uses the metric system of weights and measures. Despite the change from the imperial to the metric system in the 1970s, a 183cm person is still frequently referred to as being "6 feet tall" and some people still give their weight in stones (14lb to the stone).

The main conversions are as follows:
1 metre = 3.28 feet
1 kilometre = 0.62 miles
1 kilogram = 2.2 pounds
1 litre = 2.1 pints (US)
1 litre = 1.8 pints (UK)
0°C (Centigrade) = 32°F (Fahrenheit)

What to Wear

Generally, Australians are informal dressers, especially when the weather is warm: comfort trumps formality. However, for special occasions or dining in fine restaurants, formal attire or neat casual dress is appropriate. While a jacket and tie are rarely required for men, the more elegant establishments would not welcome gym shoes or shorts. In other words, dress more or less as you would in other cosmopolitan cities.

If you visit Australia during summer, include at least one warm garment for the occasional cold snap. If travelling to the southeastern states during winter, include warm clothing, a raincoat and an umbrella – temperatures in Melbourne can reach freezing at night. The weather in northern Queensland and the Top End of the Northern Territory is rarely chilly, even in August.

At any time of the year, solid, waterproof walking shoes are essential if you intend to go bushwalking. If exploring the Great Barrier Reef, bring along an old pair of trainers for reef walks. And always pack a hat.

Women Travellers

Women are generally safe in Australia, though the same degree of caution should be used as you would elsewhere. Some backpacker hostels such as Base Backpackers (www.stayatbase.com) offer women-only dorms and floors.

TRANSPORT

A – Z

FURTHER READING

GENERAL

The Australian Wine Annual by Jeremy Oliver. Rigorous guide to everything good in a bottle.
The Age/Sydney Morning Herald Good Australian Wine Guide by Nick Stock. Formerly branded as the Penguin guide.
Unreliable Memoirs by Clive James. Aussie expat and wit looks back at his formative years in Sydney and possibly finds rationale for being an expat.
The Sydney Morning Herald and ***The Age Good Food Guides***. Definitive guides to eating out in, respectively, Sydney and Melbourne.
The Rise and Fall of Australia by Nick Bryant. A forensic look at the Lucky Country from an outsider's perspective.
Australia's Second Chance by George Megalogenis. The most important questions confronting Australia now – how to maintain the country's winning streak.

HISTORY

At Home in Australia by Peter Conrad. The pictures are the draw in this analysis of a nation.
Australia: A Biography of a Nation by Phillip Knightley. Wide-ranging history, particularly good in its snapshots of key individuals.
Australia: A New History of the Great Southern Land by Frank Welsh. Dependable assessment of the growth of a country.
Australians: Origins to Eureka by Thomas Keneally. The first of three volumes aimed at anatomising the people of the continent.
A Concise History of Australia by Stuart Macintyre. Reliable and thoroughly up-to-date account, including the Gillard ascent.
The Explorers edited by Tim Flannery. A compendium of accounts from the early days of European settlement.
The Fatal Shore by Robert Hughes. Landmark laying bare of convict transportation and its impact.

Gallipoli by Les Carlyon. Detailed account of the formative Anzac engagement of World War I.
Kokoda Spirit: In the Footsteps of Australia's World War Two Heroes by Patrick Lindsay. Analysis of searing experiences in Papua New Guinea.
A Secret Country by John Pilger. Provocative analysis of the political and commercial foundations of modern Australia.
The Making of Australia by David Hill. The story of how a struggling convict settlement grew into six dynamic colonies and then a remarkable nation.

NATURAL HISTORY

Country: A Continent, a Scientist and a Kangaroo by Tim Flannery. Palaeontology, natural history and memoir nicely combined.
Field Guide to the Birds of Australia by Ken Simpson and Nicolas Day. Comprehensive identification guide.
Green Guide: Mammals of Australia by T. Lindsey. Handbook to the country's weird and wonderful wildlife.
Green Guide: Snakes and Other Reptiles of Australia by G. Swan. As above but with more venom.
The Slater Field Guide to Australian Birds by Peter, Pat & Raoul Slater. Fully illustrated spotter's tool.
Wild Australia: A Guide to the Places, Plants and Animals by Graham Edgar, Robert Edgar and Allan Edgar. Extends to insects and aquatic life as well.

TRAVEL

Down Under by Bill Bryson. The urbane, breezy style is deceptive – some serious research has gone into this entertaining travelogue.
Explore Australia by 4WD by Craig Lewis and Cathy Savage. How to source the right equipment and find the right tracks.
Into the Blue: Boldly Going Where

Captain Cook Has Gone Before by Tony Horwitz. Penetrative retracing of Cook's Pacific voyages.
One for the Road: An Outback Adventure by Tony Horwitz. One man's breezy journey and the people he encounters.
The Songlines by Bruce Chatwin. Remarkable outback journey into Aboriginal tradition and lore.
Tracks by Robyn Davidson. The adventures of a woman crossing the continent by camel.
Walks in Nature: Australia by Viola Design. Over 100 trails in and around major Australian cities.
Wild Swimming: Sydney Australia by Sally Tertini. Gorgeous outdoor swimming locations within reach of Sydney.

ABORIGINAL AUSTRALIA

Aboriginal Art of Australia by Carol Finley. Concise guide to art in all media, which includes a walk through some of the symbolism employed.
Aboriginal Australians by Richard Broome. An analysis of the impact of white settlement from 1788.
Aboriginal Myths, Legends and Fables by A.W. Reed. Straightforward retelling of some of the key stories.
The Artist is a Thief by Stephen Gray. Prize-winning detective story that delves into cultural clashes in modern Australia.
Balanda: My Year in Arnhem Land by Mary Ellen Jordan. A move from Melbourne to unfamiliar Arnhem Land with the predictable and unpredictable cultural collisions implicit in that.
My Place by Sally Morgan. Morgan's investigation of her family history reveals some wider truths of Aboriginal repression.
Wings of the Kite-Hawk: A journey into the heart of Australia by Nicholas Rothwell. Starting with the routes of early explorers and expanding to take in current issues.

Aboriginal Australians by Diana Marshall. Describes the history, culture and traditional and modern lifestyles of Aboriginal Australians.
Aboriginal Designs by Polly Pinder. The unique and vibrant artwork of Aboriginal people.

AUSTRALIAN LANGUAGE

The Dinkum Dictionary by Susan Butler. Bonzer stickybeak into Aussie lingo.
My Life As Me by Barry Humphries. Reminiscence of growing up in 1950s Melbourne, the genesis of his various characters and the path to a level of worldwide acclaim that saw Dame Edna Everage given the city keys.
Unpolished Gem by Alice Pung. Leaving the Cambodia of Pol Pot as a child, Pung's assimilation into life in Footscray along with her family is the core of this revealing memoir.

FICTION

The Art of the Engine Driver by Steven Carroll. Suburban Melbourne post-World War II is the setting for this measured look at how progress distorts the lives of ordinary people.
All the Birds Singing by Evie Wyld. Centres on an Aussie woman who has fled trauma and is living in an unnamed wind and rain-swept English island.
Barracuda by Christos Tsiolkas. Shows the absurdity of the idea that Australia is a classless society, or a place in which anyone can succeed if only they try hard enough.
Breath by Tim Winton. The surf is as much the focus as the relationships in this accomplished novel.
The Broken Shore by Peter Temple. A sophisticated crime novel that reaches to the very heart of Australian society.
Capricornia by Xavier Herbert. Sweeping narrative from the 1930s that partly inspired Baz Luhrmann's film, *Australia*.
Carpentaria by Alexis Wright. Hefty and densely lyrical account of an Aboriginal community in the far north.
Cloudstreet by Tim Winton. A family saga in the West mirroring the growth of the nation in the 20th century.
Cocaine Blues by Kerry Greenwood. The first in a series of detective novels set in 1920s Melbourne.
Death of a River Guide by Richard Flanagan. A man drowning in

Tasmania's Franklin River spools back through his family's history and struggle in this unforgiving land.
English Passengers by Matthew Kneale. Prize-winning novel about an 1857 voyage to Tasmania, by turns stark and hilarious.
Eucalyptus by Murray Bail. From its fairy-tale conceit, Eucalyptus evolves into a magical love story.
Fly Away Peter by David Malouf. Life on Queensland's bucolic coastal region plays counterpoint to the Great War.
For the Term of His Natural Life by Marcus Clarke. The great convict pot-boiler published in 1874.
A Fortunate Life by A.B. Facey. Rough-hewn yet classic autobiography of an outback farmer.
Gould's Book of Fish by Richard Flanagan. Tasmania's Sarah Island in the 1830s is the setting for this wildly ambitious freewheeling novel.
The Harp in the South by Ruth Park. Part of a trilogy of loved, if soapy, novels set in the slums of Sydney in the first half of the 20th century.
The Idea of Perfection by Kate Grenville. Beautifully honed romance in small-town New South Wales.
Illywhacker by Peter Carey. An expansive narrative by the 139-year-old self-confessed liar of the title takes us on a journey through history and the forging of the larrikin spirit.
It's Raining in Mango by Thea Astley. Saga stretching over a century and takes in gold-digging in Queensland and Aboriginal dispossession.
Last Drinks by Andrew McGahan. Multi-award-winning crime thriller.
Loaded by Christos Tsiolkas. Loaded unflinchingly sifts the problems of a gay Greek teenager coming to terms with both himself and a hostile city.
The Man from Snowy River by Banjo Paterson. Derring-do in the southern mountains has taken on mythical status in Australian literature.
Monkey Grip by Helen Garner. Captures the tedium of life with self-obsessed hippies and junkies in 1970s Melbourne.
Morgan's Run by Colleen McCullough. The tale of a man convicted and sentenced to prison on Norfolk Island.
My Brilliant Career by Miles Franklin. Feisty teenager grapples with the stifling constraints of early 20th-century Australia.
Of A Boy by Sonya Hartnett. The story of nine-year-old Adrian, adrift in 1977 without family anchors and when three other children have just disappeared.

On the Beach by Nevil Shute. Melbourne is the last redoubt of humanity as the fallout from nuclear annihilation in the northern hemisphere heads southward.
Oscar and Lucinda by Peter Carey. Booker winner, film and calling card for the precociously talented Carey.
Oyster by Janette Turner Hospital. The arrival of a cult-like community in a remote desert settlement is the catalyst for upheaval.
Picnic at Hanging Rock by Joan Lindsay. An eerie story of schoolgirls disappearing in the picturesque Macedon Ranges.
Remembering Babylon by David Malouf. Moving story of a white youth taken in by a Queensland Aboriginal community in the 1840s.
The Secret River by Kate Grenville. Deftly explores the ramifications of Aboriginal and white communities interacting with each other, this time in early 19th-century NSW.
The Slap by Christos Tsiolkas. Skewers suburban Melbourne values in this bestselling, Man Booker prize-nominated novel.
The Sound of One Hand Clapping by Richard Flanagan. A woman walks out into a snowstorm, leaving her family in the Tasmanian wilderness.

Send Us Your Thoughts

We do our best to ensure the information in our books is as accurate and up-to-date as possible. The books are updated on a regular basis using local contacts, who painstakingly add, amend and correct as required. However, some details (such as telephone numbers and opening times) are liable to change, and we are ultimately reliant on our readers to put us in the picture.

We welcome your feedback, especially your experience of using the book "on the road". Maybe we recommended a hotel that you liked (or another that you didn't), or you came across a great bar or new attraction we missed.

We will acknowledge all contributions, and we'll offer an Insight Guide to the best letters received. Please write to us at:

**Insight Guides
PO Box 7910
London SE1 1WE**
Or email us at:
hello@insightguides.com

The Thorn Birds by Colleen
McCullough. The romantic
blockbuster of life on the station.
Tree of Man by Patrick White.
Dissecting an Outback marriage.
The True History of the Kelly Gang
by Peter Carey. The Kelly story
in Ned's own words from "newly
discovered" letters.
The Vivisector by Patrick White.
Sydney Nolan was the model for this
dissection of an Australian artist.

CHILDREN'S BOOKS

**The Complete Adventures of Blinky
Bill** by Dorothy Wall. Tales of a
mischievous koala.
The Magic Pudding by Norman
Lindsay. The absurd and amusing
adventures of Bunyip Bluegum, Bill
Barnacle, Sam Sawnoff and their
pudding companion.
Possum Magic by Julie Vivas and
Mem Fox. A beautifully illustrated
children's classic.
Snugglepot & Cuddlepie by May
Gibbs. One of Australia's best-loved
children's books, first published in
1918.
Wombat Divine by Mem Fox and
Kerry Argent. An endearing Christmas
tale about a stage-struck wombat.
Wildlife by Fiona Wood. A book for
young adults about friendship, love
and identity.
Rivertime by Trace Balla. A tender
tale of a boy and his bird-watching
uncle on a paddling trip.

OTHER INSIGHT GUIDES

Insight Guide Australia is a top-selling
title in the Insight Guides series, with
superb photography and in-depth
background reading on the history
and culture of the Land Down Under.
Other titles include *Insight Guide
Queensland & the Great Barrier Reef*
and *Insight Guide New Zealand.*
    Insight Explore Guides provide
illuminating walks and tours around a
destination, showing you the smartest
way to link the sights and taking
you beyond the beaten tourist track.
Titles in the Explore series include
*Explore Sydney, Explore Melbourne,
Explore Queensland* and *Explore New
Zealand.*

CREDITS

Photo Credits

Alamy 243, 284B, 291TR, 311B
Andrew Tauber/Apa Publications
158, 160T, 163
Australia Reptile Park 125T
Australia Tourism 43, 130, 174,
175T, 177B, 203, 204, 234BL, 239,
275B, 286
Bigstock 123T
Chris Phutully 61
Corbis 69, 182B, 202
Dreamstime 9TR, 93BR, 101T,
101B, 109B, 136, 138T, 143T, 178,
221, 226, 234BR, 235TR, 237,
246/247, 255
FLPA 244BL, 245BL
Fotolia 206/207
Fremantle Media 70
Getty Images 4/5, 7ML, 9BR,
10/11, 12/13, 14/15, 16, 18, 19,
24, 37, 39, 42, 44, 45, 46, 47,
48/49, 51, 52, 53, 58, 59, 60, 65,
66BR, 67BR, 67BL, 67TR, 68, 71,
72, 74, 75, 76, 77, 82, 83, 84, 85,
87TR, 93BL, 94/95, 96/97, 98/99,
100, 104, 105, 115, 117B, 119B,
120, 121, 122, 127, 128, 134, 139,
140, 141, 142, 146, 147B, 148,
153, 173B, 175B, 184, 194, 205,
230B, 231, 233B, 251, 253, 262,
268, 277, 278B, 282, 283,
290/291T, 292/293, 294, 295,
298B, 299, 300B, 303B, 304, 305B,
307B, 308B, 310, 312, 313, 314BR,

314BL, 315BR, 315BL, 315TR, 316
Glyn Genin/Apa Publications 6ML,
6MR, 7TR, 7MR, 9BL, 27, 54, 62,
67ML, 86BR, 107, 108B, 110, 111,
112B, 113, 114, 116T, 116B, 191,
192, 193, 195, 197T, 197B, 199,
248, 249, 252, 254B, 254T, 256T,
256B, 257B, 257T, 259, 260B,
260T, 263, 264/265T, 264BR,
264BL, 265ML, 265BR, 265TR,
266/267, 269, 271, 272T, 273,
275T, 278T, 279T, 284T, 326
iStock 1, 6BL, 8M, 17T, 23, 25, 28,
29, 50, 56, 57R, 57L, 63, 64, 78,
81, 92/93T, 92BR, 92BL, 93TR,
123B, 126, 129, 132, 133, 138B,
144, 145B, 156, 168, 171T, 176B,
177T, 181, 182T, 183, 186/187,
188, 200, 201, 224, 230T,
234/235T, 235ML, 236, 242,
244/245T, 244BR, 245ML, 245BR,
245TR, 279B, 288B, 291BR, 296,
306, 309B, 314/315T, 315ML, 332
Jerry Dennis/Apa Publications
6MR, 108T, 109T, 112T, 119T, 135,
137T, 145T, 147T, 150, 151T, 161,
169, 172B, 173T, 176T, 179, 180,
232, 233T, 241T, 297T, 298T, 300T,
302, 305T, 307T, 308T, 311T, 309T,
319, 323
Jungle Surfing 229, 235BR
Kevin Hamdorf/Apa Publications
327

Kobal Collection 73
Mary Evans Picture Library 32, 35
Naomi Everton 171B
National Gallery of Australia
66/67T
New South Wales Tourism 117T,
125B, 143B
Niamh Sheehy/Apa Publications
7BL, 17B, 20, 280, 281, 285, 287,
288T
**Peter James Quinn/Apa
Publications** 79, 80
Peter Stuckings/Apa Publications
8MR, 21, 55, 86/87T, 86BL, 87BL,
88, 89, 90, 208, 209, 211T, 211B,
213T, 213B, 214, 216, 217, 218,
219, 220, 222, 223T, 225, 228,
235BL
Pro Dive Cairns 8BL, 91, 223B
Queensland Tourism 240
Robert Harding 241B
Shutterstock 22, 118, 131, 137B,
149, 151B, 152, 189, 258, 272B,
290BR, 290BL, 291ML, 291BC,
297B, 303T
The Art Archive 26, 30, 31, 34, 36,
38, 66BL
TopFoto 33, 41
Virginia Star/Apa Publications
7BR, 7TL, 9TL, 40, 87BR, 154/155,
157, 159, 160B, 162, 164, 165B,
165T, 166T, 166B, 167, 172T, 185T,
185B, 318, 324, 329, 330

Cover Credits

Front cover: Great Barrier Reef
Shutterstock
Back cover: Uluru *iStock*
Front flap: (from top) Glenelg beach,
Adelaide *Shutterstock*; Mine in

Coober Pedy *iStock*; West Coast
Wilderness Railway, Tasmania
iStock; Sydney Harbour *Shutterstock*
Back flap: Mungo National Park
iStock

Insight Guide Credits

Distribution
UK, Ireland and Europe
Apa Publications (UK) Ltd;
sales@insightguides.com
United States and Canada
Ingram Publisher Services;
ips@ingramcontent.com
Australia and New Zealand
Woodslane; info@woodslane.com.au
Southeast Asia
Apa Publications (SN) Pte;
singaporeoffice@insightguides.com
Hong Kong, Taiwan and China
Apa Publications (HK) Ltd;
hongkongoffice@insightguides.com
Worldwide
Apa Publications (UK) Ltd;
sales@insightguides.com
Special Sales, Content Licensing and CoPublishing
Insight Guides can be purchased in
bulk quantities at discounted prices.
We can create special editions,
personalised jackets and corporate
imprints tailored to your needs.
sales@insightguides.com
www.insightguides.biz

Printed in China by CTPS

All Rights Reserved
© 2016 Apa Digital (CH) AG and
Apa Publications (UK) Ltd

First Edition 1992
Eighth Edition 2016

No part of this book may be
reproduced, stored in a retrieval
system or transmitted in any form or
means electronic, mechanical,
photocopying, recording or
otherwise, without prior written
permission from Apa Publications.

Every effort has been made to
provide accurate information in this
publication, but changes are
inevitable. The publisher cannot be
responsible for any resulting loss,
inconvenience or injury. We would
appreciate it if readers would call our
attention to any errors or outdated
information. We also welcome your
suggestions; please contact us at:
hello@insightguides.com

www.insightguides.com

Editor: Kate Drynan
Author: Małgorzata Anczewska
Head of Production: Rebeka Davies
Update Production: AM Services
Picture Editor: Tom Smyth
Cartography: original cartography
Polyglott Kartographie, updated by
Carte

Contributors

This new edition of *Insight Guide:
Australia* was thoroughly updated
by Małgorzata Anczewska, a travel
writer based in Canberra. It builds
on the previous work of the
following writers: **Ron Banks**,
Jerry Dennis, **Ute Junker**,

Victoria Kyriakopoulos, **Kerry
McCarthy**, **Fran Severn**, **Tania
Sincock**, **Dorothy Stannard** and
Hermione Stott.
    The text was copy-edited by **Tim
Binks** and **Kate Drynan**, and
indexed by **Penny Phenix**.

About Insight Guides

Insight Guides have more than
45 years' experience of publishing
high-quality, visual travel guides. We
produce 400 full-colour titles, in both
print and digital form, covering more
than 200 destinations across the
globe, in a variety of formats to meet
your different needs.
    Insight Guides are written by
local authors, whose expertise is
evident in the extensive historical
and cultural background features.

Each destination is carefully
researched by regional experts to
ensure our guides provide the very
latest information. All the reviews
in **Insight Guides** are independent;
we strive to maintain an impartial
view. Our reviews are carefully
selected to guide you to the best
places to eat, go out and shop, so
you can be confident that when
we say a place is special, we really
mean it.

Legend

City maps

	Freeway/Highway/Motorway
	Divided Highway
	Main Roads
	Minor Roads
	Pedestrian Roads
	Steps
	Footpath
	Railway
	Funicular Railway
	Cable Car
	Tunnel
	City Wall
	Important Building
	Built Up Area
	Other Land
	Transport Hub
	Park
	Pedestrian Area
	Bus Station
	Tourist Information
	Main Post Office
	Cathedral/Church
	Mosque
	Synagogue
	Statue/Monument
	Beach
	Airport

Regional maps

	Freeway/Highway/Motorway (with junction)
	Freeway/Highway/Motorway (under construction)
	Divided Highway
	Main Road
	Secondary Road
	Minor Road
	Track
	Footpath
	International Boundary
	State/Province Boundary
	National Park/Reserve
	Marine Park
	Ferry Route
	Marshland/Swamp
	Glacier Salt Lake
	Airport/Airfield
	Ancient Site
	Border Control
	Cable Car
	Castle/Castle Ruins
	Cave
	Chateau/Stately Home
	Church/Church Ruins
	Crater
	Lighthouse
	Mountain Peak
	Place of Interest
	Viewpoint

INDEX

Main references are in bold type

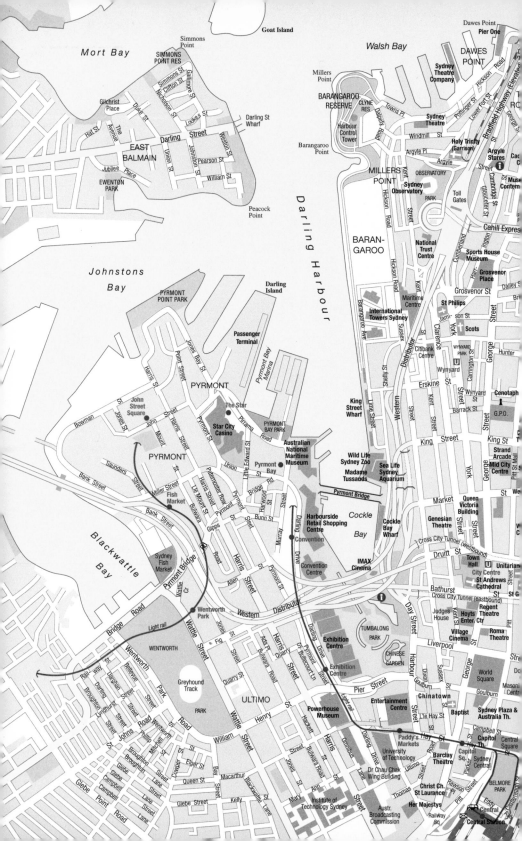